PRINCIPLES OF INTERCULTURAL COMMUNICATION

PRINCIPLES OF INTERCULTURAL COMMUNICATION

IGOR E. KLYUKANOV

Eastern Washington University

Boston ▪ New York ▪ San Francisco
Mexico City ▪ Montreal ▪ Toronto ▪ London ▪ Madrid ▪ Munich ▪ Paris
Hong Kong ▪ Singapore ▪ Tokyo ▪ Cape Town ▪ Sydney

Executive Editor: *Karon Bowers*
Series Editor: *Brian Wheel*
Series Editor Assistant: *Heather Hawkins*
Marketing Manager: *Mandee Eckersley*
Production Administrator: *Janet Domingo*
Packager: *Lifland et al., Bookmakers*
Compositor: *Publishers' Design and Production Services, Inc.*
Composition Buyer: *Linda Cox*
Manufacturing Buyer: *JoAnne Sweeney*
Cover Coordinator: *Kristina Mose-Libon*

For related titles and support materials, visit our online catalog at www.ablongman.com.

Library of Congress Cataloging-in-Publication Data

Klyukanov, Igor.
Principles of intercultural communication / Igor Klyukanov.
p. cm.
Includes bibliographical references and index.
ISBN: 0-205-35864-0
1. Intercultural communication. I. Title.

HM1211.K58 2005
303.48'2—dc22

2004057272

Printed in the United States of America

To Galya and Anya

CONTENTS

ACKNOWLEDGMENTS xiii

INTRODUCTION 1

CHAPTER ONE

Creating Cultural Boundaries: Punctuation Principle 7

INTRODUCING THE PROBLEM QUESTION 8

DEFINING BASIC TERMS 8

Culture 8

Communication 9

THE PROCESS OF CULTURAL IDENTIFICATION 11

Identity as Group Membership 11

Cultural Identity as a Reflective Self-Image 13

INTRODUCING THE PUNCTUATION PRINCIPLE 16

Boundary Lines as Conceptualizations 16

Constructive and Destructive Boundary Lines 17

Boundary Fit as the Goal of Intercultural Communication 20

THE PUNCTUATION PRINCIPLE DEFINED 21

SUMMARY 22

CASE STUDY: A HISTORY OF THE RUSSO-JAPANESE FRONTIER 23

SIDE TRIPS 26

CHECK YOURSELF 26

REFERENCES 26

CHAPTER TWO

Constructing Knowledge in Intercultural Communication: Uncertainty Principle 29

INTRODUCING THE PROBLEM QUESTION 30

EPISTEMOLOGY AND INTERCULTURAL COMMUNICATION 30

Objective Approach to Knowledge 31
Subjective Approach to Knowledge 32

INTRODUCING THE UNCERTAINTY PRINCIPLE 36

Uncertainty and Horizon of Knowledge 36
Uncertainty and Dis-closure 39
Order out of Uncertainty 42

THE UNCERTAINTY PRINCIPLE DEFINED 43

SUMMARY 44

CASE STUDY: THE SHOCK OF THE OTHER 46

SIDE TRIPS 49

CHECK YOURSELF 49

REFERENCES 49

CHAPTER THREE

Intercultural Communication as Enactment of Meaning: Performativity Principle 51

INTRODUCING THE PROBLEM QUESTION 52

LANGUAGE AS A MEANS OF COMMUNICATION: AN OVERVIEW 52

Definition of Language 52
Dimensions of Language 56
Language and Rules 57

INTRODUCING THE PERFORMATIVITY PRINCIPLE 60

The Dramaturgy of Performativity: From Rules to Roles 60
Performativity as a Reiterative Process 62
The Structure of Performativity 67

THE PERFORMATIVITY PRINCIPLE DEFINED 70

SUMMARY 71

CASE STUDY: PERFORMING AL-HALQA IN MOROCCO 72

SIDE TRIPS 76

CHECK YOURSELF 76

REFERENCES 77

CHAPTER FOUR
Charting Out a Cultural Map: Positionality Principle 79

INTRODUCING THE PROBLEM QUESTION 80

FROM BELIEFS ABOUT THE WORLD TO WORLDVIEWS: INTERCULTURAL COMMUNICATION AND PERCEPTION 80

CULTURAL GAZE: LOOKING OUT, LOOKING IN 86

CULTURAL GAZE AND ETHNOCENTRISM 88

Ethnocentric Reduction 89

Ethnocentric Negation 90

Ethnocentric Affirmation 91

INTRODUCING THE POSITIONALITY PRINCIPLE 92

Positionality as Grounding 92

Positionality and Authority 95

Positionality as a Process of Engagement 96

THE POSITIONALITY PRINCIPLE DEFINED 98

SUMMARY 99

CASE STUDY: ARGUMENT IN ISRAELI-PALESTINIAN ENCOUNTERS 101

SIDE TRIPS 104

CHECK YOURSELF 105

REFERENCES 105

CHAPTER FIVE
Comparing Cultural Maps: Commensurability Principle 107

INTRODUCING THE PROBLEM QUESTION 108

LOOKING FOR MEANING IN INTERCULTURAL COMMUNICATION 108

Semiotic Look: What's in a Word? 109

Cognitive Look: What's on Our Mind? 115

Corporeal Look: What's in the World? 117

INTRODUCING THE COMMENSURABILITY PRINCIPLE 119

The Nature of Commensurability 119

The Forms and Levels of Commensurability 120

The Implications of Commensurability 123

THE COMMENSURABILITY PRINCIPLE DEFINED 126

SUMMARY 127

CASE STUDY: TRANSLATING CULTURAL DIFFERENCES: THE PROBLEM OF *CHOU* 128

SIDE TRIPS 132

CHECK YOURSELF 132

REFERENCES 132

CHAPTER SIX
Creating a Shared Intercultural Space: Continuum Principle 135

INTRODUCING THE PROBLEM QUESTION 136

GLOBAL CULTURAL DIMENSIONS: HOW MANY? 136

INTRODUCING THE CONTINUUM PRINCIPLE 142
Overcoming Binary Thinking 142
Intercultural Continuum and Digital Communication 147
Intercultural Continuum and Analogic Communication 148

THE CONTINUUM PRINCIPLE DEFINED 152

SUMMARY 153

CASE STUDY: THE 1999 COCA-COLA SCARE IN EUROPE 154

SIDE TRIPS 157

CHECK YOURSELF 157

REFERENCES 157

CHAPTER SEVEN
Dynamics of Intercultural Communication: Pendulum Principle 161

INTRODUCING THE PROBLEM QUESTION 162

TENSIONS IN INTERCULTURAL COMMUNICATION: CULTURAL NEEDS 162

INTERCULTURAL COMMUNICATION AND ETHNOLINGUISTIC VITALITY 165

"VOICE" IN INTERCULTURAL COMMUNICATION 168

INTRODUCING THE PENDULUM PRINCIPLE 169
The Contradictory Nature of Intercultural Communication 170
Intercultural Communication as Praxis 174
Intercultural Communication and Change 176

THE PENDULUM PRINCIPLE DEFINED 177

SUMMARY 178

CASE STUDY: DIALECTICS OF COLONIAL ENCOUNTER: INTERACTING WITH THE KOBON 180

SIDE TRIPS 183

CHECK YOURSELF 183

REFERENCES 184

CHAPTER EIGHT
Resolving Intercultural Tensions: Transaction Principle 187

INTRODUCING THE PROBLEM QUESTION 188

APPROACHING CONFLICT 188
Roots 188
Routes 192

INTRODUCING THE TRANSACTION PRINCIPLE 198
Intercultural Transactions: Perception and Reality 198
Intercultural Communication as a Negotiation Zone 202
Back to the Future: From Positions to Interests 204

THE TRANSACTION PRINCIPLE DEFINED 205

SUMMARY 206

CASE STUDY: "THE WALL OF DEATH": A CONFLICT BETWEEN JAPANESE AND WESTERN CULTURES 208

SIDE TRIPS 211

CHECK YOURSELF 211

REFERENCES 212

CHAPTER NINE
Cooperation between Cultures: Synergy Principle 213

INTRODUCING THE PROBLEM QUESTION 214

PERCEPTION: SEIZING THE WORLD 214
Stereotype: Not All Swans Are White 215
Prejudice: The U.S. and the Rest-of-the-World Soccer Cup 220

INTERCULTURAL INTEGRATION: BREAKING DOWN THE WALL 224

INTRODUCING THE SYNERGY PRINCIPLE 226

Intercultural Synergy and Flow Dynamics 227
Intercultural Synergy and Nonsummativity 229
Toward Pareto Optimality 230

THE SYNERGY PRINCIPLE DEFINED 232

SUMMARY 232

CASE STUDY: THE CASE OF AMD: UNLEASHING INTERCULTURAL POTENTIAL 234

SIDE TRIPS 237

CHECK YOURSELF 237

REFERENCES 237

CHAPTER TEN
Intercultural Ethics as Rationality: Sustainability Principle 239

INTRODUCING THE PROBLEM QUESTION 240

ETHICS AND INTERCULTURAL COMMUNICATION: AN OVERVIEW 240

APPROACHES TO ETHICS IN INTERCULTURAL COMMUNICATION 242

INTRODUCING THE SUSTAINABILITY PRINCIPLE 245
Nature of Sustainability: Thinking about Forever 246
Strategies of Intercultural Sustainability: Tolerance, Trust, and Resistance 247
Formula for Intercultural Sustainability 252

THE SUSTAINABILITY PRINCIPLE DEFINED 257

SUMMARY 258

CASE STUDY: AN ETHIC OF CULTURAL EXCHANGE 260

SIDE TRIPS 266

CHECK YOURSELF 266

REFERENCES 266

CONCLUSION 269

GLOSSARY 275

INDEX 281

ACKNOWLEDGMENTS

Everything we say exists only as a dialogue with other people. I have carried on conversations about culture and communication with many people—over the years, over national borders, over the phone, over e-mail, over dinner. Their voices have entered this book and influenced my overall approach.

First and foremost, I owe my interest in communication and culture to my parents—Lyudmila A. Klyukanova and Engel N. Loitsker. I could never thank them enough for their love, support, and faith in me.

I am grateful to my teachers, colleagues, and friends: Roman R. Gel'gardt, Kalinin State University (Russia); Mara B. Borisova, Saratov State University (Russia); Alexandra A. Zalevskaya, Boris L. Goubman, and Mikhail L. Makarov, Tver State University (Russia); Antonina A. Khar'kovskaya, Samara State University (Russia); Yurii A. Sorokin, Russian Academy of Sciences, Moscow (Russia); Deborah D. K. Ruuskanen, University of Vaasa (Finland); Pedro J. Chamizo Domínguez, Universidad de Málaga (Spain); U. S. Bahri, Bahri Publications (India); Richard Lanigan, Southern Illinois University (U.S.A.); Jackie Martinez, Arizona State University (U.S.A.); Fritz Rosekrans and Thomas F. Puckett, Eastern Washington University (U.S.A.); Richard Abraham (England); Olga Stroganova and Alexander Balashov (Russia); Merrie and Bill McIvor (U.S.A.); Marsha Reiley and Craig Holstine (U.S.A.); Mary and David Daugharty (U.S.A.); and the Narducci-Filippetti family (Italy).

The ideas presented in this book are also the result of years of classroom testing. I thank all my students for their interest and contributions. Through interaction with them, this book began to take shape.

I am grateful to Dan Tylman, an Allyn and Bacon representative, who encouraged me to put my ideas on paper in book form and submit my proposal. I thank all those at Allyn and Bacon who have helped me with this book—Karon Bowers for her commitment to my project and constant support, Brian Wheel and Jennifer Trebby for their assistance through the production process. I also thank Sally Lifland and her staff at Lifland et al., Bookmakers for their careful copyediting of the manuscript.

I am grateful to the following reviewers of the manuscript for their helpful comments and suggestions: Carlos Aleman, James Madison University; Bernardo Attias, California State University–Northridge; Thomas Baglan, Arkansas State University; Rebecca Dumlao, East Carolina University; Scherrie A. Foster, Fond du Lac Tribal and Community College; Kelby Halone, University of Tennessee; Antonio C. La Pastina, Texas A&M University; Victoria Leonard, College of the Canyons; C. B. Stiegler, Northern Kentucky University; and Karl V. Winton, Marshall University.

I would like to especially recognize two people at Eastern Washington University for helping me with this book—Paul Lindholdt for thoroughly editing the entire manuscript and offering his encouragement throughout and Judy McMillan for her clear, creative graphics.

Finally, I am grateful to my wife and daughter for their love and understanding. To them, this book is dedicated. Last but not least, I thank my cat Kuzya, a beautiful Bengal, for closely monitoring the process of writing this book. Each day he would jump on my desk and sit close to the monitor of my laptop, staring at it. Then, he would close both his eyes knowingly and nod with approval.

INTRODUCTION

Organization of the Book

An Approach to Intercultural Communication

Concepts. In the study of intercultural communication, the first step is to identify and label the main concepts. The word *concept* is derived from the Latin *conceptus* and means a thing conceived—that is, an idea or a notion. For example, some important **concepts** in the field of intercultural communication are the ideas of identity, ethnocentrism, culture shock, and prejudice. In most texts on intercultural communication, a list of concepts is found at the end of each chapter under the heading "Key Terms" or "Key Words" and at the end of the book under the heading "Index" or "Glossary."

Propositions. Different concepts relate to one another, forming propositions. The word *proposition* comes from the Latin *proponere* and means to put or set something forth or to declare something. In other words, in the study of intercultural communication, certain **propositions,** or statements, are put forth about how concepts are interrelated. For example, one might come across a proposition (statement) such as "Prejudice is never a productive part of intercultural communication" or "Language plays a central role in establishing the identity of a particular culture." In most texts on intercultural communication, important propositions are found in the summary at the end of each chapter or as a separate list of "bullet" statements under the heading "Key Ideas" or "Take-Aways."

Theories. Different propositions relate to one another, forming theories. A **theory** is a system of interrelated concepts and propositions that explains the nature of a certain object—in our case, intercultural communication. No single theory can explain a complex object in its entirety; that is why there are several theories of intercultural communication. Each theory brings together a number of concepts and a number of propositions to form a coherent system of knowledge, explaining intercultural communication from a certain perspective. For example, Ting-Toomey (1999) has developed the Identity Negotiation Theory, with a number of important concepts (e.g., "identity") and propositions (e.g., "There are eight domains of identity that play a critical role in intercultural communication"). According to Gudykunst, "Today, there are at least 15 theories covering different aspects of intercultural communication" (2002: 183), which can be divided into theories focusing on accommodation and adaptation, theories focusing on identity negotiation, theories focusing on communication networks, and so forth.

Principles. In this book, we approach intercultural communication using a number of principles. The word *principle* is derived from the Latin *principium* and means first or basic (cf. Morris, 1982: 1041). A **principle** can be viewed as an essential quality or a basic source of an object—in our case, intercultural communication. A principle is like an axiom in geometry, a starting point from which an object can be studied. For example, one of the principles (Positionality Principle) formulated in this text is stated as follows: *Intercultural communication is a process whereby people from different cultures engage in interaction and claim authority for their vision of the world.*

Principles are broad statements that cut across various concepts, propositions, and theories, revealing the general nature of intercultural communication. To use a metaphor, principles are like points of the compass required for successful orientation in the world. There are over a thousand concepts in the field of intercultural communication, hundreds of propositions about the nature of intercultural communication, and at least several dozen theories explaining its nature. Because principles are basic or fundamental qualities of an object, they are fewer in number than theories, propositions, and, of course, concepts (see Figure 1).

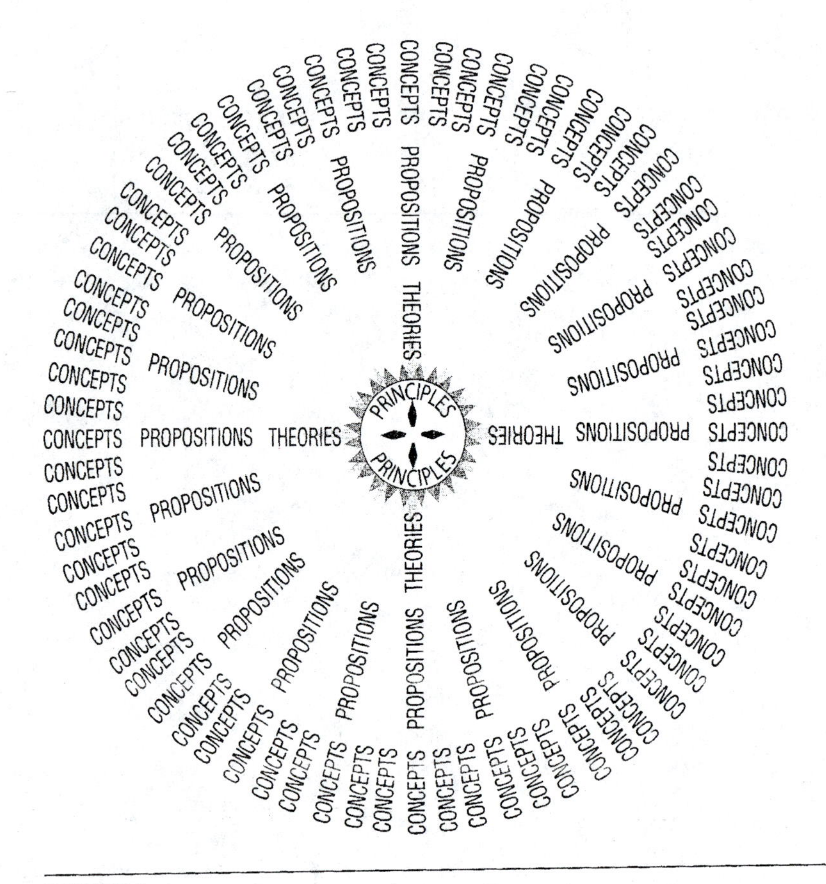

FIGURE 1

In this book, ten fundamental principles are formulated, based on the study of the most important concepts, propositions, and theories that exist in the field of intercultural communication. These ten principles constitute the core of intercultural communication and must be viewed as the points of the compass essential for your successful orientation in intercultural journeys.

Chapter Organization

Before you start your intercultural journey, you should know how this text is organized.

- *Problem question.* At the beginning of each chapter, you will find a problem question that frames the chapter and invites you into the discussion that follows. Here is an example of such a problem question: What happens to cultural meanings as they are performed and enacted?
- *Discussion.* Once a problem question has been stated, it is then discussed. Such discussion draws upon the existing scholarship in the field of intercultural communication and promotes interest in the topic. As a problem question is discussed, the groundwork is laid for introducing a principle.
- *Introduction of a principle.* A principle is labeled and briefly introduced. The three main aspects of the principle are then discussed in detail.
- *Formulation of a principle.* After the main aspects of a principle have been discussed, they are brought together, and the principle is formulated in a nutshell.
- *Summary.* At the end of each chapter, the key ideas presented in the chapter are summarized. At the very end of each summary, a new problem question is formulated to lead you into the next chapter. This continuity is extremely important; this text is one whole narrative, with each new chapter being the continuation of its predecessors. Thus, all ten principles are interconnected, an idea that is explicitly emphasized in the book's conclusion.
- *Case study.* The case study shows how the principle can be applied in a real situation of intercultural interaction. At the beginning of each case study, you are given certain topics to keep in mind. After the case study, a detailed discussion of these topics is presented.
- *Side trips.* If you have time and curiosity and are willing to make an effort, you can take various side trips. Several venues are presented for you to explore, such as articles or websites that are related to the subject of the chapter but that take it a bit further. Questions are provided to guide you on your side trips.
- *Check yourself.* At the end of each chapter is a list of key terms. Where they are explained or defined in the chapter, the key terms appear in boldface. So, if you cannot define or explain a term, you can easily find it in the chapter and review its definition.

With the help of the ten principles, this text aims to reach its main goal—helping you to develop your intercultural communication competence.

Goal of the Book: Intercultural Communication Competence

Studying intercultural communication is important for a number of reasons. Such reasons are sometimes called imperatives. For example, the following six imperatives have been isolated (Martin & Nakayama, 2004):

1. *Technological imperative.* New technologies are creating complex relationships between different cultures.
2. *Demographic imperative.* Cultural diversity is a fact of life.
3. *Economic imperative.* Having the ability to communicate with other cultures is good business.
4. *Peace imperative.* The ability to communicate with other cultures brings peace and stimulates healthy relationships.
5. *Self-awareness imperative.* The better we communicate with other cultures, the better we understand ourselves as individuals.
6. *Ethical imperative.* Intercultural communication forces us to think about the consequences (good and bad) of our actions and words.

These imperatives can be viewed as challenges that must be met. For instance, we must study intercultural communication if we want to build good relationships with new immigrants (demographic imperative) or if we want to prevent violence (peace imperative).

It is clear that, in order to meet these challenges, we must develop **intercultural communication competence** (henceforth, **ICC**). ICC is a system of knowledge and skills enabling us to communicate successfully with people from other cultures (Chen & Starosta, 1996; Wiseman, 2002; Wiseman & Koester, 1993). The ICC system comprises several components. Before we label these components, however, let's consider a specific example: meeting the challenge of having a successful vacation in Cyprus.

Some research on the culture and history of Cyprus would reveal, among many other things, that the northern part of the island has belonged, since 1974, to Turkey and that Greek Cypriots consider that territory to be "a zone of occupation" (for more information, see Broome, 2004: 277–278). First suppose that you did not do any research and hence failed to treat this issue with sensitivity: You made the cultural faux pas of asking your hosts to take you to the beautiful resort of Famagosta, a town that used to be a famous resort in Cyprus but now is part of the Turkish territory. This is a sore topic for Greek Cypriots. If you made this mistake, your request might be taken at best as a display of ignorance or at worst as an attempt to cause your hosts emotional pain. In either case, intercultural communication would be unsuccessful, failing to convey the meaning you intended.

Now suppose that you did your research and hence didn't make any cultural mistakes in your interactions with your hosts. What enabled you to communicate effectively?

First, you were able to learn an important fact about the present-day situation in Cyprus—an example of the cognitive component of ICC. This component is your knowledge base and can be represented by the expression "I know ____." When you learn new information about people from other cultures and how to interact with them, you fill in the blank, as it were, and the cognitive component of your ICC becomes more complex—for example, "I know *that the northern part of Cyprus now belongs to Turkey.*"

Second, you were able to develop a certain attitude toward the fact that you learned—sensitivity, in this case. (It could be any attitude—rejection, indifference, anger, etc.) This attitude is an example of the affective component of ICC. The affective component includes various attitudes, feelings, and emotions that arise in intercultural situations, and it can be represented by the expression "I feel ____." As we face new situations of an intercultural nature, the blank is repeatedly filled; for instance, "I feel *angry that Greek Cypriots must suffer because of the loss of part of their island.*" As a result, our attitudes change; ideally, we become more open-minded, sensitive, and fair.

Third, when in Cyprus, you were able to discuss the delicate issue of the divided island with tact; you behaved as a good listener, asking the right questions and not asking wrong ones. These abilities are examples of the behavioral component of ICC. As the name suggests, this component includes all those things that you actually do or say (or do *not* do or say, in cases where silence is more appropriate). The behavioral component can be represented by the expression "I do ____." Our ICC grows as we interact with people from other cultures—listening, gesturing, paying a compliment, or carrying on a casual conversation.

So, the ICC system is made up of three interconnected components—cognitive, affective, and behavioral. All these components are equally important; together, they enable us to communicate successfully with people from other cultures. The ICC system can be represented as shown in Figure 2.

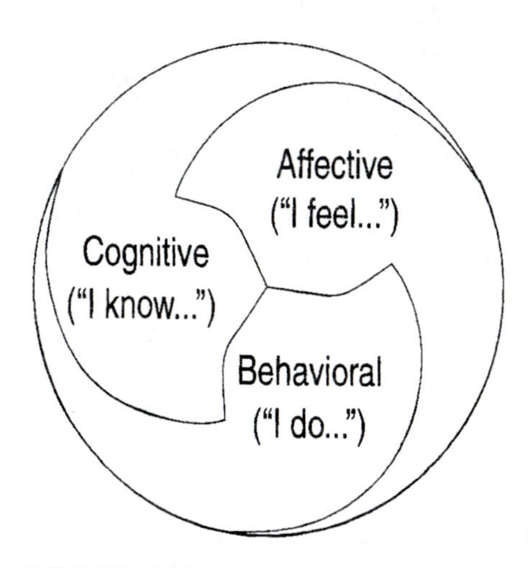

FIGURE 2 The ICC System

There are a number of challenges posed by life itself that make it imperative for us to study intercultural communication. We can meet these challenges by developing the ICC system. The goal of this text is to help you become more competent in intercultural communication—that is, to help you build up your system of ICC, based on ten fundamental principles.

Let us emphasize one more time that this text unfolds as a story. All ten principles are interconnected, and so each chapter can be seen as a step in your intercultural journey. Learning these ten principles will make your travel in today's intercultural world more successful and rewarding. And now, let the journey begin!

CHECK YOURSELF

Concept
Proposition
Theory
Principle
Intercultural communication competence (ICC)

REFERENCES

Broome, B. (2004). Building a shared future across the divide: Identity and conflict in Cyprus. In Fong, M., & R. Chuang (Eds.), *Communicating ethnic and cultural identity* (pp. 275–294). Lanham, MD: Rowman & Littlefield.

Chen, G., & Starosta, W. (1996). Intercultural communication competence: A synthesis. In Burleson, B. (Ed.), *Communication yearbook*, Vol. 19 (pp. 353–383). Thousand Oaks, CA: Sage.

Gudykunst, W. (2002). Intercultural communication theories. In Gudykunst, W., & B. Moody (Eds.), *Handbook of international and intercultural communication* (pp. 183–206). Thousand Oaks, CA: Sage.

Martin, J., & Nakayama, T. (2004). *Intercultural communication in contexts*. New York: McGraw-Hill.

Morris, E. (Ed.). (1982). *The American Heritage dictionary of the English language*. Boston: Houghton Mifflin.

Ting-Toomey, S. (1999). *Communicating across cultures*. New York: Guilford.

Wiseman, R. (2002). Intercultural communication competence. In Gudykunst, W., & B. Moody (Eds.), *Handbook of international and intercultural communication* (pp. 207–224). Thousand Oaks, CA: Sage.

Wiseman, R., & Koester, J. (Eds.). (1993). *Intercultural communication competence*. Newbury Park, CA: Sage.

CHAPTER ONE

CREATING CULTURAL BOUNDARIES: PUNCTUATION PRINCIPLE

What's in a Line?

- *Key Theme:* Boundaries
- *Key Objective:* To help you understand how and why cultural identities are formed

INTRODUCING THE PROBLEM QUESTION

DEFINING BASIC TERMS

Culture
Communication

THE PROCESS OF CULTURAL IDENTIFICATION

Identity as Group Membership
Cultural Identity as a Reflective Self-Image

INTRODUCING THE PUNCTUATION PRINCIPLE

Boundary Lines as Conceptualizations
Constructive and Destructive Boundary Lines
Boundary Fit as the Goal of Intercultural Communication

THE PUNCTUATION PRINCIPLE DEFINED

SUMMARY

CASE STUDY: A HISTORY OF THE RUSSO-JAPANESE FRONTIER

SIDE TRIPS

CHECK YOURSELF

REFERENCES

Introducing the Problem Question

In an article entitled "Alas, What to Call Non-Caucasians?" Leonard Pitts Jr., a well-known American journalist, writes

> In a saner world, when somebody asked a non-Hispanic, black Native American Indian, what he preferred to be called, he wouldn't have to give the currently acceptable term for his genus, his group or his type. He'd only have to give one thing. His name. (2003: A12)

Very elegantly phrased. Nobody will dispute the importance of personality, but people—with their individual names—also identify with other people and come together into groups. It is important to study not only individual personalities, but also groups of people and how they communicate with one another. We cannot study intercultural communication without understanding the process of cultural identification.

Let's then begin by asking the following problem question: *What is the process of cultural identification?*

In this chapter we will

- Define the basic terms *culture* and *communication*
- Discuss identity as group membership and as a reflective self-image
- Show how cultural identities are created with the help of boundary lines
- Look at the nature of boundary lines in the formation of cultural identities
- Discuss the constructive and destructive sides of boundary lines
- Present the overall goal of intercultural communication in terms of boundaries.

Defining Basic Terms

The subject of this book is intercultural communication, so we will begin by defining its basic terms—*culture* and *communication*.

Culture

The word *culture* goes back to the Latin *cultura*, derived from *cultus* and meaning cultivation or tillage (Morris, 1982: 321). Just as crops are produced by nature, people cultivate and share their own "crop"—a system of symbolic resources. So, **culture** can be defined as a system of symbolic resources shared by a group of people. Let's highlight briefly the main components of this definition.

Culture is a system of *symbolic* resources shared by a group of people. A symbol is anything that represents meaning to us. For example, for many Western companies, a field rich with oil means the potential to create a lot of consumer goods and services. And in some Asian cultures, making sounds while eating (slurping) means appreciation of the food and a tribute to the chef. These meanings might seem natural to those who share them, but they are not: Meanings are symbolic creations, produced and reproduced by people themselves, not by nature. A field rich with oil does not always mean consumer goods and services; for the U'wa Indians, oil is sacred as the blood of Mother Earth and cannot be drilled. In most Western cultures, slurping sounds indicate a lack of respect and bad manners.

Culture is a system of symbolic *resources* shared by a group of people. A resource is anything that makes it possible for people to accomplish a task. Just like natural crops, symbolic resources allow us to accomplish various tasks. Symbolic resources can be seen as the *source* to which people *re*sort when needed—hence the word *re*sources. For example, people use oil when they need to produce gas for their vehicles or when they need to connect to Mother Earth. People resort to slurping when they want to show appreciation of the food or display a lack of respect.

Culture is a *system* of symbolic resources shared by a group of people. A system is a group of interrelated elements forming a whole entity. Symbolic resources are meanings that form a system; they interconnect to form a whole entity—culture. For example, we understand the meaning of a handshake only insofar as it relates to other forms of greeting, such as a hug or a kiss; and greetings relate to other forms of behavior, such as farewells.

Culture is a system of symbolic resources *shared* by a group of people. Symbolic resources "are shared with others and constructed jointly through interaction" (Littlejohn, 2002: 165). Symbolic resources are meaningful only insofar as people agree on what these resources mean. For example, although people from the same culture might agree that slurping represents a lack of respect and bad manners, a person who does not share this meaning, common in Western cultures, may inadvertently come across as disrespectful or rude by making slurping sounds during a meal.

Culture is a system of symbolic resources shared by a *group of people*. The term *culture* can be applied to any group of people based, for example, on nationality, ethnicity, gender, sexual orientation, or physical (dis)ability. "This inclusive conception of culture allows for the viewing of all communication encounters as potentially 'intercultural'" (Kim, 2001: 140). In this respect, the concepts of "stranger" (Rogers, 1999; Simmel, 1950) and "cultural Other" (Blommaert, 1998; Jandt & Tanno, 2001) are sometimes used to incorporate different types of groups.

So, culture is a system of symbolic resources shared by a group of people. In every intercultural situation, groups of people with different systems of symbolic resources come into contact—that is, they communicate with each other.

Communication

The word *communication* goes back to the Latin *communicare*, derived from *communis* and meaning to make common (Morris, 1982: 269). The idea of making something common implies mixing or exchanging something. In the process of communication, cultural meanings as symbolic resources are created and exchanged. Thus, **communication** can be defined as the practice of creating and exchanging meanings or symbolic resources.

It is clear that culture and communication are interconnected. "Culture and communication are not separate entities or areas. Each is produced through a dynamic relationship with the other" (Shirato & Yell, 2000: 2). Communication practices make it possible for cultural meanings to be created and exchanged, while culture as a system of symbolic resources makes it possible for communication practices to continue. For example, through the process of communication, people in many Asian cultures assigned to the practice of slurping during a meal its meaning as appreciation of the food. This cultural meaning, in turn, now makes it possible for people in these cultures to communicate with one another (resort to this practice over and over again) and also exchange this meaning (share this symbolic resource) with people from other cultures.

Thus, culture and communication as "resources and practices are tightly connected and cannot really be separated. Resources are constructed in practice, and practices are shaped by resources. This is the recursive loop of resources and practices" (Littlejohn, 2002: 165). So, culture and communication form a circular and dynamic relationship, as shown in Figure 1. Based on this understanding of culture and communication, we can define **intercultural communication** as a process of interaction between groups of people with different systems of symbolic resources.

As you can see, in intercultural communication we deal with "the identification of communications of a shared system of symbolic verbal and nonverbal behavior that are meaningful to group members" (Fong, 2004a: 6). So, let's take a closer look at how and why people identify with each other and form cultures. In other words, let's discuss the process of cultural identification.

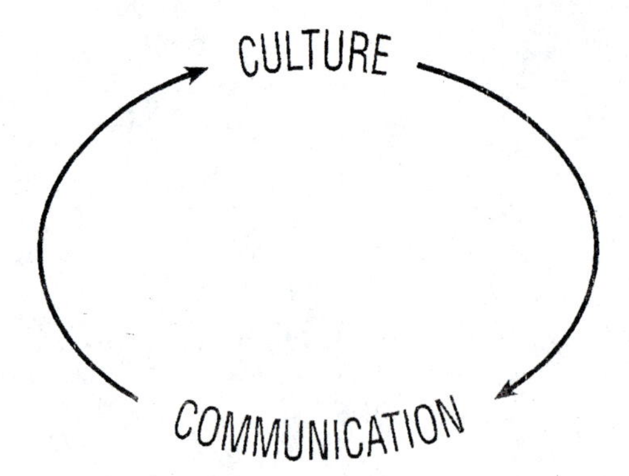

FIGURE 1 Relationships of Culture and Communication

The Process of Cultural Identification

Identity as Group Membership

In this world, people have their individual names, but people also form groups and are categorized "as members of our cultures or not members of our cultures" (Gudykunst & Kim, 2003: 189). This way, "culture serves the *group inclusion function,* satisfying our need for membership affiliation and belonging. Culture creates a comfort zone in which we experience in-group inclusion and in-group/out-group differences" (Ting-Toomey, 1999: 13). Members of our culture form an **in-group,** and members of another culture form an **out-group** (Tajfel, 1981). In technical terms,

> **In-group** refers to group members who identify and associate with each other. Members of the group see themselves and other members as part of their "in-group." . . . People who are kept at a physical and emotional distance are considered the **out-group** from the view of in-group members. . . . For example, athletes and cheerleaders may consider themselves as the in-group at their school and see the student government leaders as the out-group. (Fong, 2004a: 8)

Such perceptions of out-groups often lead to stereotyping and prejudice; we will discuss these barriers to effective intercultural communication in Chapter 9 (Synergy Principle).

Now, take a sheet of paper and divide it in two parts with a line down the middle. On the left, list some groups of which you personally are a member. Next, look around you and put groups different from yours on the right side of the sheet of the paper. You can use words, such as Jewish, Spanish, Democrat, or Muslim, or you can get more creative and use pictures such as religious symbols, to represent different groups. It is a simple exercise, but it will help you to see—literally—how many different groups of people exist in this world. As an example, see Figure 2.

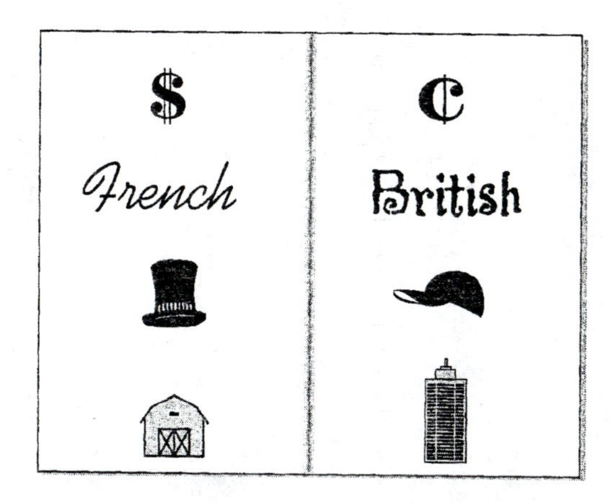

FIGURE 2

As you can see, the process of cultural identification begins with drawing boundaries between an in-group and an out-group. So, the key to answering our problem question is found on the sheet of paper in front of you: The process of cultural identification is based on boundaries that are perceived to exist between different groups of people. Just look at the boundary line down the middle of Figure 2. Boundary lines play a crucial role in the process of construction of cultures.

As a member of an in-group, one shares certain meanings or symbolic resources with other members. For example, as a Muslim, one shares with other Muslims certain ideas about what it means to be a Muslim; one identifies with certain meanings, such as serving Allah. When we draw a boundary line between ourselves and others, we identify with those similar to us, creating our cultural identity. All people who identify with the same meanings or symbolic resources have a collective cultural identity. The word *identity* is derived from the Latin *idem* meaning the same (Morris, 1982: 654). Thus, cultural **identity** can be viewed as membership in a group in which all people share the same symbolic meanings. Naturally, cultural identities vary in terms of scope (the number of people who share the identity), salience (the importance of the identity), and intensity (the strength with which the identity is communicated to others) (Collier & Thomas, 1998).

There are a large number of cultural identities. We "identify with many groups as we are growing up. Groups may be based on gender, race, ethnicity, class, sexual orientation, religion, and nationality" (Martin & Nakayama, 2000: 112). All these cultural identities are marked by different boundary lines. In this textbook, we will often be concerned with racial, national, and ethnic identities.

The concept of **racial identity** refers to group membership based on alleged biological and physical characteristics. Racial identities are marked by such boundary lines as facial features, skin pigmentation, and hair texture. Race, however, can be controversial because it is difficult to establish a true identity based only on physical marks. For instance, attempts to determine racial identity through DNA testing are usually met with resistance. Racial identity, which is grounded in the natural "lines of descent," is always further constructed to reflect a hierarchy of symbolic meanings. Consequently, reliance on the body as the site of racial identity is inadequate because race is constructed through various communicative behaviors. For example, the meaning of the "white race" is enacted in a number of different verbal and nonverbal behaviors; it cannot be identified only with the skin color (for more information, see Warren, 2001).

The concept of **national identity** refers to group membership based on a historico-political formation with a specific space and an administrative apparatus. Usually, national identity refers to "a person's legal status or citizenship in relation to a nation" (Fong, 2004b: 30). If one has dual citizenship, one has a dual national identity. National identities are usually marked by such boundary lines as borders—on land, in the air, or in the water. For instance, it is possible to speak of a French national identity. National identities have an impact on how people from different cultures interact. For instance (see Vatikiotis & Schwartz, 1995), on May

31, 1995, six Thai fishing boats were set upon by Vietnamese coastal-patrol vessels in waters claimed by both Thailand and Vietnam, prompting the Thai navy to intervene. For Thailand the incident was a reminder of how serious the competition for resources in these waters had become, whereas for Vietnam it was a worrisome signal that Thailand was willing to use force to uphold its interests. The Thais said that the incident occurred 213 kilometers east of the coastal town of Songkhla, which would place the incident area within Thailand's exclusive economic zone. For their part, the Vietnamese said only that the incident occurred within Vietnam's southwestern territorial waters. The timing of the skirmish was particularly awkward, occurring just days before bilateral talks in Ho Chi Minh City on the disputed boundary of Thai and Vietnamese waters. Needless to say, the incident had an impact on the Thai and Vietnamese perceptions of each other and on their future intercultural interactions.

The concept of **ethnic identity** refers to group membership based on a common symbolic heritage. Just think of such ethnic groups as the Kurds in the Middle East and the Zulu in southern Africa. Ethnic identities are marked by such boundary lines as shared language, beliefs, and rituals. So, ethnic identity "can be sustained by shared objective characteristics (language, religion, etc.) or by more subjective contributions to the sense of 'groupness'" (Edward, 1979: 10)—for instance, a sense of origin and history.

It must be emphasized that "identities are contingent and unstable cultural creations with which we identify. They are not universal or absolute existent 'things'" (Barker, 2000: 193). This statement applies to any group of people perceived to be different. Cultural identities are marked not only by tangible boundaries, such as national land borders or skin color, but also by more intangible boundaries, such as shared beliefs and values. Based on these tangible and intangible boundaries, people constantly construct their identity as a reflective image of themselves.

Cultural Identity as a Reflective Self-Image

As we saw earlier, cultural identity refers to conceptualizations of the self that derive from membership in groups (Brewer & Miller, 1996). To put it simply, cultural identity is the way we see ourselves; it is our self-image. For example, people from the United States might identify with characterizations of themselves as hard-working, friendly, tolerant, and freedom-loving (for more information on American cultural patterns, see Stewart & Bennet, 1991).

How a Cultural Self-Image Is Formed. People in each in-group construct an image of themselves—their self-image or identity. However, "what we think of as our identity is dependent on what we think we are *not*" (Barker, 2000: 195). Each cultural identity "is symbolically constructed and defined" (Eisenstadt, 1998: 138). Cultural identities are created and maintained in the process of interaction. As a result of interaction, "within our own cultural context, we have unconsciously built our 'self-image'" (Usunier, 1996: 386).

So, our cultural identity as an image of ourselves is the result of our interaction with other people. Cultural identity, therefore, is not simply group membership. The term *identity* is also used "to denote the reflective self-image or self-conception that we each derive from our cultural group membership" (Ting-Toomey, 1999: 28). Every situation of "intercultural communication takes place in the confrontation of a cultural self and a cultural other" (Nöth, 2001: 240). The genesis of Self from the mirror image of the Other is elaborated in many developmental theories of social interaction (Lacan, 1968; Vygotsky, 1962). Common to all these theories is the premise that Self is but a reflection of the Other. This premise is captured very well by Karl Popper in the following quote:

> It seems to me of considerable importance that we are not born as selves, but that we have to learn that we are selves; in fact we have to learn to be selves. . . . How do we obtain self-knowledge? Not by self-observation, I suggest, but by becoming selves, and by developing theories about ourselves. Long before we attain consciousness and knowledge of ourselves, we have, normally, become aware of other persons. . . . I suggest that a consciousness of self begins to develop through the medium of other persons: just as we learn to see ourselves in a mirror, so the child becomes conscious of himself by sensing his reflection in the mirror of other people's consciousness of himself. (Popper & Eccles, 1977: 109–110)

G. H. Mead, a well-known American scholar who studied language and communication at the beginning of the last century, called this reflection of ourselves the **looking-glass self** (Mead, 1934). As members of an in-group, we acquire our view of ourselves based on the view of us held by people from other cultures. Our cultural identity, then, is a *reflective* self-image. Cultural identity as a reflective self-image is projected differently by different cultures. Intercultural communication always puts us in a hall of mirrors with multiple and ever-changing reflections. It is as if all other cultures were holding up a huge mirror in which we could see ourselves (see Figure 3).

FIGURE 3

Thus, cultural identity is a *reflective* self-image; it is how we see ourselves as seen by people from other cultures. If we fail to present the image that we desire, intercultural communication cannot be considered successful. As was said earlier, Americans may view themselves as hard-working, friendly, tolerant, and freedom-loving. However, there are often differences between this self-construal and the reflective self-image—that is, the way people from other cultures see Americans. For instance, the book *Learning to Hate Americans* (DeFleur & DeFleur, 2003) presents the image teenagers around the world have of Americans. According to surveys conducted in 12 countries, many people perceive Americans to be extremely violent and criminally inclined, and American women to be sexually immoral. The authors of the book note that they expected some difference in perceptions, but such images shocked them. Naturally, "conflict may arise when there are sharp differences between who we think we are and who others think we are" (Martin & Nakayama, 2000: 111).

Why a Cultural Self-Image Is Formed. It is important to think of cultural identity as a reflective self-image because for all people the experience of "interacting with a person from a different culture triggers an awareness of their own cultural identities" (Lustig & Koester, 2003: 145). For example, interacting with people from other cultures can help Americans get a better understanding of their self-image and make changes in it, if necessary. People from every culture try to define themselves as members of an in-group. In this respect, "culture provides the frame of reference to answer the most fundamental question of each being: Who am I?" (Ting-Toomey, 1999: 12). This question cannot be answered adequately without including information on how people from other cultures define one's identity; intercultural communication is all about people's self-definition as cultural beings.

Thus, intercultural communication consists not only of interpreting behaviors of people from other cultures but also of interpreting our own behavior based on others' reactions to it. We cannot count on a self-construal as our true identity; we need to look at ourselves through the eyes of the Other and see our identity as a reflective self-image. Any interaction between people from different cultures reveals—not only to each other, but also to themselves—an important part of their cultural identities. We may not always like this reflective self-image, but blaming the mirror, so to speak, is never helpful.

So, "collective identity is produced by the social construction of boundaries. These boundaries . . . establish a demarcation between inside and outside, strangers and familiars" (Eisenstadt, 1998: 139). Every cultural identity can be viewed as group membership and as a reflective self-image. We can define ourselves as cultural beings only in the process of interaction with people from other cultures. Without boundary lines, there would be no Others. Without Others, there would be no Selves. In a word, intercultural communication makes it possible for us to understand ourselves and others.

Introducing the Punctuation Principle

Let's now formulate, based on the discussion above, the first principle of intercultural communication: the Punctuation Principle. We will isolate three parts that make up this principle. Each part deals with intercultural communication as a process of drawing boundary lines between groups of people. First, we will present boundary lines in intercultural communication as conceptualizations. Next, we will look at constructive and destructive boundary lines. Finally, we will discuss the goal of intercultural communication as a process of looking for a boundary fit. After discussing each part separately, we will formulate the Punctuation Principle as a whole.

Boundary Lines as Conceptualizations

The Concept of "Punctuation." You may be wondering what punctuation has to do with intercultural communication. It must be said right away that the Punctuation Principle is not about punctuation marks, even though the word *punctuation* has the same origin in the case of punctuation marks and in the case of the Punctuation Principle. Etymologically, *punctuation* is derived from the Latin *punctuare* and means to break or to mark with a point (Morris, 1982: 1060). This is exactly what traditional punctuation marks do—they break the stream of writing into separate elements and tell us what the divisions between these elements are. Punctuation marks help us to understand the correct meaning; as we all know, a simple comma, put in the wrong place, can change meaning dramatically. But the term **punctuation** can also be applied to communication in general, not just writing (see Bateson & Jackson, 1964; Watzlawick, 1984). "In the study of communication, *punctuation* is a process of perception through which people organize their ongoing interactions into recognizable openings, closings, causes, and effects" (Anderson & Ross, 2002: 147).

Intercultural communication can be viewed from the same perspective. In intercultural communication, as shown above, we find marks such as skin color and land and water borders. Our experiences are divided through such marks, or boundary lines, into different cultures with their own identities. In essence, the Punctuation Principle is the Principle of Boundary Lines.

If you were asked now "What is a boundary line?" you would probably give examples such as land borders, sea lines, shared language, or shared beliefs and values. And you would be absolutely correct: All these are examples of boundary lines. But think how these boundaries change as we move from skin color to land borders to sea lines to shared beliefs and values. They become less and less tangible, and more and more difficult to detect. You can (literally) put your finger on a land border, but how can you grasp lines in the universe of beliefs and values? What about people who have the same skin color and yet do not communicate at all or, even worse, are ready to kill each other? Where does the boundary line between these people lie? What is a boundary line, first and foremost?

A Boundary Line as an Idea. Earlier, Barker was quoted as saying "What we think of as our identity is dependent on what we think we are *not*" (2000: 195). The word *think*, used twice in the quote, is the key to the origin of boundary lines: They are, above all, our thoughts, perceptions, and expectations. Boundary lines are born in people's minds, as conceptualizations, and later turn into borders, walls, lines in the water, language barricades, and such. There is a wonderful short film called *Boundary Lines*, directed and written by Philip Stapp in 1946. In this film, we see two friendly neighbors peacefully settling a dispute over a little fence. But we also see an arrow shot by a primordial hunter flying across time and turning into various types of weapons, eventually ending as an atomic bomb, ready to descend on a city. The film makes a powerful statement about the conceptual nature of boundary lines.

Of course, sometimes nature pushes us, allowing us to draw boundary lines more readily—by giving us different skin pigmentation, for instance. But even then, as we saw earlier in the example of race, our thoughts affect the process of identity construction. For example, in the 2000 U.S. Census, almost half of all Hispanic respondents refused to identify themselves as belonging to any of the five racial categories on the form: white, black, Asian, American Indian or Alaska native, or native of Hawaii or the Pacific Islands. Forty-two percent of all Latino respondents marked the box labeled "some other race" and wrote in such identities as Mayan, Tejano, and mestizo (Navarro, 2003). So, even skin color is a moving target, and the North American construct of race is making room for new groups of people.

It is people who create boundary lines, for better or for worse. A boundary line, first and foremost, is an idea, or conceptualization.

Constructive and Destructive Boundary Lines

Identity Confirmation and Disconfirmation. During intercultural communication, people present their identity by taking a line. Naturally, people try to take an appropriate line, aiming to project the image that they desire. People from other cultures may respond to our self-presentation positively, or they may respond negatively. Positive responses can be equated with **identity confirmation,** the "process through which individuals are recognized, acknowledged, and endorsed" (Laing, 1961: 83). Identity-confirming messages may include showing empathy toward others and using supportive language. Negative responses can be equated with **identity disconfirmation,** "the process through which individuals do not recognize others, do not respond sensitively to dissimilar others, and do not accept others' experiences as valid" (Ting-Toomey, 1999: 47). Identity-disconfirming messages may include ignoring others and using racist language. People "can suffer real damage, real distortion" if people from another culture "mirror back to them a confining, or contemptible picture of themselves" (Taylor, 1992: 25).

Confirming or disconfirming messages affect the process of cultural identification. If people can freely take the line they want—that is, use the verbal and nonverbal behaviors they want—their identity as a self-construal is confirmed. In this case, people achieve their goals, and boundary lines are perceived as constructive. If people take a line, using certain verbal and nonverbal behaviors, but their identity as a self-construal is disconfirmed, they do *not* achieve their goals, and boundary lines are perceived as destructive.

Destructive Boundary Lines. When most people hear the words *boundary lines* and *boundaries,* their first image is of separation and breakdown in communication; hence, boundary lines are perceived as negative and destructive. Unfortunately, this view is supported by numerous real-life examples. In fact, many illustrations discussed in this text are examples of intercultural failures due to destructive boundary lines. Boundary lines are destructive when they fail to help people realize their goals and define themselves—that is, construct their cultural identities (see Figure 4).

Any boundary that physically separates people from different cultures, preventing them from taking their line in interacting with each other, is an example of a destructive boundary line; the Berlin Wall was one such boundary. People from different cultures can also be separated by other destructive boundary lines—for example, those of language. In the Texas town of Amarillo, two women who were fluent in Spanish and English were fired from their jobs because they chatted in Spanish in their workplace. The owner of the company asked the women to speak only English while at work; the owner allegedly even demanded that they sign a pledge not to speak Spanish. Both women refused, and they lost their jobs (see Verhovek, 1997). It is clear that the boundary line in this intercultural interaction was destructive: The owner was perceived by the women as overstepping his boundary, while the two women were perceived by the owner as uncooperative and lacking flexibility.

Constructive Boundary Lines. Let us not forget that without boundary lines there would be no cultures, so boundary lines cannot be all bad! Besides, the Latin root of *punctuation* refers simply to "marking with points," and the Latin root

FIGURE 4

of *boundary* refers to "a field within limits." Nowhere do we find any evaluation; the meanings of the words *punctuation* and *boundary* are neutral. Boundary lines could be perceived as negative and destructive, or they could (and should!) be perceived as positive and constructive. Boundary lines are constructive when they make it possible for people to take a certain line in communication and define (construct) their cultural identity, regulating interaction with others. If the cultures involved in communication see the boundary lines as serving them well, then the boundary lines are perceived as constructive and positive. The idea of constructive boundary lines is highlighted in Figure 5.

Take the example of St. Martin, the smallest parcel of land in the world ruled by two sovereignties. Part French and part Dutch ever since the partition treaty was signed back in 1648 (for more information, see Jermanok, 1999), the island even has two names—St. Martin and Sint Maarten. People from both cultures have merged to create arguably the most cosmopolitan island in the Caribbean. The island's inhabitants are proud of their peaceful coexistence for over 350 years. A boundary line running from Cupecoy Bay in the west to Cortalita Beach in the east apportioned 21 square miles to the French and 16 square miles to the Dutch. Legend has it that two soldiers, one Dutch and one French, were chosen to divide the island in half. They started back to back and began walking. However, the Dutch soldier stopped to have a drink, while the French soldier remained sober and continued his duty, hence the difference in size. (More likely, though, the French received 21 square miles because of their superior naval presence in the region when the treaty was signed.) Today, one is free to cross sides without a passport.

Thus, the nature of boundary lines is two-fold. A boundary line can cause disputes and even wars; then a boundary line is perceived as destructive and does not lead to effective intercultural interactions. Or a boundary line can create peaceful borders (think of a fence between two friendly neighbors); then it is perceived as constructive and leads to effective intercultural communication. Again, the origin of boundary lines is in people's minds, and so it is people who make those boundary lines destructive (dysfunctional, negative) or constructive (functional, positive).

FIGURE 5

Boundary Fit as the Goal of Intercultural Communication

The main goal of intercultural interactions is to make sure boundary lines are respected and agreed upon—that is, are perceived as constructive by people from all cultures engaged in the interaction. Then all cultures can function successfully, reaching a boundary fit in their interactions. A **boundary fit** is an agreement among people from interacting cultures on the function of a boundary line between them. An example of a successful boundary fit would be the relationship between the Amish and people from the Anglo-Saxon culture. Although interactions between the Amish and Anglo-Saxons are not perfect, the Amish have managed to fulfill their philosophy of maintaining cultural separateness and still succeed in their businesses and be accepted and respected by the Anglo-Saxon culture (Petronio et al., 1998).

But now look at another example—an excerpt from a guided tour of one of the so-called heritage museums in Israel:

> I'll tell you a story, do you remember the story about the Patriarch Abraham? Oh, he was quite a man! Phee (Wow), he had lots of cows and sheep and lots of people working for him, and he used to wander from place to place, and he lived in the desert. He was the first Bedouin, the Bedouins weren't there yet, but he was there already. He was sitting in a tent, what was his wife's name? Sara, Sara sat with him in the tent, and three angels are coming, they are going around in the desert, and they see some old man sitting with a young and beautiful woman, so they say: "Let's go visit them," so they come, and Abraham says to them: "Tefadalu, please, come in and be our guests," so he says, what does he say to Sara? He whispers a loud whisper in her ear: "Go get three measures of flour (seot kemah)." Here are the measures (pointing to the wall), from the Bible straight here on this wall. You see, this is what they used to measure in, imagine, the Patriarch Abraham in his time. How many years already? Oh, it's impossible, I wasn't there, you weren't there, your parents weren't there, and he was already using this to measure with this. (Katriel, 1994: 14)

To Jewish audiences, this kind of story sounds like a playful elaboration of a well-known biblical tale. To Arab audiences, however, the strategy of renaming Abraham as the first Bedouin and endowing a familiar agricultural object (the measure) with a biblical career is an act of **cultural appropriation**—the taking away of symbolic resources. It might be that the Israeli crossed an imaginary line here, or it might be that the Arabs simply overreacted. Whatever the case, it is hardly possible to speak of a true boundary fit in this intercultural interaction.

Or take the example of a dramatic change in the boundary lines in the former Yugoslavia, where people from the same communities suddenly saw themselves as members of different ethnic groups. The aggressive behavior of former neighbors, friends, and even spouses, which the international community found difficult to understand, was the consequence of a changed boundary fit (Petronio et al., 1998).

Sometimes it seems that the boundary line between people from different cultures is so negative and deeply engraved that no boundary fit is possible. However, it must be remembered that boundary lines are, first and foremost, ideas that are manifested in many different forms. Some of these forms, like skin color, appear as almost natural creations; others, like the Berlin Wall, simply seem rock solid. But even these seemingly eternal boundary lines undergo dramatic—and sometimes rapid—changes; think of the fall of the Berlin Wall.

Boundary lines can be hard or soft, depending on how difficult or easy it is for an out-group to communicate with an in-group. **Hard boundaries** are lines that are deeply engraved within a culture and difficult to change in the process of intercultural interaction. **Soft boundaries** are lines that are not as deeply engraved within a culture and easier to change in the process of intercultural interaction. What is important to remember, however, is that even the hardest boundaries change because our conceptualizations change. It is said that nothing can stop the idea whose time has come, and that is true for boundary lines in intercultural communication. Boundary lines change because people can always change their conceptualizations of themselves and others.

Thus, effective intercultural communication requires that people from different cultures agree on their boundary lines, or negotiate a boundary fit. In a way, the whole process of intercultural communication is looking for that boundary fit. We will discuss specific routes for negotiating a boundary fit later in this book when we take up the Transaction Principle of intercultural communication. In the meantime, let's define our first principle—the Punctuation Principle.

The Punctuation Principle Defined

We will provide a more concise formulation of the Punctuation Principle, based on the discussion of its three parts above.

First, intercultural communication can be seen in terms of boundary lines, which originate in people's minds and mark distinctions between in-groups (Self) and out-groups (the Other). Any boundary line is, first and foremost, an idea, or conceptualization.

Second, boundary lines between people from different cultures can be perceived as destructive or constructive, resulting in less effective or more effective communication, respectively. If boundary lines prevent people from realizing their goals and defining themselves, they are considered destructive; if they allow people from different cultures to define themselves and realize their goals, they are considered constructive.

Third, people from different cultures have certain boundary demands. Effective intercultural communication requires that people from different cultures agree on their boundary lines, or negotiate a boundary fit.

In a nutshell, the Punctuation Principle can be formulated as follows:

> *Intercultural communication is a process whereby people from different cultures define their collective identities by drawing boundary lines between themselves, looking for a mutually acceptable boundary fit.*

Thus, effective intercultural communication involves establishing a boundary fit; people from different cultures can then realize their goals and function successfully.

So, what's in a line? A lot, it turns out.

Summary

In this chapter, the following problem question was posed: What is the process of cultural identification? In other words, we set out to find out how and why cultural identities are formed.

We showed that cultural identities are created by drawing a boundary line between one group and another group (in-group and out-group, Self and the Other). We gave examples of cultural identities (racial, national, and ethnic identities), emphasizing that cultural identities are marked not only by tangible boundaries (e.g., national borders or skin color) but also by more intangible boundaries (e.g., shared beliefs and values). Thus, all cultural identities were presented as fluid constructions.

Next we showed that cultural identities are constructed in the process of interaction. We can understand who we are only by understanding who we are *not*—through the eyes of the Other(s). It was emphasized that people from other cultures make it possible for us to define our own cultural selves. From this perspective, intercultural communication was presented as a process of our self-definition as cultural beings.

Based on these ideas, we formulated the Punctuation Principle of intercultural communication. In essence, the Punctuation Principle is the Principle of Boundary Lines because all cultural encounters are divided ("punctuated") by certain marks or boundary lines. We showed that boundary lines are, first and foremost, conceptualizations, born in people's minds. Also, we demonstrated that boundary lines can be perceived as destructive or constructive. Destructive boundary lines prevent people from realizing their goals, while constructive boundary lines allow people to realize their goals and function successfully. Finally, intercultural communication was presented as a process of searching for a mutually acceptable boundary fit—an agreement among people from interacting cultures on a boundary line between them.

We now know that cultural identities are created by drawing boundary lines between different groups of people. The success of intercultural communication depends on establishing a boundary fit between people from different cultures. But, to negotiate this boundary fit, people must gain knowledge about each other—they must venture beyond their boundary lines. In the next chapter, we'll discover the nature of knowledge, in general, and how it affects intercultural interactions.

CASE STUDY
A HISTORY OF THE RUSSO-JAPANESE FRONTIER

This case study is based on an article entitled "Lines in the Snow: Imagining the Russo-Japanese Frontier" (Morris-Suzuki, 1999). It is recommended that you read the article in its entirety; below is a summary of the article.

Be ready to identify and then discuss the following topics:

1. Boundary lines as conceptualizations
2. Boundary lines as marks of cultural identity
3. Searching for a boundary fit

In August of 1945, a three-week war between the Soviet Union and Japan broke out. As a result, Soviet troops seized the islands of Shikotan, Kunsashir, Iturup, and the Habomai group, along with the rest of the Kurile Islands and the southern half of Sakhalin. These territories—a few dots in the ocean with a population of about 20,000—are called in Russia the Southern Kuriles, while Japan refers to them as its Northern Territories (Hoppo Ryodo).

Three periods can be isolated in the formation of this Russo-Japanese frontier.

Period 1

During the first period (up to the 18th century), the Okhotsk peoples, sometimes referred to as "Asian Vikings," used the Okhotsk Sea for fishing and hunting marine animals and occupied its shores and islands. Early attempts to classify these peoples were not very successful because the imagined boundaries between them were too complex and confusing. Today, scholars use a simple terminology, identifying two ethnic cultures of the Okhotsk Sea people: the Ainu, who inhabit the southern fringes of the region, and the Nivkh, who inhabit northern Sakhalin and the region around the mouth of the Amur River.

Period 2

During the second period (from the 18th century to the beginning of the 20th century), the region became a frontier zone between expanding Russian and Japanese nations. People from both Russia and Japan began to penetrate the world surrounding the Okhotsk Sea, and the naming of this mysterious region created a framework for rival and shifting claims to the frontier. For Russia, this remote frontier became known as Siberia or, sometimes, Great Tartary—an exotic colonial possession, rich in "soft gold" (fur). For Japan, this region became known as Ezo, its most important resources being "golden fertilizer" (kinpi), herring, and other fish. At this point, Russian goods started to reach Japan, and Japan became conscious of a new presence to the north.

Gradually, trading posts were built, and the frontier became (somewhat literally) a series of points that created boundary lines. Russia claimed the territory to be a natural extension of its coastal regions, granted by the ambiguous terms of the 17th-century Treaty of Nerchinsk. The Japanese argued that the Ainu people, who inhabited Hokkaido, the south Kurile Islands, and the southern half of Sakhalin, had traditionally been under the Japanese domain of Matsumae and that their territory was therefore Japanese territory. In 1859, the negotiations ended in a compromise, with the Kurile archipelago divided between Russia and Japan. As a result, the indigenous people on both sides of the boundary line became national subjects.

(continued)

A HISTORY OF THE RUSSO-JAPANESE FRONTIER CONTINUED

After that, both Russia and Japan continued to appropriate and to redefine this frontier zone. For Russia, the whole area bordering on the Okhotsk Sea was no longer a remote fringe of Siberia but a region integrated by the label "Maritime region" (Primorye) or "Amur region" (Priamur). This set the stage for a newly defined group of people, the Amurians (amurtsy), later Trans-Amurians (zaamurtsy), who promoted the study and exploration of and expansion into Manchuria. The region became associated with the triumphal image of the march of progress. For Japan, the name Ezo was replaced by Hoppo (the Northern Regions). The new name located Japan in the center, as it were, and offered an imaginary panorama of the country as a long chain of islands stretching from the frozen north to the subtropical south, embodying a potential for expansion in either direction.

Period 3

In the postwar period (1945–today), the term *Hoppo* survives, though now it is largely confined to the small region of the Hoppo Ryodo—the Northern Territories claimed as Japan's own territories. Russia insists that they belong to the Kurile chain, discovered by Russian explorers, and are part of the Sakhalin District. Meanwhile, some Ainu activists point out that it is the Ainu people who historically have the oldest claims to the islands. And the frontier is, once again, being renegotiated.

Throughout the postwar decades, Soviet ideology emphasized the image of the border zone as the vulnerable interface with the threatening forces of capitalism and glorified the courage of the soldiers and settlers who guarded the limits of the Motherland. On the Japanese side, the frontier became in many ways a forgotten region, even though posters demanding the "return of the Northern Islands" are still seen along the roads in Hokkaido. When KL007, a Korean airliner, was shot down by the Soviets, the image of the boundary line as a sealed border, rather than a point of contact and exchange, was reinforced.

In the post-Soviet era, the vision of the frontier was again transformed, with many changes taking place at a local level. For instance, a series of visa-free visits to the Kurile Islands by Japanese ex-residents, school groups, and others provided a forum for exchanges of ideas across the disputed frontier. The need for collaboration intensified with common concerns such as environmental issues. Joint resource-based projects also generated increasing flows of people across the frontier. Russian tourists became an important source of income for Japanese small businesses, while in Eastern Siberia Japanese firms became engaged in logging and timber-milling.

The so-called Yeltsin-Hashimoto Plan of 1997 calls for the resolution of the border issue between people from the two cultures. How and when this will be accomplished remains to be seen.

DISCUSSION

Now let us see how this case can be viewed as an illustration of the Punctuation Principle of intercultural communication.

1. Boundary lines as conceptualizations. Clearly, the boundary lines described in the case study are conceptual—that is, arbitrary and moveable. They can, and must, be discussed not only in geographical terms but also in cultural terms. Until the 18th century, the Okhotsk peoples, sometimes referred to as "Asian Vikings," had used the Okhotsk Sea for fishing and hunting marine animals and occupied its shores and islands. Early attempts to classify these peoples were not very successful because the imagined boundaries between them were too complex and confusing. As a result, scholars today identify two main ethnic cultures of the Okhotsk Sea people: the Ainu, who inhabit the southern fringes of the region, and the Nivkh, who inhabit northern Sakhalin and the region around the mouth of the Amur River. Thus, the Ainu and Nivkh ethnicities are, to a degree, creations of modern scholars and their vocabulary.

Also, it is clear that the genesis of these cultural identities is in the confrontation between Self and the Other—a process whereby people from Russia and Japan become aware of themselves by seeing their reflection in the other's mirror of consciousness.

2. Boundary lines as marks of cultural identity. The fuzzy water lines marked many small indigenous communities (ethnic identities), which occupied the shores of the Okhotsk Sea and its islands. Also, the boundary lines of the trading posts marked the identities of two emerging powers (national identities).

Marking cultural identities with names is very important. For example, people in Russia at one point labeled this remote frontier "Great Tartary" and viewed it as an exotic colonial possession, rich in "soft gold" (fur). Later, a new cultural identity was marked by the new geographic label "Maritime region" (Primorye) or "Amur region" (Priamur). As a result, a newly defined group of people, the Amurians (amurtsy), later Trans-Amurians (zaamurtsy), was created. For Japan, replacing the name Ezo with Hoppo (the Northern Regions) located Japan in the center and offered an imaginary panorama of the country as a long chain of islands, embodying a potential for expansion in either direction. The shift in names symbolizes changing perceptions of the region and the cultural identities of the people inhabiting it.

Today, this Russo-Japanese region is the subject of many negotiations and treaties, and the conflict between people from these two cultures has not been resolved. In other words, the boundary lines between them are not clearly marked, making it important to search for a boundary fit.

3. Searching for a boundary fit. The symbolic meanings of the boundary lines changed over time. For example, for both Russia and Japan this frontier initially had been an exotic place full of magic and monsters. Much later, Russia associated the same region with progress, and Japan saw in it a potential for expansion. During the Cold War years, the frontier became for Russia a border zone to be guarded against the threatening forces of capitalism, and on the Japanese side the frontier became in many ways a forgotten area.

All these symbolic changes took place because people from different cultures had different boundary demands. Effective intercultural communication requires that people from different cultures agree on their boundary lines—that is, negotiate a boundary fit. In this sense, the history of the Russo-Japanese frontier conflict must be viewed as a search for a boundary fit. People from both sides first saw this region as a mysterious place, and later claimed it as a possession of their territorial expansion. At one point, the idea that the KL007 airliner (supposedly) had crossed the invisible air frontier made the search for a boundary fit more difficult.

Today, the prospects of establishing a boundary fit seem to be better than before. The region seems to have a more similar meaning for people from both sides, with shared concerns such as environmental issues. The need for collaboration intensifies with joint resource-based projects, generating increased flows of people across the frontier. How and when the positive boundary fit will be established remains to be seen.

SIDE TRIPS

1. After the September 11, 2001, terrorist attacks, many U.S. legislators began pushing for racial profiling. Critics pointed out, however, that racial profiling is not reliable because, among other things, it does not denote clear biological lines. As a result, it cannot tell us what its proponents claim it can. What is your opinion of racial profiling?
2. We tend to forget that people from other cultures often see us differently from how we see ourselves. For example, people from the United States have a certain image of themselves (cultural self-concept). However, when people from the United States interact with people from other cultures, this image changes! It is as if people from the United States see themselves differently depending on whose eyes reflect their self-concept. Discuss some of these mirror reflections, using the book *Images of the U.S. Around the World* (Kamalipour & Tehranian, 1998).
3. It is argued that forceful erasure of boundaries may lead to "the degeneration and even dissolution of the identity" (Puddifoot, 1997: 252). Do you agree with this statement? If so, can you think of examples of erasure of cultural boundaries?

CHECK YOURSELF

Culture
Communication
Intercultural communication
In-group
Out-group
Identity
Racial identity
National identity
Ethnic identity
Looking-glass self
Punctuation
Identity confirmation
Identity disconfirmation
Boundary fit
Cultural appropriation
Hard boundaries
Soft boundaries

REFERENCES

Anderson, R., & Ross, V. (2002). *Questions of communication: A practical introduction to theory.* Boston: Bedford/St. Martin's.

Barker, C. (2000). *Cultural studies: Theory and practice.* London: Sage.

Bateson, G., & Jackson, D. (1964). Some varieties of pathogenic organization. In McRoach, D. (Ed.), *Disorders of communication* (pp. 270–283). N.P.: Association for Research in Nervous and Mental Disease.

Blommaert, J. (1998). Different approaches to intercultural communication: A critical survey. http://africana.rug.ac.be/texts/research..._on-line/Intercultural_Communication.htm

Brewer, M., & Miller, N. (1996). *Intergroup relations.* Pacific Grove, CA: Brooks/Cole.

Collier, M., & Thomas, M. (1988). Cultural identity. In Kim, Y., & W. Gudykunst (Eds.), *Theories of intercultural communication.* Newbury Park, CA: Sage.

DeFleur, M., & DeFleur, M. (2003). *Learning to hate Americans: How U.S. media shape negative attitudes among teenagers in twelve countries.* Spokane: Marquette Books.

Edward, A. (1979). *Language in culture and class.* London: Heinemann.

Eisenstadt, S. (1998). Modernity and the construction of collective identity. *International Journal of Comparative Sociology,* Vol. 39, No. 1, pp. 138–159.

Fong, M. (2004a). Identity and the speech community. In Fong, M., & R. Chuang (Eds.), *Communicating ethnic and cultural identity* (pp. 3–18). Lanham, MD: Rowman & Littlefield.

Fong, M. (2004b). Multiple dimensions of identity. In Fong, M., & R. Chuang (Eds.), *Communicating ethnic and cultural identity* (pp. 19–34). Lanham, MD: Rowman & Littlefield.

Goffman, E. (1967). *Interaction ritual.* Garden City, NY: Anchor.

Gudykunst, W., & Kim, Y. (2003). *Communicating with strangers: An approach to intercultural communication.* New York: McGraw-Hill.

Hall, B. (2002). *Among cultures: The challenge of communication.* Belmont, CA: Wadsworth.

Jandt, F., & Tanno, D. (2001). Decoding domination, encoding self-determination: Intercultural communication research process. *The Howard Journal of Communication,* Vol. 12, pp. 119–135.

Jermanok, S. (1999). A tale of two countries. *Boston Globe,* March 28, p. M1.

Kamalipour, Y., & Tehranian, M. (1998). *Images of the U.S. around the world: A multicultural perspective.* Albany: State University of New York Press.

Katriel, T. (1994). Sites of memory: Discourses of the past in Israeli pioneering settlement museums. *The Quarterly Journal of Speech,* Vol. 80, No. 1, pp. 1–20.

Kim, Y. Y. (2001). Mapping the domain of intercultural communication: An overview. In Gudykunst, W. (Ed.), *Communication yearbook,* Vol. 24 (pp. 139–157). Thousand Oaks, CA: Sage.

Lacan, J. (1968). The mirror-phase as formative of the function of the I. *New Left Review,* Vol. 51, pp. 71–77.

Laing, D. (1961). *The self and others.* New York: Pantheon.

Littlejohn, S. (2002). *Theories of human communication.* Belmont, CA: Wadsworth.

Lustig, M., & Koester, J. (2003). *Intercultural competence: Interpersonal communication across cultures.* Boston: Allyn and Bacon.

Mead, G. H. (1934). *Mind, self, and society.* Chicago: University of Chicago Press.

Morris, E. (Ed.). (1982). *The American Heritage dictionary of the English language.* Boston: Houghton Mifflin.

Morris-Suzuki, T. (1999). Lines in the snow: Imagining the Russo-Japanese frontier. *Pacific Affairs,* Vol. 72, No. 1, pp. 57–77.

Navarro, M. (2003). Going beyond black and white: Hispanics in census pick "other." *The New York Times,* November 9, pp. 1, 21.

Nöth, W. (2001). Towards a semiotics of cultural other. *The American Journal of Semiotics,* Vol. 17, No. 2, pp. 239–251.

Petronio, S., Ellemers, N., Giles, H., & Gallois, C. (1998). (Mis)communicating across boundaries: Interpersonal and intergroup considerations. *Communication Research,* Vol. 25, No. 6, pp. 571–595.

Pitts, L. (2003). Alas, what to call non-Caucasians. *The Spokesman-Review,* May 27, p. A12.

Popper, K., & Eccles, J. (1977). *The self and its brain.* Berlin: Springer.

Puddifoot, E. (1997). Psychological reaction to perceived erasure of community boundaries. *The Journal of Social Psychology,* Vol. 137, No. 3, pp. 343–356.

Rogers, E. (1999). Georg Simmel's concept of the stranger and intercultural communication research. *Communication Theory,* Vol. 9, No. 1, pp. 58–74.

Shirato, T., & Yell, S. (2000). *Communication and culture.* London: Sage.

Simmel, G. (1950). The stranger. In Wolff, K. (Ed.), *The sociology of George Simmel.* New York: Free Press.

Stewart, E., & Bennet, M. (Eds.). (1991). *American cultural patterns.* Yarmouth, ME: Intercultural Press.

Tajfel, H. (1981). *Human groups and social categories.* Cambridge: Cambridge University Press.

Taylor, C. (1992). *Multiculturalism and "the politics of recognition."* Princeton, NJ: Princeton University Press.

Ting-Toomey, S. (1999). *Communicating across cultures.* New York: Guilford.

Usunier, J.-C. (1996). *Marketing across cultures.* London: Prentice Hall.

Vatikiotis, M., & Schwartz, A. (1995). Crossed lines: Thailand and Vietnam clash over fishing rights. *Far Eastern Economic Review,* Vol. 158, p. 16.

Verhovek, S. H. (1997). Clash of cultures tears Texas city. *The New York Times,* September 30, p. A10.

Vygotsky, L. (1962). *Thought and language.* Cambridge, MA: MIT Press.

Warren, J. (2001). Doing whiteness: On the performative dimensions of race in the classroom. *Communication Education,* Vol. 50, No. 2, pp. 91–108.

Watzlawick, P. (1984). Self-fulfilling prophecies. In Watzlawick, P. (Ed.), *The invented reality: How do we know what we believe we know?* (pp. 95–116). New York: Norton.

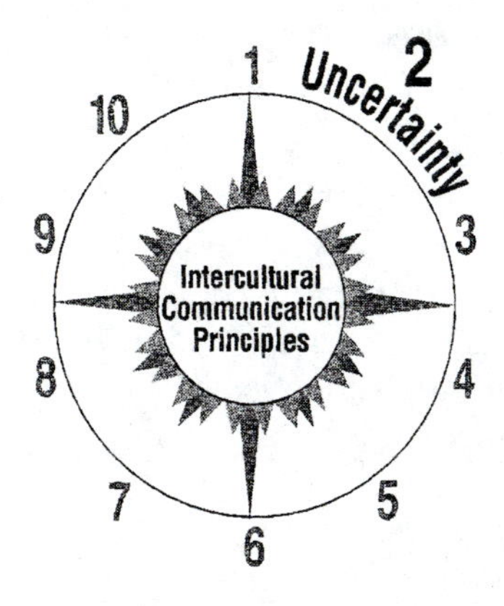

CHAPTER TWO

CONSTRUCTING KNOWLEDGE IN INTERCULTURAL COMMUNICATION: UNCERTAINTY PRINCIPLE

Let the Mystery Be!

- *Key Theme:* Uncertainty
- *Key Objective:* To help you understand and appreciate the inherent uncertainty of intercultural interactions

INTRODUCING THE PROBLEM QUESTION

EPISTEMOLOGY AND INTERCULTURAL COMMUNICATION

Objective Approach to Knowledge
Subjective Approach to Knowledge

INTRODUCING THE UNCERTAINTY PRINCIPLE

Uncertainty and Horizon of Knowledge
Uncertainty and Dis-closure
Order out of Uncertainty

THE UNCERTAINTY PRINCIPLE DEFINED

SUMMARY

CASE STUDY: THE SHOCK OF THE OTHER

SIDE TRIPS

CHECK YOURSELF

REFERENCES

Introducing the Problem Question

In the previous chapter, we discussed the process of cultural identification, showing how and why cultural identities are formed. We emphasized the importance of drawing boundary lines and how the success of communication is determined by the boundary fit between people from different cultures in various situations of interaction. To establish this boundary fit, people must learn how to interact with one another, venturing beyond their boundary lines.

More specifically, for intercultural communication to be effective, people from each culture must know, first, who they are (their self-image); second, what people from the other culture think of them (their reflective self-image); and, third, who people from the other culture are (the Other's cultural identity). Then people from different cultures can interact with one another successfully. The nature of knowledge is quite complex, however, and that has a profound impact on our ability to interact with other people.

So, let's take up the following problem question: *How does the nature of knowledge affect intercultural communication?*

In this chapter we will

- Emphasize the importance of knowledge in the study of intercultural communication
- Discuss the two main approaches to knowledge
- Distinguish different levels of awareness in intercultural communication
- Demonstrate how people from different cultures share information about each other and try to understand this information as completely as possible
- Show how order is created out of uncertainty.

Epistemology and Intercultural Communication

Epistemology is defined as "the branch of philosophy that studies knowledge, or how people know what they claim to know" (Littlejohn, 2002: 26). Applied to intercultural communication, this process involves, as was said earlier, knowing who we are (our self-image), what people from the other culture think of us (our reflective self-image), and who people from the other culture are (the Other's cultural identity). "The more important our group memberships are to how we define ourselves, the greater our predictive certainty regarding strangers' behavior" (Gudykunst & Kim, 2003: 33). In other words, intercultural communication is more effective when we "have a solid self-concept" (Martin & Nakayama, 2000: 210).

People from different cultures try to gain knowledge about each other's identities and represent it as completely and precisely as possible. But what is the nature of knowledge? This question is not as simple as it might seem at first glance. Two broad approaches to human knowledge, with different assumptions about its nature, are usually isolated: the objective approach and the subjective approach. Let's take a look at these two approaches to human knowledge.

Objective Approach to Knowledge

The **objective approach** to knowledge is also often called the scientific (Littlejohn, 2002: 10), or social science (Martin & Nakayama, 2004: 48), approach. In this approach, knowledge is viewed as an objective reality (an object), external to people as subjects of inquiry. In other words, the world is viewed as made up of hard and tangible variables. As a result, people are considered to rely on such variables and behave "in patterned, predictable ways, often seen in terms of cause and effect" (**determinism**) (Baldwin et al., 2003: 26). Hence, the goal of the objective inquiry is clear: to find all such variables and formulate laws of cause and effect in order to predict people's interactions. If you approach knowledge objectively, you assume that you can always find it through careful observation of the world—in our case, the world of intercultural interactions. The objective observer "attempts to look at the world in such a way that all other observers . . . would see the same thing" (Littlejohn, 1999: 10).

Suppose you want to know how travelers adapt overseas (cf. Kim, 2001). You start looking for variables and find them, for example, in travelers' language, age, and gender. Now you can formulate laws; for instance, if one is young(er), she or he finds it easier to adapt overseas. You can then use such laws to predict future intercultural interactions.

So, according to the objective approach, knowledge exists objectively and is external to people; the careful observer discovers this knowledge and represents it in a meaningful form. Seen from this perspective, meanings are like butterflies: some more common, flying right in front of us, and some more rare, living in remote places. However, it is only a matter of time before they all are discovered by scientists, pinned down, and exhibited in a museum (a Museum of Meanings?). Then we can take these meanings out of the "museum" when necessary and use them in communicating with people from other cultures. The essence of the objective approach is as follows: To know something is to capture and represent its meaning (Figure 1).

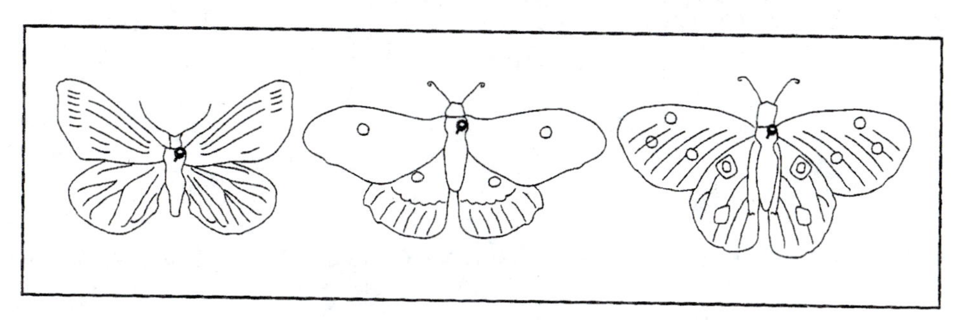

FIGURE 1 The Objective Approach to Knowledge

But, is knowledge really found (discovered) in things? Is a researcher someone who walks around with a net, observes things, and captures their meanings? If meaning were a part of things, how would we know where the meaning ended and the thing began? Obviously, knowledge does not simply exist in things; it is constructed in the dynamic relationships between objects and people as subjects of inquiry.

Subjective Approach to Knowledge

The **subjective approach** is also often called the humanistic (Littlejohn, 2002: 10), or interpretative (Martin & Nakayama, 2004: 53), approach. According to this approach, knowledge is constructed by people in various situations of interaction; that is, cultural meanings are internal to people. "For example, love is not something external to us, with five dimensions that cover all types of love in all cultures. Rather, each culture defines love and dating in its own way" (Baldwin et al., 2003: 26). Any knowledge, therefore, "can only be understood from the point of view of the individuals who are directly involved in the activities which are to be studied" (Burrel & Morgan, 1979: 5). Because "people do not behave on impulse but rather make decisions on free will" (**voluntarism**) (Baldwin et al., 2004: 27), the goal of the subjective inquiry is to understand or interpret people's interactions. For example, you might discover that younger people find it easier to adapt overseas because they can process complex information much faster or, on the contrary, because they avoid complex information.

According to the subjective approach to knowledge, everything in this world is interrelated with other things. What things mean changes as people interact with each other, and our knowledge can never be final or complete. When we study intercultural communication, we try to be "scientifically objective"—that is, detached from the object of our study. But "humanists often are suspicious of the claim that there is an immutable world to be discovered, and they tend not to separate the knower from the known" (Littlejohn, 1999: 10). We may *think* we observe something objectively, but in reality we do not! We ourselves are a part of this objective world (its objects, so to speak), and we are interrelated with what we study, in spite of our best intentions to be "scientific" and objective. The observer tries to be neutral and collect "objective knowledge" of something—in our case, knowledge of how to interact with people from other cultures. But the observer must come into contact with the object of study, and the scientific findings are thus influenced by the observer's subjective viewpoint. This situation is known as the **observer's paradox**. As the physicist Max Bohr pointed out decades ago:

> We may compare the observer . . . with that of a football game where the act of watching, accompanied by applauding and hissing, has a marked influence on the speed and concentration of the players, and thus on what is watched. . . . It is the action of the experimentalist who designs the apparatus, which determines essential features of the observations. Hence there is no objectively existing situation, as was supposed to exist in classical science. (1956: 35)

So, we live in a world where everything is interrelated and where not all of the relationships are known or can be known. Moreover, when we try to know something we consider to be an object, such as another culture, we cannot help interacting with it. As a result, knowledge changes depending on the viewpoint of the observer, and the observer changes, too.

Why does the observer change? Because the observer is not a neutral, perfectly detached outsider who simply studies people from different cultures for scientific purposes. The observer not only affects the cultures observed, but is affected by his or her interaction with people from those cultures. You might be familiar with the term **culture shock,** which is the reaction people have when they attempt to adjust to new situations (Oberg, 1960). Usually, people make some changes in their behavior in order to communicate more effectively with those from the new culture. People tend to think that when they stop interacting with people from another culture they leave the changes in their behavior behind, too. Not so! They are often surprised to find that they now look at the world with somewhat different eyes. The term **self-shock** (cf. Zaharna, 1989) is used to refer to people's reaction to changes in their own cultural identity while trying to adjust to new situations. Self-shock proves that you cannot simply observe a situation and then forget about it; that experience will remind you of itself, to your surprise.

Thus, according to the subjective approach, to know something is to capture and represent its meaning as it relates to other things, including the observer. According to this view, meanings, like butterflies, are constantly changing their shape and color, and just when you think you have pinned them down, they come to life—upon contact with you or another butterfly—and fly away (Figure 2).

FIGURE 2 The Subjective Approach to Knowledge

The two approaches to knowledge can be summarized as shown in Table 1.

TABLE 1

	OBJECTIVE	SUBJECTIVE
View of Knowledge	Knowledge is external	Knowledge is internal
Basis of Behavior	Determinism	Free will
Goal of Inquiry	Prediction	Explanation
Result of Inquiry	Laws of interaction	Interpretation of interaction

Thus,

> Objectivists . . . see a "real world" external to individuals, look for regularities in behavior, and see communication as "determined" by situations and environments. Subjectivists, in contrast, contend that there is no "real world" external to individuals, try to understand individual communicators' perspectives, and view communication as a function of "free will." (Gudykunst, 2002: 183)

Neither approach by itself can reveal the complexity of knowledge in intercultural communication. Let's see where each approach to knowledge might lead, in an extreme case.

Combining the Two Approaches. Suppose knowledge existed only externally to people. Theoretically, it would be possible for people, as subjects, to discover all the knowledge of the object of their inquiry—say, intercultural communication. But, if people discovered all possible variables and formulated all possible laws, they would cease to exist as subjects. In essence, people as subjects would disappear, having turned into the object (become part of it). Intercultural communication then would amount to a predetermined order, and people would function like robots (objects) without any free (subjective) will.

Now suppose knowledge existed only internally—that is, it was constructed by people as subjects. Theoretically, all knowledge would reside in people, and every situation of intercultural interaction would have to be viewed as unique, with meaning understood only by the individuals directly involved in the encounter. Then there would be nothing external to people in this world that they could rely on in their interactions, so intercultural communication would become a chaotic experience. In essence, knowledge as object would disappear, having turned into subject (become part of people). Intercultural communication would amount to a new experience each time people interacted with one another, and they would have no objective patterns to follow.

Predetermined Order ---- Determinism ⟵——⟶ Free Will ---- Chaos

As you can see, these two extremes fail to reveal the epistemological picture of intercultural communication. If free will is taken out of the picture, the subject disappears, and determinism turns into predetermined order. If determinism is taken out of the picture, the object disappears, and free will turns into chaos.

We interact "in situations which lie between the two extremes. . . . At one extreme, we are so confident of our predictions that we no longer experience doubt at all [predetermined order]; at the other, what will happen is so absolutely unpredictable it can only be treated fatalistically [chaos]" (Marris, 1996: 18). In other words, "between the two extremes, we have to deal with our uncertainties" (Gudykunst & Kim, 2003: 30).

Clearly, the two approaches discussed above are two sides of the same coin—the nature of our discovery of knowledge. They simply focus on its two different sides. In a nutshell, the objective approach "focuses on the discovered world," while the subjective approach "focuses on the discovering person" (Littlejohn, 1999: 11). The complexity of intercultural communication can be revealed only if these two views are combined. Their joint operation "emphasizes the processual, relational, and contradictory nature of intercultural communication, which encompasses many different kinds of intercultural knowledge" (Martin & Nakayama, 2004: 62). We will witness the processual and relational nature of knowledge in intercultural communication many times throughout this book.

So, the nature of knowledge is, indeed, very complex. Knowledge cannot be completely predicted or completely explained. As shown above, the two forms of inquiry—scientific and humanistic—complement each other and cannot exist separately. It turns out that the line between "objective" reality and its "subjective" interpretation is always uncertain. How does all this affect intercultural communication? You are now perhaps a bit uncertain, and that is a good thing! For this whole chapter is, first and foremost, about the uncertainty of our knowledge.

You might have heard of Werner Heisenberg, the German physicist and Nobel laureate, who put forward his famous Indeterminacy Principle during the first part of the last century. According to that principle, it is impossible to determine the exact location and speed of small pieces of matter (their exact "meaning," if you will) independently of the observer's viewpoint. When the observer tries to pinpoint their location and speed, they change; thus, something in their meaning must remain unknowable (uncertain). This principle presents basic elements of matter as having a dual nature—that of particles and waves.

To understand the significance of Heisenberg's ideas, consider the example discussed by Danesi and Perron in their book *Analyzing Cultures:*

> Let's suppose that a scientist reared and trained in North America sees a physical event that she has never seen before. Curious about what it is, she takes out a notebook and writes down her observations in English. At the instant that our North American scientist observes the event, another scientist, reared and trained in the Philippines and speaking only the indigenous Tagalog language, also sees the same event. He similarly takes out a notebook and writes down his observations in Tagalog. Now, to what extent will the contents of the observations, as written in the

> two notebooks, coincide? The answer of course is that the two will not be identical. The reason for this discrepancy is clearly not due to the nature of the event, but rather to the fact that the observers were different, psychologically and culturally. So, as Heisenberg would have suggested, the true nature of the event is indeterminable. (1999: 64)

In every intercultural interaction, we try to capture and represent meaning so that we can use it in the future. In a way, we approach every situation of intercultural interaction as if it consisted of "things," or small particles, and strive to discover their exact meaning; this approach is found in the objective view of knowledge. But, as you remember, every situation is dynamic because "things" relate to other things, creating continual motion like that of a wave; this approach is found in the subjective view of knowledge. Thus, it is possible to discover the exact meaning of something with only a degree of certainty, which implies a degree of uncertainty as well.

Introducing the Uncertainty Principle

Now, on the basis of the discussion above, we can introduce the second principle underlying intercultural communication: the Uncertainty Principle. There are three parts to this principle, and each deals with the nature of our knowledge about our interactions with people from other cultures. First, we will discuss uncertainty in terms of horizon of knowledge. Next, we will present intercultural communication as a process of dis-closure. Finally, we will show how uncertainty is linked to order. We will discuss each part separately and then formulate the Uncertainty Principle as a whole.

Uncertainty and Horizon of Knowledge

Uncertainty refers to our cognitive inability to predict or explain "our own or others' feelings and behaviors in interactions" (Chen & Starosta, 1998: 122). Two kinds of uncertainty are often isolated: predictive and explanatory. **Predictive uncertainty** is the inability to predict what someone will say or do, while **explanatory uncertainty** is the inability to explain why people behave as they do (Martin & Nakayama, 2000: 210).

Uncertainty usually evokes **anxiety,** which is considered to be its affective equivalent (Gudykunst & Kim, 2003: 329). Higher levels of uncertainty and anxiety directly correlate with increased communication apprehension (Neuliep & Ryan, 1998).

The Uncertainty Management Theory (Gudykunst, 1995; Gudykunst & Lee, 2002) sees the goal of intercultural communication as seeking information to reduce uncertainty and increase the predictability of our interactions with the Other. Ideally, it seems, uncertainty would be eliminated from our intercultural interactions, but can it be? Can we be absolutely confident that our knowledge is certain and complete? Can we honestly say that the way we have predicted or explained something excludes all other predictions or interpretations made in the past or to be made in the future? We can try to know everything there is to know about ourselves, about people from other cultures, and about how to interact with them, but can we succeed?

Earlier, it was shown that the line between objective reality and its subjective interpretation is always uncertain. Now let's take this thesis a step further and look at intercultural communication, using a modification of the **Johari Window model** (Luft, 1970). Our model consists of four areas of awareness (or "window panes") in the context of interaction (see Figure 3).

The first area, the Open Window, contains the information that others know about you and that you are aware of. The second area, the Closed Window, contains the information that you know about yourself, but others do not know about you. The third area, the Blind Window, contains the information that other people know about you, but you do not know. And the fourth area, the Unknown Window, contains the information that is unknown to both you and others.

In their interactions, people from different cultures share some information about themselves (Open Window). At the same time, people from one culture keep to themselves some information that people from the other culture are not aware of (Closed Window) and are unaware of some information that people from the other culture have about them (Blind Window). Intercultural communication takes place against the backdrop of some information that is not known to people from either culture (Unknown Window).

Consider the following situation (see Cohen, 1999: 224). Two persons, one from an Asian culture and the other from a Western culture, are engaged in business negotiations. At some point it becomes obvious to both parties that the negotiations are leading nowhere, yet the Asian suggests that a document be signed, presenting the negotiations as a success. The Westerner might view this behavior as frustrating or even ethically questionable. The Westerner might take offense and withdraw from the negotiations or, on the contrary, vow not to go away and insist that the negotiations continue. That behavior, in turn, might be perceived by the Asian as unnecessarily unpleasant and excessively persistent. To the Asian, accord is essential, to preserve appearances and maintain the impression that the

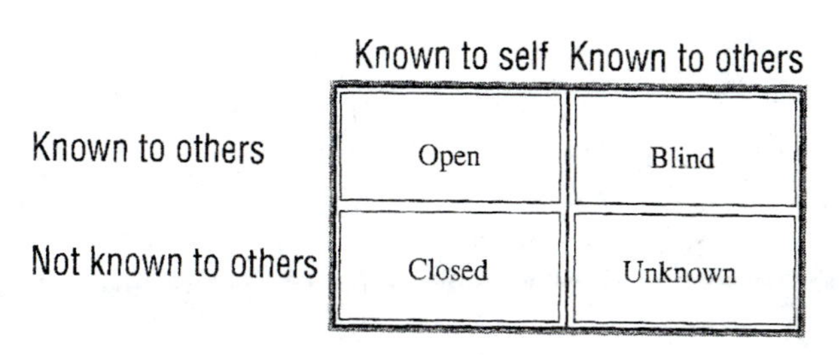

FIGURE 3 Application of Johari Window to Intercultural Communication

negotiations have concluded on a basis of mutual respect and equal standing. Besides, there is always a hope that, in the future, things might change and turn out all right.

First, these two people share some information about themselves: The Asian suggests that a document be signed, and the Westerner objects. This part of the intercultural exchange forms its Open Window. Second, each person holds some information that the other is not aware of: The Asian wants to preserve appearances, while the Westerner wants to be straightforward. This part of the intercultural exchange forms its Closed Window. Third, both parties are unaware of some information about them held by the other: The Asian is unaware that he or she is coming across as lazy or unethical, while the Westerner is unaware that he or she is coming across as stubborn and inconsiderate. This part of the intercultural exchange forms its Blind Window. Fourth, there is always the possibility that this situation may change, taking a new twist. Thus, this exchange contains information that is not known to either party (Unknown Window).

Figure 4 shows intercultural interactions in terms of the areas of awareness discussed above. The shared area in the middle represents the Open Window; the areas on the left and right represent the Closed Window (Self's view of Self) and the Blind Window (Other's view of Self); and the background area represents the Unknown Window.

Every situation of intercultural interaction appears before us like a horizon: It seems to stand still, but in reality it does not. We move closer trying to reach it, and it moves away. Thus, the picture we see is always somewhat different—and limited to our view. What we have in front of us, in fact, is a viewing window. We try to see more of what is behind the left edge, and we inevitably lose some information on the right. We try to see more of what is behind the right edge, and we inevitably lose some information on the left. And something always remains unknowable. We must stress "the function of the unknown" because "concerned as we are with what we do, we cannot forget that we are all limited individuals, most interested in those facts relevant to the course of our lives, having to make decisions before we have all the information a pure seeker after knowledge would require" (Fleischacker, 1994: 50–51).

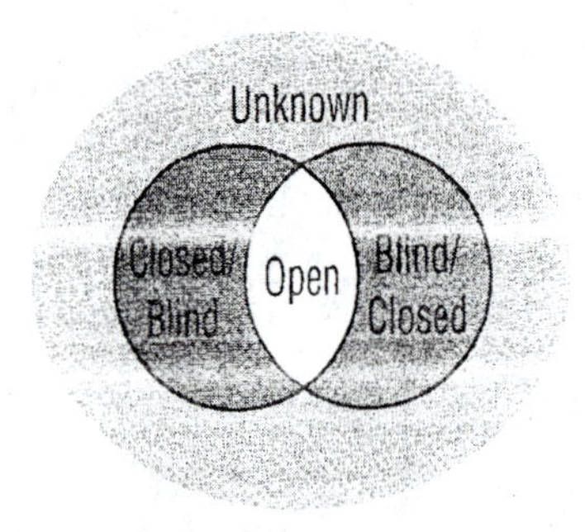

FIGURE 4

Thus, every situation of intercultural communication is characterized by a **horizon of knowledge**—that is, a different degree of reach of knowledge. Like a horizon, knowledge in intercultural communication is never completely reached. In other words, seemingly static cultural realities are, in fact, dynamic by nature and always open to new interpretation. One of Gary Larson's cartoons makes this point very well. In the cartoon, an ostrich, sitting in a bar holding a cocktail glass, is saying to the woman next to him, "Well, according to the dictionary, I'm just a large, flightless bird from East Africa . . . But believe me, Doris—once you get to know me, you'll see I'm much, much more than that."

So, we cannot be absolutely confident that our understanding is certain and complete; intercultural communication is inherently variable and subject to reinterpretation. We can never say that the way we have predicted or explained something excludes all other predictions or interpretations made in the past or to be made in the future. We must acknowledge uncertainty as an unavoidable aspect of intercultural communication.

Since uncertainty in intercultural communication cannot be avoided, we must deal with it. That is to say, we must share information with others and understand their information ourselves. As a result, intercultural communication can be seen as a process of dis-closure.

Uncertainty and Dis-closure

Disclosure is usually defined as the process of "regulation of information flow between the self and the outer world" (Ting-Toomey, 1999: 188). Often, this process is also labeled "self-disclosure" (Gudykunst & Kim, 2003: 333).

"Self-disclosure occurs among people of all cultures" (Lustig & Koester, 2003: 284), although there are cultural differences in the breadth, depth, valence, and targets of the self-disclosure (for more information, see Gudykunst & Kim, 2003: 333–334; Lustig & Koester, 2003: 284–285; Ting-Toomey, 1999: 188–189). Breadth refers to the range of topics of self-disclosure—for example, whether they include interests, tastes, financial matters, and physical condition. Depth refers to the level of information revealed in the process of self-disclosure—superficial or intimate. Valence refers to whether the information revealed in the process of self-disclosure is positive (favorable to self) or negative (unfavorable to self). The target of self-disclosure is the person to whom information is given, such as a same-sex friend, opposite-sex friend, spouse, or acquaintance.

When people engage in self-disclosure, they aim to open up their cultural identity, as it were, and share it with people from other cultures. In this respect, disclosure can be viewed as a process of opening up all the windows of awareness. During this process, people from each culture share information about themselves, which varies in terms of its breadth, depth, valence, and targets. However, as we saw earlier, they can never be confident that this information is certain and complete. First, people from one culture keep to themselves some information that people from the other culture are not aware of (Closed Window). Second, there is always some information that people from one culture are unaware that people from the other culture have about them (Blind Window). Third, in every intercultural situation there is some information that is not known to people from either of the interacting cultures (Unknown Window). So, disclosure always contains some missing information for people from another culture. From this perspective, intercultural communication between Self and the Other can be represented as shown in Figure 5.

Now, let's see how the Other reacts to information revealed by Self. In this process, three strategies for dealing with uncertainty can be isolated—passive, active, and interactive (Berger, 1979):

> *The passive strategy* entails reflective observations concerning the verbal and nonverbal performance of the individual whom you are interested in getting to know. *The active strategy* refers to seeking out information from a third person about the interests and hobbies of the individual of interest. Lastly, *the interactive strategy* refers to the direct interaction between yourself and that person. (Ting-Toomey, 1999: 189)

Using these three strategies, people from another culture (the Other) try to understand the new information they receive, based on the previous knowledge they have. This way, people aim to build a bridge between what they know and what they want to know. When a connection between the two is made, a pattern is established; that is, closure is reached. Closure involves a process of filling in missing information. In other words, **closure** is a process for dealing with uncertainty whereby an incomplete stimulus is perceived to be complete (cf. Bernstein et al., 1988: 632). It is as if people tried to close the windows of awareness, thereby reducing uncertainty in intercultural interactions. However, as we saw earlier, uncertainty cannot be completely removed from intercultural interactions; we can never reach the horizon, and the windows of awareness cannot be shut down once and for all. Thus, closure is a process of closing down windows of awareness that always contains some missing information. From this perspective, intercultural communication between Self and the Other can be represented as shown in Figure 6.

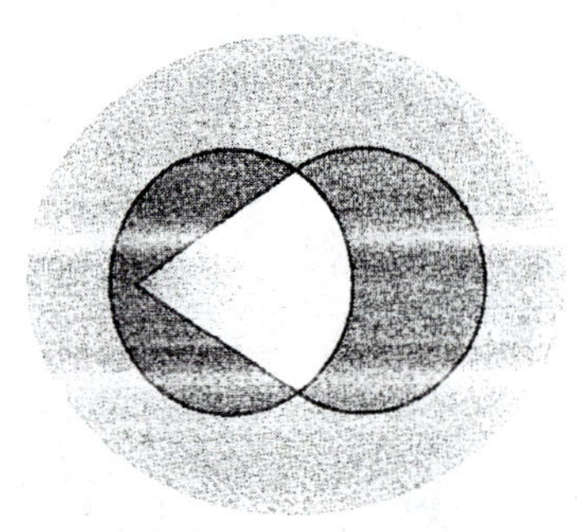

FIGURE 5 Intercultural Communication from the Perspective of Disclosure

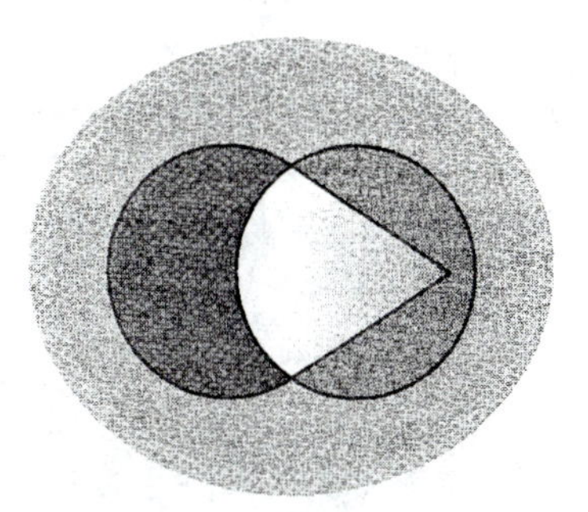

FIGURE 6 Intercultural Communication from the Perspective of Closure

In intercultural communication, every culture acts as both Self and the Other, sending and receiving information and thus using both disclosure and closure. So, overall, intercultural communication can be presented as a process of **dis-closure** (see Figure 7).

In this process, people from different cultures together construct knowledge of their own and each other's identities and how to interact with each other. This knowledge must be viewed like a giant dynamic puzzle, in which some pieces are always missing. You remember that disclosure was defined as a process of opening up the windows of awareness that always contains some missing information, while closure was defined as a process of closing down the windows of awareness that always contains some missing information. Notice that, in both cases, some information is always missing—the knowledge constructed in the process of disclosure always contains some uncertainty.

This view of interactions between people from different cultures seems to be quite pessimistic. It is tempting, on the one hand, to fight this view with full determination to find all missing pieces, aiming to complete the giant puzzle of intercultural communication. As we saw earlier, however, this extreme approach is unproductive because it leads to a predetermined order. On the other hand, it is tempting to give in to this view, allowing the giant puzzle of intercultural

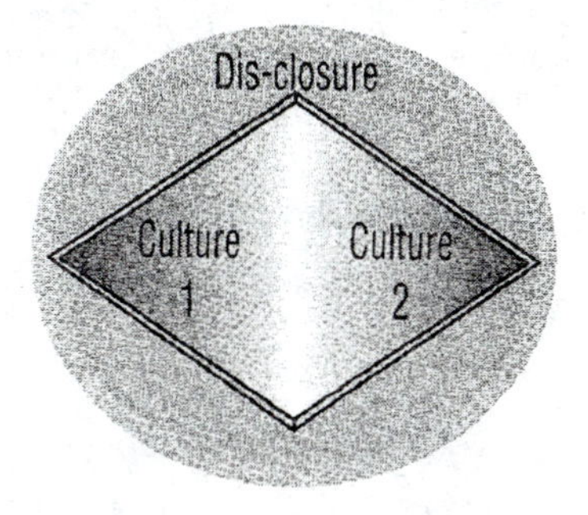

FIGURE 7

communication to break into countless pieces and dealing with each piece individually. As we saw earlier, however, this extreme approach is also unproductive because it leads to chaos.

So, what should we do with the uncertainty that is built into all intercultural interactions?

Order out of Uncertainty

The view of intercultural communication as a process of dis-closure with a horizon of knowledge is not really pessimistic. We must not equate uncertainty with impossibility of intercultural communication. In fact, the opposite is true! We must acknowledge uncertainty as an unavoidable aspect of intercultural communication and, because it *is* unavoidable, deal with it. The rich history of intercultural communication shows eloquently how people, over the centuries, have dealt with uncertainty.

Recall the example cited earlier of the North American and Tagalog scientists observing the same event and taking notes. It continues as follows:

> So, as Heisenberg would have suggested, the true nature of the event is indeterminable, *although it can be investigated further, paradoxically, on the basis of the notes taken by these two scientists.* (Danesi & Perron, 1999: 64; italics added)

Not only can it be, but it must be! For that is the only way to communicate—by comparing your notes or, figuratively, your perspectives of the same event from your respective "viewing windows." In Chapter 5, we will discuss in depth how and why different cultures compare their perspectives. Right now, let's emphasize that knowledge—in spite of or thanks to its unavoidable uncertainty—must be seen as a basis for intercultural communication. Order is created out of uncertainty.

You might be having mixed feelings about the Uncertainty Principle, thinking that it sounds too philosophical, too academic, and too impractical. True, a person with an uncertainty approach to intercultural communication might be seen as lacking self-confidence and unable to make decisions. Uncertainty values are not always encouraged, especially by Western cultures. But "humans should recognize that the possibility of certainty or complete predictability is an illusion and that believing this possibility is a product of an erroneous Western attempt to control nature" (Bradac, 2001: 546). We should also remember that "indeterminate organisms possess expandable or 'open' boundaries that enable them to continue to grow and alter their patterns indefinitely" (Hoffmeyer, 1999: 337). Uncertainty opens a free space for change and evolution; it is the major force of creativity.

In this dynamic world, to be always certain might not be to your advantage. When you go beyond the boundary lines of your culture, you will discover, sooner or later, that the world cannot always be relied upon to meet your expectations. Being always certain often leads to intolerance, prejudice, and violence. To recognize the Uncertainty Principle means to encourage humility and creativity and to take responsibility for your actions, admitting errors and seeking improvement. Without a degree of uncertainty, there would be no advancement of knowledge. Remember that "the development of self requires a kind of 'enlightened indeterminacy'—a willingness to embrace ambiguity and uncertainty as an integral part of everyday life" (Eisenberg, 2001: 534).

So, think of the Uncertainty Principle in a positive sense. Think of it the way Mary Bateson does. In her book *Full Circles, Overlapping Lives: Culture and Generation in Transition*, she has this to say:

> We live with strangers. Those we love most, with whom we share a shelter, a table, a bed, remain mysterious. Wherever lives overlap and flow together, there are depths of unknowing. Parents and children, partners, siblings, and friends repeatedly surprise us, revealing the need to learn where we are most at home. We even surprise ourselves in our own becoming, moving through the cycles of our lives. There is strangeness hidden in the familiar. (2000: 27)

So—let the mystery be!

The Uncertainty Principle Defined

Let's now give a more concise formulation of the Uncertainty Principle, based on the above discussion of its three parts.

First, we cannot be absolutely confident that our understanding of intercultural interactions is certain and complete. Intercultural communication is inherently variable and subject to reinterpretation; in other words, our interpretations of new cultural experiences have a degree of uncertainty. We can never say that the way we have predicted or interpreted something excludes all other predictions or interpretations made in the past or to be made in the future. We must acknowledge uncertainty as an unavoidable aspect of intercultural communication.

Second, intercultural communication can be presented as a process of disclosure, or simultaneous opening up and closing down of the windows of awareness. In this process, people from different cultures together construct knowledge of their own and each other's identities (Self and the Other) and how to interact with each other. This knowledge is like a giant dynamic puzzle with some pieces always missing.

Third, different interpretations of the same experiences form the basis of intercultural communication, as shared order is created out of uncertainty.

In a nutshell, the Uncertainty Principle can be formulated as follows:

> *Intercultural communication is a process whereby people from different cultures constantly search for knowledge of how to interact with one another against the background of uncertainty.*

So, the Uncertainty Principle views intercultural communication as a joint search for knowledge with an unavoidable degree of uncertainty. The Uncertainty Principle must be seen as encouraging tolerance, civility, cooperation, creativity, and growth.

Summary

In this chapter, we set out to find out what happens when people venture beyond their cultural boundary lines. The following problem question was posed: How does the nature of knowledge affect intercultural communication?

To answer the problem question, we first turned to the field of epistemology, which studies knowledge, or how people know what they claim to know. We emphasized that the process of intercultural communication involves knowing who we are (our self-image), what people from the other culture think of us (our reflective self-image), and who people from the other culture are (the Other's cultural identity).

We looked at two broad approaches to human knowledge with different assumptions about its nature—the objective approach and the subjective approach. We showed that knowledge cannot be completely predicted or completely explained; thus, the two approaches complement each other. We concluded that section by stating that the line between objective reality and its subjective interpretation is always uncertain.

Based on these ideas, the Uncertainty Principle of intercultural communication was introduced.

First, we presented intercultural communication in terms of four windows of awareness, showing that every intercultural situation is characterized by a horizon of knowledge. In other words, our interpretations of a seemingly static cultural reality can never be absolutely complete.

Next, we presented intercultural communication as a process of dis-closure, whereby the windows of our awareness are constantly and simultaneously opened up and closed down by each culture. In this process, people provide and interpret information, together constructing knowledge of themselves, of each other, and of how to interact with each other. Because of inherent uncertainty, some pieces of this knowledge are always missing.

We emphasized that this view of intercultural interactions is not pessimistic. On the contrary, different interpretations of experiences form the basis of intercultural communication. Shared order is created out of uncertainty.

Based on these ideas, the Uncertainty Principle was formulated.

We now know that intercultural communication involves drawing boundary lines. When we cross boundary lines, we search for knowledge of how to interact with each other against the background of uncertainty. Intercultural communication is a process that is inherently variable and subject to interpretation. At the same time, the inherent uncertainty of communication makes it possible for people from different cultures to find meaning and create a shared order. So, how do people find their way out of the maze of uncertainty, creating order? What is the means to meaning in intercultural communication?

CASE STUDY
THE SHOCK OF THE OTHER

The following case study is based on the video "The Shock of the Other," one of the programs in the series *Millennium: Tribal Wisdom and the Modern World,* produced by Biniman Production Limited in 1992 and distributed by PBS Video. It is recommended that you watch the video in its entirety; below is a summary of the video.

Be ready to identify and then discuss the following topics:

1. Uncertain nature of intercultural search
2. Looking for closure
3. Uncertainty as a basis for intercultural communication

"The Shock of the Other" follows its host, David Maybury-Lewis, the head of the Cultural Survival organization, and his crew on their journey into the Peruvian Amazon to learn about the Mascho-Piro tribe, hidden from the outside world.

The video begins with Maybury-Lewis visiting the chief of the Xavante tribe in Brazil, whom he had met 30 years ago and now considers his "brother." Maybury-Lewis is looking for the chief's wisdom and encouragement before setting out on a journey to Peru. According to a custom of the Xavante tribe, he and his "brother" lie down and talk about their fears and hopes—"two mysteries to the Other," as Maybury-Lewis puts it, full of respect for each other.

Another stop Maybury-Lewis makes before setting out on his journey is at the monastery in Spain where Christopher Columbus had planned his journey several hundred years before. Maybury-Lewis cannot help noting the destruction of the Old World that Columbus's discovery brought, and he also sees the ugly side of the New World—pollution, ground bereft of life. He faces a dilemma: Should he set out on his own journey or stay home? He does not understand why, while we learn from the Other, we want the Other to be just like us. For him, the decision as to whether to travel to Peru is tied to solving this paradox. He remembers his Xavante "brother" and decides to set out on his journey.

Next we see him, accompanied by two Peruvians, traveling through the jungle. He sees this jungle, more than half of which is impenetrable, as hiding from the main predators—people. On the boat that is taking him to his camp, he feels like a stranger—to those Peruvians who accompany him and to himself. But he has a noble goal: to save the Mascho-Piro tribe from extinction, the fate of so many other tribes. The only information he has about the tribe is a photo of three women, along with some stories told by the locals of their contact with the tribe. Maybury-Lewis looks up and feels as if the whole jungle is watching him. He thinks he sees a distant figure in the river, but then thinks it must be just a dream.

He makes a stop at the last settlement before the virgin jungle, known as the "Park." This settlement, which looks like a half-way house, has an appropriate name, he thinks: "Labirinto," a place in limbo, caught between the past and the present. He goes to a saloon ("Where else?" he wryly smiles to himself) and looks around. Again, he wonders how those people see him—"as a monster?" He looks out the window and sees a funeral procession, finding it to be an omen. What for those people is loss of a human life, for him is death of a culture, destruction of the web of life.

At his camp, Maybury-Lewis finds out that the authorities in Lima are reluctant to let the group move on and photograph the tribe. Another decision needs to be made. He and his crew talk about this on a cold night, and he feels uncertainty sneaking up on him. "It all used to be so simple," he thinks. "When did certainty break?" He traces uncertainty back to the end of the 19th century and beginning of the 20th century, when Nietzsche announced there was no God, Freud and Darwin came up with their theories, and physicists proved that truth was relative. Yet Maybury-Lewis hopes that it is possible to meet the Other and have pluralism of opinions. And so they journey on.

The Peruvians accompanying the crew insist that they go up the river. "I think they sensed the tribe's closeness," Maybury-Lewis says. And he sees several women from the Mascho-Piro tribe peering out of the jungle. One of the women seems to call someone. "The rest of the tribe?" wonders Maybury-Lewis. Even at that distance, he feels, mystery comes across. "I stood at the edge of mystery," he says. He takes a small boat and sails closer to the northern boundary of the Mascho-Piro territory. On the bank of the river he sees their footprints, only hours old, and waits. Nobody comes out of the jungle, but he is sure they are watching him. He leaves some gifts for the tribe—pots and a knife. Leaving, he thinks: "Let the mystery be. Someday, we will meet, when we both are ready. And maybe we will still be brothers in a thousand years."

DISCUSSION

Now let's see how this case can be seen as an illustration of the Uncertainty Principle of intercultural communication.

1. Uncertain nature of intercultural search. The video shows the very nature of our knowledge—what happens when we understand our experiences or think that we do. The theme of intercultural contact being always mysterious runs through the whole story. The tape begins with Maybury-Lewis and his Xavante "brother" lying down and talking together, "two mysteries to the Other," and it ends with Maybury-Lewis leaving the Mascho-Piro territory thinking "Let the mystery be." "I stood at the edge of the mystery," he says, and this phrase is a nice metaphor for intercultural communication in general.

Another good metaphor is that of the impenetrable jungle. It suggests that there is always something unknowable about the jungle, just as there is always something unknowable about people from other cultures. We can view people from other cultures (and ourselves!) only up to a point; the Unknown Window is always present in all our interactions.

Maybury-Lewis specifies when certainty broke and the age of uncertainty was born. The discoveries of Nietzsche, Freud, Darwin, and early-20th-century physicists, seemingly unrelated, all proved that truth was elusive and our knowledge inherently uncertain.

2. Looking for closure. The video shows how people, in their search for knowledge, tend to complete incomplete stimuli. Wherever he looks, Maybury-Lewis tries to put pieces of a puzzle together. He looks at the jungle and sees (or thinks he sees) a distant figure. Unlike most other people, he looks at the funeral procession and sees destruction of the web of life. He looks at a candle and mosquito net on a cold night and sees the age of uncertainty being born.

(continued)

THE SHOCK OF THE OTHER CONTINUED

The Peruvians who accompany Maybury-Lewis and his crew, in their turn, sense the closeness of the Mascho-Piro tribe—sense it, maybe, with their very skin. All these perceptions are based on their previous knowledge. Obviously, Maybury-Lewis draws on his experiences as an anthropologist and the head of the Cultural Survival organization, while the Peruvians draw on their experiences of living in the jungle.

Intercultural interactions are difficult because the Mascho-Piro tribe's self-disclosure is reduced to a minimum: One of the women seems to peer out of the jungle, calling someone. As a result, Maybury-Lewis and his crew must deal with a lot of missing information as they construct knowledge of how to interact with the tribe. So, closure in this case is difficult to achieve, making intercultural interactions not very effective.

3. Uncertainty as a basis for intercultural communication. The video shows that, in spite of the inherent uncertainty of our knowledge, people from different cultures still communicate and hope for a peaceful pluralism of opinions. The video begins and ends with Maybury-Lewis visiting his Xavante "brother." They lie down and talk, "two mysteries to the Other," yet brothers, full of respect for each other. This, then, is the main goal of intercultural communication—to overcome the shock and meet the Other.

Intercultural contact often brings negative consequences, and we see several examples in the video—from both the New World and the Old World. But that should not stop you from setting out on intercultural journeys. You should just remember not to make the Other in your own image, and then it is possible to meet the Other and to understand who you are. In a way, everybody who sets out on an intercultural journey is like Columbus. It is crucial that, instead of bringing a destructive light, you make sure the web of life continues—for the Other and for yourself.

In that context, another metaphor in this story should be noted: the journey. Perhaps this metaphor is the most important one in the video. Maybury-Lewis sails off in his boat, searching for the Mascho-Piro tribe and also for his own identity. Intercultural communication is a journey.

SIDE TRIPS

1. In his article "Indeterminacy and History in Britton Goode's Western Apache Place-names: Ambiguous Identity on the San Carlos Apache Reservation," David Samuels (2001) discusses a number of strategies the Western Apache use in their intercultural interactions. The author shows how indeterminacy becomes a means of constituting and maintaining the culture on the San Carlos reservation. He argues that ambiguity and indeterminacy play important roles in creating meanings of place for San Carlos Apaches, and he shows how they make the landscape vibrate with contingency. Read the article and see whether you can appreciate this tolerance for uncertainty.
2. In her article "Making Better 'Scents' in Anthropology: Aroma in Tuareg Sociocultural Systems and the Shaping of Ethnography," Susan Rasmussen states: "At the heart of aroma, therefore, is ambiguity" (1999: 57). Do you agree with this statement? You will be able to provide a better answer if you read the entire article.
3. Chinese are said to use ambiguous verbal strategies to establish and redefine relationships. Sometimes such strategies are presented as a part of the indeterminate linguistic space. Read the article where this linguistic framework is discussed (Chang, 1999) and, based on these ideas, think how you would construct your message while interacting with Chinese.

CHECK YOURSELF

Epistemology
Objective approach
Subjective approach
Determinism
Voluntarism
Observer's paradox
Culture shock
Self-shock
Uncertainty
Predictive uncertainty
Explanatory uncertainty
Anxiety
Johari Window model
Horizon of knowledge
Disclosure
Closure
Dis-closure

REFERENCES

Baldwin, J., et al. (2003). *Communication theories for everyday life.* Boston: Allyn and Bacon.

Bateson, M. C. (2000). *Full circles, overlapping lives: Culture and generation in transition.* New York: Random House.

Berger, C. (1979). Beyond initial interaction. In Giles, H., & R. St. Clair (Eds.), *Language and social interaction.* Oxford: Blackwell.

Bernstein, D., et al. (1988). *Psychology.* Dallas: Houghton Mifflin.

Bohr, M. (1956). *Physics in my generation.* London: Pergamon.

Bradac, J. (2001). Theory comparison: Uncertainty reduction, problematic integration, uncertainty management, and other curious constructs. *Journal of Communication,* Vol. 51, No. 3, pp. 456–476.

Burrel, G., & Morgan, G. (1979). *Sociological paradigms and organizational analysis.* London: Heinemann.

Chang, H-C. (1999). The 'well-defined' is 'ambiguous'—indeterminacy in Chinese conversation. *Journal of Pragmatics*, Vol. 31, pp. 535–556.

Chen, G. M., & Starosta, W. J. (1998). *Foundations of intercultural communication*. Boston: Allyn and Bacon.

Cohen, R. (1999). *Negotiating across cultures*. Washington, DC: United States Institute of Peace Press.

Danesi, M., & Perron, P. (1999). *Analyzing cultures: An introduction and handbook*. Bloomington: Indiana University Press.

Eisenberg, E. (2001). Building a mystery: Toward a new theory of communication and identity. *Journal of Communication*, Vol. 51, No. 3, pp. 534–552.

Fleischacker, S. (1994). *The ethics of culture*. Ithaca, NY: Cornell University Press.

Gudykunst, W. (1995). Anxiety/uncertainty management (AUM) theory. In Wiseman, R. L. (Ed.), *Intercultural communication theory* (pp. 8–58). Thousand Oaks, CA: Sage.

Gudykunst, W. (2002). Intercultural communication theories. In Gudykunst, W., & B. Moody (Eds.), *Handbook of international and intercultural communication* (pp. 183–205). Thousand Oaks, CA: Sage.

Gudykunst, W., & Kim, Y. (2003). *Communicating with strangers: An approach to intercultural communication*. New York: McGraw-Hill.

Gudykunst, W., & Lee, C. (2002). Cross-cultural communication theories. In Gudykunst, W., & B. Moody (Eds.), *Handbook of international and intercultural communication* (pp. 25–50). Thousand Oaks, CA: Sage.

Hoffmeyer, J. (1999). Order out of indeterminacy. *Semiotica*, Vol. 127, No. 1/4, pp. 321–343.

Kim, Y. Y. (2001). *Becoming intercultural: An integrative theory of communication and cross-cultural adaptation*. Thousand Oaks, CA: Sage.

Littlejohn, S. (2002). *Theories of human communication*. Belmont, CA: Wadsworth.

Luft, J. (1970). *Group process: An introduction to group dynamics*. Palo Alto, CA: Mayfield.

Lustig, M., & Koester, J. (2003). *Intercultural competence: Interpersonal communication across cultures*. Boston: Allyn and Bacon.

Marris, P. (1996). *The politics of uncertainty*. London: Routledge.

Martin, J., & Nakayama, T. (2000). *Intercultural communication in contexts*, 2nd ed. London: Mayfield.

Martin, J., & Nakayama, T. (2004). *Intercultural communication in contexts*, 3rd ed. New York: McGraw-Hill.

Neuliep, J., & Ryan, D. (1998). The influence of intercultural communication apprehension and socio-communicative orientation on uncertainty reduction during initial cross-cultural interaction. *Communication Quarterly*, Vol. 46, pp. 88–99.

Oberg, K. (1960). Cultural shock: Adjustment to new cultural environments. *Practical Anthropology*, Vol. 7, pp. 177–182.

Rasmussen, S. (1999). Making better 'scents' in anthropology: Aroma in Tuareg sociocultural systems and the shaping of ethnography. *Anthropological Quarterly*, Vol. 72, No. 2, pp. 55–73.

Samuels, D. (2001). Indeterminacy and history in Britton Goode's Western Apache placenames: Ambiguous identity on the San Carlos Apache reservation. *American Ethnologist*, Vol. 28, No. 2, pp. 277–302.

Ting-Toomey, S. (1999). *Communicating across cultures*. New York: Guilford.

Zaharna, R. (1989). Self-shock: The double-binding challenge of identity. *International Journal of Intercultural Relations*, Vol. 13, No. 4, pp. 501–526.

CHAPTER THREE

INTERCULTURAL COMMUNICATION AS ENACTMENT OF MEANING: PERFORMATIVITY PRINCIPLE

The Deed Is Everything.

- *Key Theme:* Action
- *Key Objective:* To help you understand how intercultural communication is performed

INTRODUCING THE PROBLEM QUESTION

LANGUAGE AS A MEANS OF COMMUNICATION: AN OVERVIEW
- Definition of Language
- Dimensions of Language
- Language and Rules

INTRODUCING THE PERFORMATIVITY PRINCIPLE
- The Dramaturgy of Performativity: From Rules to Roles
- Performativity as a Reiterative Process
- The Structure of Performativity

THE PERFORMATIVITY PRINCIPLE DEFINED

SUMMARY

CASE STUDY: PERFORMING AL-HALQUA IN MOROCCO

SIDE TRIPS

CHECK YOURSELF

REFERENCES

Introducing the Problem Question

As was shown in the previous chapter, intercultural communication is a process that is inherently variable and subject to interpretation. Our search for knowledge always takes place against a backdrop of uncertainty. At the same time, the inherent uncertainty of communication makes it possible for people from different cultures to look for meaning. Now we need to find out how people deal with uncertainty. We need to discover how people find their way out of the maze of uncertainty, creating shared order.

Thus, the problem question for this chapter is this: *What is the means to meaning in intercultural communication?*

In this chapter we will

- Provide a brief overview of language as a means of communication
- Outline the main types of verbal and nonverbal language
- Look at intercultural communication as a dramaturgical performance
- Present intercultural communication as a complex reiterative activity
- Show the structure of intercultural communication as performance
- Demonstrate that meanings are enacted in the process of intercultural interactions.

Language as a Means of Communication: An Overview

Definition of Language

Language is most commonly defined as a means of communication (Fromkin & Rodman, 1993). Indeed, people cannot communicate with one another unless they have a language to use in their interactions. Language is typically identified with verbal languages such as the English language. However, nonverbal means can also qualify as language. Consider the following example:

> A student in class, John, might successfully communicate, by coughing, that he wants the attention of another student, Mary. First, he uses a distinct vocal (but not verbal) sign exhibiting rhythm and intonation . . . semanticised as a sociolinguistic norm (in John's community, as elsewhere, coughing is used to attract attention discretely). Moreover he followed appropriate turn-taking rules (John waited until Mary had finished taking a note to be sure she would hear). (Boylan, 2002: 169)

One often hears of other nonverbal languages, such as the language of gestures or the language of flowers. If we take a broad approach to language and look at its general nature, such languages appear no different from the verbal language that we all are familiar with. Below is a very brief overview of language as a means of communication.

Language, in general, is made up of some basic elements. For example, spoken language at the basic level is made up of sounds; the language of gestures is made up of some elementary movements of various body parts; and the language of music is made up of notes. The list of such basic elements is finite; however, we are able to create an infinite number of combinations of these basic elements, using them for various purposes. For example, we can chat with our friends or write a poem; we can send a message of love with our eyes; or we can compose a symphony. Both verbal and nonverbal languages are built from the ground up. In this process, as basic elements are combined to form complex messages, cultural knowledge is created. So **language,** as a means of communication, is, in fact, combinations of elements used to accomplish various tasks.

Verbal Language. Verbal language can be spoken or written.

Spoken Language. The basic elements of spoken language are distinctive sounds, or **phonemes**. In this sense, "knowing a language means knowing what sounds are in that language and what sounds are not" (Fromkin & Rodman, 1993: 4). For instance, for Russians and people from many other cultures, the English phoneme *th* (as in *thing* or *this*) is not a distinct sound. In other words, people from these cultures do not differentiate between *th* and *z*, pronouncing both as "z," or between *th* and *s*, pronouncing both as "s." As a result, such words as *thong* and *song* are pronounced by people from these cultures the same way, with the sound "s." Naturally, this may create problems in communication. Thus, learning a foreign language as a step toward effective intercultural communication must begin with mastering the sound system of that language by learning to hear and pronounce new sounds.

Written Language. The basic elements of written language are distinctive graphic characters. Just like sounds or phonemes, they help people to differentiate between meanings; for example, the difference between *cat* and *mat* is only one written character. Written characters, like phonemes, are symbolic creations and can represent sounds, as in phonetic writing (e.g., the English language), or ideas associated with objects, as in ideographic writing (e.g., the Chinese and Japanese languages). As a result, Chinese and Japanese written characters may appear strange to people whose language is English, and English characters may look odd to people whose language is Chinese or Japanese, posing a challenge to intercultural communication.

Nonverbal Languages. A nonverbal language is any language that uses elements other than verbal (spoken or written) means. Several main kinds of nonverbal languages can be isolated.

Environment. The natural elements of the **environment,** such as the physical landscape, temperature, and humidity, affect the way people communicate.

People do not actually use the natural elements of environment; rather, people are "used," or affected, by such elements and can only try to adjust to them. For example, a person born and raised in Hawaii may find it difficult to adapt to a culture with a cold climate, such as Finland, and, as a result, may find the people there cold and reserved, with a low level of self-disclosure.

Artifacts. *Artifacts* refers to "elements of the environment that communicate by virtue of people's use of them" (Jandt, 2001: 103). A cultural **artifact** is any object created and used by people for a specific purpose and includes clothing, vehicles, and houses. People actually use these elements of their environment for various purposes. For example, they build houses to show their status or apply makeup to reflect their idea of beauty. Artifacts are artificial creations, and their meaning is symbolic. Obviously, when people interact with people from other cultures, artifacts play an important role. In Egypt, for example, tensions between the Coptic minority and the Muslim majority are manifested in two competing bumper stickers. Those who identify with the Coptic identity use the fish as a symbol of their Christianity; the Muslims respond with the shark (Michael, 2003). Thus, two simple artifacts add to intercultural tensions.

Paralanguage. **Paralanguage** refers to all meaningful sound characteristics that are not phonemes, including rate, volume, and pitch. These nonverbal elements, used along with spoken language, often dramatically affect people's interpretations of one another. For example, Hall noted that African Americans tend to be very intense in the way they speak (paralanguage), though not necessarily in what they say (language); as a result, "many White Americans see African Americans as loud, pushy, and aggressive to the point of being out of control. Many African Americans see White people as too controlled, hypocritical, and lacking real feeling" (2002: 180).

Kinesics. **Kinesics** refers to the use of body movements, such as gestures and facial expressions, as a means of communication. These nonverbal elements seem to be natural, as we perform such movements almost unconsciously; yet, like any language, they are symbolic creations and vary from culture to culture. For example, the ring gesture (forming a circle with the thumb and forefinger) means OK to people in the United States. However, "things certainly would not be 'A-OK' if the ring gesture were used in cultures that attached other meanings to it" (Knapp & Hall, 1997: 258). For example, this gesture "indicates 'you're worth zero' in France and Belgium; 'money' in Japan; and 'asshole' in parts of southern Italy; and in Greece and Turkey it is an insulting or vulgar sexual invitation" (Knapp & Hall, 1997: 258).

Proxemics. **Proxemics** refers to the use of space in communication. The basic elements of proxemics are spatial zones, which reflect distances between people who are communicating with each other. Usually, four main spatial zones are isolated—intimate, personal, social, and public (Hall, 1966). The distances vary in different cultures, with elaborate rules about how close people may stand to each other and various objects. For example, the Amish and Anglo-Saxon cultures have different ideas about how close teenagers can stand to powerful equipment. Anglo-Saxon lawmakers try to prohibit teenagers from working near dangerous machines, such as those in sawmills or on farms, while many Amish groups say that such laws threaten their cultural tradition of "learning by doing" (Jordan, 2003).

Haptics. **Haptics** refers to the use of touch in communication. Different cultures vary as far as who may touch whom, where, when, and how. People in the United States, for example, are said to be touch deprived, with one of the world's lowest rates of the use of touch (Jandt, 2001: 117). When people from other cultures, such as the Mediterranean, come to the United States, the way they use touch is sometimes perceived as inappropriate and may even lead to sexual harassment charges.

Chronemics. **Chronemics** refers to the use of time in communication. The basic elements of chronemics are periods or moments of time as conceptualized by people from different cultures. How long something lasts, when something takes place, the relative importance of past, present, and future—all these factors are part of chronemics. In India, for example, wedding dates may be determined (often by the parents) after consulting Hindu priests who compare astrological readings and determine compatibility for the prospective bride and groom (Wang, 2003). This practice may pose a challenge when the bride is from India and the groom is from another culture, or vice versa.

Following Hall (1959), two main conceptualizations of time are usually isolated: monochronic and polychronic. Cultures with a **monochronic time orientation** emphasize "schedules, the compartmentalization and segmentation of measurable units of time," while cultures with a **polychronic time orientation** see "time as much less tangible" and stress "involvement of people and the completion of tasks" (Neuliep, 2000: 122).

Basic elements make it possible for people to build language from the ground up. By combining basic verbal (sounds or written characters) and/or nonverbal elements, people make language more and more complex, using it to accomplish various tasks such as arguing, joking, or giving a lecture. In summary, language as a means of communication can be classified as shown in Figure 1.

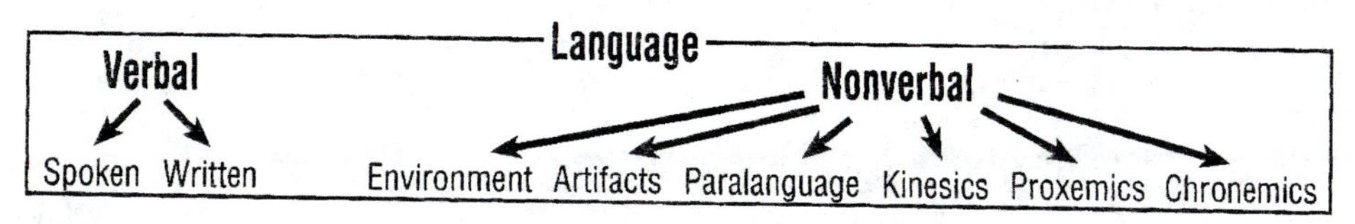

FIGURE 1

Dimensions of Language

Language, either verbal or nonverbal, has three dimensions—semantic, syntactic, and pragmatic (see Nöth, 1995: 50–51).

The **semantic dimension** of language covers the relations between its elements and what they designate in the world. For example, the character "c" designates a sound that is different from the sound of "a" or "t." The word *cat* designates "a carnivorous mammal, *Felis catus,* domesticated since early times as a catcher of rats and mice and as a pet" (Morris, 1982: 210). The gesture of turning one's head from side to side designates (in most cultures) contradiction of what is being presented.

The **syntactic dimension** of language covers the relations between its elements—how one element relates to all the other elements of a language. For example, for language elements to designate "a carnivorous mammal domesticated since early times as a catcher of rats and mice and as a pet," they must be combined in a certain order: *c, a, t.* The more combinations of elements that are established, the more complex the language becomes and the more diverse the meanings that can be created.

The **pragmatic dimension** of language covers the relations between its elements and the people who use them. For example, the word *dog* not only designates "a domesticated carnivorous mammal, *Canis familiaris,* raised in a wide variety of breeds and probably originally derived from several wild species" (Morris, 1982: 388) and appears as a sequence of the three written characters *d-o-g,* but also, as part of language, is interpreted by people as a faithful companion (in most cultures) or a part of cuisine (in some cultures). The gesture of turning one's head from side to side not only designates contradiction of what is being presented and appears as a sequence of head movements, but also can be interpreted as an act of defiance, arrogance, courage, or cowardice.

The three dimensions of language exist together in every act of communication. For example, to understand the meaning of the utterance "This painting is beautiful," one must have knowledge of all three dimensions. First, one must know what each of the elements designates—what the meaning of *this* is, what the meaning of *is* is, what the meaning of *painting* is, and what the meaning of *beautiful* is. This way, one comes to understand what segment of the world is designated by the utterance. Second, one must know the order in which these elements are combined—how sounds or written characters form words and words form sentences. Third, one must be able to interpret this utterance—why it was created, which depends on its use in a certain situation of interaction. Depending on the situation of interaction, it may be interpreted as a compliment or sarcasm or a subtle request. Thus, language as a means of communication requires knowledge of *what* elements designate, *how* they are combined, and *why* they are used, as shown in Figure 2.

When we use language, we select elements available from a certain system; for example, we choose between "painting," "work of art," and simply "piece." Also, we combine elements together in a certain order; for example, we say "This

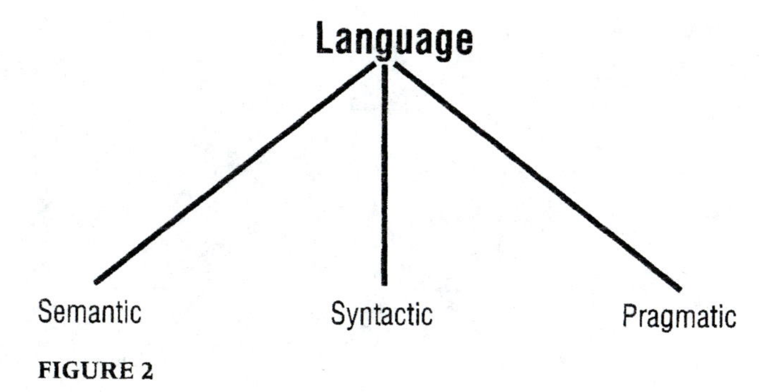

FIGURE 2

painting is beautiful" and not "Beautiful painting is this." Finally, we select and combine all these elements for a purpose—for example, to make the artist feel appreciated (if she or he interprets our statement as a compliment) or embarrassed (if she or he interprets it as sarcasm).

Figure 2 seems to present the use of language as a step-by-step process, whereby we first select from among available elements, then combine them together, and then use them to accomplish a certain task. In real interactions, of course, these three dimensions exist together and are activated simultaneously. If you take one away, language can no longer function as a means of communication. In this sense, language can be viewed as a giant dynamic tripod, constantly creating and re-creating various meanings (see Figure 3).

Language and Rules

Language as a giant tripod does not move at random, but follows rules. In other words, language is a rule-governed means of communication. "Rules allow us to organize and coordinate our lives. They create order out of chaos, uncertainty, and confusion. Football, flirting, solitaire, business meetings, and even friendships are

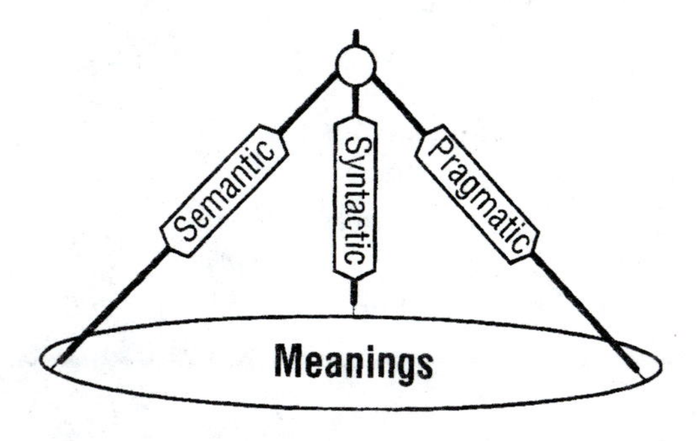

FIGURE 3

guided by different sets of formal or informal rules" (Anderson & Ross, 2002: 152). Every rule can be represented by the formula "If situation X occurs, do (do not do) Y." Based on this formula, "rules may be followed, or not, as the actor chooses" (McLaughlin, 1984: 21).

According to rules theorists (Shimanoff, 1980), all rules are followable, prescriptive, and contextual. To be followable, a rule must be understandable and accessible enough for people to adhere to it. "Communication scholars associate rules with actions rather than motions, and actions and behaviors that one may choose to perform; hence a rule must be capable of being followed" (Shimanoff, 1980: 39). One may be motivated to create a new rule for doing something—for example, watching people with closed eyes. However, if no one is able to perform such an action, the rule cannot operate (is not followable).

To be prescriptive, a rule must tell us what we must do to follow it or what will happen if we do not follow it. For example, in Russian Orthodox churches, a woman must cover her head with a scarf and everybody must remain standing during the service; those who do not follow these prescribed rules will be looked upon with disapproval.

To be contextual, a rule must be applicable only in particular situations. For example, it is appropriate to tell jokes in certain contexts, such as at a party. At a funeral, however, joke-telling may be interpreted as rude and insensitive.

Thus, all cultural meanings are created, or constituted, based on rules. In this respect, "rules are called constitutive because they 'constitute,' or make up, people's inner sense of meaning" (Anderson & Ross, 2002: 155). The term **enculturation** is used to describe the primary socialization process of people in their own culture; in other words, enculturation refers to how people learn various rules that constitute their own cultural identity. Rules of language as a means of communication make it possible for people from one culture to interact "in ways that would be confusing to someone who is just learning the language, or just entering the culture" (Anderson & Ross, 2002: 153). The term **acculturation** is used to describe the secondary socialization process of people in another culture; in other words, acculturation refers to how people learn various rules that constitute a cultural identity different from their own.

Whenever we interact with other people, we engage in various language games; the more we are able to identify, and play by, certain rules, the more coordinated and effective our games are. "Here, 'game' is not a negative or trivializing term" (Anderson & Ross, 2002: 156). Instead, using the ideas of Wittgenstein (1953) and others (Pearce, 1994), **language games** are viewed as dynamic structures created by people for accomplishing various tasks.

As language gets more complex, it can be used for accomplishing more diverse tasks. Consequently, it becomes more difficult to state explicitly all rules of interaction, so rules become more implicit. Following rules becomes more difficult, yet more important. It may be easy to select and combine language elements, taking care of the semantic and syntactic dimensions. However, it is difficult to use language appropriately in a particular situation, taking care of its pragmatic dimension. In intercultural communication, pragmatic failures, involving inability to understand "what is meant by what is said" (Thomas, 1983), are very common. In such cases, people cannot play the language game successfully because they are not familiar with its (subtle and implicit) rules. For example, if a person from Saudi Arabia offered you coffee, you might say "Thank you, but I have already had breakfast." You would interpret the offer as a mere offer of a beverage rather than as an expression of hospitality; the implicit rule in such a situation is to be gracious and say "yes" (see Neuliep, 1996: 247–248).

So, the constitutive view of language posits "that the elements of communication, rather than being fixed in advance, are reflexively constituted within the act of communication itself" (Craig, 2001: 128). Rather than creating rules for the games that people play, language is created by people in the process of their interaction.

People create meanings within certain language constraints. For example, every language has a system of basic sounds at people's disposal, and people must create language games using these sounds only. People use certain gestures because of the basic shape and size of their body. At this basic level, language constraints seem fixed in place, not subject to any change. However, even these language elements may change if they fail to meet people's needs. Nothing prevents people from using different sounds or gestures if they decide to play new games, games that cannot be performed with the old system of sounds or gestures. Nothing, in principle, prevents people from creating new rules as long as they are followable, prescriptive, and contextual. Thus, people create new language games by overcoming constraints. In this sense, language use must be viewed as a constant process of creating and overcoming constraints or breaking rules creatively (cf. Pearce & Cronen, 1980). So, the constitutive view of language makes it clear that meaning is created by people in the process of interaction (see Figure 4).

Coming back to our problem question, What is the means to meaning? It is the overall process of using language as a means of communication. What is the nature of this process? You might have noticed that in discussing this process we have used such terms as *game, play, acting out,* and *performance*. Indeed, the overall process of using language—both verbal and nonverbal—is a performance, and "performance is an important way of both knowing and being. In other words, performances are a means to knowing about experiences and they are also ways that we define our personal, social, and cultural identities" (Wood, 2000: 122).

Thus, people deal with uncertainty in intercultural communication through performances. This view of intercultural communication as performance is

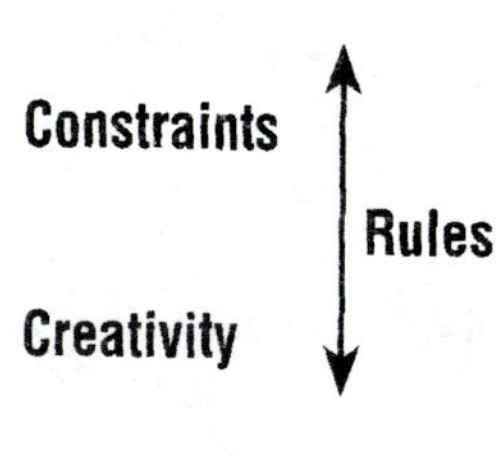

FIGURE 4

consistent with the so-called performative approach in social studies (Kapchan, 1995; Schechner, 2002; Warren 2001). According to this approach, to perform is to carry something into effect; hence, intercultural communication can be viewed as a process of carrying meaning, or cultural identity, as such, into effect.

When we speak of performativity or performance in intercultural communication, we must remember that "**performance** is the manifestation of performativity. This is to say, **performativity** refers to the reiterative process of becoming, while performance refers to the materialization of that process—the individual acts by human players in the world" (Warren, 2001: 106; boldface added)

The performative approach suggests that intercultural communication is performed, like music. There are a variety of verbal and nonverbal elements (notes), with which people create various language games (music). Some games are quite simple (a routine greeting), while others are more complex (business negotiations). In all cases, though, meanings are performed; that is, they are created and re-created in the process of interaction. People perform various activities repeatedly, and through repetition these movements become symbolic resources making up cultural identity. In intercultural interactions, to use Nietzsche's expression, "the deed is everything" (quoted in Butler, 1990: 25).

Introducing the Performativity Principle

Looking at intercultural communication as performance, we will formulate our third principle of intercultural communication: the Performativity Principle. There are three parts to this principle, and each deals with intercultural communication as creating and enacting meaning in the process of interaction. First, we will discuss the dramaturgy of intercultural performativity, or how people move from rules to roles. Next, we will present intercultural communication as a reiterative process. Finally, we will show the structure of intercultural communication as performance. We will discuss each part separately and then formulate the Performativity Principle as a whole.

The Dramaturgy of Performativity: From Rules to Roles

Communication as Drama. When people communicate with one another, they try to reach their goals by using various language means. Every act of communication is a performance whereby people face each other (either literally or in a mediated fashion, such as via the telephone or the Internet) and, as if on stage, present themselves—their very identities—dramatically to each other.

The theatrical or dramaturgical metaphor for communication does not suggest that people perform actions according to predetermined scripts or that performances are insincere and deceitful. Nor does the theatrical metaphor suggest that people think of themselves as actors, always conscious of performing on stage. What the dramaturgical view of performativity states is that all people engage in role enactment, playing out their identities. The premise of this view is that "people are not, originally and in some factlike way, 'mothers,' 'surgeons,' or 'crazy.' Instead, they are cast into these roles by themselves and by others" (Brown, 1977: 199). In other words, all roles are created in the process of communication. Even in the most mundane situations, such as a casual conversation with a friend, the interaction is always a performance, a process of playing a certain role and presenting a certain impression, or "face."

Performance and Face. The concept of **face** refers to the cultural identity we present to others (Goffman, 1959). Our cultural face embodies all meanings with which we identify, and, obviously, we want to present it according to our goals. Naturally, people from other cultures want to present their face according to their goals. In this light, intercultural communication can be seen as **facework**—an elaborate process whereby people from different cultures present their identities to each other, trying to play a language game together and accomplish their tasks. In this process, roles are enacted and impressions of identities are managed. In fact, there is a special theory—Identity Management Theory—that discusses how people from different cultures manage face in their encounters (Cupach & Imahori, 1993). This theory argues that cultural identities are revealed through the presentation of face and that "the maintenance of face is a natural and inevitable condition of human interaction" (Cupach & Imahori, 1993: 116). Therefore, "intercultural communication competence involves successfully managing face" (Gudykunst & Kim, 2003: 120). If people fail to present the face that they desire, a role fails to be enacted, and intercultural communication as a performance cannot be considered successful.

Performance and Frames. So, in every intercultural encounter, people from one culture present a certain image of themselves and act so that this image is understood by people from another culture. This is done by using various forms of verbal and nonverbal language, as we discussed earlier—"insignia of office or rank; clothing; sex, age, and racial characteristics; size and looks; posture; speech patterns; facial expressions; bodily gestures; and the like" (Goffman, 1959: 13). As a result, every intercultural encounter is framed; a **frame** is a definition or an interpretation of what a certain situation means (Goffman, 1974). People from various cultures have their own frames for such interactions as weddings, job interviews, and lectures. Every cultural frame can be viewed as a language game played according to certain rules. Naturally, if the same situation is framed differently by people from different cultures, intercultural communication as performance cannot be effective. The offer of a cup of coffee discussed earlier is one such situation; what was meant (framed) as an invitation to establish a friendly relationship was interpreted (framed) as a mere offer of a beverage.

Cultural identities spotlight every act of communication as performance. In other words, people find themselves in the spotlights provided by their respective cultures. This area, illustrated in Figure 5, constitutes the stage where intercultural performances take place and roles are enacted.

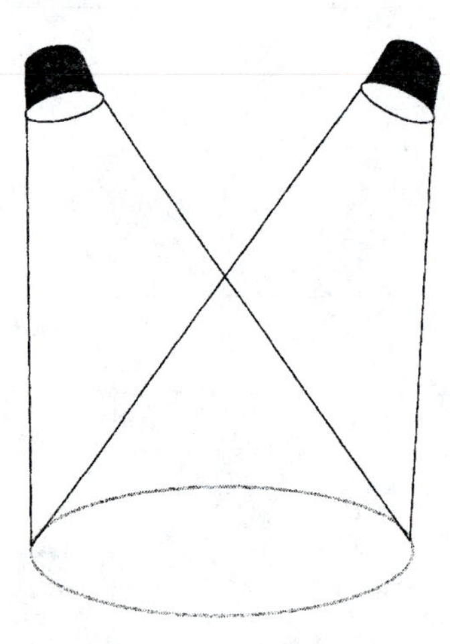

FIGURE 5

Thus, the dramaturgical view of performance shows us that intercultural communication is a process of playing out our identities by moving from rules to roles. We must emphasize that this enacting of roles is a process and takes time and effort.

Performativity as a Reiterative Process

We will begin this section by looking at intercultural communication in two ways. We will view it first as an ethnographic encounter and second as culture shock. We will then explain what both views have in common and how it all relates to the concept of performativity.

Intercultural Communication as an Ethnographic Encounter. **Ethnography** is "a method of interpreting actions in a manner that generates understanding in the terms of those performing the actions" (Wood, 2000: 130). Ethnographers "study the diversity and unity of cultural performance as a universal human resource for deepening and clarifying the meaningfulness of life" (Conquergood, 1985: 1). Interpretation of different cultural experiences is not only the province of trained ethnographers; it is what all people do when they meet one another. In this respect, intercultural communication can be viewed as a constant series of ethnographic encounters.

What are the main steps Self takes as it interacts with the Other? Let's look at a simple example of an intercultural encounter. Suppose you, a person from England, find yourself in Saudi Arabia and want to buy a Valentine's Day gift for a friend.

You go into a store and ask a simple question, "Where can I buy Valentine's Day gifts?" To your surprise, the salesperson is horrified and quickly disappears. Obviously, your intercultural encounter was not successful, and your ethnographic experience produced a negative result. But why did you act that way in the first place? Because you assumed that Valentine's Day was celebrated everywhere and expected to perform such a routine business transaction as buying a gift without any difficulty. This first step you took on your way to understanding the Other can be called "introspection." **Introspection** refers to using one's own frame of reference in dealing with others. In our intercultural encounters, we cannot help relying on our own working models and expectations, and we become aware of cultural differences when they are brought to light by an unsuccessful encounter. Introspection is our default mechanism, so to speak, and it is activated each time we have an intercultural encounter.

You might have failed to buy a Valentine's Day gift, but you have not given up on buying one—and gaining more knowledge about the culture of Saudi Arabia. So you decide to stay in the store; you want to see if other buyers will have more luck. Soon another customer comes in, and another salesperson, who seems to be more perceptive and less scared, shows him a large selection of Valentine items and sells him a Valentine's Day gift. Now you know that Valentine's Day gifts are available in Saudi Arabia, and you are proud of having gained this piece of cultural knowledge. This step can be called **observation**—paying attention or noting a phenomenon. This is exactly what you did; you acted as an observer (by not stepping out of the store), and it paid off.

Now you know that Valentine's Day gifts are available in Saudi Arabia, but you are still far from understanding the meaning of the behaviors you have observed. You decide to dress in your best Western clothes and try another store. You strike up a conversation with a salesperson, telling him you come from England and want to send your friend a Valentine gift. Your guess is that the salesperson will have nothing to fear and will be eager to help you. You guess right, and minutes later you walk out of the store with a nice teddy bear, with "Love" and "Me" traced on two paws. The step you just took can be called **experiment**—examining the validity of a hypothesis. This is exactly what you did; you came up with a guess, set up the situation, and confirmed your guess. The result is the teddy bear—and another insight into the culture of Saudi Arabia.

However, you still cannot quite see the practice of buying a Valentine gift in Saudi Arabia from the point of view of those native to that culture—salespeople and customers, whose encounters seemed to you like a well-choreographed dance. You feel that something is still missing, and you cannot be sure that your next intercultural encounter in a similar situation will be successful. Fortunately, you are on your way to meet a young person from Saudi Arabia who had stayed at your house back in England as an exchange student. He speaks good English and seems to be very open-minded and eager to talk. So you describe your shopping adventure to him and ask for an explanation. This is how you find out that officially Valentine's Day is prohibited in Saudi Arabia, but it is difficult to ban people, especially young people, from celebrating the holiday. You learn that the feared muttawa, or religious police, visit stores to try to ensure that everyone obeys the law. You also learn that salespeople can usually tell real buyers (especially those dressed in Western clothes or obviously from other cultures) from undercover religious police. Finally, you are told that stores usually sell the gift items weeks in advance; as February 14 gets closer, it becomes more difficult to find Valentine gifts in stores because the religious police begin looking for anything suggesting the holiday. You are amazed to learn all this information and feel that now you can really understand the meaning of the cultural practices associated with Valentine's Day from the point of view of the people native to Saudi Arabia. This last step that you took can be called **interview,** for this is exactly what you did—you asked questions, as in an interview.

With each step, you have come closer to the Other (culture of Saudi Arabia). You have become more actively involved in intercultural communication, moving from simply using your own frame of reference (introspection) to passively looking at the situation (observation) to setting up a situation and validating your guess (experiment) to asking questions (interview). As a result of this ethnographic encounter, you have gained important knowledge about the people of Saudi Arabia, and you should be able to communicate with them more successfully the next time you find yourself in that country and need to buy a Valentine gift. Thus, in your ethnographic encounter, you have taken several important steps, coming back to Self and changing your own frame of reference (see Figure 6).

Intercultural Communication as Culture Shock. When people act as ethnographers in intercultural communication, they may find it difficult to adjust to new situations. For example, one might react to the situation described above with a variety of thoughts ("Why did that salesperson refuse to talk to me?"), emotions ("This is very frustrating!"), and behaviors ("I'm leaving this country tonight!"). As was mentioned earlier in the book, culture shock, as the name suggests, is people's reaction to an attempt to adjust to new situations (Oberg, 1960). Intercultural communication is a process of constantly dealing with culture shock.

Culture shock can be viewed as a process involving several stages (see Fumhan & Bochner, 1986; Winkelman, 1994). Let's break down your experience in Saudi Arabia into its main stages.

First of all, even before getting to Saudi Arabia, you formed some expectations about people from that culture and how to interact with them. This first stage of culture shock can be called the **preliminary stage**; it sets the tone for your intercultural journey.

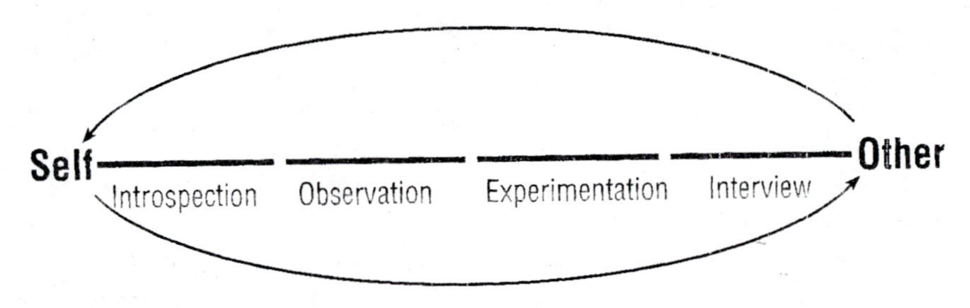

FIGURE 6 Ethnographic Encounter

As soon as you got to Saudi Arabia, you became excited about all the new things you encountered in the culture. You were fascinated by the exotic foods, beautiful architecture, and peculiar dress. This stage of culture shock can be called the **"honeymoon" stage.** Back home in England, you had done your homework, read travel books, and formed your expectations. And now, finally, you were in Saudi Arabia for the first time, and of course you were very excited!

Then you remembered that February 14 was coming up and decided to send your friend back home a gift for Valentine's Day. You stepped into a store and asked that simple question: "Where can I buy Valentine's Day gifts?" To your surprise, the salesperson was horrified and quickly disappeared. Naturally, you were puzzled and frustrated. You felt confused and rejected. This is the **crisis stage** of culture shock. As the name suggests, it is a critical stage; either you give up and leave the store (and perhaps the country) or you try to find out what is going on. Fortunately, you started to observe other customers and then decided to set up an experiment. As a result, you learned that Valentine's Day gifts are available in Saudi Arabia, and you felt better about your stay there.

Later, you spoke with your Saudi friend about your experience, learning much more about Valentine's Day in that culture. Your confusion and feelings of hostility and rejection disappeared. You decided you could live with the cultural practices associated with Valentine's Day. This is the **adjustment stage** of culture shock.

When you plan your next trip to Saudi Arabia, you will keep these travel experiences in mind. The next time you need to buy a Valentine gift there, you will be able to accomplish that task successfully, without as much shock. Thus, in dealing with culture shock, you went through several important stages, coming back to Self and changing your preliminary expectations (see Figure 7).

Intercultural Communication as a Hermeneutic Circle. What is common to viewing intercultural communication as an ethnographic encounter and as culture shock? Both views show how Self goes through certain steps, or stages, in order to understand how to interact with the Other. In both cases, Self moves closer and closer to understanding the Other and then goes back to square one (one's own frame of reference). Thus, in this complex process, Self operates

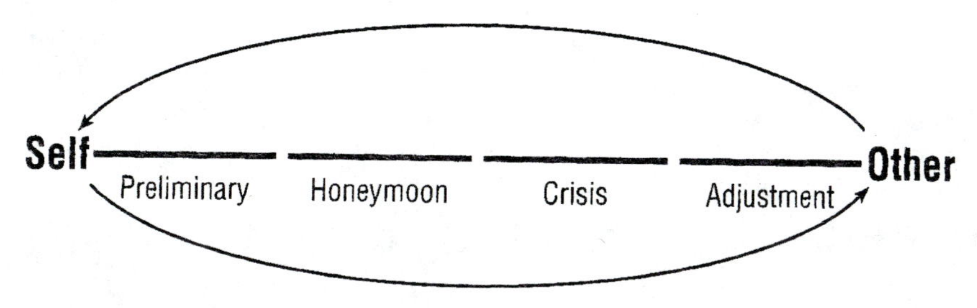

FIGURE 7 Stages of Culture Shock

between two extremes—identifying with the Other and keeping distant from the Other. This process of understanding meaning is sometimes described as a **hermeneutic circle,** where distance-experiences and near-experiences are in constant rotation (Geertz, 1983). First, Self looks at the Other from a distance (distance-experience). Then Self gets closer to the Other, trying to understand its meanings from within (near-experiences). These meanings, however, can be understood only if Self steps back and checks how these new experiences fit his or her own frame of reference (distance-experiences). But then Self must again move back closer to the Other (near-experiences), and the cycle continues.

In this process, Self has to balance two roles: those of insider and outsider, or actor and spectator. If Self completely identifies with the people from the other culture—that is, becomes an actor—Self ceases to see how she or he is different from the Other and thereby loses the framework from which to approach the Other. As a result, Self can no longer be a spectator of the language game being created and is no longer able to evaluate the intercultural experience and decide what meanings should and should not be enacted. This scenario of intercultural interactions can be viewed as **assimilation,** in which individuals disregard their own cultural tradition in favor of the tradition of another culture. Of course, if Self chooses to completely distance himself or herself from contact with the Other, no intercultural communication takes place. Then Self is merely a spectator, unable to act together with the Other and create meanings. This scenario of intercultural interactions can be viewed as **separation,** in which individuals tend to favor their own cultural tradition and disregard the tradition of a new culture. The best way to balance the roles of insider and outsider, or actor and spectator, is through integration, in which individuals have a truly bicultural identity. (We will discuss the nature and value of intercultural integration in Chapters 8, 9, and 10.)

The hermeneutic circle can be viewed as the stage where all intercultural performances take place. It is important to remember, however, that no spectators exist separately from the actors on that stage; people are both actors and spectators. As actors, people simultaneously write and perform their script together, creating and re-creating their world. As spectators, people watch the results of their creations. But they exist on the *same* stage, in the *same* world. Remember Shakespeare—"*All* the world's a stage" (italics added)? Only people who interact with one another can take care of their world and write a good script in which everybody tries to get along with everybody else.

For the sake of the example, we have assumed that you as Self are comfortable with the role you have enacted in the intercultural performance—that of a Western customer willing to perform, in essence, an illegal act in order to show affection for your friend back in England. However, your performance could take a different route; for instance, you might decide to insist that a Valentine gift be sold to you openly, thus acting in defiance of the existing cultural practices. In this scenario, another role is enacted—that of a critic of the existing cultural order. Salespeople, on their part, will need to decide on their roles in this intercultural performance: Do they support you and let you have your way, go against your

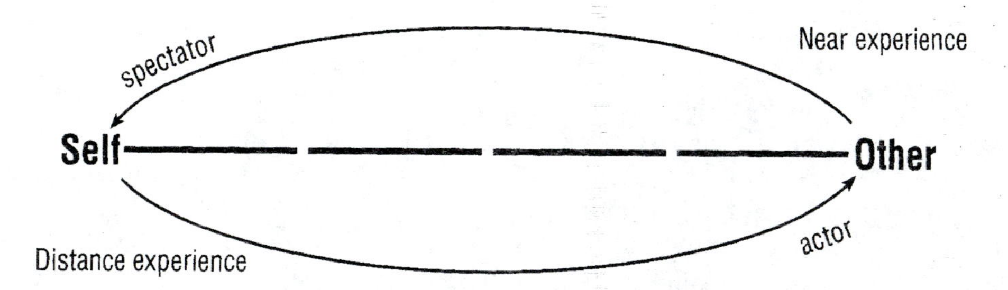

FIGURE 8 Hermeneutic Circle of Intercultural Communication

wishes, or take some other course of action? In this scenario, intercultural tensions are much higher, causing more severe culture shock and leading to a serious conflict. There are a number of models describing the types of identity change that can be related to role enactment (see Ting-Toomey, 1999: 254–256). Overall, our experiences in understanding people from other cultures in terms of the hermeneutic circle are shown in Figure 8.

Thus, enactment of meanings that constitute cultural identity is a reiterative process. We all want to be part of a culture—that is, belong to a certain culture. However, belonging is not simply a matter of be-ing, but of longing, and hence belonging (Bell, 1999: 1). Belonging is always an achievement, an effect performatively produced. But cultural identity can never be achieved once and for all; in a way, we can never simply "be" (completely identify with) Self or the Other. We can only repeatedly work on the construction of cultural identities; that is, we can only "long for" cultural identities. Thus,

> Performativity denies, in some fundamental ways, the stability of identity, moving toward a notion of repetition as a way of understanding that those markers used to describe one's identity (i.e., gender, class, race, sexuality) get *constructed through the continual performance* of those markers. (Warren, 2001: 95; italics added)

The view of performativity as a reiterative process is not pessimistic at all; on the contrary, it is liberating. It suggests that any identity can be constructed as long as Self and the Other go through the hermeneutic circle—as many times as is necessary for meaning to be enacted.

But how many times? How do we know when meaning is enacted? We need to learn about the structure of performativity to answer this question.

The Structure of Performativity

The following discussion of the structure of intercultural performance is based on the ideas of the Activity Theory initiated in Russia in the 1920s and 1930s (for more information, see Leont'ev, 1978; Wertsch, 1998). A simple example will help us to understand how any activity is performed.

Levels of Performance. Suppose you are visiting the United States and your American friends invite you to attend a baseball game. Their friendship is important to you, and you are determined to show them that you enjoy this entertainment experience as much as they do. Having formulated for yourself the cultural frame ("sports entertainment") and the motive ("enjoying the game together with one's friends"), you must successfully attain a variety of specific goals. Some of the actions you must take to achieve those goals include purchasing your ticket, handing it to the gatekeeper, following the score, and visiting the concession stand. Some of these actions are relatively simple (purchasing the ticket); some are more complex (following the score).

Suppose your friends are willing, and even happy, to introduce you to the game and teach you as much as possible about this popular American sport. They do their best to explain to you the rules of the game and how to keep score, and they provide a lot of other useful information about the overall performance. What impact will all this have on your future interactions in a similar intercultural situation? Obviously, you will feel much more comfortable performing all the necessary actions. Even more importantly, you will think less about how to, say, purchase a ticket or hand it to the gatekeeper. The activity of attending a baseball game will have flown through actions to operations; in other words, the activity will have become operationalized. As a result, you will start performing this activity almost automatically.

So, the structure of performativity can be analyzed in terms of three levels:

1. The first level is called the **activity level**; it is performance driven by a certain motive. This level focuses on a certain culturally defined context, or frame, as discussed earlier. The activity in our example can be framed as "sports entertainment," and the motive is "enjoying the game together with one's friends" (someone else might have a different motive for performing this activity, such as obligation or to please a boyfriend or girlfriend).
2. Every activity can be carried out only through actions; hence, the second level of behavior is the **actions level.** Actions are performances directed toward specific goals. In our example, you must purchase your ticket, hand it to the gatekeeper, and so forth.
3. Finally, the third level is the **operations level** because every activity can be performed through different operations, depending on conditions. Operations adjust actions to current conditions. In our example, you may bring along an umbrella, if it is a rainy day, or binoculars, if your seats are too far from the field. Without such adjustments you cannot realize your main motive—enjoying the game.

Thus, the structure of your performance takes on the form shown in Figure 9.

Every performance can be seen as an activity that is carried out through actions and results in the formation of operations (skills). In other words, successful communication as performance requires knowledge of *why* an encounter takes place, *what* goals must be attained through what actions, and *how* they can be ac-

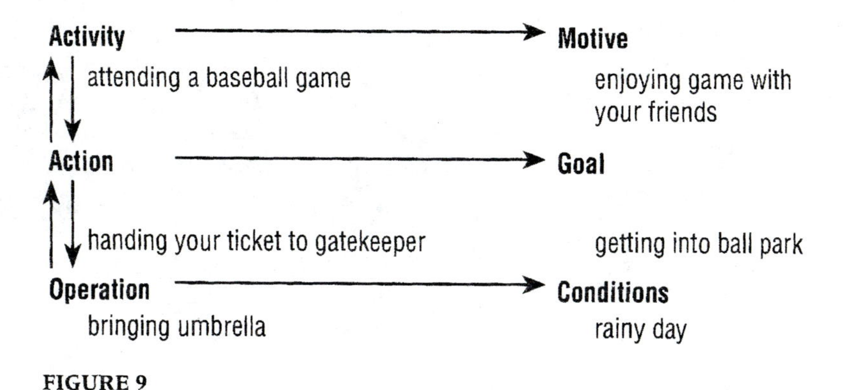

FIGURE 9

complished under specific conditions. Thus, every performance is seen at the highest level as an activity, at the intermediate level as a series of actions, and at the lowest level as a number of concrete operations. It is important to emphasize that these three levels can be isolated only for the sake of analysis; in real life, every intercultural encounter is one whole performance.

At the highest level, intercultural communication is framed, to use the term discussed earlier; that is, it takes place within certain culturally defined contexts. For communication to be successful, people must, first of all, understand what the frames are and what motivates people to behave in a certain way. If one fails to identify the appropriate frame and to see the motive for other people's behavior, intercultural communication may be unsuccessful.

In his ethnographic descriptions of the Western Apache culture, Basso tells about a young Apache woman who, while attending a girl's puberty ceremony, had her hair in pink plastic curlers. Here is how Basso describes what happened to that young woman at a birthday party two weeks later:

> When the meal was over casual conversation began to flow, and the young woman seated herself on the ground next to her younger sister. And then—quietly, deftly, and totally without warning—her grandmother narrated a version of the historical tale about the forgetful Apache policeman who behaved too much like a white man. Shortly after the story was finished, the young woman stood up, turned away wordlessly, and walked off in the direction of her home. Uncertain of what had happened, I asked her grandmother why she had departed. Had the young woman suddenly become ill? "No," her grandmother replied. "I shot her with an arrow." (Basso, 1990: 122)

It became clear to the ethnographer that the girl's grandmother had told her a moralistic story (arrow) to teach her a lesson and to remind her that, at puberty ceremonies, hair should be worn loose to show respect for Apache customs. Basso describes this Western Apache cultural frame as "stalking with stories"—telling a moralistic historical narrative. At first, however, the ethnographer was unable to identify the frame and understand the motives for the girl's and the grandmother's behavior; as he admits, he was "uncertain of what had happened." When he found out what had happened, all their actions made sense to him.

So, the outcome of intercultural communication depends on how successfully we can understand meanings of other people's behavior. If we do not understand why people from a different culture behave in a certain way, we need to go back to our ethnographic drawing board, so to speak, and gather more information.

The Flow of Performance. The flow of every performance is from activity through actions to operations and back to activity. In this flow, roles of intercultural performance are constantly enacted and re-created.

Why is it important for our performances to become operationalized? The simple answer is "so we can focus on more important things." You could hardly enjoy a baseball game if you were constantly thinking about how to keep score or how to purchase a beverage at the concession stand. However, if we started performing our intercultural interactions only as operations, then we as actors would become no different from robots, simply going through the motions. We must never forget about our other role—that of spectators. We must always evaluate our performance and, if we feel we are only going through the motions, create new meanings, whatever they might be. Our performances become operationalized only to give us more freedom to be creative and come up with new motives and new meaningful activities. The flow of intercultural communication as enactment of meaning is from activity through actions to operations and then back to activity. That is why the arrows in Figure 9 go from the activity level down to the level of operations and back up to the level of activity. Communication as performance is always a loop—a reiterative process of enactment of meaning.

Now we know that meaning is enacted when our performance is operationalized. How long or how much effort it takes depends on the complexity of the performance. If the goal is simply to greet a fellow student, this meaning can be enacted fairly quickly. If, however, you need to act as a chief negotiator, working with people from another culture on a joint business project, the enactment of your role will take much more time and effort.

The Performativity Principle Defined

Let's now give a more concise formulation of the Performativity Principle, based on the above discussion of its three parts.

First, intercultural communication is a process of playing out our identities by moving from rules to roles. In every intercultural encounter, people from one culture present a certain image of themselves and act so that this image is understood by people from another culture. This is done by using various verbal and nonverbal language means. As a result, every intercultural encounter is framed or defined in a certain way.

Second, enactment of meanings that constitute cultural identity is a reiterative process. In this process, Self and the Other go through the hermeneutic circle as many times as is necessary for meaning to be enacted.

Third, the structure of intercultural communication as performance is as follows: from activity through actions to operations and then back to activity.

In a nutshell, the Performativity Principle can be formulated as follows:

> *Intercultural communication is a reiterative process whereby people from different cultures enact meanings in order to accomplish their tasks.*

Thus, intercultural communication is a joint effort of creating and enacting meanings.

Summary

In this chapter, the following problem question was posed: What is the means to meaning in intercultural communication?

We began the chapter by presenting language as a means of communication. We showed that both verbal and nonverbal means are used to create certain language games, which constitute cultural identities. The overall process of using language was presented as a performance. Thus, performance was shown to be the main means to meaning in intercultural communication.

Based on these ideas, we discussed the dramaturgical nature of intercultural communication as a process of moving from rules to roles. In this process, people from different cultures act and create meanings together. Thus, we defined performativity as a process of enactment of meaning.

Next, we showed that the process of enactment of meaning is reiterative. We looked at the reiterative nature of intercultural communication, using the example of a hermeneutic circle as an interplay between distance-experiences and near-experiences. In this process, people constantly balance the roles of actors and spectators, together creating and re-creating their world. Cultural meanings are enacted through a reiterative and ongoing process of performance.

Finally, we presented the structure of intercultural performativity. We showed that the flow of performativity is from activity through actions to operations and back to activity.

Based on these ideas, the Performativity Principle was formulated.

We now know that intercultural communication is always a joint effort, an activity performed by Self and the Other. As a result of this activity, cultural meanings are enacted. But what happens to cultural meanings as they are enacted? This question will be answered in the next chapter.

CASE STUDY
PERFORMING AL-HALQA IN MOROCCO

This case study is based on two articles: "Performance," by Deborah A. Kapchan (1995), and "Al-halqa Performance in Morocco from the Open Space to the Theater Building," by Khalid Amine (2001). As usual, it is recommended that you read each article in its entirety; below is a summary of the articles.

Be ready to identify and then discuss the following topics:

1. An ethnographic encounter with al-halqa
2. Al-halqa and culture shock
3. Structure of an al-halqa performance

Imagine that during your stay in the Middle Atlas region of Morocco you decide to visit one of its open-air marketplaces. Back home, you had heard how exotic and wonderful these places are, and you are eager to make a trip to the marketplace not far from where you are staying to see for yourself. Besides, you have taken some classes in Arabic from a private tutor and now want to see how successfully you can communicate; buying something in a marketplace seems like a good way to do so. And, of course, you want to learn more about how people in the Moroccan culture think and feel so that you can interact with them better.

Once there, you notice a woman in her forties, seated on a small mat, with a variety of herbs in front of her. You go up to her and ask if you could buy some herbs from her. To your surprise, the woman either does not understand you or simply does not want to sell you anything. She is talking to several people around her, waiting for something. You wonder what goal she might have in mind and decide to wait around to observe what happens next. Soon, when her audience has grown to about twenty men and women, some squatting down in front of her in a semicircle and some standing behind them, the woman begins to perform. She addresses the crowd, while drawing their bodies and their words into the circle. You are both captivated and somewhat shocked by her eloquent and bawdy language, as well as her gestures, pointing to the lower part of her body. You decide to stay on, though, and mimic the words and actions of the crowd around you. You think that to enjoy this performance you must blend in with the crowd as much as you can.

You see the woman herbalist hold forth one of her herbs and address the audience: "This little bit that I'm going to give you, what is it used for? By God, I won't tell you what it's used for until you ask 'what?' "

She clearly expects a response from her audience, and it comes from the crowd right away: "What is it used for, allala?"

"By God, I didn't hear you!" calls out the herbalist.

Now you know what to say, so you do, together with the crowd: "What is it used for?"

And so it goes on and on, with the audience participating in the performance. At one point, while describing the miraculous powers of her homemade herbal remedies to cure a disease, she picks you out, along with several more people from the crowd, and designates you "a witness to God." You do not quite understand this part of the performance, but you play along, putting your hands together like everyone else in the audience. The herbalist continues her performance by placing small samples of her herbs into everyone's hands and pouring a single glass of tea. The audience eats together, washing down the remedy with the tea, which is passed from person to person. Again, you find this behavior a bit strange, but toward the end of the performance you feel that you have actually enjoyed it, including the part of eating and drinking together. You leave the marketplace with a sense of accomplishment, and you look forward to doing it again on the next market day.

By the next market day, you have asked some people you know in Morocco to tell you more about this fascinating experience. You find out that this performance is called *al-halqa* and literally means a link in a chain. It is a cultural practice in Morocco that involves a circular assembly of people surrounding a performer in a public setting, usually a marketplace. This cultural practice does not exist without an audience, and the performer does not begin to perform until the audience reaches a certain density. The spirit of the performance is spontaneous and liberating, with the topics often revolving around ills, excesses, and desires of the body. This form of cultural expression often challenges the existing social hierarchies and interacts with daily life and ideology in a number of other ways. You learn that, since Islamic law requires twelve witnesses to establish something as a legal fact, you were picked out as one of the "witnesses to God" to testify to the potency of the herbs. As you suspected, common ingestion of food is a symbol of sociability and friendship in Morocco (that is why, after the performance, you felt good about that experience).

So, the next time you visit a marketplace and see the al-halqa performance, you feel more confident of your actions, and you try to focus more on what the performer actually says. Earlier you simply wanted to practice your language and buy some herbs; now you are more inclined to learn about life in Morocco and how it is changing.

DISCUSSION

Now let's see how this case can be seen as an illustration of the Performativity Principle of intercultural communication.

1. An ethnographic encounter with al-halqa. When you found yourself in Morocco, you acted as an ethnographer because you wanted to learn about that culture. You wanted to find out how people there thought and felt so that you could interact with them better. In other words, you wanted to get inside their culture and understand its meanings from within.

Your first encounter with the woman herbalist was a failure. What you thought would be a routine interaction (buying-selling) turned out to be a small disaster. Your own frame of reference (remember introspection?) failed you, as the woman did not sell you anything but instead kept talking to several other people. You decided not to give up, however, and stayed on, observing the situation. You saw that, once about twenty people had gathered around the woman, she began her performance. At that moment, you thought you would join the audience and mimic their actions—verbal and nonverbal. In a way, this was a little experiment you set up; it proved quite successful, for you enjoyed the experience and learned quite a lot about the culture of Morocco. What you had failed to understand during the performance (for example, suddenly becoming a "witness to God") you were able to learn with the help of some questions you asked of your Moroccan friends.

Overall, your ethnographic encounter was quite successful. You managed to balance the distance-experiences and near-experiences and seemed to establish the right relationship between Self and the Other.

(continued)

PERFORMING AL-HALQA IN MOROCCO CONTINUED

2. Al-halqa and culture shock. While you were trying to understand this cultural practice, you went through several stages of culture shock.

Back home, during the preliminary stage, you heard how exotic and wonderful many places in Morocco were. Also, you took some classes in Arabic from a private tutor and were eager to find out how successfully you could communicate with people there.

When in Morocco, you got quite excited, anticipating your first real encounter with the Moroccan culture. You had read a lot about its exotic marketplaces, and you could not wait to see how well you could get by with the language you had learned back home. That "honeymoon" stage, though, quickly gave way to the crisis stage. Your first encounter with the herbalist was unsuccessful, and you could have given up on the Moroccan marketplace (and your overall intercultural experience).

Fortunately, you did not give up, and soon you were an active part of the audience. By the end of the performance, you felt you had adapted nicely to this Moroccan cultural practice and were even eager to take part in a similar performance again on the next market day. Thus, you reached the adjustment stage of culture shock.

3. Structure of an al-halqa performance. Clearly, the performance of al-halqa is a joint effort; meanings can never be communicated and enacted unless there is interaction between a performer and an audience. Thus, meanings are truly performed—created and enacted in the process of interaction. These enactments of meanings appear as a reiterative process; they come into being through a series of repeated performances. To put it simply, it takes time and perseverance for cultural meanings to take hold. In a way, the performer tests the waters: Which of her or his behaviors will be enjoyed, tolerated, rejected by the audience?

Overall, the performance of al-halqa can be seen as an activity that is carried out through a series of actions and results in the formation of operations. As an activity, the performance must fit a certain cultural frame—for example, entertainment, the selling of merchandise, or a call for the transformation of society. Initially, this activity appears to most as a form of entertainment, which it definitely is. But, more deeply, it often functions as a form of social commentary. It acts as a mirror, reflecting daily life, ideology, and the social organization of the country and contributing to the shaping of the Moroccan cultural identity.

As actions, the performance appears as a series of verbal and nonverbal movements, which include waiting for the performance to begin, responding to the performer, obeying his or her commands, and sharing herbs and tea with the rest of the audience. These actions form an elaborate piece of music, so to speak, that is played by the performer and the audience. The more successfully it is performed, the more automatic the activity becomes at the lowest level of operations. This means that the performer does not think much about how to place the herbs on the ground or how to make a certain gesture and that people in the audience do not think much about how to form a circle or how to pass a glass of tea from person to person. These actions are performed almost automatically, as operations.

Once the actions get operationalized, those who engage in the interaction can focus on the more important aspects of the performance, attending to why it takes place (activity) and what must be said and done (actions), rather than how it all is accomplished (operations). When you go back to participate in al-halqa on the next market day, you will probably try to figure out, at a deeper level, why this performance takes place. It is not just about selling herbs and entertaining crowds of people. After you have visited the marketplace several times, you may notice that there is only one woman performing al-halqa, as opposed to a dozen men. Thus, you may understand the deeper meaning of this cultural practice, reframing this performance as the construction of feminine public authority in Morocco.

Finally, the result of any intercultural encounter depends on how smoothly this activity is performed, which is determined by how well the cultural meanings are understood and enacted by Self and the Other. If, for example, you failed to see the al-halqa performance as an attempt to establish feminine public authority and saw it simply as a form of cheap entertainment, the intercultural encounter could hardly be called very successful, as the cultural meanings that the performer tried to get across are unlikely to be enacted. If, however, you found the performance truly liberating, from both an aesthetic and a social point of view, and decided to support this cultural practice, attending more performances while in Morocco or perhaps writing an article about it when you got back home, then the intercultural encounter would be more successful, and the cultural meanings would have a much better chance of being enacted.

Overall, by following rules you contributed to the enactment of certain roles making up cultural identities—that of the woman herbalist (the Other) and your own (Self).

SIDE TRIPS

1. Concern for design and visual appeal is a distinctive characteristic of Japanese cuisine. Food is often prepared in full view of the customer, and appreciation of the chef's skills becomes an integral part of the eating experience. The ideal meal is a visual as well as a gastronomic delight. Might a visit to a Japanese restaurant be framed differently by Japanese people and people from another culture, affecting their interaction?
2. On September 8, 2001, the *Los Angeles Times* published an article with the following headline: "Trekking to Cloud 9." The subhead read "Some U.S. women find love, even marriage, with their Sherpas. But often, the romances in the Himalayas have led to broken hearts."

   Sherpas are a small ethnic group in Nepal, and, according to the article, many American women go to Nepal looking for more than the beauty of the mountains or the golden glow of the sunsets. In turn, some Sherpas want to come to the United States because they have heard "this is the place where they can make it."

   How would you analyze such intercultural encounters in terms of cultural frames and motives?
3. In his article "Doing Whiteness: On the Performative Dimensions of Race in the Classroom," Warren (2001) tries to find out what it means to be "white." He discovers that reliance on the body as the site of racial identity is inadequate because race is constructed through various communicative performances. In the article, he locates a number of such reiterative moments of racial enactment and shows how they might affect intercultural interactions. How do you think whiteness is performed—both verbally and nonverbally? Think of some examples of the enactment of the meaning of "whiteness," and compare them with those discussed in the article.

CHECK YOURSELF

Language
Phoneme
Environment
Artifact
Paralanguage
Kinesics
Proxemics
Haptics
Chronemics
Monochronic time orientation
Polychronic time orientation
Semantic dimension (or language)
Syntactic dimension (of language)
Pragmatic dimension (of language)
Enculturation
Acculturation
Language game
Performance
Performativity
Face
Facework
Frame
Ethnography
Introspection
Observation
Experiment
Interview
Preliminary stage (of culture shock)
"Honeymoon" stage (of culture shock)
Crisis stage (of culture shock)
Adjustment stage (of culture shock)
Hermeneutic circle
Assimilation
Separation
Activity level (of performativity)
Actions level (of performativity)
Operations level (of performativity)

REFERENCES

Amine, K. (2001). Al-halqa performance in Morocco from the open space to the theater building. *The Drama Review*, Vol. 45, No. 2, pp. 55–69.

Anderson, R., & Ross, V. (2002). *Questions of communication: A practical introduction to theory*. Boston: Bedford/St. Martin's.

Basso, K. (1990). *Western Apache language and culture: Essays in linguistic anthropology*. Tucson: University of Arizona Press.

Bell, V. (1999). Performativity and belonging: An introduction. *Theory, Culture & Society*, Vol. 16, No. 2, pp. 1–10.

Boylan, P. (2002). Language as representation, as agency, as being. In Cormeraie, S., et al. (Eds.), *Revolutions in consciousness: Local identities, global concerns in languages and intercultural communication* (pp. 165–174). Leeds, UK: Leeds Metropolitan University.

Brown, R. (1977). *A poetic for sociology: Toward a logic of discovery for the human sciences*. Cambridge, UK: Cambridge University Press.

Butler, J. (1990). *Gender trouble: Feminism and the subversion of identity*. New York: Routledge.

Conquergood, D. (1985). Performing as a moral act: Ethical dimensions of the ethnography of performance. *Literature in Performance*, Vol. 5, pp. 1–13.

Craig, R. (2001). Communication. In Sloane, T. (Ed.), *Encyclopedia of rhetoric* (pp. 125–137). Oxford, UK: Oxford University Press.

Cupach, W., & Imahori, T. (1993). Identity management theory. In Wiseman, R., & J. Koester (Eds.), *Intercultural communication competence*. Thousand Oaks, CA: Sage.

Fromkin, V., & Rodman, R. (1993). *An introduction to language*. Fort Worth, TX: Harcourt Brace Jovanovich.

Fumhan, A., & Bochner, S. (Eds.). (1986). *Culture shock: Psychological reactions to unfamiliar environment*. London: Methuen.

Geertz, C. (1983). *Local knowledge: Further essays in interpretive anthropology*. New York: Basic.

Goffman, E. (1959). *The presentation of self in everyday life*. Garden City, NY: Doubleday Anchor.

Goffman, E. (1974). *Frame analysis: An essay on the organization of experience*. Cambridge, MA: Harvard University Press.

Gudykunst, W., & Kim, Y. (2003). *Communicating with strangers: An approach to intercultural communication*. New York: McGraw-Hill.

Hall, B. (2002). *Among cultures: The challenge of communication*. Belmont, CA: Wadsworth/ Thomson Learning.

Hall, E. T. (1959). *Beyond culture*. New York: Doubleday.

Hall, E. T. (1966). *The hidden dimension*. Garden City, NY: Anchor Books/Doubleday.

Jandt, F. (2001). *Intercultural communication: An introduction*. Thousand Oaks, CA: Sage.

Jordan, L. (2003). Amish group seeks relaxed labor laws for children. *The Spokesman-Review*, October 9, p. A4.

Kapchan, D. (1995). Performance. *Journal of American Folklore*, Vol. 108, No. 430, pp. 479–508.

Knapp, M., & Hall, J. (1997). *Nonverbal communication in human interaction*. Fort Worth, TX: Harcourt Brace.

Leont'ev, A. N. (1978). *Activity, consciousness, personality*. Englewood Cliffs, NJ: Prentice-Hall.

McLaughlin, M. (1984). *Conversation: How talk is organized*. Beverly Hills, CA: Sage.

Michael, M. (2003). Muslim shark stickers annoy Egyptian Christians. *The Spokesman-Review*, November 30, p. A12.

Morris, W. (Ed.). (1982). *The American Heritage dictionary of the English language*. Boston: Houghton Mifflin.

Neuliep, J. (1996). *Human communication theory: Applications and case studies*. Boston: Allyn and Bacon.

Neuliep, J. (2000). *Intercultural communication: A contextual approach*. Boston: Houghton Mifflin.

Nöth, W. (1995). *Handbook of semiotics*. Bloomington: Indiana University Press.

Oberg, K. (1960). Cultural shock: Adjustment to new cultural environments. *Practical Anthropology*, Vol. 7, pp. 177–182.
Pearce, W. (1994). *Interpersonal communication: Making social worlds.* New York: HarperCollins.
Pearce, W., & Cronen, V. (1980). *Communication, actions, and meaning.* New York: Praeger.
Schechner, R. (2002). *Performance studies: An introduction.* London: Routledge.
Shimanoff, S. (1980). *Communication rules: Theory and research.* Beverly Hills, CA: Sage.
Thomas, J. (1983). Cross-cultural pragmatic failure. *Applied Linguistics*, Vol. 4, pp. 91–112.
Ting-Toomey, S. (1999). *Communicating across cultures.* New York: Guilford.
Wang, A. (2003). Thousands of weddings tie India in knots. *The Spokesman-Review*, November 28, p. A12.
Warren, J. (2001). Doing whiteness: On the performative dimensions of race in the classroom. *Communication Education*, Vol. 50, No. 2, pp. 91–108.
Wertsch, J. (1998). *Mind as action.* New York: Oxford University Press.
Winkelman, M. (1994). Cultural shock and adaptation. *Journal of Counseling and Development*, Vol. 73, pp. 121–127.
Wittgenstein, L. (1953). *Philosophical investigations.* Oxford, UK: Basil Blackwell.
Wood, J. (2000). *Communication theories in action.* Belmont, CA: Wadsworth/Thomson Learning.

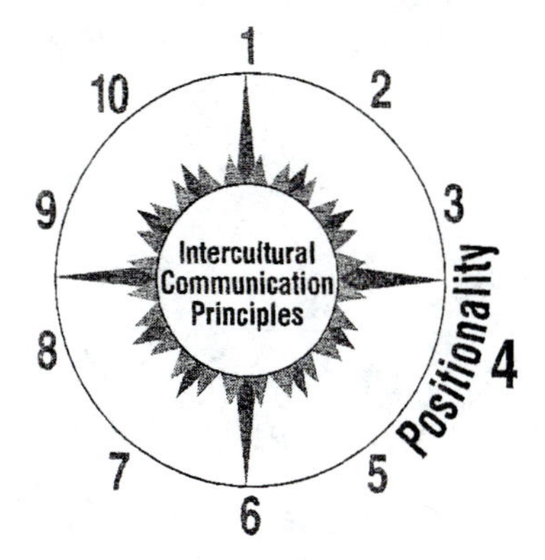

CHAPTER FOUR

CHARTING OUT A CULTURAL MAP: POSITIONALITY PRINCIPLE

It All Depends.

- *Key Theme:* Specificity
- *Key Objective:* To help you understand how every cultural system of knowledge can be seen as unique

INTRODUCING THE PROBLEM QUESTION

FROM BELIEFS ABOUT THE WORLD TO WORLDVIEWS: INTERCULTURAL COMMUNICATION AND PERCEPTION

CULTURAL GAZE: LOOKING OUT, LOOKING IN

CULTURAL GAZE AND ETHNOCENTRISM

Ethnocentric Reduction
Ethnocentric Negation
Ethnocentric Affirmation

INTRODUCING THE POSITIONALITY PRINCIPLE

Positionality as Grounding
Positionality and Authority
Positionality as a Process of Engagement

THE POSITIONALITY PRINCIPLE DEFINED

SUMMARY

CASE STUDY: ARGUMENT IN ISRAELI-PALESTINIAN ENCOUNTERS

SIDE TRIPS

CHECK YOURSELF

REFERENCES

Introducing the Problem Question

The process of constructing a system of meanings combines taking in various stimuli through the senses, organizing those stimuli, and interpreting them. In this process, people from different cultures move from sensing this world to making sense of it. We will look at this process as charting out a cultural map. This approach is similar to seeing intercultural communication as a process of building a virtual warehouse of various meanings (Neuliep, 2000: 142) or developing a cultural orientation system (Klopf, 1998: 16). In essence, every cultural map is an orientation system, allowing people from different cultures to navigate this world. Let's see how people chart out their cultural maps.

The problem question for this chapter is this: *What happens to cultural meanings as they are performed and enacted?*

In this chapter we will

- Present the main types of cultural meanings and see how they form a cultural map
- Define cultural gaze and see how it relates to ethnocentrism
- Discuss the two main ethnocentric dangers in the process of intercultural interactions
- Demonstrate how cultural meanings are positioned as they are enacted
- Emphasize the relationship between cultural positioning and power
- Show why it is important for different cultural maps to be engaged in interaction.

From Beliefs about the World to Worldviews: Intercultural Communication and Perception

Every day we interact with a great variety of people. All our interactions are influenced by **perception**—"the process by which people select, organize, and interpret sensory stimulation into a meaningful and coherent picture of the world" (Berelson & Steiner, 1964: 88).

First, our perceptions are selective. In the process of interacting with other people, we use all our senses (eyesight, hearing, touch, smell, and taste). We cannot pay attention to every stimulus in our environment: sensory information is too diverse and unlimited. Instead, we select only certain stimuli, such as skin color, dress, or form of greeting; the list goes on and on. For instance, some people with light skin color may notice only other people's dark skin color, paying no attention to the texture of their skin, the color of their hair, or their occupations.

Second, our perceptions are organized. We organize our experiences into categories. Categorization makes it possible for us "to structure and give coherence to our general knowledge about people and the social world, providing typical patterns of behavior and the range of likely variation between types of people" (Cantor et al., 1982: 34). For example, we may organize all people with dark skin color into a separate group as members of a certain culture, such as African American.

Third, our perceptions involve interpretation. For instance, we may come to interpret people with dark color as beautiful, athletic, suspicious, violent, or friendly. Such interpretations influence our interactions with them. According to one study, Afro-Brazilians are more likely than whites to be the victim of assault, and they are more likely to be assaulted by the police (Mitchell & Wood, 1998).

Through the process of perception we become aware of what takes place around us, turning sensory stimulation into a meaningful world. Thus, we move from sensing this world to making sense of it. Below we look at this process and the main types of meaning that form our cultural maps.

Beliefs. Let's take the Masai of Kenya as our first example. They are a nomadic warrior tribe whose life centers around cattle herding. For the Masai, a cow is not simply a source of meat. They drink its milk, use every bit of the cow for clothing and decorations, and even use its dung in the construction of their huts. It is not surprising, therefore, that the Masai believe God entrusts cattle to them, and that they measure wealth in number of cattle. Also, they believe that blood from the cow, mixed with milk, makes them stronger.

Now let's hit the Inca Trail, a 25-mile trek to Machu Picchu, the sacred city of the ancient Incas. During that trip, it is common to leave three coca leaves as an offering to Pachamama. Why? Because Pachamama in the Quechua language means Mother Earth, thought to be the giver of life and a source of energy in Inca culture.

Or take the sandstone canyon southwest of Billings, Montana. To the Anschutz Exploration Corp. of Denver, this land is a potential site for drilling oil. To the numerous Native American tribes, this place is known as the Valley of the Chiefs. These tribes believe the canyon serves as a living link to their collective past.

More examples from other cultures could be given, but the main point is clear: Whenever people perceive a connection between two things, they turn it into a meaningful mental construct—a belief. A **belief** is the attribution of some characteristic to an object. In other words, it is a perceived connection between a characteristic and an object. It could be a connection between cow's blood and wealth or strength, between a river and energy, or between land and a collective past. While most Western cultures believe that illness is caused by the invasion of malignant microorganisms into our bodies, some Azande and Navajo people believe that illness is caused by witchcraft. Belief structures, as mental constructs, can be quite complex and abstract, especially when the connection between things is perceived very indirectly. For instance, how do you deal with beliefs about time or beliefs in a just world, which vary so much from culture to culture?

The influence of cultural beliefs on behavior is beyond any doubt. Obviously, the above-mentioned Westerners and Navajos will treat illness very differently. Similarly, if Anglo and Latino women do not share the same belief as to the connection between regular Pap exams and cervical cancer, they will treat visits to a doctor and screening tests differently (Chavez et al., 2001). The practice of female circumcision, now outlawed in Africa but still practiced in secret by many tribes including the Masai, is based on the belief that women's reproductive activities are a service to the whole tribe. In most other cultures, women believe that they should control their own reproductive activities.

Forming beliefs is a starting point for charting out a cultural map. What happens next? Let's take another look at some of the cultures mentioned above.

Attitudes. Cows are at the center of life for the Masai, so it is not surprising that they cherish cows almost as much as they cherish their children and plots of land. In fact, these are the three most cherished things the Masai can offer as a gift. So, following the September 11 attacks on the United States, the Masai held a special ceremony and blessed 14 cows, giving them to the people of the United States. During the ceremony, the Masai elders chanted in Maa, the local language, and walked in a circle around the group of cows (Lacey, 2002). The significance of giving their sacred animals as a gift cannot be overestimated.

The interaction over the canyon southwest of Billings, Montana, ran a different course. For the Anschutz Exploration Corp., the canyon is Federal Lease MTM-74615; should the company's wells pan out, it could be worth millions of dollars. The Native American tribes revere the canyon for its ancient rock drawings of warriors, shields, and animals. Tribes from the Comanche to the Crow have long used the canyon as a place of worship; for them, the spot is holy and has no price. So, when the company's representatives and tribal representatives met to discuss the fate of the canyon, their arguments were very different: The Anschutz executives invoked their legal rights, while an Arapaho elder offered a short prayer and invoked the place's sacredness. At the end of the meeting, no agreement had been reached (Kirn, 2001). In both examples of intercultural communication, one successful and the other not, two mental constructs stood out—attitudes and values.

An **attitude** is a predisposition to respond positively, negatively, or neutrally to certain objects and practices. The Masai's attitude toward cows is very positive, and they may have a negative attitude to wild animals that pose a danger to cows. Similarly, the attitude of the Native American tribes to the canyon is highly positive, while they may develop a negative attitude to the oil executives who want to destroy that holy spot.

Values. Attitudes naturally grow into **values**—shared ideas within a culture about what is important or desirable. What people from one culture consider important, people from another culture might not; thus, cultures vary with respect to the salience (the perceived importance) of specific values. The Masai offered as a gift their cows—one of their most valuable possessions. The gift was duly appreciated by the United States, even though a cow itself is not as highly valued by the American culture. The value appreciated was the extension of good will. (Because of the difficulty of transporting cows, the United States asked that beads from the Masai culture be sent as a gift instead.)

The interaction between the Native American tribes and the oil company was not as successful. Negotiation was difficult because the cultures attached entirely different values to the same land. While for the oil company the canyon's worth consisted of millions of dollars in profit, for the tribes the value of the canyon was as a holy spot, connecting them to their past and inestimable in monetary terms. There is no doubt, however, that in both examples intercultural contact was influenced (positively and negatively) by cultural attitudes and values.

Successful intercultural communication requires that attitudes and values be taken into consideration. For instance, if a company wants to market a new commercial product internationally, it will be more successful if it targets values a country emphasizes, such as peacefulness in Japan, ruggedness in the United States, or passion in Spain (Aaker et al., 2001). Some cultural values are difficult to identify and even more difficult to understand. For example, a group of British tourists pursuing their hobby of plane-spotting found themselves arrested and then convicted in a Greek court on charges of obtaining national secrets (Hoge, 2002). The British reacted to the charges with incredulity and outrage. This peculiar British pastime appears incomprehensible to most other cultures, while in Britain it attracts thousands and thousands of devoted fans. In other words, most people do not understand the value in spending hours alongside landing-strip fences at major airports with binoculars and notebooks. The British, on the other hand, appreciate this pastime because it involves patience, precision, deliberation, and the occasional moment of jubilation.

It is important to emphasize the relationship among beliefs, attitudes, and values. As cultural beliefs are being formed, attitudes are developed. Once you perceive a connection to exist between two things, you tend to respond to this fact positively or negatively. And, based on that response, cultural values are established. To put it in simple terms, people form ideas about the world (beliefs); based on these ideas, people come to like or dislike the world around them (attitudes); and, based on their likes and dislikes, people come to appreciate that which is worthy, useful, and significant to their culture (values).

Norms. What is the next step in charting out a cultural map? The answer should be obvious: If you value certain things and practices more than others, you should try to preserve them. Now the main cultural task is protecting certain meanings. And this, of course, is accomplished with the help of cultural norms.

A cultural **norm** can be defined as a shared standard for accepted and expected behaviors. If you violate a cultural norm, you are subject to some form of sanction. Cultural norms are often divided into three categories: folkways, mores, and laws (Gudykunst & Kim, 1992: 58–59; Sumner, 1940).

Folkways are everyday cultural practices that are widely accepted. They include the ways people dress, eat, drive, and keep up their dwellings. For example, the Masai men are responsible for tying fence branches together to protect their cattle and maintain their huts, while the women are expected to milk the cows and fetch water.

Mores are cultural practices that, as the name suggests, carry moral connotations and impose stricter constraints on people's behavior. For instance, although their sexual practices are quite complex, the Masai obey a strict morality. The warrior takes as a lover a prepubescent girl, but he cannot marry until he has served his tribe. When the girl reaches puberty and is able to conceive, she is returned to her mother until she can marry. Before her marriage, she is circumcised. The Masai boys, too, have a coming-of-age ceremony when they reach the age of 15. They make headdresses of ostrich plumes and eagle feathers, shave their heads, are circumcised, and become Morani, or young warriors. Traditionally, in order to pass into manhood, they are expected to hunt a lion with only a spear. Violations of these mores, which may be interpreted as cowardice, defiance, or reluctance to serve one's tribe, may bring about severe sanctions such as ostracism.

Laws are cultural practices that are codified and usually written down. They serve to protect the most cherished values, such as freedom, and their violation brings about legal sanctions. When people from different cultures come into contact, their norms are tested and redefined. For instance, the Masai nowadays boost their income by performing ceremonies and selling beads to tourists. These practices do not appear to affect their folkways; in fact, the Masai often set up huts where they tend cows and dance strictly for tourism, while their real settlements are miles away. At the same time, exposure to other cultures—particularly to the Western values of individuality, human rights, and so on—has had an impact on the Masai norms. Today, the practice of female circumcision, known in the West as female genital mutilation, is outlawed in Africa. Similarly, the initiation ceremony in which Masai boys hunt a lion with a spear has been made illegal by the government of Kenya. These activities, still practiced in secret, reflect the struggle between cultural mores and laws.

Numerous difficulties arise in intercultural communication because of different norms. For instance, Brigitte Bardot, the French film star and animal-rights activist, has publicly condemned the custom of eating dogs in South Korea. She is quoted as saying, "Eating dogs is not culture, it is grotesque. Culture is composing music like Mozart." As a result, she has reportedly received 7,000 death threats (Dogs' lives, 2002).

Another example of intercultural conflict is seen in a letter to Northwest Airlines from the Council on American-Islamic Relations. The letter demanded that the Minnesota-based carrier apologize for allegedly forcing a Muslim high school student to remove her head scarf at an airport security checkpoint. According to the letter, for a Muslim woman to be forced to take off her head scarf in public is a violation of her rights. Muslim women believe that covering their hair in public—essential to being modest—is mandated by God.

These examples not only illustrate a crucial role played by norms in intercultural communication but also show how norms are connected with beliefs, attitudes, and values. In the Bardot example, we see how different beliefs ("Dogs are a source of food" vs. "Dogs are living beings, not food") help to develop certain attitudes (positive vs. negative toward eating dogs), which lead to certain values ("Eating dogs is an important part of culture" vs. "Eating dogs cannot be valued as something cultural"). And values, in turn, are protected by cultural norms ("It is OK to eat dogs" vs. "It is wrong to eat dogs").

In the head scarf example, different beliefs ("God mandates that Muslim women cover up their hair in public" vs. "Covering up hair may be potentially dangerous") give rise to certain attitudes (positive vs. negative toward wearing a head scarf), which form the foundation for certain values (modesty vs. security). These values then turn into norms (on the Muslim side, women must wear a head scarf or else experience shame; on the air carrier's side, head scarves must be checked or else there may be a breech of security and appropriate punishment).

Worldview. Now the picture of how people from different cultures construct their systems of meaning is almost complete. We must add only one more mental construct, the most complex and abstract—worldview. **Worldview** "refers to a set of interrelated assumptions and beliefs about the nature of reality, the organization of the universe, the purposes of human life, God, and other philosophical issues that are concerned with the concept of being" (Jain & Kussman, 1997: 79). As the overall way people from a certain culture see reality, worldview "helps us locate our place . . . in the universe" (Samovar & Porter, 1991: 16). Thus, worldview is the way people from a certain culture view themselves in relation to everything else (other cultures). It is not by chance that, in many languages, one of the meanings of the word *see* is know. In this sense, the worldview is our overall knowledge of the world and our place in this world. Naturally, this knowledge is broader than beliefs, attitudes, values, and norms taken separately. In fact, the worldview combines all these mental constructs and transforms them into a number of fundamental ideas.

The following ideas are said to underpin the African-centered worldview (Graham, 1999: 112):

- The interconnectedness of all things.
- The spiritual nature of human beings.
- Collective/individual identity and the collective/inclusive nature of family structure.
- Oneness of mind, body, and spirit.
- The value of interpersonal relationships.

In the same vein, the Indian worldview, grounded in Hinduism, is said to comprise the following four fundamental ideas (Hesselgrave, 1978: 162):

- The law of karma, which binds the person to the universe and necessitates the round of transmigration.
- The concept of maya, which means that the experienced cosmos is illusionary.
- The idea of the absolute or pure being, which lies behind the world of experience and is viewed as the atman (the self or soul), the Brahman (the absolute objectively understood), or nirvana (the highest good, peace).
- The means or techniques of gaining liberation, called Yoga.

It is critical that people pay attention to worldviews when communicating interculturally. For example, social work services cannot be successfully provided to African American communities without an understanding of their worldview (Graham, 1999), and successful Christian missionary work in India requires knowledge of that culture's worldview (Hesselgrave, 1978: 167–171).

Now we know how people chart out their cultural maps. Every culture develops ideas about the world and its place in it. It must be emphasized that all these ideas are interconnected. As people establish what they perceive to be true about the world (beliefs), they tend to respond to these perceived facts positively or negatively (attitudes); decisions are made as to what is important and what is not (values); standards for behavior (norms) are developed in order to keep what is of more worth and guard against what is undesirable; and, finally, all ideas are transformed into a worldview, which underpins the culture in its entirety.

Thus, as meanings are enacted, cultures move from sensing this world to making sense of it. This way, people from every culture develop their collective cultural gaze.

Cultural Gaze: Looking Out, Looking In

Every culture faces the task of understanding itself and its place in the world—that is, charting out a map by developing a system of meanings. Such cultural maps allow us to "structure and give coherence to our general knowledge about people and the social world, providing expectations about typical patterns of behavior and the range of likely variation between types of people and their characteristic actions and attributes" (Cantor et al., 1982: 34).

So, people from every culture develop their own **cultural gaze**—a projection beam, looking outward into the world. This gaze, of course, is not limited to the visual aspect of our perception; it involves all senses. Thus, looking out (gazing) is the way we establish our orientation in the world. In various intercultural situations, the "visibility" of our cultural gaze can be quite different. Sometimes we can see (know) more clearly, and sometimes our gaze is quite hazy. Consequently, the meanings we bring back home after our intercultural travels can be very complex or quite simple, correct or incorrect.

Today, certain intercultural interactions are specifically set up for our gaze. For example, **ethnic tourism** is a special practice whereby people are invited to experience other cultures. Ethnic tourism brings together "(1) the *tourist*, who travels to seek an experience that cannot be duplicated in ordinary life; (2) the *touree*, the performer who modifies his or her behavior to suit the tastes of the tourists for gain; and (3) the *middleman*, who mediates the two groups and profits by their interaction" (Hiwasaki, 2000: 395). Through ethnic tourism, one can gaze at the Ainu tourist villages scattered across Hokkaido, Japan, or visit the Tana Torajia culture in Indonesia (McGregor, 2000). In such cases, tourists are exposed to carefully chosen and presented aspects of a culture, such as ritual performances.

Their cultural experience is commodified, and their gaze is heavily structured. Yet this experience is an important step in the quest for the Other.

We all engage in this quest, of course, whenever we come into contact with people from other cultures. We may not think of ourselves as tourists in the strict sense of the word (travelers in foreign lands), but the experience is essentially the same, just less structured. We gaze out at people from different cultures, trying to represent the results of our interactions with them as fully and correctly as possible. We hope that these meanings are authentic, reflecting other cultures accurately. In other words, we hope that our quest for authenticity is successful.

McGregor (2000: 48) cites the example of tourists' experiences at the animal market in Tana Torajia. Those tourists who relied on the guidebooks' description of that cultural site—a buffalo and pig market held every six days—gazed upon the event with little enthusiasm. However, those with more information about the position of the market, as a centerpiece of the Tana Torajia economy and lifestyle, gazed upon it with more appreciation and interest. In the second case, the gaze revealed more complex and authentic meanings about the Tana Torajia culture. This, in turn, had an impact on the tourists' attitude toward that part of the culture.

Every culture looks out at the world, and this gaze is reflected back in various meanings, so our cultural gaze looks both out and in. The meanings generated by our cultural gaze form a mental space, showing what place our culture occupies in the world. First and foremost, this mental space is found in verbal language, which is central to any culture. Like a map, language allows us to set off on a journey and become explorers.

People also create their cultural maps (views of the world) literally—with maps. Every map is a cultural artifact, or a kind of nonverbal language. Like languages, maps are mental constructs and serve the same main function—a culture's self-identification. Unlike languages, though, which are extremely complex and can hardly be grasped at a glance, most maps reveal a fascinating tendency: Cultures tend to map themselves as world-centered, with all other cultures as relatively peripheral! Blair (2000) provides many examples of such maps, which prove that geography is often a function of culture. For instance, an American map centers its east-west axis on the United States, resulting in land-area distortions based on distance from the equator. A map made in Switzerland centers its east-west axis on Western Europe, with a visible difference from the American map in the representation of relative landmasses. A Russian map centers on Moscow; a map from the People's Republic of China centers on the Western Pacific and shows Western Europe and the United States in a peripheral position. How strange, you might think. But maps tend to "share an arbitrariness that reflects their historical emergence in one particular cultural setting at one particular time" (Blair, 2000: 32). In other words, what is visible on world maps is "the ethnocentrism enjoyed by every culture in the world" (Blair, 2000: 24).

You probably knew that, sooner or later in the chapter, the word *ethnocentrism* would come up. Indeed, it is impossible to discuss how people from different cultures look at each other without using this concept.

Cultural Gaze and Ethnocentrism

Two main views of ethnocentrism can be isolated. One is negative and widespread; the other is positive and much less common.

According to the first view, ethnocentrism is a perceptual prism through which people from one culture, with an attitude of superiority, evaluate all other cultures, whose practices are judged as inferior or simply wrong. In this respect, ethnocentrism is portrayed as a barrier to effective intercultural communication. It is interpreted as "the inability to believe that other cultures offer viable alternatives for organizing reality" (Klopf, 1998: 130). Jandt states that "to be ethnocentric is to believe in the superiority of one's own culture" (2001: 53). Ethnocentrism is treated as the tendency for any culture to put itself in a position of centrality and worth, while showing negative attitudes toward people from other cultures (Segall, 1979). Similarly, ethnocentrism is presented as "our defensive attitudinal tendency to view the values and norms of our culture as superior to other cultures, and we perceive our cultural ways of living as the most reasonable and proper ways to conduct our lives" (Ting-Toomey, 1999: 157). There are numerous examples of such ethnocentric attitudes. Remember the story about Brigitte Bardot, the French film star and animal-rights activist, who publicly condemned the custom of eating dogs in South Korea? By the same token, many Hindus in India might find it shocking that in some cultures, especially in the West, people eat cows.

According to the second view, ethnocentrism is a positive attitude that helps every culture maintain its integrity. This view emphasizes surviving threats from external forces and taking pride in what your culture represents. Ethnocentrism is said to be functional, satisfying the needs of people in a certain culture when that culture becomes strengthened and more cohesive (Gudykunst & Kim, 1992: 86–97). Also, "if people view their own group as central to their lives and as possessing proper standards of behavior, they are likely to come to the aid of other group members when they are in trouble" (Brislin, 1993: 39).

Often ethnocentrism is viewed negatively—as a prism that distorts our perception of other cultures, taking the form of a "we are right, they are wrong" bias. Not surprisingly, calls are made to overcome ethnocentrism and make sure that this barrier to effective intercultural communication is removed. But can it be done? Can we develop magic interaction skills and help people to get rid of their ethnocentrism, once and for all?

The two views we have just discussed share the same approach to ethnocentrism: They put evaluative judgments into their interpretation of this concept (one negative, the other positive). But what does the term itself mean? It is derived from the Greek words *ethnos* (nation) and *kentron* (center of a circle). Thus, the term *ethnocentrism* simply means something like "our nation is in the center." Sumner, who was one of the first to start using this term in the study of culture and group relations, defined it as "the technical name for the view of things in which one's own group is the center of everything, and all others are scaled and rated with reference to it" (1940: 13). Notice that the etymology of the word, like Sumner's definition, is devoid of any evaluative component; both simply state that people from every culture put themselves in the center and, from that position, view all other cultures. It is important to remember that "culture is of its nature ethnocentric" (Chen & Starosta, 1998: 296). From that central position, every culture makes judgments about all other cultures. But can it be otherwise? Where can our understanding come from if not from within our own culture? It is from within our own culture—from the "center"—that our cultural gaze is projected out into the world.

Instead of interpreting ethnocentrism as a danger to be avoided at great cost (negative view) or as a celebrated stand (positive view), we need to think of ethnocentrism, first and foremost, in neutral terms—as an inherent human condition, a necessity dictated by human diversity. **Ethnocentrism** is a point of reference that every culture needs in order to understand the world and itself. To put it simply, we perceive the world from where we are—from a particular location and time period. In this sense, ethnocentrism is universal, with people from different cultures viewing the world from their own positions, which, for them, are central. It is possible, therefore, to speak of ethnocentrism*s* (in the plural), all of which "have, in principle, an equal claim on legitimacy" (Blair, 2000: 32). The very nature of ethnocentrism is, above all, to admit the centrality of every cultural gaze. In a manner of speaking, no map of the world can be said to be definitive. And this means, of course, that people from different cultures can define themselves—in the form of cultural or geographical maps—only by interacting with one another.

Ethnocentrism is an inherent human condition—ground zero, so to speak. Like explorers, we travel and come into contact with people from other cultures, setting our gaze on their practices and representing them in a meaningful way, with the hope that these meanings are accurate (authentic). Each time we come across a new intercultural experience, we judge it against our point of reference. If it is something we like, we might borrow it; if it is something we think the Other lacks and should have, we might share it; if it is something we feel we do not need, we might bypass it; and if it is something that gets in our way or presents a danger, we might take flight or fight. In each case, we make a decision as to how new experiences measure up against our frame of reference—and respond accordingly. With each decision, our frame of reference changes yet remains central (ethnocentric). We need to respond adequately to our intercultural experiences, making sure that our cultural gaze is clear and our travels are rewarding. We need to ensure that ethnocentrism serves us—and people from other cultures—well. However, in doing so, we confront two main dangers: ethnocentric reduction and ethnocentric negation.

Ethnocentric Reduction

One danger—the "we are right and they are wrong so let's force them to be like us" attitude—was mentioned earlier. It is dangerous because one culture imposes its system of meanings on another culture, reducing that culture to a shadow of

Self. **Ethnocentric reduction** takes place when people from one culture look (gaze) at another culture, make a negative judgment about the way things are done there, and force the people from that other culture to start doing things according to the first culture's frame of reference. This negative ethnocentric attitude finds its extreme manifestation in such horrors as ethnic cleansing, discrimination, and wars. This danger of ethnocentrism is presented graphically in Figure 1.

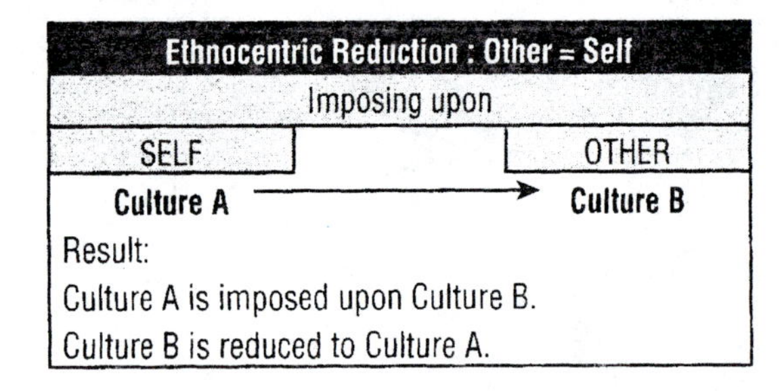

FIGURE 1

Ethnocentric Negation

The other danger associated with ethnocentrism is less obvious and perhaps less significant than ethnocentric reduction, but nevertheless cannot be overlooked. Let's look at the now-famous example of the drunken Indian and the kidney machine, discussed by Clifford Geertz in his paper "The Uses of Diversity" (1986). This story is about a Native American alcoholic who was given access to a kidney dialysis machine but refused to stop drinking. His doctors became angry because they felt that another patient could make better use of the machine. They did not take him off the machine, however, and the man continued drinking until he died. Geertz argues that neither side in this story made any attempt to make sense of the other's position and thus question its own position. The two parties failed to understand "what it was to be on the other (side), and thus what it was to be on (their) own (side)" (1986: 117). Each side was blinded by its own ethnocentrism, and no real engagement with the Other took place. This danger, therefore, is exactly the opposite of ethnocentric reduction. Instead of reducing another culture to Self, one culture simply disregards another culture as not Self, or a negation of Self. Let's call this danger **ethnocentric negation.**

Examples of such an ethnocentric attitude are more common than one might think. Abdel-Nour has this to say in his article "Liberalism and Ethnocentrism":

> When European travelers and scholars "produced" and exoticized the "Other," . . . their ethnocentric lack of engagement with the alienness of the other led them to see others as simply not self, and Arabs and Muslims in particular became imprisoned in Western images of them as either "exotic" or "dangerous," simply *not us.* (2000: 22)

The portrayal of Arabs and Muslims as "dangerous" has a special significance today, when intercultural engagement with them is very challenging.

Other examples of ethnocentric negation can be found in the world's trouble spots where international citizens, mostly representing the United Nations, have the job of helping newly established countries create a social order. For instance, when the Indonesians pulled out of East Timor, after more than 20 years of brutal rule, the United Nations sent in its administrators, consultants, and police. The Timorese put all those people in the category of "internationals"—a large culture of new colonialists whose very lifestyle "walls them off from the people they serve" (Lee, 2002: 35). With expensive cars, air conditioning, and bottled water, among other things, most of these people feel superior in their new environment. "This affects the way internationals talk. The locals quickly become *they*. A foreign visitor hears that *they* can't drive. *They* can't fix a computer. *They* can't organize a press conference or march in a parade" (Lee, 2002: 36). Because internationals do not stay in such spots long, they do not feel any need to engage in real interaction with the culture they are helping; it is as if they lived in a parallel universe. This danger of ethnocentrism is presented graphically in Figure 2.

Ethnocentric Negation : Other = Not Self		
Ignoring		
SELF		OTHER
Culture A	**X**	**Culture B**
Result:		
Culture A ignores Culture B.		
Culture B is negated by Culture A.		

FIGURE 2

Ethnocentric Affirmation

The two dangers of ethnocentrism identified above are negative because they are extreme manifestations of our cultural gaze. In both cases, one culture's gaze is blind to another culture. As a result, people from both cultures suffer: Culture B is either reduced or ignored, while culture A deprives itself of external diversity. Thus, people from both cultures have no chance to realize their symbolic resources freely and fully. It is only by avoiding these two dangers of ethnocentrism that intercultural interactions can be made effective. This scenario is presented graphically in Figure 3.

In this scenario of **ethnocentric affirmation,** people from cultures A and B exercise equal authority. In other words, both cultures have equal power to make decisions about what should happen to their frames of reference as a result of an intercultural encounter. They defend their positions and affirm each other; that is, they each treat the Other as both Self and Not-Self. Such a cultural gaze

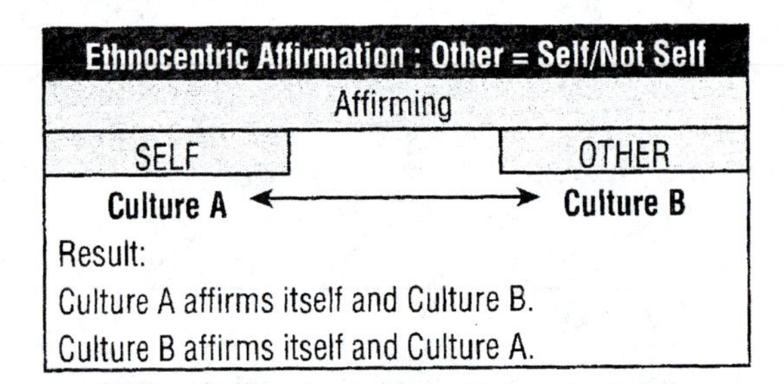

FIGURE 3

makes it possible for them to negotiate how to maintain their position (positive ethnocentrism) and allows the Other to maintain its position, as well.

Introducing the Positionality Principle

Now it is time to formulate our fourth principle underlying intercultural communication: the Positionality Principle. As usual, we will isolate three parts that make up this principle. Each part deals with the nature of positioning in intercultural interactions. First, we will discuss the Positionality Principle in terms of grounding. Next, we will show the relationship between grounding and authority. Finally, we will present grounding as a process of intercultural engagement. We will discuss each part separately and then formulate the Positionality Principle as a whole.

Positionality as Grounding

At the beginning of the chapter, we set out to understand what happens to meanings as they are enacted. We now know that cultures construct their systems of meanings and see the world differently because people are located in space and time. Obviously, people from different cultures cannot be located in the same place at the same time; they have to occupy different locations. It is by virtue of these different positions that cultures develop different systems of knowledge. All cultures, therefore, are characterized by different **cultural loci**—positions from which they view the world and their own place in it.

When we speak about meanings as our cultural maps, we must remember that our cultural knowledge is situated—that is, generated in specific situations. These situations are concrete in the sense that they provide physical settings for constructing a cultural mental framework. Based on these settings, every culture defines itself and the world from a certain point of view. Every culture looks outward from its own point of view; reflected back, this look becomes its cultural gaze. Cultural gaze is a projector beam, as it were, that allows people from every culture to navigate in the world. With the help of this gaze, every culture looks both inward to its own identity and outward to its relation with other cultures. The better the "cultural visibility," the more successful the intercultural encounters.

Thus, intercultural communication is a matter of positionality. As cultures occupy different positions and interact, their cultural gaze makes it possible for them to see the world and their own place in it. In this process, cultural meanings are generated, or—to put it another way—each culture is grounded. Everything that we experience as a result of an intercultural encounter and find meaningful is framed and becomes part of our culture, our "common ground." These cultural frames are constructed as a product of our perception and can be presented in terms of figure/ground effects. You might be familiar with these terms from Gestalt psychology (Koehler, 1969), where the distinction between figure and ground is usually illustrated by a visual example such as the image in Figure 4, which can be perceived either as four black squares (figure) on a white surface (ground) or as a white cross (figure) on a black surface (ground) (Koch, 2001: 203).

The figure/ground distinction is not limited, of course, to the visual realm; one can experience this effect using any other senses. Whatever senses people use, the nature of the figure/ground distinction is the same: Experiences are grouped together and either form a foundation or stand out as a figure. It is a foundation that is cultural ground. In this sense, ground is a culturally accepted system of meanings that is shared and seems so natural that it is often taken for granted. Ground is not highly visible, yet its significance cannot be overestimated. Its importance is highlighted when it comes under threat—just think of such expressions as "Stand your ground" or "Defend your ground" (both figuratively and literally!). Ground is what holds cultures together; it is their center. Being ethnocentric means being grounded.

FIGURE 4

Grounding, therefore, is a process of establishing a cultural system of meanings. What meanings? Recall the main cultural constructs we discussed at the beginning of the chapter. Grounding of meanings begins with a perceived connection between two things—this is the way cultural beliefs are developed. Then cultural ground becomes more complex and takes the form of attitudes, values, norms, and worldview. As a result of developing these dispositions, people from different cultures position themselves.

In intercultural encounters, the same experience can be categorized as either ground or figure, depending on cultural position. If an experience is perceived as different from your own cultural system of meaning, it is figure. Thus, "the figure or difference . . . stands against everything else (ground)" (Roth, 2001: 31). Consider the sight of someone riding a motorcycle during the day with the headlights on (Enfield, 2000: 40). In Australia, this sight is part of the cultural ground because Australian traffic authorities recommend that motorcyclists keep their headlights on at all times for reasons of safety. In Laos, this sight is part of the cultural figure because headlights are put on only in emergency situations when the right of way is needed. It is easy to foresee how an Australian biker might be stopped by Laotian traffic authorities and fined for riding with headlights on. In this example, grounding takes the form of different values (safety vs. emergency) and norms (folkways vs. laws).

In other cases, grounding finds its manifestation in cultural attitudes. Mitchell and Wood (1998) report that the state authorities in Brazil have a negative attitude toward Afro-Brazilians, perceiving them as potentially more criminal than other Brazilians. As a result, they are more likely to be assaulted by police. Afro-Brazilians suffer discrimination because they stand out as figure, mostly because of their skin color.

So, all new experiences appear to us as figure; if accepted, they become part of our cultural ground. Intercultural communication can be seen as a process of trying to figure out (pun intended!) new experiences.

It must be emphasized that, even though cultural meanings arise and are grounded in specific concrete situations, they are never set in concrete. What is perceived by a certain culture at a certain point in time as figure may become part of its ground, and vice versa. For instance, people in Laos might decide to make it a norm that headlights be kept on by motorcyclists at all times, or the state authorities in Brazil might change their attitude toward Afro-Brazilians and stop discriminating against them. The negative attitude toward Afro-Brazilians is likely to be more difficult, yet more necessary, to change: No one likes to be discriminated against, and so Afro-Brazilians will fight to stop discriminatory practices. In the case of the headlights, changing a cultural position may be less pressing; it is possible to imagine, though, how safety might become a priority and the traffic regulation change accordingly. In all cases, people from every culture must decide what their position on this or that issue should be. If a culture feels that it is unable to establish a desirable position, it will make an effort to bring about a change, whether through a new traffic rule or a new rule in the criminal justice system.

Grounding, therefore, is a dynamic process, driven by relationships between cultures and their constant search for authority. And this brings us to the second aspect of the Positionality Principle, which deals with the issues of power and control.

Positionality and Authority

Every culture tries to establish its own position in the world, or ground itself. In other words, people from every culture try to create a system of authentic or true meanings. By doing so, cultures claim authority for their vision of the world. **Authority** can be equated with the ability to lay claims that are accepted. In this sense, "authority is ultimately a matter of power" (Fleischacker, 1994: 84), or the ability to make decisions as to what a cultural position should be. In the example of East Timor, discussed earlier, the "internationals" are basically creating a new order; their power, or their authority, is much greater than that of the Timorese people. These administrators, consultants, police, and soldiers are making most of the decisions and having a huge impact on what the culture of East Timor shall be in the future.

So, positionality is not simply a matter of cultures establishing their specific positions; it is a matter of power relationships between these positions. As Clifford says, "Self-other relations are matters of power and rhetoric rather than of essence" (1988: 14). Cultures (Self and the Other) are not stable categories (essences), but shifting positions, which are determined by complex relations of power enacted by verbal and nonverbal means (matters of rhetoric).

Every culture claims authority for its vision of the world by using its cultural map to create stories, or narratives. **Narrative** "refers to a recounting of a sequence of events that is told from a particular point of view" (Hall, 2002: 71)—that is, from a particular position. In a way, every culture tells its own story of the world, or creates its own narratives. In Chapter 1, we discussed the example of the heritage museum in Israel where the story about the patriarch Abraham is narrated by a tour guide (Katriel, 1994: 14). We noted that to Jewish audiences this kind of story sounds like a playful elaboration of a well-known biblical tale, while to Arab audiences the strategy of renaming Abraham as the first Bedouin and endowing a familiar agricultural object with a biblical career is an act of cultural appropriation. Thus, two cultural authorities clash as a certain segment of the world is narrated from two very different positions.

There are different ways to understand the main functions of narratives. Hall discusses four teaching functions of narratives in intercultural communication. He notes that "narratives function to teach us how the world works, our place in the world, how to act in the world, and how to evaluate what goes on in the world" (2002: 73). Also, there are different ways to categorize narratives, from everyday conversations with friends to **grand narratives**—"stories that can give us certain knowledge of the direction, meaning and moral path of human 'development'" (Barker, 2000: 21). It might be said that every cultural worldview can be seen as a grand narrative. For example, Jewish culture "is incomprehensible without the supernatural history in which it is embedded, while Christianity (perhaps Buddhism as well) is virtually all story" (Fleischacker, 1994: 71).

Regardless of how narratives are categorized and their functions understood, two criteria for narratives can be isolated: coherence and fidelity (Fisher, 1984). First, for a cultural story to be meaningful, all parts of the narrative must fit together; then a narrative meets the criterion of coherence. Second, for a cultural story to be meaningful, the narrative must resonate with people's beliefs, attitudes, values, norms, and worldviews; then a narrative meets the criterion of fidelity. When both criteria are met, a narrative turns "into a tradition, something passed down from one generation to another" (Fleischacker, 1994: 80), meeting the needs of, and making sense to, people from that culture.

So, "authority is a position" (Fleischacker, 1994: 82). Every culture claims authority for its vision of the world by projecting its gaze, charting out a cultural map, and creating narratives. In other words, every culture collectively claims that the world is thus and so. In this sense, all cultures can be viewed as "just so stories." Every culture claims authority for its understanding of the world by creating narratives; to people from all cultures, their own stories are the authentic ones. The story of the world is told in many tongues.

Thus, to people from any culture, their cultural maps and their narratives seem true, authentic, and natural (central). It might seem that people from every culture would have the best knowledge of their own position—that is, could speak with authority about the world and their place in it. This ethnocentric view, though, is constantly tested in intercultural encounters. When a culture's gaze is blind to other cultures, that culture fails to understand what its *real* position is and how much authority (power) it *really* has. Therefore, the best way for cultures to determine their positions and power dynamics is through interaction. Positionality presupposes that different cultural positions are engaged in acts of communication.

Positionality as a Process of Engagement

The cartographic metaphor (Munshi & McKie, 2001) sees the world in terms of a number of mental maps on which cultures see themselves occupying different positions; for example, the West sees itself occupying a superior position. These cultural maps are dynamic, though. So, the essence of intercultural communication can be better represented by the kaleidoscope metaphor, which views cultural positions as constantly changing through the process of **engagement,** whereby people from different cultures present claims that their narratives represent the true vision of the world.

Cultural positions are situated (grounded), not given; they are developed through intercultural communication as complex dynamics of authority, or power relations. When people from different cultures come into contact, their positions are engaged. For instance, the U.S. position on its role in winning the Second World War is seen differently when the British and Russian perspectives are engaged. The U.S. position shifts, as if in a kaleidoscope, from that of a crucial player to that of a minor player in the last phase of the war.

In intercultural interactions, whether a culture's authority is a source of power depends on whether it is accepted or rejected by other cultures. The authority of what a culture presents as its knowledge of the world depends on acknowledgment by people from other cultures. Hence, the more others accept a culture's system of meanings, the more authority the culture has and the more ground it covers, so to speak. As a result, its position becomes more powerful. People from one culture may not accept another culture's position on something—that is, they may deny its authority. They may feel that their core values are being undermined by foreign influence such as advertising or media. As a result, resistance may become one of their main rhetorical intercultural strategies.

The strategy of resistance comes into play when a culture feels that its authority is being threatened or weakened by other cultures. The ethnocentric, or central, position the culture has held so naturally is now challenged; the culture starts losing ground, as it were, to other cultures whose positions may now become central, establishing new ground. Interesting evidence of this phenomenon is found in the practice of self-labeling, whereby people from a certain culture identify themselves through various verbal labels. One recent study revealed resistance of white Americans to self-labels such as "White" and "Caucasian" (Martin et al., 1996). Many subjects mocked the survey, and a large number of unusable responses were generated. These results illustrate that white Americans occupy a privileged (central) position; for them, this position is situated as "natural." They have more power because they make more decisions about how things should be done. They resist (consciously or not) looking at themselves from another (peripheral) position because that suggests other cultures might see them differently, which would challenge their central position. In other words, white Americans do not consider—or refuse to consider—that their whiteness (as ground) may lose its central place and be replaced by another color (another culture). Thus, resistance is a natural strategy aimed at keeping undesirable cultural positions at bay and reinforcing one's own cultural position. We will discuss the nature of resistance as a strategy of intercultural communication in more detail in Chapter 10.

Earlier we showed how every culture aims to establish authority for its vision of the world by creating narratives. It is now clear that different cultures engage in interaction with each other, claiming their own visions of the world. Overall, "no one narrative can capture every possible aspect of a series of events, so what is told and how it is told inescapably express a point of view" (Hall, 2002: 71). It is not surprising, therefore, to find any grand narrative claiming universal truth attacked or "deconstructed" (see Young, 1996).

"Positionality is thus determined by where one stands in relation to 'the other'" (Merriam et al., 2001: 411). It is impossible for a culture to determine its real position without engaging other cultures' perspectives. Of course, dealing with positionality as engagement is easier when intercultural encounters are successful and people from all interacting cultures feel good about themselves. It is more difficult, yet more important, to engage other perspectives when relationships between cultures are very asymmetrical. Richard Rorty, a well-known American philosopher, reminds Americans how important it is for their national pride to remember the horrors of the past, such as slavery, massacres, segregation, discrimination, and wars; similar horrors can be found in many nations' histories. He advocates that Americans never engage in such behaviors again (Rorty, 1998). However, this laudable approach must be taken a step further; in addition to promising never to do it again, the United States should engage the perspectives of others, such as the descendants of the enslaved and the massacred tribes and the survivors of Vietnam. "Without the help of the face of the other (the victim). . . , the latter's perspective cannot begin to comprehend the enormity of the act" (Abdel-Nour, 2000: 223). In other words, people from different cultures must engage each other's perspectives if they truly want to comprehend themselves, to understand their real positions. In a sense, people must face reality through intercultural interactions. In Chapters 9 and 10, we will discuss in detail what may happen if people from different cultures go against reality and fail to see each other's positions.

Speaking of intercultural engagement, an analogy can be drawn between learning intercultural communication and learning foreign languages (Blair, 2000: 33). It is known that a second language is easier to learn than the first one, and the reason for that may have less to do with the structure of a particular language than with a change in our relation to the native language. We come to realize that our native language is only one way of looking at the world, and not the "key" to reality! It turns out there are other views of the world, reflected in language. Once we come to terms with this fact, it becomes easier to learn and appreciate other languages. The same goes for communicating with people from other cultures. Intercultural communication is a matter of multiple positions, and ours, no matter how natural and authoritative it may seem, is just one of many. If we want to learn more about the world (and ourselves!), we need to engage in intercultural communication.

The Positionality Principle Defined

Let's now give a more concise formulation of the Positionality Principle, based on the above discussion of its three parts.

First, our cultural knowledge is always situated, and people from every culture look at the world and their place in it from a particular point of view. The process of establishing a specific cultural position is called grounding.

Second, positionality is not simply a matter of cultures establishing their specific positions; it is a matter of power relations between these positions. When cultures establish their positions (ground themselves), they claim authority for their vision of the world. But the authority of what a culture presents as its knowledge depends on acknowledgment by other cultures. In intercultural interactions, a culture's power depends on whether its system of meanings is accepted or rejected by other cultures.

Third, it is impossible for a culture to determine its real position without engaging other cultures' perspectives. When people from different cultural groups come into contact, their positions are activated, and changes in their systems of meanings take place.

In a nutshell, the Positionality Principle can be formulated as follows:

Intercultural communication is a process whereby people from different cultures claim authority for their vision of the world.

The Positionality Principle is important because it reveals the nature of ethnocentrism as an inherent human condition, while also highlighting its dangers for intercultural communication. The Positionality Principle helps us to look at intercultural communication in a more relational way. It is important to understand that our cultural knowledge is always specific—that is, relative to a particular point of view—and we cannot help engaging in intercultural communication from that particular point of view. This is true for all cultures: Their knowledge is relative to *their* point of view. In intercultural communication, "it all depends!" When we communicate, our specific perspectives are engaged, and we all strive to keep our ground.

So, now we know what happens to cultural meanings as they are performed and enacted. They are grounded, helping cultures to position themselves in the world.

Summary

In this chapter, the following problem question was posed: What happens to cultural meanings as they are performed and enacted? To answer that question, we looked at the process of constructing cultural meaning as charting out a cultural map.

We saw that cultural maps are dynamic formations and contain such categories as beliefs, attitudes, values, norms, and worldviews. This way, people from different cultures move from sensing the world to making sense of it.

With the help of a cultural gaze, we establish our orientation in the world. The starting point of our cultural gaze is ethnocentrism as an inherent human condition. Ethnocentrism was presented, first and foremost, as a central point of reference that every culture needs in order to understand the world and itself. We discussed two dangers of ethnocentrism: ethnocentric reduction and ethnocentric negation. It was shown that effective intercultural communication, based on positive ethnocentrism, requires treating people from other cultures as both Self and Not-Self at the same time.

Based on these ideas, intercultural communication was presented as a matter of positionality. We demonstrated that cultures occupy specific positions.

When they interact, their cultural gaze makes it possible for them to see the world and their own place in it. In this process, cultural meanings are generated; that is, our culture is grounded. Everything that we experience as a result of an intercultural encounter and find meaningful is framed and becomes part of our culture, our "common ground."

Also, we saw that positionality is not simply a matter of people from different cultures establishing their specific positions; it is a matter of power relations between these positions. Intercultural encounters were presented as sites of power distributions. Every culture claims authority for its understanding of the world by creating narratives. To people from all cultures, their own stories are authentic. However, the real power of every culture depends on whether its system of meanings is accepted or rejected by people from other cultures. That is why it is impossible for a culture to determine its real position without engaging other cultures' perspectives.

Based on these ideas, the Positionality Principle was formulated.

You might be wondering how, if everything in intercultural communication is a matter of a specific point of view, it is possible for cultures to communicate. Can cultures engage in interaction at all? There must be something general that people from *all* cultures can relate to—some common ground. We will discuss this question in the next chapter. We will try to find out whether there are any general standards that make intercultural communication possible.

CASE STUDY
ARGUMENT IN ISRAELI-PALESTINIAN ENCOUNTERS

This case study is based on an article entitled "Going to Ground: Argument in Israeli-Jewish and Palestinian Encounter Group," by Ifat Maoz and Donald G. Ellis (2001). As usual, it is recommended that you read the article in its entirety; below is a summary of the article.

Be ready to identify and then discuss the following topics:

1. The role of grounding in the Israeli-Palestinian encounters
2. The power relations revealed in these encounters
3. The Israeli-Palestinian encounters as an engaged dialogue

The article discusses a series of workshops conducted by an Israeli-Palestinian organization within the framework of a peace education project. These workshops brought together about 30 Israeli and 30 Palestinian youths, who were engaged in discussions of the conflict between their two cultures. The goal of the workshops was to foster interaction between the two sides.

In the article, argument is presented as an interactional practice of managing dilemmas. The main dilemma in the article is for each side to give an account of its own vision of reality and, at the same time, successfully challenge the other side's view. For example, the Israeli Jews want to appear committed to civil rights, while defending their distrustful feelings toward Palestinians. The article shows how such dilemmas can be worked out in encounters between these two cultures.

In one of the encounters, the following exchange took place between Danny and Gil, two Israeli males, and Bashir, a Palestine male:

Bashir: He [his brother's friend] was killed . . . because he wanted his land back.

Danny: But you tried to conquer the land from us in 1948. The U.N. gave it to us and you tried to conquer it.

Bashir: Give me proof that this, that this is your land.

Danny: I give you proof of the Bible, of Jerusalem that we built.

Gil: What is the Bible for them?

Danny: We are exiled from our country. This was our land and we wanted to come back to it.

The authors of the article discuss how the two sides defend their positions without appearing overly biased. The term *argumentative ground* is used for the point at which one can argue no further. For instance, in the excerpt above, the two sides import the sacred issues of the Bible, land, and freedom of movement as such ground. Both sides give prominence to historical subjects.

According to the authors of the article, a key strategy in presenting arguments is for each culture to project itself as rational and its position as "objectively" acceptable. Each side lays claims to legitimacy for its own argument, trying to naturalize its position. Here is an excerpt from one such Palestinian argument (PM = Palestinian Male; PF = Palestinian Female):

(continued)

ARGUMENT IN ISRAELI-PALESTINIAN ENCOUNTERS CONTINUED

PM1: If we go into Tantur not through the Machson [Hebrew word for checkpoint] I can go in. They see me and they don't care. It is that they want to make it difficult for me.

PF1: There are three ways to go from Bethlehem to Jerusalem.

PM2: If I want to go to Jerusalem, I am there in five minutes.

PM3: 60,000 Palestinians every day go to Israel without permission, every day. 40,000 with permission. So it's not security, it's politics. This is the information. I am not saying this to support.

From the Palestinian perspective, the checkpoints restricting their movement into Israel do not really work because many people enter Israel every day illegally, avoiding those checkpoints. So, the Palestinians look for a connection between checkpoints and illegal entry into Israel; from their point of view, the Israelis are more interested in punishing Palestinians than in security.

The authors of the article pay special attention to a large number of questions used to trigger an argument sequence. Most of these questions shape the power distribution in the debate, as each group tries to restrict the answer (voice) of the other side. The following examples are taken from one of the excerpts of the debate:

JEWISH-ISRAELI QUESTIONS

1. If we permit every Palestinian to go to Tel Aviv, what will happen?
2. If there is no closure, can you assure me there are no bombings?
3. Isn't there a border between two countries?

PALESTINIAN QUESTIONS

1. Do you want to punish the whole people for one bomber?
2. Name one water resource. If I give you Tel Aviv and tell you to live only in Tel Aviv, will you be able to do it?
3. How many times did you run out of water in your house, no water to wash your hands?
4. When will we have water? After ten, twenty, fifty years?

According to the authors of the article, the Palestinian questions have a plaintive quality; they complain about water, restrictions of movement, and so on. The Israelis present their positions as easily defensible, and their questions are more assertive.

DISCUSSION

Now let's see how this case study can be an illustration of the Positionality Principle of intercultural communication.

1. The role of grounding in the Israeli-Palestinian encounters. The two cultures involved in the debate definitely look at the Israeli-Palestinian conflict from different points of view. In other words, their cultural knowledge is differently positioned. These positions are grounded in a number of beliefs, values, and norms. For instance, the Israeli Jews (more than the other side) believe that violence is defensible because of historical events. The Palestinians believe that the actual reason for the Israeli checkpoints is to punish Palestinians, not to prevent illegal entry into Israel.

Both sides try to reconcile their justification of violence with egalitarian values such as human rights. Yet their norms often clash. Consider the example of checkpoints. What the Israelis find normal, the Palestinians find unwarranted (not normal). Thus, the gaze of each culture is grounded and affects the discussions described in the article. Especially important is the so-called argumentative ground—the point at which the culture can argue no further.

2. The power relations revealed in these encounters. The Israeli-Palestinian encounter described in the article is not simply a situation of two cultures arguing from two established positions. In this encounter, structural asymmetries between these positions are revealed. When people from each culture present their arguments, they claim authority for their vision of the situation in order to gain more power.

In these discussions, the tone of the questions in the Palestinian arguments suggests that the Palestinian side has a secondary power position. The Israeli Jews are more successful at limiting the size and development of answers by the Palestinians. The Israeli arguments are presented, and seem to be accepted, as more defensible. The Palestinians present more collaborative arguments in which a speaker states a position and other participants supply support (consider the excerpt involving three Palestinian Males and one Palestinian Female, presented above). Such strategies are usually used by subordinate groups, which must operate within the constraints imposed on them by the more dominant culture. By joining forces, a subordinate culture tries to find ways to be heard.

3. The Israeli-Palestinian encounters as an engaged dialogue. It is impossible for a culture to determine its real position without engaging other cultures' perspectives. This is exactly what participants from the two cultures try to accomplish in the encounters described in the article. They are engaged in discussions with the goal of improving communication between the two sides.

Their interaction is very difficult, as people from the two cultures try to balance the tensions between egalitarian values and distrustful feelings about each other. Sometimes the two sides fail to move the discussion beyond initial confrontation. Yet the Israeli-Palestinian encounters described in the article, which took place within a peace education project, are based on the premise that the two cultures can coexist successfully only if they continue to communicate with each other—that is, engage in a constructive dialogue.

Such intercultural encounters continue to take place within the Seeds of Peace project, which celebrated its tenth year in 2002. The tenth Seeds of Peace camp was held in Otisfield, Maine, where young Palestinians and Israelis, along with young people from Pakistan and India, participated in "coexistence sessions," trying to find solutions to the conflicts in their regions (Kim, 2002).

SIDE TRIPS

1. The following excerpt is taken from John Lee Anderson's article "The Assassins" (2002). See if you can identify the clash of two different cultural positions (particularly in terms of mores and values) in the interaction he describes.

> I met Bismillah Khan [the Northern Alliance commander] again in late May, at his base in Kabul. He shared it with a Swedish contingent of the I.S.A.F. [International Security Force in Afghanistan]. He has an office on the rooftop of a building that has a rose garden and a lawn and a huge, sixties-style swimming pool. The Swedes were giving a Taste of Sweden barbecue when I arrived, and Bismillah Khan and his men were lined up with paper plates and plastic utensils to get their food. They were obviously ill at ease, and not a little offended, since at an Afghan feast a guest sits and is served.
>
> Some of the Afghans didn't know how to eat with forks and knives, and those who did helped them. They whispered about what was on their plates: barbecue beef, chicken, potatoes, and bamboo shoots. They didn't know what bamboo was, and most of them didn't touch it. They had never eaten potatoes with the skins on. A few of the men cracked jokes in Dari about the meat, which they thought might be dog, or pork. Others said that it wasn't *halal*, that is, that a butcher had not uttered "God is great" when the animal's throat was cut.
>
> At the end of the meal, the Swedish chef, a burly soldier, announced that he wanted to wish one of the other soldiers a happy birthday, and, as was the custom in Sweden, he would present him with a gift. This was all translated to the Afghans, who were puzzled, since they don't celebrate birthdays. The chef unwrapped a bottle of whiskey and handed it to the soldier. "And now," the chef said, "our friend must share his gift, as is the custom in Afghanistan, with everyone here. It will take, I estimate, five minutes." And he laughed at his joke.
>
> Two of Bismillah Khan's aides ran over to the Swede's translator and pointed out that this was a big mistake. Fridoun, my translator, muttered, "Don't they learn anything at all about Afghan culture before they come?" The whiskey bottle was removed, and Bismillah Khan, who had politely eaten everything on his plate during dinner, rose and thanked his hosts and shook the officers' hands.

2. Shortly after the tragic events of 9/11, President Bush called his battle against Arab terrorists "a crusade." The White House had to apologize for that remark because, in the Middle East, that word is seen quite differently. See if you can identify the clash of two different cultural positions (particularly in terms of attitudes). You might find helpful an article in the *New York Daily News* by Helen Kennedy (2001).
3. At the Fourth U.N. World Conference on Women that took place in Beijing in 1995, delegates from many different cultures discussed the proposed "Platform for Action"—the document to be taken back home as a guideline for improving women's status. The delegates spent hours discussing single words and phrases. For instance, the phrase "sexual rights" had many interpretations, from the right to say "No" to sex within marriage to freedom from discrimination based on sexual orientation. Intercultural communication during such debates, in spite of a large number of translators and interpreters, was challenging, to say the least. Yet the conference was definitely a success. How can this event be analyzed in terms of positionality and engagement?

CHECK YOURSELF

Perception
Beliefs
Attitudes
Values
Norms
Folkways
Mores
Laws
Worldview
Cultural gaze
Ethnic tourism
Ethnocentrism
Ethnocentric reduction
Ethnocentric negation
Ethnocentric affirmation
Cultural loci
Grounding
Authority
Narrative
Grand narrative
Engagement

REFERENCES

Aaker, J., Benet-Martinez, V., & Garolera, J. (2001). Consumption symbols as carriers of culture: A study of Japanese and Spanish brand personality constructs. *Journal of Personality and Social Psychology*, Vol. 81, No. 3, pp. 492–508.

Abdel-Nour, F. (2000). Liberalism and ethnocentrism. *Journal of Political Philosophy*, Vol. 8, No. 2, pp. 207–226.

Anderson, J. L. (2002). The assassins. *The New Yorker*, June 10, p. 80.

Barker, C. (2000). *Cultural studies: Theory and practice*. London: Sage.

Berelson, B., & Steiner, G. (1964). *Human behavior: An inventory of scientific findings*. New York: Harcourt.

Blair, J. (2000). Thinking through binaries: Conceptual strategies for interdependence. *American Studies International*, Vol. 38, No. 2, pp. 23–38.

Brislin, R. (1993). *Understanding culture's influence on behavior*. Fort Worth, TX: Harcourt Brace.

Cantor, N., Mischel, W., & Schwartz, J. (1982). Social knowledge. In Isen, A., & A. Hastorf (Eds.), *Cognitive social psychology*. New York: Elsevier North-Holland.

Chavez, L., et al. (2001). Belief matters: Cultural beliefs and the use of cervical cancer-screening tests. *American Anthropologist*, Vol. 103, No. 4, pp. 1114–1129.

Chen, G.-M., & Starosta, W. (1998). *Foundations of intercultural communication*. Boston: Allyn and Bacon.

Clifford, J. (1988). *The predicament of culture: Twentieth-century ethnography, literature and art*. Cambridge, MA: Harvard University Press.

Dogs' lives. (2002). *The Spokesman-Review*, June 3, p. B2.

Enfield, N. (2000). The theory of cultural logic: How individuals combine social intelligence with semiotics to create and maintain cultural meaning. *Cultural Dynamics*, Vol. 12, No. 1, pp. 35–64.

Fisher, W. (1984). Narration as a human communication paradigm: The case of public moral argument. *Communication Monographs*, Vol. 51, pp. 1–22.

Fleischacker, S. (1994). *The ethics of culture*. Ithaca, NY: Cornell University Press.

Geertz, C. (1986). The uses of diversity. *Michigan Quarterly Review*, Vol. 25, pp. 105–123.

Graham, M. (1999). The African-centered worldview: Toward a paradigm for social work. *Journal of Black Studies*, Vol. 30, No. 1, pp. 103–122.

Gudykunst, W., & Kim, Y. (1992). *Communicating with strangers: An approach to intercultural communication.* New York: McGraw-Hill.

Hall, B. (2002). *Among cultures: The challenge of communication.* Belmont, CA: Wadsworth/Thomson Learning.

Hesselgrave, D. (1978). *Communicating Christ cross-culturally.* Grand Rapids: Zondervan.

Hiwasaki, L. (2000). Ethnic tourism in Hokkaido and the shaping of Ainu identity. *Pacific Affairs,* Vol. 73, No. 3, pp. 393–412.

Hoge, W. (2002). Plane-spotters found guilty in Greek court in secrets case. *The New York Times,* April 28, p. A5.

Jain, N., & Kussman, D. (1997). Dominant cultural patterns of Hindus in India. In Samovar, L., & R. Porter (Eds.), *Intercultural communication: A reader* (pp. 89–97). Belmont, CA: Wadsworth.

Jandt, F. (2001). *Intercultural communication: An introduction.* Thousand Oaks, CA: Sage.

Katriel, T. (1994). Sites of memory: Discourses of the past in Israeli pioneering settlement museums. *Quarterly Journal of Speech,* Vol. 80, No. 1, pp. 1–20.

Kennedy, H. (2001). White House apologizes for crusade remark. *New York Daily News,* Sept. 19.

Kim, A. (2002). War-weary teens find peace at camp. *The Spokesman-Review,* June 27, p. A3.

Kirn, W. (2001). Crossing the divide. *Time,* July 16, p. 32.

Klopf, D. (1998). *Intercultural encounters: The fundamentals of intercultural communication.* Englewood, CO: Morton.

Koch, P. (2001). Metonymy: Unity in diversity. *Journal of Historical Pragmatics,* Vol. 2, No. 2, pp. 201–244.

Koehler, W. (1969). *The task of Gestalt psychology.* Princeton, NJ: Princeton University Press.

Lacey, M. (2002). Masai offer cattle in sympathy over Sept. 11. *The Spokesman-Review,* June 3, p. A2.

Lee, M. (2002). The internationals. *The Atlantic Monthly,* July/August, pp. 35–36.

Maoz, I., & Ellis, D. G. (2001). Going to ground: Argument in Israeli-Jewish and Palestinian encounter group. *Research on Language and Social Interaction,* Vol. 34, No. 4, pp. 399–419.

Martin, J., Krizek, R., Nakayama, T., & Bradford, L. (1996). Exploring whiteness: A study of self-labels for white Americans. *Communication Quarterly,* Vol. 44, No. 2, pp. 125–144.

McGregor, A. (2000). Dynamic texts and tourist gaze: Death, bones, and buffalo. *Annals of Tourism Research,* Vol. 27, No. 1, pp. 27–50.

Merriam, S., Johnson-Bailey, J., Lee, M. Y., Kee, Y., Ntseane, G., & Muhamad, M. (2001). Power and positionality: Negotiating insider/outsider status within and across cultures. *International Journal of Lifelong Education,* Vol. 20, No. 5, pp. 405–416.

Mitchell, M., & Wood, C. (1998). Ironies of citizenship: Skin color, police brutality, and the challenge to democracy in Brazil. *Social Forces,* Vol. 77, No. 3, pp. 1001–1020.

Munshi, D., & McKie, D. (2001). Toward a new cartography of intercultural communication: Mapping bias, business, and diversity. *Business Communication Quarterly,* Vol. 64, No. 3, pp. 9–22.

Neuliep, J. (2000). *Intercultural communication: A contextual approach.* Boston: Houghton Mifflin.

Rorty, R. (1998). *Achieving our country: Leftist thought in twentieth-century America.* Cambridge, MA: Harvard University Press.

Roth, W.-M. (2001). Situated cognition. *The Journal of the Learning Sciences,* Vol. 10, Nos. 1 & 2, pp. 27–62.

Samovar, L., & Porter, R. (Eds.). (1991). *Intercultural communication: A reader.* Belmont, CA: Wadsworth.

Segall, M. H. (1979). *Cross-cultural psychology: Human behavior in global perspective.* Monterey, CA: Brooks/Cole.

Sumner, G. (1940). *Folkways.* Boston: Ginn.

Ting-Toomey, S. (1999). *Communication across cultures.* New York: Guilford.

Young, R. (1996). *Intercultural communication: Pragmatics, genealogy, deconstruction.* Clevedon, UK: Multilingual Matters.

CHAPTER FIVE

COMPARING CULTURAL MAPS: COMMENSURABILITY PRINCIPLE

It's Everybody's World.

- *Key Theme:* Generalness
- *Key Objective:* To help you realize the inherent common nature of people from different cultures

INTRODUCING THE PROBLEM QUESTION

LOOKING FOR MEANING IN INTERCULTURAL COMMUNICATION

Semiotic Look: What's in a Word?
Cognitive Look: What's on Our Mind?
Corporeal Look: What's in the World?

INTRODUCING THE COMMENSURABILITY PRINCIPLE

The Nature of Commensurability
The Forms and Levels of Commensurability
The Implications of Commensurability

THE COMMENSURABILITY PRINCIPLE DEFINED

SUMMARY

CASE STUDY: TRANSLATING CULTURAL DIFFERENCES: THE PROBLEM OF *CHOU*

SIDE TRIPS

CHECK YOURSELF

REFERENCES

Introducing the Problem Question

In the previous chapter, we saw that everything in intercultural communication is a matter of a specific point of view, so it is only natural to wonder whether it is possible for people from different cultures to communicate at all. There must be something general, though, that all people can relate to—something that makes intercultural communication possible in principle. We will try to find out if there are any general standards that make intercultural communication possible.

So, the problem question for this chapter is this: *Is there anything general that makes intercultural communication possible?*

In this chapter we will

- Look at meaning in intercultural communication from the semiotic perspective (i.e., in terms of signs)
- Look at meaning in intercultural communication from the cognitive perspective (i.e., in terms of mental constructs)
- Look at meaning in intercultural communication from the corporeal perspective (i.e., in terms of material experiences)
- Present the main forms and levels for comparing different cultures
- Discuss the implications of comparing different cultures, or why cultures can and must be compared.

Looking for Meaning in Intercultural Communication

A universal is usually understood as something that "appears under the same form in each and every culture" (Pinxten, 1976: 122). In this sense, universals include housing, tools, and gender roles. A list of universals would be very long, if not endless. However, the key to all these constructs is meaning. So, we will treat universals in terms of how people are able to agree on meaning. If we can prove that this is a general human capacity, we can indeed say that intercultural communication is possible.

Let's look at a simple example of cultural meaning: The gesture of forming a circle with the thumb and index finger is interpreted as representing a physical object (money) in Japan and a psychological state (things are OK) in the United States. So, what is needed to generate meaning?

First, we need the world in general—any reality that people can perceive, including physical objects and psychological states. We all live in this world, perceive it with our senses, and try to understand it. There are many things we now understand and many other things hidden from our view, waiting to be discovered (remember the Uncertainty Principle?). The world is the object of exploration, and people are its explorers.

Second, we need something to represent the results of our explorations. People from each culture represent the world using different symbols—words, gestures, artifacts. We use all these systems of symbols to *re*present objects; that is, we make the world present again in symbols.

Third, we need a special place for storing mental constructs associated with symbols. The mind can be viewed as a dynamic storage place for such constructs.

Let's look again at the example above. We have a symbol for representing a certain segment of the world—the formation of a circle with the thumb and index finger. We have certain segments of the world that are represented—a physical object (money) and a psychological state (things being OK). And we have two cultural interpretations of this symbol in the form of mental constructs in our mind—"money" in Japan and "things are OK" in the United States. Meaning is created when these three components—symbol, world, and mind—are activated in the process of communication. When objects are represented and interpreted in meaningful ways, culture as a shared system of resources is created.

Intercultural communication is a process whereby people with different systems of resources come into contact, generating meaning. In intercultural communication, people from different cultures search for meaning together, trying to reach some common ground. But do people have the capacity to understand one another and agree on meaning? Let's start looking for meaning in intercultural communication.

Semiotic Look: What's in a Word?

Where do we start our search for meaning? There are three suspects, so to speak: symbol, world, and mind. Right away, our attention is caught by a large number of symbols that vary from culture to culture. A **symbol** is anything that can stand for something else and has meaning. Words, gestures, and dress are all symbols. For example, the English symbol *snow* stands for white or translucent ice crystals of various shapes originating in the upper atmosphere as frozen particles of water vapor. Any system of symbols can be viewed as a language (e.g., spoken/written language, the language of music).

Symbols are studied by the discipline of **semiotics.** The term *semiotics* is derived from the Greek word *semeion* (sign). Semiotic analysis can be applied to any language. Let's take a semiotic look at meaning in intercultural communication. The verbal language system is one of the most visible and important parts of any culture, and a word is the most common language symbol. So, what's in a word?

It is safe to assume that people from the same culture are familiar with the meanings of most language symbols and communicate with each other without much problem. However, outside of our culture we find ourselves on unfamiliar ground. We are so overwhelmed by the diversity of the world's cultures and their symbols that it is only fair to ask if understanding is possible at all. Can people from diverse cultures understand one another when their symbols are often so different?

Linguistic Relativity: Strong Version. Such questions have been raised since early antiquity. Present-day ideas along these lines are usually associated with the names of Sapir and Whorf and the term *linguistic relativity.* Sapir and Whorf studied Aztec, Maya, and Hopi languages, which are very different from what Whorf called "Standard Average European" (SAE) language. They discovered that those languages, through their vocabulary and grammatical structure, provide different segmentations of experience. Because of different language segmentation, different cultures think and act differently—that is, have different views of the world.

In Sapir's words,

> Human beings do not live in the objective world alone . . . , but are very much at the mercy of the particular language which has become the medium of expression for their society. . . . The fact of the matter is that the "real world" is to a large extent unconsciously built up on the language habits of the group. . . . We see and hear and otherwise experience very largely as we do because the language habits of our community predispose certain choices of interpretation. (Whorf, 1956: 134)

Whorf echoes these ideas:

> These automatic, involuntary patterns of language . . . are specific for each language and constitute the formalized side of language, or its "grammar." . . . From this fact proceeds what I have called the "linguistic relativity principle," which means, in informal terms, that users of markedly different grammars are pointed by their grammars toward . . . somewhat different views of the world. (Whorf, 1956: 221)

Grammar here is a broad term, covering not only traditional grammatical structures (e.g., tense, agreement, mood) but lexical structure (words and expressions) as well. Whorf's famous example of a different "grammatical" segmentation of the world is the fact that the Hopi language has no grammatical forms referring to what Europeans call "time" (Whorf, 1956: 58).

The use of the term **linguistic relativity** for this phenomenon is now easily understood: It is linguistic because prime value is placed on a culture's language, or linguistic signs, and it is a matter of relativity because the way in which a culture thinks and acts depends on its language. Graphically, linguistic relativity can be represented as shown in Figure 1.

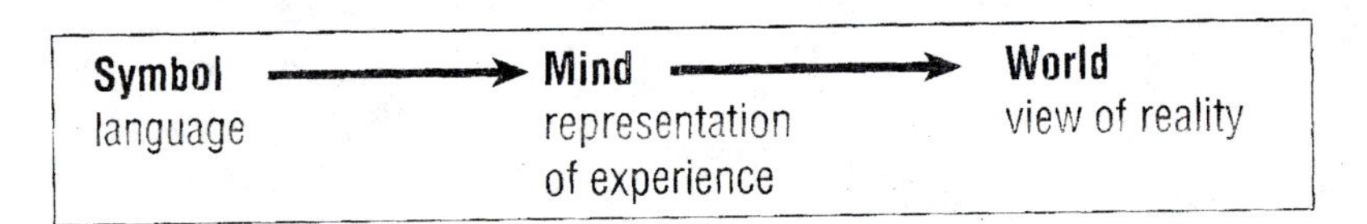

FIGURE 1

If different languages segment and represent experiences in different ways, these representations must create divergent views of the world. According to Sapir (1964), cultures appear to be arranged into formally complete yet incommensurable systems, based on linguistic classifications of experience. It appears that the structures of different languages may be fundamentally incommensurable—not "able to be measured by a common standard" (Morris, 1982: 267). Let's take a simple example and see what conclusions can be drawn if we follow this strand of thought all the way through.

Consider a simple language symbol from the U.S. culture. The meaning of the word *snow* is represented as follows: "solid precipitation in the form of white or translucent ice crystals of various shapes originating in the upper atmosphere as frozen particles of water vapor" (Morris, 1982: 1223–1224). Everybody views this particular piece of the world in the same way and acts accordingly—understands the song "Let It Snow" and knows that snow is cold, that you can make snowballs with it, that you can ski when there is enough of it, and so forth. In this case, there is complete agreement on meaning; the language symbol (*snow*) is interpreted in the same way by all people from the United States (see Figure 2).

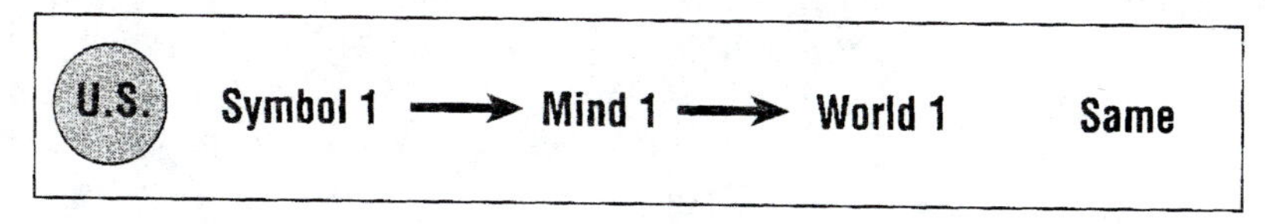

FIGURE 2

Now, let's see how this simple symbol may be interpreted by people from other cultures. Looking at what Whorf labeled "Standard Average European" (SAE) language, we find similar symbols with very similar meanings in German and in French, for example. People in these cultures understand snow in basically the same way and act accordingly. That the interpretation of *snow* is much the same in the U.S. and SAE cultures is shown by the significant overlap of the two circles shown in Figure 3.

In the language of the Inuits, however, we find a large number of other symbols for snow—for example, words for falling snow, snow on the ground, snow packed hard like ice, and slushy snow. We see that the divergence between the meanings of *snow* is now more significant and have to admit that the Inuits view

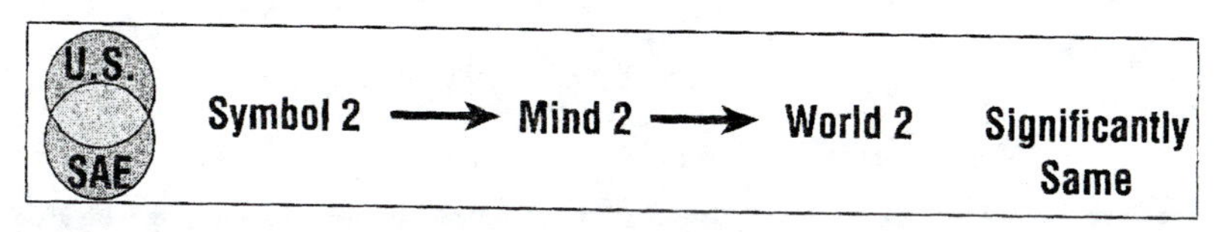

FIGURE 3

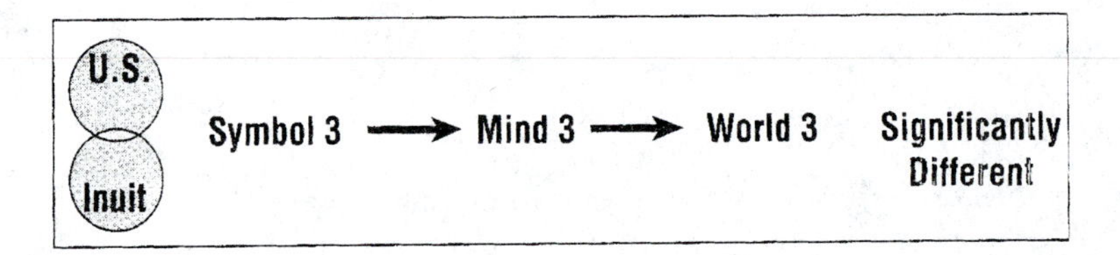

FIGURE 4

the world differently (at least as far as snow is concerned). Because the interpretation of *snow* varies more significantly and the worldviews are noticeably different, the overlap between the two circles is not as large in Figure 4 as in Figure 3.

Let's take this strand of thought even further. Suppose a tribe X is discovered that has no symbol (word) for snow; they simply have never experienced snow. Such a gap in a symbol system is called a lacuna; a **lacuna** is an empty space or missing part (usually in a language system). One might say that there is a lexical (word) lacuna for *snow* in the language of tribe X. People from tribe X have no knowledge of the symbol *snow*, so they cannot understand the song "Let It Snow" and do not know that snow is cold and that you can make snowballs with it. They cannot create any messages with the symbol *snow*. Thus, there seems to be a true gap between their view of the world and that of the U.S. culture. Because the word for snow does not exist in the language of the tribe, its people will not understand what people from the United States mean when they use *snow* in different situations of interaction. There is nothing to agree on here. The worldview of tribe X is not the same as that of the U.S. culture, as shown by the gap between the two circles in Figure 5.

The preceding view of the relationship between language and cultural knowledge is sometimes known as the **strong version of linguistic relativity,** or "linguistic determinism" (Steinfatt, 1989). According to the strong version of linguistic relativity, linguistic structure determines the way people think and act. When people from different cultures use different symbols, they think and act differently, creating different messages. These ideas can be taken to mean that the segmentation of experience reflected in one system of symbols is not commensurable with that reflected in systems of symbols of other cultures. As a result, it appears reasonable to speak about the superiority of cultures with a more developed system of symbols or to defend the impossibility of communication between people from different cultures due to a gap between their systems of symbols.

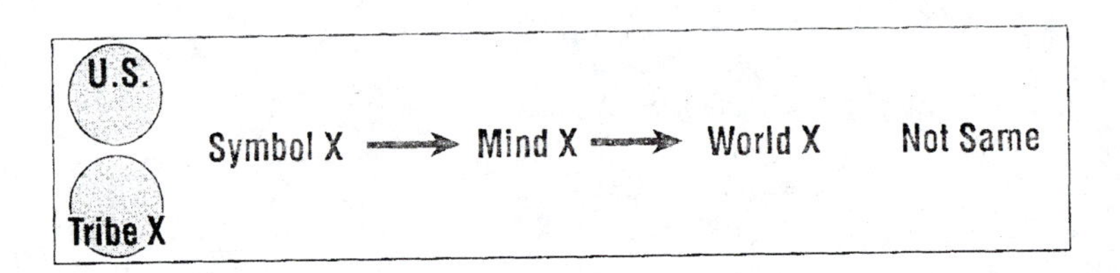

FIGURE 5

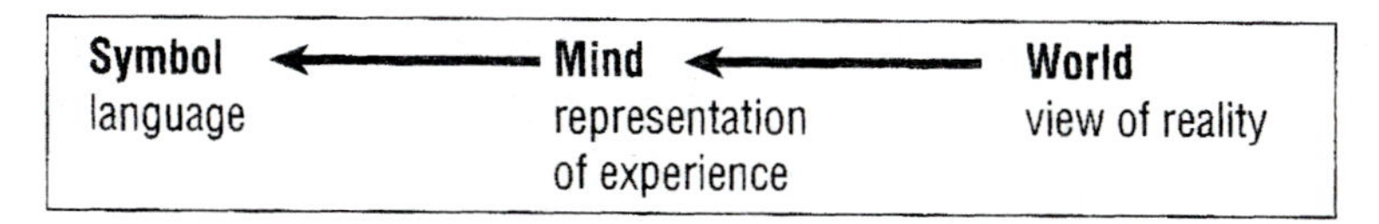

FIGURE 6

So, the strong version of linguistic relativity states that language shapes our mind and creates a unique worldview. This approach is usually criticized for being too deterministic: "There is no evidence for the strong version of the hypothesis—that language imposes upon its speakers a particular way of thinking about the world" (Wason & Johnson-Laird, 1977: 442). Such a view overestimates the role of language as a system of symbols.

Symbols do not determine the way we think and act. Rather, they reflect the segmentation of the world as performed by people from different cultures and based on cultural foci; for instance, if snow is an important part of a certain culture, this fact is reflected in the large number of words pertaining to snow. Thus, the arrows do not go from Symbol to World, as in Figure 1, but in the opposite direction, as in Figure 6. Symbols—verbal or nonverbal—are more of a mirror of the world than a creator of our worldviews.

However, the role of symbols such as language symbols should not be underestimated either; meaning cannot be constructed without them. Symbols do matter. The view that there is a connection between linguistic structure and the way people think and act is called the **weak version of linguistic relativity.**

Linguistic Relativity: Weak Version. According to the weak version of linguistic relativity, which is usually accepted by scholars (Steinfatt, 1989), language does influence communication. In Figure 6, we reversed the arrows, contradicting the strong version of linguistic relativity; the arrows originate in World and go to Symbol, wherein our view of reality is reflected. However, Symbol cannot be completely disregarded; symbols do influence the way people from different cultures see the world. So let's represent this connection between Symbol and World as shown in Figure 7. Broken, not solid, arrows emphasize that symbols do not determine anything; they simply influence our perception of reality.

As an example, we can look at two broad perceptions of time mentioned in Chapter 3: monochronic and polychronic. As you may remember, monochronic

Symbol --------->	**Mind** --------->	**World**
language	representation of experience	view of reality

FIGURE 7

time orientation emphasizes "schedules, the compartmentalization and segmentation of measurable units of time," while polychronic time orientation sees time as "much less tangible" and stresses "involvement of people and the completion of tasks" (Neuliep, 2000: 122). The fact is that these two conceptualizations of time are grounded, to a degree, in language symbols.

The first worldview (the teleological view) is based on perceiving time as a separate entity that is "figured out" as part of the culture, as in traditional European cultures. As a figure carved out of the world, time receives a number of language labels, including *time, clock,* and *5 p.m.* Not surprisingly, most of these language symbols are nouns, and they cannot help but influence the way the world is perceived by the people of the culture. It becomes possible to "do" things with time—create schedules, plan activities, meet deadlines. This gives people a sense of power over the world, as far as time goes. People think that they make time move, controlling the world.

The second worldview (the organic view) is based on perceiving time as part of the world; time is not a figure, separate from this world. What moves, in this case, is not the hands on the clock, but the sun or the clouds or human activity—whatever is chosen to measure and represent time. Such a conceptualization of time finds its manifestation in language; most symbols are verbs. These expressions, too, influence the way the world is perceived. People do not think that time moves because of them; it moves with the world, exercising its control over people. It comes to people naturally, as if from the environing world. In that sense, people live more naturally because their actions are based on the movement of this world, not the movement of the clock. The first worldview, of course, is also natural to those who share it; those people are used to the clock, measuring time in accordance with their symbolic segmentation. The two views can be represented as shown in Table 1.

The conclusions one draws with respect to intercultural communication depend on whether one subscribes to the strong or the weak version of linguistic relativity.

If we accept that language, as a system of symbols, shapes our mind and creates a unique worldview, we have to admit that communication between people from different cultures is doomed to failure; in theory, symbols of different cultures can be entirely different. This pessimistic point of view is based on the assumption that language, as a system of symbols, is omnipotent; unless people from different cultures have the same symbols, they can never arrive at the same meaning while communicating with each other.

TABLE 1

TELEOLOGICAL VIEW	ORGANIC VIEW
Time figured, as a separate entity, into culture's ground (its symbols)	Time *not* figured, as a separate entity, into culture's ground (its symbols)

If we accept that meaning cannot be equated with our segmentation of experience by symbols, we can claim that people from different cultures are able to understand each other. Our common sense tells us that it is possible for us to understand people from another culture even if our culture lacks a symbol in its system of language that is present in the language system of that other culture. Learning a foreign language often requires us to achieve such understanding. This assumption finds a more logical formulation:

> Our question is "Are there Cultural Universals?" I propose *a reductio ad absurdum* proof for an affirmative answer as follows. Suppose there were no cultural universals. Then inter-cultural communication would be impossible. But there is inter-cultural communication. Therefore, there are cultural universals. (Wiredu, 1995: 52)

It is not the intent of theorists of linguistic relativity to condone cultural superiority or predict the failure of intercultural communication. The implications of Sapir and Whorf's ideas are more benign—and more profound. We will discuss them later in the chapter.

So, in spite of discrepancies existing between their systems of symbols, people from different cultures can still communicate with one another. In other words, lack of symbols is not an insurmountable obstacle to understanding meaning in intercultural communication. Therefore, there must be more to meaning than what is encapsulated in symbols. We have "forgotten" the very place where meanings as interpretations of our experiences are stored—the mind. Can we try to look in that "black box"? Let's continue our search by taking a cognitive look at meaning.

Cognitive Look: What's on Our Mind?

The **cognitive look** at meaning in intercultural communication deals with the mental process, or faculty, by which meaning is acquired and represented. People have always dreamed of "a universal method whereby all human problems, whether of science, law, or politics, could be worked out rationally, systematically, by logical computation" (Davis & Hersh, 1986: 7). Such logical representation can be found in concepts, representing reality in the form of abstract notions. In other words, "the raw, unorganized information that comes from seeing, hearing, and the other senses is organized into useful concepts" (Sebeok & Danesi, 2000: 7). Concepts are the result of our mental segmentation and categorization of the world; they can be concrete or abstract. For example, "the concept CAR brings together objects which share certain observable features, while the concept FRIENDSHIP denotes behaviors and mental states which share less directly manifest properties" (Boyer, 1996: 205).

Every culture believes that its system of conceptual meanings is a true representation of the world. In a way, every culture tries to encapsulate meaning in its collective mind, where it is supposed to exist in the purest form. This way, all cultures try to capture, once and for all, the true meaning of their experiences in the universal form of concepts. This conceptual notation aims to be the most truthful (authoritative) view of the world.

People from every culture create concepts when they find similarities in their experiences: "Concepts put together things that are supposed to have something in common" (Boyer, 1996: 207). Thus, people group together, say, lemons and oranges in the concept of fruit. Different cultures provide different segmentations of experiences, resulting in different conceptual representations. This happens because, as we discussed in Chapter 4, cultural meanings are grounded, or positioned, differently. In intercultural communication, different conceptualizations of experiences are highlighted. For example, the Japanese concept of "shibui" has been described as "not showy or gaudy but serene, self-possessed, with presence of mind, austere, understated" (Jandt, 2001: 187). However, "there is no equivalent term in English, so the concept cannot be easily explained. . . . You would have to be exposed to a number of objects classified as shibui to determine what the critical attributes are" (Jandt, 2001: 187).

An example of such cultural exposure is provided by Agar, who tells this story about his anthropological work in a village in South India:

> In that kinship system, the father is called *baap*. Only the actual biological father is called *baap*. . . . Let's say the father's brother ambles by, and Nate Notebook, as I referred to myself then, asks what he is called. *Motobaap*, they say. . . .
>
> Another brother stops in, and the anthropologist, chest swelling with pride, points at him and calls him *motobaap*. The group members laugh, do the South Indian village equivalent of slapping their knees, and once again prove that the only reason Nate was ever tolerated was because of his entertainment value. . . .
>
> No, they say, he is called *kaaka*. . . .
>
> Now, since a wedding is brewing, the mother's brothers show up from another village. Confused and perplexed, Nate tries *motobaap* and *kaaka* and gets that look like he just stepped out of a flying saucer. No, they are called *masi*. All of them are *masi*.
>
> There are three types of uncles, *motobaap*, *kaaka*, and *masi*. . . .
>
> *Motobaap* labels the older brothers of the father, and *kaaka* labels his younger brother. *Masi* labels the brothers of the mother. (1994: 52–53)

In this example, our anthropologist was able to understand the conceptual system of kinship of that village in South India even though the language symbols were new to him. As he himself puts it, "Nate figured it out—give him credit for that" (Agar, 1994: 53). Similarly, we can figure out the meaning of *shibui*, discussed above. The fact is that language meaning, found in symbols, must not be confused with conceptual meaning, found in our mind. Lack of a symbol to express a certain concept does not mean people are unable to understand that concept. Any meaning can be understood by people from all cultures, even though they might lack (yet!) a concept and, consequently, a symbol (or symbols) to express it. The question is, How? How did Nate figure it out? How do people from different cultures understand each other? There must be more to meaning than what is encapsulated in symbols and what exists as concepts.

Earlier, it was mentioned that one must be exposed to a number of objects classified as a certain concept, such as "shibui," in order to determine its meaning. In other words, one must turn to the objective reality—the world. It is only natural to turn to the world in general, because it is the starting point of intercultural communication (as the arrows in Figure 6 indicate). Let's continue our search by taking a corporeal look at meaning.

Corporeal Look: What's in the World?

We have discovered that cultures provide different symbolic and conceptual segmentations of experiences. Yet, based on common sense, intuition, and a *reductio ad absurdum,* we assume that people from different cultures can still communicate with each other—that is, operate with the same meaning in communication. Let's see now whether we can provide a more scientific proof for this assumption by looking at the world in general. After all, all people, with their languages and minds, are part of this world, or universe. Where, if not in the universe, should we look for universals?

We experience this world through our senses: We see, hear, smell, taste, and touch it. It might seem, with so many cultures in this world, that our experiences would always be unique and incommensurable. People from different cultures do communicate with one another, though, so there must be something that all cultures share. What is it that everybody shares? You will be surprised to learn that the answer to this question is found in the previous sentence, and you may at first be disappointed to learn how simple this answer is. What we all share is *body*. But just think about it: Every*body* has the same experience, as a warm-blooded creature that is three-dimensional, laterally symmetrical, front-back asymmetrical, moving on this planet according to the law of gravity. True, in this approach human beings are reduced to a highly schematic creature—just a body with a basic front-back orientation, eyes pointed ahead, legs moving forward more readily than backward, and so forth. But this approach to human meaning proved to be revolutionary in the 1970s and 1980s, when it became clear that mind was embodied.

For centuries, meaning was thought to be encapsulated in the human mind. People were thought to be human because they could think, creating and using meaning. Remember René Descartes with his famous "Cogito ergo sum"—"I think; therefore I am"? Toward the middle of the 20th century, however, a new perspective on meaning—the "embodiment perspective"—took shape. In their celebrated publications (e.g., Lakoff & Johnson, 1980; Lakoff & Johnson, 1999), Lakoff and Johnson showed that meaning grows out of the experiences of the body. They drew our attention to primary experiences that all people share, such as feeling warm when being held affectionately, feeling energetic when having an upright posture, and finding that big things (e.g., parents) exert major forces. These experiences are so natural that people do not think much about them. They are natural because they are evolutionarily older than any concepts or language; they are *pre*linguistic *and pre*conceptual. Meaning, then, goes beyond symbol and mind! We are equipped with the general capacity to deal with this world in terms of such experiential gestalts (structured wholes) as *up, down, inside, outside, close, far, light,* and *heavy.* Thus, meaning is grounded in the body. As Johnson puts it, body is "central to human meaning" (1987: xiv). So, it is possible to paraphrase René Descartes and state "Sum ergo cogito"—"I am; therefore I think."

The most natural experiences of the body provide the universal foundation for meaning in intercultural communication. People from different cultures can communicate with each other because, above all, the same image-schemas are activated in the process of their interaction. **Image-schemas** are mental structures that grow out of primary bodily experiences. One example of an image-schema is verticality, derived from feeling energetic when in an upright posture. Balance is another example of an image-schema, derived from the balancing activity of the body. The balance image-schema, for example, is the source of expressions in the areas of finance (*balancing* a checkbook), art, and psychology, to name a few.

There are several often-discussed types of image-schemas (for more information, see Lakoff & Johnson, 1999). Orientational image-schemas such as verticality and impediment are derived from our bodily experiences of orientation (up, down, front, back). Ontological image-schemas such as containment and movement are derived from our experiences associated with substances and entities. These image-schemas underlie the formation of more abstract meanings.

It is important to point out two things. First, image-schemas are not replicas of the world; they are not the same as the primary experiences of the body. Image-schemas are the result of human activity—structures created in our mind with the help of language symbols. (In theory, image-schemas could be very different if our bodies changed drastically because of some changes in the world—for example, if we started to walk on our hands.) Second, image-schemas as "mental icons" (Danesi & Perron, 1999: 168) of our bodily experiences must not be identified only with visual images.

Thus, the **corporeal look** at meaning is grounded in sensory experiences of the body. The word *corporeal* comes from the Latin *corporeus* (of the body) and means "pertaining to, or characteristic of, the body; of a material nature, tangible" (Morris, 1982: 298). The human mind "does not understand anything of which it had no previous impression from the senses" (Bergin & Fisch, 1984: 123)—that is, from the experiences of the body.

By using the same image-schemas, people from different cultures begin to understand each other's messages made up of language symbols and existing as mental concepts. For example, the English sentence "I've been feeling up for the past two days" is understood because people from all cultures share the same image-schema of verticality.

Now is a good time to introduce the fifth principle underlying intercultural communication: the Commensurability Principle.

Introducing the Commensurability Principle

We have been trying to understand whether intercultural communication is possible and, if so, what makes it possible. In other words, we have been trying to find a common measure for messages exchanged by people from different cultures. We have looked for meaning in (language) symbols, inside our mind, and in the world. Now let us bring all these ideas together in the form of another fundamental principle underlying intercultural communication—the Commensurability Principle. As usual, we will isolate the three most important parts of this principle. First, we will discuss the dynamic nature of commensurability. Next, we will isolate its main forms and levels. Finally, we will discuss the implications of commensurability. We will discuss each part separately and then formulate the Commensurability Principle as a whole.

The Nature of Commensurability

We started with the question of whether there is anything universal that makes interaction between people from different cultures possible. The answer to this question often appears quite pessimistic. For example, the famous anthropologist Claude Levi-Strauss writes, "Cultures are like trains moving each on its own track, at its own speed, and in its own direction" (1985: 10). Sometimes there are trains, he says, that are "rolling alongside ours" so that "through the windows of our compartments, we can observe at our leisure the various kinds of cars, the faces and gestures of the passengers." But if "a train passes in the other direction, we perceive only a vague, fleeting, barely identifiable image." No wonder many find this "an impressive image of the incommensurability of cultures which renders communication between them impossible. But does this image really describe what is going on between cultures . . . ?" (Bredella, 1994: 295).

At the beginning of the chapter, three components were introduced that are necessary for people to create and understand meaning—symbol, mind, and world. It is certainly meaning that should be taken as a standard measure, which people from different cultures must agree upon while communicating with each other.

First, we saw that while meaning can be encapsulated in language symbols, different cultures have different systems of symbols and can create entirely different messages. However, people can grasp any meaning in spite of a lack of symbols for that meaning in their language. Therefore, there is more to meaning than what is encapsulated in (language) symbols.

Second, we saw that our minds strive to develop a system of concepts as a universal cognitive representation. Different cultures have different conceptualizations of experience; however, people can still grasp any new meaning in spite of a lack of the concept in their culture. Therefore, there is more to meaning than what is encapsulated in our mind.

Third, we saw that the world is the same for everybody grounded in the natural experiences of the body. Different cultures occupy different positions in this world; to put it simply, one cannot be everybody—in all places at all times. However, people can still understand any new meaning; therefore, there must be more to meaning than what is encapsulated in our generic (i.e., genetic) body.

These three components seem to play a game with us, as it were. When we are ready to pinpoint meaning, each component refers us to the other two, as if to say "Search for meaning there." Is it a vicious circle? No. The fact is that none of these three components, taken separately, can present us with *the* key to meaning. It is only when they are taken together that they make it possible for humans to make and understand meaning. Intercultural communication is a process of agreeing on what meaning is.

The nature of commensurability does not lie in the world, symbols, or mind alone. At the core of commensurability is people's ability to bring these three components together in a meaningful way. Meaning is a process, not something that some cultures have and other cultures do not and cannot have. Meanings, as common ground, are dynamic and generated by some basic "processes that make these meanings possible" (Turner, 1996: 11). In this light, any meaning can be created and understood by people from different cultures. Commensurability must be thought of, first and foremost, as a universal human capacity, which is realized through the same levels and forms of meaning.

The Forms and Levels of Commensurability

Based on the discussion above, three forms of commensurability can be isolated as standard measures of meaning that make intercultural communication possible—symbols, concepts, and image-schemas. You may have noticed that we started with the most abstract level of symbols, the semiotic level, where meanings are very diverse and relatively culture-specific. Next, we moved down to the cognitive level of concepts, where meanings are still abstract but less diverse and more general. Finally, we isolated the most basic level of image-schemas, the corporeal level, where meanings are very concrete and most universal. Thus, the three forms of commensurability can be said to operate at three different levels: semiotic, cognitive, and corporeal (Figure 8).

Form	Level
Symbols	Semiotic
Concepts	Cognitive
Image-schemas	Corporeal

FIGURE 8

In real communication, the levels and forms of meaning representation are interconnected; they all converge in the creation and understanding of meaning. It is possible to dissect meaning (the way we do in this chapter) only for the purpose of analysis. Figure 9 shows how these universal forms and levels of meaning are interconnected. Also, each of these forms and levels gravitates toward one of the components discussed at the beginning of the chapter: Image-schemas (corporeal level) are closer to World; concepts (cognitive level) are closer to Mind; and symbols (semiotic level) are closer to Symbol.

Notice that all three forms are connected with arrows, and the number of arrows increases as we go up. This illustrates the somewhat limited number of image-schemas, the larger number of concepts, and the practically unlimited number of symbols. In this sense, meaning grows up, out of the World. Using a metaphor, we might say that meaning can be seen in terms of a forest (image-schemas), trees (concepts), and leaves (symbols). It is most important not to "miss the forest for the trees," but it is also important not to overlook the leaves—the very "flesh" of meaning. For symbols are a part of this world, and they, too, are of a material nature. After all, we perceive the world through our language; we can hear, see, or even touch our language. Language has a physical manifestation; it is also an object of this world. So, language symbols are connected to the cognitive and corporeal levels, affecting both our mind and the world.

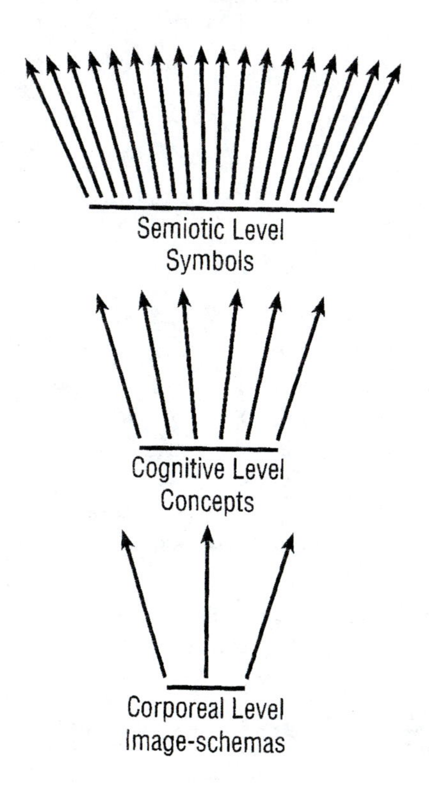

FIGURE 9

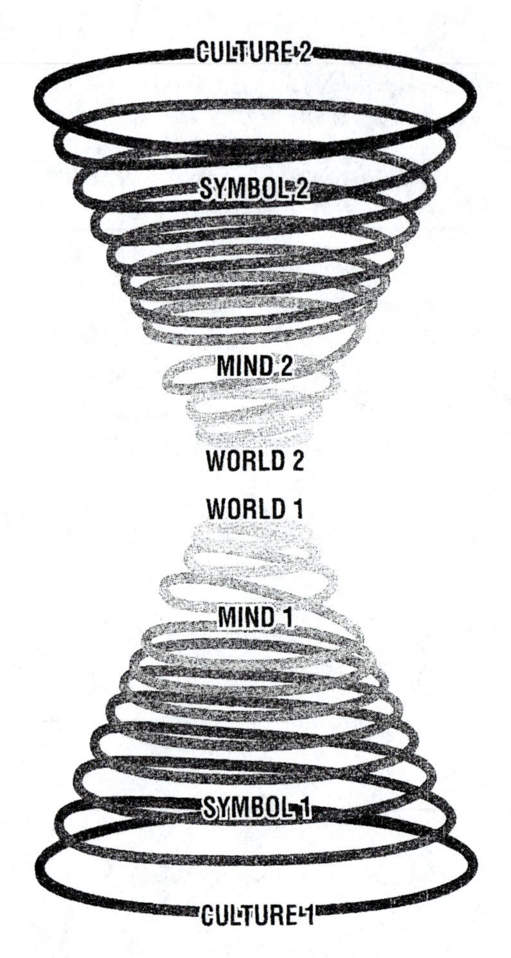

FIGURE 10

The three forms and levels of meaning cannot exist separately; they can be visualized as a triangle, within which meaning exists—everywhere. In intercultural communication, two such triangles representing people from two different cultures (1 and 2) come into contact to form a spiral (Figure 10).

The potential for misunderstanding becomes larger as we move from lower to higher levels. Notice how close to each other World 1 and World 2 are; here, it is easy to reach an agreement on meaning because meaning is very concrete, existing in the form of image-schemas. The most serious potential for breakdown in intercultural communication exists at the semiotic level; notice how far apart Symbol 1 and Symbol 2 are. At this level, meaning is more abstract because of the conventional relation between symbols and reality. As a result, meanings of the world, incorporated in cultural worldviews and mediated by language symbols, can appear very different. It takes more effort to understand such meanings and reach common ground, but such efforts are more important and rewarding.

The higher the level of meaning, the more effort it takes to reach common ground, because there is more ground to cover. Meaning becomes more abstract and culture-specific because we look less closely at the world in general and more closely at the real conditions under which cultural symbols are used—that is, at the different cultural worlds.

In the spiral of intercultural communication, different levels and forms of meaning representation are interconnected, so interpretation can move both down and up. It is possible to express and understand any meaning in intercultural communication because we can move freely along this spiral, representing abstract and new experiences through familiar and concrete ones. When we cannot understand a new and abstract message, we simply go down and identify experiences in terms of image-schemas. For instance, the two different views of time discussed earlier—polychronic and monochronic—are based on the same image-schema of movement. That is why people from polychronic and monochronic cultures can understand each other's worldviews and communicate with each other successfully.

Once we understand or create a new concept, we can label it with a new symbol (or symbols), thus getting back to the highest (semiotic) level. For example, from the image-schema of verticality it is but one step to such concepts as "up," "happiness," "down," and "sadness," and one more step to such common expressions (made up of symbols) as "My mood sank" and "I'm feeling up today."

So, what are the implications of all this?

The Implications of Commensurability

Possibility of Intercultural Communication. Let's take the example of John, a businessman from Australia who is visiting culture X. People from that culture have never seen a watch or a clock, and their language has no word for "time." Before he leaves, John hands his friends from culture X a box and says, "Please take this watch as a gift." The question is, Will they be able to understand him? Based on the commensurability principle, this question is answered positively. If a symbol or concept is present in one culture but absent from another culture, communication between people from these two cultures is still possible because of the commensurability of meaning, which is a dynamic construct; meaning can be constructed and expressed with the help of different symbols.

How is the new experience of opening the box and seeing a strange object (a watch) handled in our example? This experience is certainly unfamiliar to the people from culture X—it is not part of their culture. The meaning of this object can be understood, however, in terms of something familiar, which is found in concrete experiences. These experiences are represented in the form of the movement image-schema (path-goal-destination). It might take a while (and a lot of creativity) for John or someone else to explain how the movement of a watch resembles the movement of the sun; other semiotic systems of symbols may have to be used (pictures, gestures). But eventually the people from culture X will figure out what this strange object does; they will understand its conceptual meaning. Then they will find a symbol (or symbols) in their language or create a new symbol (or symbols) for this object. This, too, might take a while (and a lot of creativity); for example, what is called a *watch* in English might be called *little sun* or *moving hands* in the language of culture X. Eventually, the people from culture X will start using this symbol (or these symbols) in creating new messages—that is, in communicating among themselves and with others.

The point is that successful intercultural communication does take place. Meaning is understood by mapping from one domain (John's culture) onto another domain (culture X). Now communication between these two cultures should run more smoothly because people from both cultures have symbols to denote the object (watch). Later, culture X might develop a very different view of this segment of the world, as the sign for moving hands might acquire different meanings. For instance, the watch given by John as a sincere gift might ruin the traditional fabric of culture X, causing conflicts or the deterioration of relationships. Thus, what in the Western culture is an indispensable object might become an object of contention in culture X. In other words, the symbolic meanings of this object in these two cultures might become quite different; nonetheless, at the basic corporeal level, its meaning remains the same.

Thus, in intercultural communication, gaps in meaning get bigger as we move from the corporeal to the cognitive to the semiotic level. The same segment of reality (e.g., a watch) is always represented with the help of different symbols and seen from two different positions; it cannot be otherwise. People from different cultures try to reach common ground in communicating with each other in spite of—or because of—their differences. In this sense, intercultural communication is not simply possible; it is essential.

Necessity of Intercultural Communication. You might remember that Sapir and Whorf's ideas are often taken as a rationalization for cultural incommensurability and the potential failure of intercultural communication. However, such implications go against the thrust of linguistic relativity. The main implication of the commensurability principle, based in part on the ideas of linguistic relativity, is that different cultures present equally valid experiences of the world (worldviews). Communication between people from different cultures is not only possible; it is essential. Through communication, people find out how they measure up against each other. This way, each culture does not simply learn about other worldviews; it gains a better understanding of its own view of the world as well. It was Whorf's hope that "a full awareness of linguistic relativity might lead to humbler attitudes about the supposed superiority of standard average European languages and to a greater disposition to accept a 'brotherhood of thought' among men" (Zhifang, 2002: 164). Similarly, one of the main implications of the commensurability principle is that different cultures not only can but must be compared with each other through communication. As a result, each culture is supposed to learn about other ways of seeing the world, to borrow what it needs and to reject what it does not, while also sharing its own meanings with people from other cultures. Thus, each culture tests its own standing in this world and adjusts its own position.

Manifestation of Meaning in Intercultural Communication. In intercultural communication, each culture tries to figure out and represent new experiences. Once these experiences have been figured out and represented, they become part of the culture—that is, are grounded. It is possible to draw a parallel between the figure/ground distinction discussed in Chapter 4 and the two broad categories introduced by Whorf, called "Manifested" and "Manifesting." The **Manifested category** comprises all that has been accessible to senses and represented by culture. The **Manifesting category** covers "the striving of purposeful desire, intelligent in character, toward manifestation—a manifestation which is much resisted and delayed, but in some form or other is inevitable" (Whorf, 1956: 60). The Manifested category can be said to comprise all meanings that are established (ground); the Manifesting category can be said to comprise meanings that appear in intercultural communication in the form of new experiences (figure).

Coming back to the example of John and his new friends from culture X, the meaning of a watch is part of the Manifested 1/Ground 1 segment of John's culture (see Figure 11). For his new friends, the watch appears as a new experience—Manifesting/Figure. Once understood, this meaning is translated (mapped out) into culture X and becomes part of its worldview, too—Manifested 2/ Ground 2. Intercultural communication can be seen as an attempt to figure out a new experience, or a certain figure—in our example, a watch. In this process, meanings are manifested, or translated from one culture to another. In this sense, "translation is not simply a matter of matching sentences in the abstract, but of learning to live another form of life and to speak another kind of language" (Asad, 1986: 149).

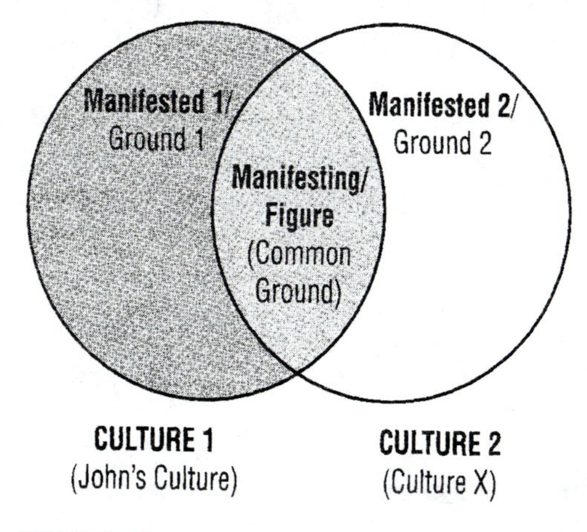

FIGURE 11

Experiences are never figured out in the exact same way; common ground does not comprise identical meanings for people from different cultures. No matter how similar cultural meanings might be, they are still part of different worldviews (different cultural positions). The discrepancy between meanings might be very small, but it is always present. In intercultural communication, this gap is continually filled in. But cultures develop, new gaps appear, and the spiral of meaning continues. In the next two chapters, we will have more to say about what drives this spiral of meaning, as we look more closely at the dynamics of intercultural communication. Right now, let's define the Commensurability Principle.

The Commensurability Principle Defined

Now we can give a more concise formulation of the Commensurability Principle, based on the above discussion of its three parts.

First, the nature of commensurability is dynamic. At its core is human ability to bring the world, symbol, and mind together in a meaningful way. Commensurability is a general human capacity that is realized in every act of intercultural communication.

Second, commensurability is realized at three levels of meaning representation. At the low (corporeal, most concrete) level, meaning is manifested in the form of image-schemas; at the intermediate (cognitive) level, meaning is manifested in the form of concepts; and at the high (semiotic, most abstract) level, meaning is manifested in the form of symbols.

Third, intercultural communication can be seen as a spiral process, in which people from different cultures compare their maps. In this process, meanings are manifested and cultural lacunas are filled in. This way, people measure themselves against one another and understand better other worldviews and their own worldview. Thus, both the possibility and the necessity of intercultural communication are emphasized.

In a nutshell, the Commensurability Principle can be formulated as follows:

> *Intercultural communication is a process whereby people from different cultures compare their maps and search for common ground, using the same forms and levels of meaning representation.*

Now we know that there are three main forms and levels of meaning representation that make intercultural communication not only possible, but necessary. Thus, we now understand that intercultural communication can and must be measured according to some general standards.

Summary

In this chapter, we set out to answer the question of whether there is something general that makes intercultural communication possible in principle. To answer this question, we looked at intercultural communication as a process whereby people with different systems of resources come into contact, generating meaning.

We looked at meaning from three different perspectives: semiotic, cognitive, and corporeal. First, we showed how meaning can be interpreted in terms of language symbols (semiotic look). Second, we showed how meaning can be interpreted in terms of concepts (cognitive look). Third, we showed how meaning can be interpreted in terms of image-schemas (corporeal look). At the same time, meaning cannot be interpreted as encapsulated only in symbols, concepts, or image-schemas. We emphasized that meaning is a process of bringing these three components together. As a result, any meaning can be conceived, constructed, and expressed.

Thus, image-schemas, concepts, and symbols were identified as the three forms of cultural commensurability. We showed how these forms of commensurability represent the world at three different levels—corporeal (most concrete), cognitive (intermediate), and semiotic (most abstract). We emphasized that these forms and levels of commensurability act together to form meaning.

We also discussed the implications of commensurability. We noted that, based on the forms and levels identified in the chapter, intercultural communication is possible in principle. At the same time, we emphasized that the general forms and levels are still relative to a specific cultural position; as a result, meaning in intercultural communication is never interpreted in exactly the same way by people from different cultures. We saw that people from different cultures try to reach common ground in communicating with each other not only in spite of, but also because of, their differences. Thus, we noted that intercultural communication is not simply possible; it is essential. We emphasized the necessity of intercultural communication as a process of meaning manifestation. In this process, people from different cultures measure themselves against one another and better understand other worldviews and their own worldview.

Based on these ideas, the Commensurability Principle was formulated.

We have established the levels and forms of commensurability. Now we know that intercultural communication can and must be measured according to some general standards. You might be somewhat confused, though. On the one hand, it is stated that cultural knowledge is always situated and that every culture looks at the world from a specific point of view; that is, all cultural knowledge is different. On the other hand, cultural knowledge comes down to some general standards; that is, it is the same. Is there a contradiction here? Can we prove that intercultural communication somehow combines both uniqueness and sameness of meaning? We will make this our next problem question.

CASE STUDY
TRANSLATING CULTURAL DIFFERENCES: THE PROBLEM OF *CHOU*

This case study is based on an article entitled "The Untranslatability of Cultural Differences: The Problem of 'Chou'," by Xin Liu Gale (1992). As usual, it is recommended that you read the article in its entirety; below is a summary of the article.

Be ready to identify and then discuss the following topics:

1. Possibility that people from other cultures can understand the meaning of *chou*
2. Possibility of translating the meaning of *chou*
3. Implications of translating *chou*

In the article, Xin Liu Gale examines the Chinese word *chou*. The author claims that it is a unique symbol and that "cultural distinctions codified in the word make the translation of it into English almost impossible" (p. 10). The author aims to show that *chou* has eluded the translators' "grasp as a word and consequently their comprehension as a human emotion" (p. 10).

Xin Liu Gale provides the etymology of the word *chou*, which is associated "both with the change of the seasons and human emotions, a kind of feeling evoked by a season that is characterized by deterioration and depression" (p. 10). Then the author cites a number of poems in which *chou* is used and gives their translations in English. The first poem begins as follows:

> Autumn winds, swish-swish, sorrow killing men.
> Going out: sorrow. Coming in: sorrow.

Xin Liu Gale notes that the translation of *chou* as sorrow

> does not quite convey the subtlety of a feeling that is alien to the Western readers. . . . On the one hand, the feeling of "chou" is so torturous that it can turn one's hair into gray overnight; on the other hand, such sufferings seem to be so necessary for a Chinese upon leaving his home that it is almost a ritual to perform, like a bride is expected to weep really hard before the wedding ceremony. (p. 11)

Later in the article, Xin Liu Gale notes that the word *chou* "embodies not only suffering but also suppression" along with "a yearning for love and freedom" (p. 12). The author admits that "the Chinese language lacks abstract nouns for abstract thinking" so "'chou' perhaps should be considered an exception"; still, the author emphasizes that this word "hardly has an English equivalent" (p. 14). The author insists that "to say that 'chou' is untranslatable may not be an exaggeration," because once translated into English, "it will never evoke the same associations in Western readers as it does in Chinese readers" (p. 15). These translations, according to the author, will never be able to convey such feelings associated with the word *chou* as "loneliness, home-sickness, strange land, the changing phases of nature, and quiet suffering" (p. 15). The author adds that for Chinese the word *chou* means "a split between the mind and the heart, . . . an eternal conflict between the bound body and the free soul" (p. 17). To Western readers, the meaning of *chou* "seems to be extremely simplistic and obvious" (p. 17).

DISCUSSION

Now let us see how this case study can be an illustration of the Commensurability Principle of intercultural communication.

1. Possibility that people from other cultures can understand the meaning of *chou*. The very title of the article claims "the untranslatability of cultural differences"—the impossibility of communication (as far as the segment of reality represented by *chou* is concerned) between Chinese and Western people. Xin Liu Gale states that *chou* conveys an emotion unfamiliar to Western readers. There is a hint that the author may consider Chinese readers superior to Western readers; the latter are unable to understand the subtlety of the symbol *chou*. All the richness and complexity of *chou* is lost on them; their interpretation of the word is simplistic and obvious.

To find out whether the meaning of *chou* is really alien to Western readers, two language systems—Chinese and, in this case, English—must be compared. This comparison reveals that the meaning of *chou* is defined as follows:

> **愁**ㄔㄡˊ 1. to worry; 2. sorrowful; sad; 3. gloomy; saddening. (*Mass modern*, 1988: 1275–1276)

The meaning of *chou*, then, does not appear to be unique; it is represented by such English words as *worry* and *sad*.

The arguments presented in the article go against its very claim and support the fact that the meaning of *chou* is not alien to Western readers. The article states that *chou* is impossible to translate because its meaning cannot be understood by Western readers; then the meaning of *chou* is explicated. In essence, the article says that you cannot understand this word because it means a feeling of being torn between a yearning for happiness and suffering. The very act of explaining what we cannot understand, though, proves that we can, and do, understand it. The article claims that the word *chou* conveys emotions unfamiliar to Western readers; then the following emotions familiar to Western readers are listed: loneliness, home-sickness, strange land, the changing phases of nature, and quiet suffering.

Thus, it appears that Western readers are able to understand the symbol *chou*. The meaning of this word is represented (in English) by a number of different symbols (words and word combinations). There may not be a single language symbol in English to denote the complex meaning of *chou*, but that does not change the fact that this meaning can be expressed and is understandable.

However, what if the author of the article is right, and all the English symbols mentioned above cannot be considered equivalents of *chou*? In other words, what if *chou is* uniquely Chinese, with no symbol or symbols in the English language that represent its meaning? Does this suggest that the strong version of linguistic relativity is correct, and the Chinese have a unique view of the world (as far as *chou* goes) that cannot be understood by Western people? No. If the experience expressed by *chou* is truly new to Western readers, its meaning can still be understood at the corporeal level. If what is missing in our understanding of *chou* is the concept of "an eternal conflict between the bound body and the free soul," the container image-schema might be taken as the source for cultural elaborations. This image-schema consists of an interior and an exterior separated by a boundary and allows us to conceptualize a conflict between the free soul and the bound body. It might take a while for Western readers to grasp this concept (with a lot of help from Chinese). Recall that this is a

(continued)

TRANSLATING CULTURAL DIFFERENCES: THE PROBLEM OF *CHOU* CONTINUED

highly abstract concept, so its meaning is not easy to ground in concrete terms; a number of different situations of its usage may be required to understand its meaning. Once grasped, however, this concept can be expressed in the new language (English).

2. Possibility of translating the meaning of *chou.* If the people of a Western culture feel that, indeed, there is a gap (lacuna) in their cultural system which needs to be filled in, they must find a way to do so. Can they? Yes. There are two basic ways of translating meanings. The first way focuses on a symbol's phonetic or graphic form, and the second way focuses on a symbol's content. The first way works well for simple and/or frequently used symbols that require little interpretation; often, such symbols denote objects that exist in many cultures. As a result, symbols like "McDonald's" and "jeans" are found in many languages, transcribed and/or transliterated according to the rules of their own semiotic systems, of course. The second way works well for more complex symbols, such as "stocks" or "harassment," that are used less often. Usually, these symbols denote specific segments of reality.

If the meaning of *chou* is found to be somewhat exotic but still having a place in a Western culture, it is likely to be introduced into the culture's language in the second way—through content. For instance, *chou* can be translated as "a feeling of anguish resulting from a struggle between liberation and containment" or "eternal conflict between body and soul." (This may not work well, of course, in poetic translations.) If, however, the meaning of *chou* is found to be quite significant by a Western culture and labeling this meaning becomes extremely important, then the translation suggested above will prove too cumbersome. Instead, an attempt can be made to introduce the meaning of *chou* in the first way—through form. As a result, a new English symbol can be created—*chou.* This approach may require (especially initially) some explanation of the symbol's content, which is often done in parentheses after the translation. This explanation is usually included until the symbol becomes familiar and accepted in its new form. Theoretically, this option is as plausible as the other one. For instance, in an article entitled "Linguistic Relativity and Cultural Communication," Zhu Zhifang notes that the "uppermost concept of morality in Chinese culture is 'Ren.' It covers the meaning associated with a number of English terms. It means humanity, universal love, the mercy of sovereignty of its subject, moral goodness, sacrifice for justice" (2002: 168–169). The author entertains the possibility of introducing this foreign term into English: "The term 'Ren' might be adapted to English" (2002: 169).

3. Implications of translating *chou.* The first implication of translating *chou* is that its meaning *can* be understood. It simply would not be translated if the meaning could not be understood. Thus, translating *chou* highlights the commensurability of cultures and the very possibility of intercultural communication. Once the gap, or lacuna, in the English system of symbols is filled in, the potential for misunderstanding between people from two cultures is reduced. It is never eliminated completely, though; *chou* in Chinese and whatever symbol(s) become(s) its equivalent in English, no matter how similar in meaning, will continue to be used by different people in different situations, causing at the very minimum some differences in interpretation. For Chinese, for example, this word is likely to have a stronger, more poignant meaning.

The second implication of translating *chou* is that it *must* be understood. It simply would not be translated if its meaning did not have to be understood. Intercultural communication as mapping of meanings takes place because it allows different cultures to measure themselves against one another. This way, people from different cultures learn about other systems of meaning and their own view of the world. If a Western culture finds the meaning of *chou* equivalent, say, to that of *sorrow* and dismisses the claims of its uniqueness, that culture will feel no need for another symbol to express a familiar emotion. The Chinese then may question their own worldview, thinking "Maybe we read too much into this word. Maybe it is really nothing but the expression of sorrow." Or, more likely, the Chinese culture may reject equating *chou* with *sorrow* and continue to feel alienated from the West (as far as this segment of reality is concerned). If, on the other hand, people from a Western culture find the meaning of *chou* unique (missing from their own conceptual system) and introduce it into their language as a new symbol (or symbols), the Chinese might have a sense of pride, having shared a piece of their worldview with another culture. Thanks to them, the system of meanings of that Western culture has now become more elaborate, and both cultures can navigate the world more successfully.

SIDE TRIPS

1. Palmer (1996: 148–149) describes his ethnographic work with speakers of Yaqui, a Uto-Aztecan language of northern Mexico and southern Arizona. He tells the story of drawing a crude picture of a stick figure and a house, meant to show a man standing by a house. When the picture was presented to Yaqui speakers, they described it, in Yaqui, as "a boy walking by a house." In the same way, a picture of a bee sitting on a wall was described as "the bee crawling on the wall," and a picture of a duck in the water was described as "the duck being carried along on the current."

   Try to prove that communication between speakers of Yaqui and English is possible. Think of some difficulties that may arise in communication between these cultures, considering that "for Yaqui speakers animate images may have greater salience than static images" (Palmer, 1996: 148).
2. The Japanese culture is said to retain a sakoku mentality in its treatment of foreigners. For example, non-Japanese are referred to as "gaijin," meaning people from outside. This term is not considered derogatory, but it still emphasizes the exclusiveness of Japanese attitudes toward outsiders. How might the Japanese sign for "gaijin" be translated into English through form and how through content? You may find the information in section 2 on page 130 helpful in answering this question.
3. In an article entitled "We Are All Americans" in the liberal Spanish newspaper *El País*, Vincente Verdu has this to say about the American influence on other cultures:

   > The American model of life repeats itself like a fractal in the many different aspects of everyday existence, be it communal life, sex, art, or money. . . . American influence consists of a whole bundle of things, of varying degrees of goodness and toxicity. . . . Thanks to the Americans, we have ecology, although the United States did not sign the Kyoto Accord, and thanks to the Americans we have hard-line feminism, militant gays, nontraditional couples, equity within couples, and acceptance of multiculturalism. (2002: 41)

   Can you identify some "distinctly American" concepts and how they are represented with verbal or nonverbal signs in other cultures? An example would be the concept of fast food and its representation by the sign "McDonald's" (verbal) or the golden arches (nonverbal).

CHECK YOURSELF

Symbol
Semiotics
Linguistic relativity
Lacuna
Strong version of linguistic relativity
Weak version of linguistic relativity
Cognitive look
Image-schema
Corporeal look
Manifested category
Manifesting category

REFERENCES

Agar, M. (1994). *Language shock: Understanding the culture of conversation.* New York: William Morrow.

Asad, T. (1986). The concept of cultural translation in British social anthropology. In Clifford, J., & G. Marcus (Eds.), *Writing culture: The poetics and politics of ethnography* (pp. 141–164). Berkeley: University of California Press.

Bergin, T. G., & Fisch, M. (1984). *The new science of Giamnattista Vico.* Ithaca, NY: Cornell University Press.

Boyer, P. (1996). Cognitive limits to conceptual relativity: The limiting-case of religious ontologies. In Gumperz, J., & S. Levinson (Eds.), *Rethinking linguistic relativity* (pp. 203–224). Cambridge, UK: Cambridge University Press.

Bredella, L. (1994). Intercultural understanding between relativism, ethnocentrism and universalism: Preliminary considerations for a theory of intercultural understanding. In Blaicher, G., & B. Glaser (Eds.), *Anglistentag 1993 Eichstatt: Proceedings of the Conference of the German Association of University Teachers of English,* No. 15 (pp. 287–306). Tubingen: Niemeyer.

Danesi, M., & Perron, P. (1999). *Analyzing cultures: An introduction and handbook.* Bloomington: Indiana University Press.

Davis, P., & Hersh, R. (1986). *Descartes' dream: The world according to mathematics.* Boston: Houghton Mifflin.

Gale, X. L. (1992). The untranslatability of cultural differences: The problem of "chou." *Language Quarterly,* Vol. 30, Nos. 3–4, pp. 10–17.

Jandt, F. (2001). *Intercultural communication: An introduction.* Thousand Oaks, CA: Sage.

Johnson, M. (1987). *The body in the mind: The bodily basis of meaning, imagination, and reason.* Chicago: University of Chicago Press.

Keesing, R. (1994). Radical cultural difference: Anthropology's myth? In Putz, M. (Ed.), *Language contact and language conflict* (pp. 3–23). Amsterdam: John Benjamins.

Lakoff, G., & Johnson, M. (1980). *Metaphors we live by.* Chicago: University of Chicago Press.

Lakoff, G., & Johnson, M. (1999). *Philosophy in the flesh: The embodied mind and its challenge to Western thought.* New York: Basic.

Levi-Strauss, C. (1985). *The view from afar.* Oxford: Blackwell.

Mass modern Chinese-English dictionary. (1988). Taipei: Wan ren chu ban she.

Morris, E. (Ed.). (1982). *The American Heritage dictionary of the English language.* Boston: Houghton Mifflin.

Morris, J. (2002). Home thoughts from abroad. *Atlantic Monthly,* November, pp. 136–138.

Neuliep. J. (2000). *Intercultural communication: A contextual approach.* Boston: Houghton Mifflin.

Palmer, G. (1996). *Toward a theory of cultural linguistics.* Austin: University of Texas Press.

Pinxten, R. (1976). Epistemic universals: A contribution to cognitive anthropology. *Universalism versus relativism in language and thought: Proceedings of a colloquium on the Sapir-Whorf hypothesis* (pp. 117–176). The Hague: Mouton.

Sapir, E. (1964). Conceptual categories in primitive languages. In Hymes, D. (Ed.), *Language in culture and society: A reader in linguistics and anthropology.* New York: Harper and Row.

Sebeok, T., & Danesi, M. (2000). *The forms of meaning: Modeling systems theory and semiotic analysis.* Berlin: Mouton de Greytor.

Steinfatt, T. M. (1989). Linguistic relativity: Toward a broader view. *International and Intercultural Association Annual,* Vol. 13, pp. 35–75.

Turner, M. (1996). *Reading minds: The study of English in the age of cognitive science.* Princeton, NJ: Princeton University Press.

Verdu, V. (2002). We are all Americans. *El País,* April 27, reprinted in English in *The World Press,* July, p. 41.

Wason, P., & Johnson-Laird, P. (Eds.). (1977). *Thinking.* Cambridge, UK: Cambridge University Press.

Weiss, T. (1987). Reading culture. *Journal of Business and Technical Communication,* Vol. 11, No. 3, pp. 321–339.

Whorf, B. (1956). *Language, thought and reality: Selected writings of Benjamin Lee Whorf.* Cambridge, MA: MIT Press.

Wiredu, K. (1995). Are there cultural universals? *The Monist,* Vol. 78, No. 1, pp. 52–64.

Zhifang, Z. (2002). Linguistic relativity and cultural communication. *Educational Philosophy and Theory,* Vol. 34, No. 2, pp. 161–170.

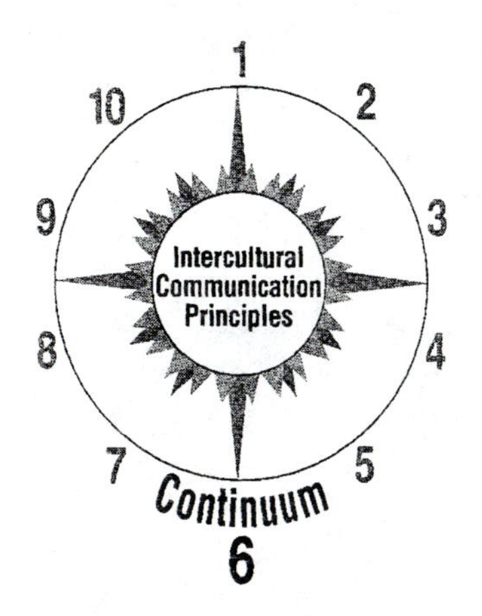

CHAPTER SIX

CREATING A SHARED INTERCULTURAL SPACE: CONTINUUM PRINCIPLE

Having It Both Ways.

- *Key Theme:* Distance
- *Key Objective:* To help you understand how people from different cultures form one continuous space

INTRODUCING THE PROBLEM QUESTION

GLOBAL CULTURAL DIMENSIONS: HOW MANY?

INTRODUCING THE CONTINUUM PRINCIPLE

Overcoming Binary Thinking

Intercultural Continuum and Digital Communication

Intercultural Continuum and Analogic Communication

THE CONTINUUM PRINCIPLE DEFINED

SUMMARY

CASE STUDY: THE 1999 COCA-COLA SCARE IN EUROPE

SIDE TRIPS

CHECK YOURSELF

REFERENCES

Introducing the Problem Question

In Chapter 4 (the Positionality Principle), we learned that every culture projects its gaze into the world and back to itself. As a result, cultural meanings are grounded (positioned). In Chapter 5 (the Commensurability Principle), we learned that intercultural communication can be explained with the help of general forms and levels of meaning. These two chapters seem to contradict each other: One states that cultural meanings are all specific (unique), while the other argues for general (same) cultural meanings. How can we find our way out of this seeming contradiction? Can we somehow reconcile the arguments put forward in Chapters 4 and 5? Can we have it both ways?

The problem question for this chapter is this: *Can we prove that intercultural communication somehow combines both uniqueness and sameness of meaning?*

In this chapter we will

- Discuss a number of global cultural dimensions
- Show why it is important to overcome binary thinking in intercultural communication
- Present intercultural interactions as a form of digital communication
- Present intercultural interactions as a form of analogic communication
- Show how people from different cultures create a shared continuous space while interacting.

Global Cultural Dimensions: How Many?

Let's begin by looking at some meanings usually presented as global cultural dimensions. These meaningful variables are very broad (hence, "global"), apply to all cultures (hence, "cultural"), and can be used for measuring cultures (hence, "dimensions").

In the past several decades, researchers have identified a number of global cultural dimensions (Hofstede, 1980, 1991; Schwartz, 1994). Based on this research, Kashima and Kashima (1998), for example, discuss the following dimensions:

- Individualism/Collectivism
- Power Distance
- Uncertainty Avoidance
- Masculinity/Femininity
- Integration
- Confucian Work Dynamism
- Human Heartedness
- Moral Discipline
- Conservatism
- Affective Autonomy
- Intellectual Autonomy

- Hierarchy
- Egalitarian Commitment
- Mastery
- Harmony
- Achievement
- Universalism
- Paternalism
- Involvement

Hampden-Turner and Trompenaars (2000) isolate the following dimensions of cultural variability:

- Universalism/Particularism
- Individualism/Communitarianism
- Specificity/Diffusion
- Achieved Status/Ascribed Status
- Inner Direction/Outer Direction
- Sequential Time/Synchronous Time

To these lists other dimensions are added, such as the so-called Big Five dimensions that link personality and culture—the variables of Neuroticism, Extraversion, Openness, Agreeableness, and Conscientiousness (Marsella et al., 2000). In other research (Keating et al., 2002), yet more dimensions are proposed, such as Performance Orientation (Do cultures reward achievement of excellence?) and Future Orientation (Do cultures encourage future-oriented behaviors, such as planning and investing?).

These dimensions are all globally concerned with how people solve different tasks—for example, how they deal with time (Future Orientation), with work (Confucian Work Dynamism), with inequality (Hierarchy, Power Distance), and with groups (Individualism/Collectivism). By taking the example of global cultural dimensions, we will begin to answer the problem question posed above. Below, we look at several dimensions that are most frequently discussed in intercultural communication texts. The question "How Many?" in the heading of this section does not refer to the total number of global cultural dimensions. As you must have noticed, this number varies from researcher to researcher. The question refers to the number of the dimensions we are about to discuss; at the end of this section you will be asked to answer this question, so be prepared. This question is not as easy to answer as it might appear at first glance.

The global cultural dimensions we will discuss in this section are concerned with certain tasks that people face: how to respond to the group, how to respond to authority, how to respond to gender roles, how to respond to ambiguity, and how to respond to messages. The corresponding global dimensions are Individualism/Collectivism, Power Distance, Masculinity/Femininity, Uncertainty Avoidance, and High-Context/Low-Context Communication. The dimensions of Individualism/Collectivism, Power Distance, Masculinity/Femininity, and Uncertainty Avoidance are based on Hofstede's cross-cultural data, gathered from questionnaires administered to the employees of the multinational corporation IBM (1980, 1991). Hofstede's research is sometimes criticized for having been developed within an organizational setting and having a Western or Eurocentric orientation (Calori, 1994; Degabriele, 2000). However, it is generally considered that "the importance of Hofstede's work cannot be overestimated" (Gannon, 2001: 51) and that his "large scale empirical study in 40 countries retains benchmark status" (Keating et al., 2002: 634). The concept of High-Context/Low-Context Communication is based on Hall's ideas (1976) and can be found in most, if not all, intercultural communication textbooks.

Individualism/Collectivism. The concepts of **Individualism** and **Collectivism** describe the degree to which people are integrated into groups. In individualistic cultures, "the ties between individuals are loose: everyone is expected to look after himself or herself and the immediate family" (Hofstede & Bond, 2001: 37; Triandis, 1995). In collectivistic cultures, on the other hand, "people from birth onward are integrated into strong, cohesive ingroups; often their extended families (with uncles, aunts, and grandparents) continue protecting them in exchange for unquestioning loyalty" (Hofstede & Bond, 2001: 37). Based on Hofstede's research, the category of individualistic cultures usually includes such countries as the United States and France, while the category of collectivistic cultures includes such countries as Brazil and Mexico. In individualistic cultures, behaviors are aimed at self-realization. In collectivistic cultures, on the other hand, people have an emotional dependence on institutions and organizations because they provide security and reward loyalty; there, behaviors aimed at self-realization may be seen as selfish. Subtle clashes between individualistic and collectivistic cultures are revealed in interviews for entry-level positions in Anglo-American multinational corporations. Chinese applicants from Singapore, for example, tend to focus on the group or family, besides being averse to self-assertion (Wong, 2000). Unless interviewers are aware of this tendency, they may not hire a strong candidate, failing to differentiate between cultural background and potential to perform work duties successfully.

Power Distance. The concept of **Power Distance** describes the degree to which people accept and expect that power is distributed unequally. Inequalities exist between people in every culture with respect to social status, prestige, and wealth; hence, high power distance and low power distance cultures can be isolated. The category of high power distance cultures usually includes such countries as India and Brazil, while the category of low power distance cultures includes such countries as Finland and Israel. In high power distance cultures, people tend to accept—with little justification—a hierarchical order with an established authority. In low power distance cultures, on the other hand, people tend to search for equality and question authority, demanding justification for any existing inequalities. In high power distance cultures, for instance, conspicuous consumption is often used to display power and status, while in low power distance cultures individuals who occupy positions of authority try to minimize inequalities between themselves and less powerful individuals, avoiding conspicuous displays of wealth. The success of empowering practices used by United States–based corporations in other countries depends on the degree of power distance in those cultures, since empowerment implies sharing of authority. Marchese (2001) found that the empowerment practices of a U.S. company were quite successful in Poland, whereas employees in India had negative reactions to such practices. Therefore, continuing with such practices may cause more harm than good in India.

Masculinity/Femininity. The concepts of **Masculinity** and **Femininity** describe the degree to which individuals' gender roles are emphasized (e.g., men are seen as breadwinners and soldiers, and women as homemakers and teachers) and also the degree to which masculine values (e.g., ambition, achievement, and competitiveness) and feminine values (e.g., nurturing, caring for others, and environmental concerns) are emphasized. The category of masculine cultures usually includes such countries as Japan and Mexico, while the category of feminine cultures includes such countries as Taiwan and Brazil. People from feminine cultures, for example, are more likely to expect government policies that ease the burden of leaving one's job to bear a child and then returning to work. If they marry into a masculine culture where such policies and services are insufficient or absent, this may put pressure on the intercultural relationship.

Uncertainty Avoidance. The concept of **Uncertainty Avoidance** describes the degree to which people feel uncomfortable in ambiguous, unstructured situations. " 'Unstructured situations' are defined as novel, unknown, surprising, or different from usual" (Hofstede & Bond, 2001: 38). People in uncertainty-avoiding cultures are intolerant of such unstructured situations and try to control ambiguity at all costs; "uncertainty-avoiding cultures try to minimize the possibility of such situations by adhering to strict laws and rules, safety and security measures" (Hofstede & Bond, 2001: 38). People in uncertainty-accepting cultures, on the other hand, are tolerant of ambiguity and often welcome it. In other words, "uncertainty-accepting cultures are more tolerant of behavior and opinions that differ from their own; they try to have as few rules as possible, and on the philosophical and religious level they are relativist, allowing many currents to flow side by side" (Hofstede & Bond, 2001: 38). The category of uncertainty-avoiding cultures usually includes such countries as Japan and France, while the category of uncertainty-accepting cultures includes such countries as the United States and Finland. People in uncertainty-accepting cultures are more tolerant of foreigners.

High-Context/Low-Context Communication. The concept of High-Context/Low-Context Communication refers to how people construct messages. Every message is made up of two parts: information called text, vested in a language code, and everything that surrounds the message (e.g., physical surrounding), called context. Thus, the concept of **High-Context/Low-Context Communication** describes the degree to which information in a message is contextualized.

> A high-context (HC) communication or message is one in which most of the information is either in the physical context or internalized in the person, while very little is in the coded, explicit, transmitted part of the message. A low-context (LC) communication is just the opposite; i.e., the mass of the information is vested in the explicit code. (Hall, 1976: 91)

People in high-context cultures do not emphasize the use of written or oral forms of expression, relying more on context—for instance, knowledge of relationship. As a result, they expect more from their interlocutors, who must put all the pieces in the interaction in place. The category of low-context communication cultures usually includes such countries as the United States and Germany, and the category of high-context communication cultures usually includes such countries as Japan and China.

These two types of communication are illustrated very well in the training video "Crosstalk: Performance Appraising Across Cultures" (1991) featuring a series of goal-setting performance-appraisal interviews between individuals from low-context and high-context cultures. In this video, individuals from low-context cultures start their interview

> with a conclusion: I did well during this past year, and here are the actions justifying this self-appraisal. In contrast, the high-context subordinates refuse to offer an initial conclusion and merely describe the situation during the past year and the activities they undertook in response to it; this description should be so accurate that the conclusion naturally emerges, and it is the responsibility of the superior to decide whether the performance warrants a salary increase based on this description and other facts known to him or her. (Gannon, 2001: 28)

For successful intercultural communication, it is important to understand all these global dimensions. For example, if you work as a financial consultant, you should remember that global dimensions are a factor in cultures' willingness to accept the risk of international stock exchanges. Riahi-Belkaoui noted that cultures where "people accept a hierarchical order in which everybody has a place that needs no justification, are expected to take care of themselves and their immediate family, and are tolerant of ambiguity" have strong conditions for high systematic risk (1998: 107). Similarly, if you work for an international advertising agency, knowledge of the main global cultural dimensions will help you to use the right rhetorical appeal in your message. For instance, in tailoring your message for uncertainty-accepting cultures you may want to stress adventure, while for high-power distance cultures you may want to stress the ornamental and status character of the product (Albers-Miller & Gelb, 1996).

So, How Many? The importance and usefulness of global dimensions in intercultural communication cannot be overestimated. However, our main task here is not so much to discuss these dimensions as to find the answer to the problem question posed at the beginning of the chapter; we must find out if intercultural communication somehow combines both the uniqueness and the sameness of meaning. Before we consider the answer to that question, though, let's see if you can answer another question: How many global cultural dimensions were discussed above? On the one hand, we made finding the right answer more difficult for you by discussing concepts rather than dimensions. On the other hand, we provided several clues along the way that should help you to answer the question. So how many global cultural dimensions did we just discuss?

It is tempting to simply count all the terms that denote different concepts and identify them with dimensions. Thus, one possible answer to the question of how many seems to be 10:

1. Individualism
2. Collectivism
3. High Power Distance
4. Low Power Distance
5. Masculinity
6. Femininity
7. Uncertainty-Avoiding
8. Uncertainty-Accepting
9. High-Context Communication
10. Low-Context Communication

But, as was mentioned earlier, concepts and dimensions are not the same. In fact, each dimension is made up of two concepts. Thus, the correct answer to the question of how many is 5:

1. Individualism/Collectivism
2. High Power Distance/Low Power Distance
3. Masculinity/Femininity
4. Uncertainty-Avoiding/Uncertainty-Accepting
5. High-Context Communication/Low-Context Communication

Did you notice the clues we provided? For instance, we mentioned that the global cultural dimensions are concerned with how people accomplish different tasks, and we listed five specific tasks: how people respond to the group (Individualism/Collectivism dimension), how people respond to authority (High Power Distance/Low Power Distance dimension), how people respond to traditional gender roles and masculine/feminine values (Masculinity/Femininity dimension), how people respond to ambiguity (Uncertainty-Avoidance/Uncertainty-Acceptance dimension), and how people respond to messages (High-Context Communication/

Low-Context Communication dimension). Also, we used such expressions as "on the one hand" and "on the other hand," suggesting that one concept—say, Masculinity—cannot exist without the other—Femininity. It takes two concepts to form a global cultural dimension. Within each dimension, *both* concepts exist at the same time.

And now it is time to introduce the Continuum Principle of intercultural communication.

Introducing the Continuum Principle

In order to see how it is possible to approach intercultural communication from this new angle, we will formulate the sixth principle underlying intercultural communication—the Continuum Principle. As usual, we will isolate three parts that make up this principle. Each part deals with the shared and continuous nature of intercultural interactions. First, we will discuss why it is important to overcome binary thinking. Next, we will discuss the intercultural continuum and digital communication. Finally, we will discuss the intercultural continuum and analogic communication. We will present each part separately and then formulate the Continuum Principle as a whole.

Overcoming Binary Thinking

It is not easy for people to come to terms with the idea of two concepts existing together. We are used to **binary thinking,** which divides everything into two separate entities (Hermans & Kempen, 1998). We like seeing things as either black or white, since such a view is so clear! According to this view, the world is made up of friends and enemies, cultures are either modern ("good") or primitive ("bad"), and so forth. This binary view is credited to René Descartes, who saw people either biologically, as bodies, or cognitively, as minds. You might remember from the previous chapter, though, that these two entities—body and mind—cannot really be separated, as they both contribute to the same task: constructing and interpreting meaning. Similarly, even though we can talk about the separate right and left hemispheres of the brain, in reality both hemispheres are needed for us to function normally; their joint activity (communication, in a way!) allows us to be creative and solve tasks. And, of course, although we can speak separately of either culture A or culture B, every culture can understand itself only through the eyes of another culture (as we discussed in Chapter 1). Thus, both cultures A and B are needed for these cultures to exist "separately." So, it is necessary to go beyond binary thinking. It is crucial that we learn how to stop seeing the world only in terms of two separate entities, whether these entities are the hemispheres of the brain, global cultural dimensions, or cultures themselves. We must learn to see the world in a more complex way, replacing "either/or" with "both/and." This shift in our thinking will

FIGURE 1 A Continuum

help us to gain a new insight into intercultural communication, seeing that it, indeed, combines both the uniqueness and the sameness of meaning.

The idea of overcoming binary thinking is captured in the concept of a continuum. You must have heard the word *continuum* used in expressions such as "it must be viewed on a continuum" or "it is only one side of the continuum." But have you really thought about what *continuum* means? The concept of a continuum is quite complex and extremely useful for our understanding of intercultural communication.

Continuum is defined as "a continuous extent, succession, or whole, no part of which can be distinguished from neighboring parts except by arbitrary division" (Morris, 1982: 289). A simple line is an example of a continuum. It can be divided into (at least) two parts, point A and point B, and it is continuous (whole). Figure 1 is an illustration of a continuum.

A continuum can be understood as a topological space that has certain characteristics. **Topology** is defined as "the study of the properties of geometric configurations invariant under transformation by continuous mapping" (Morris, 1982: 1355). Don't let this definition scare you; when we speak of something as a topological space, we simply mean that it remains stable, identical to itself (invariant) under change. Intercultural communication can be seen as a topological space or a continuum: It is continuously transformed, yet remains the same. To better understand intercultural communication as a continuum, we must discuss its two main characteristics—connectedness and compactness.

First of all, a continuum is a connected space. To put it simply, a continuum is a number of points, all connected with one another. As was shown above, we get a continuum by dividing something into parts, such as points A and B. For example, we can divide a global cultural dimension into two points—"individualistic" (point A) and "collectivistic" (point B). However, the line that divides the continuum into two parts, the left half and the right half, is itself a point where *both* parts (left and right) intersect. This division point (let's call it point X) is, in fact, part of the whole space; in this case, the space is formed by the individualistic/collectivistic dimension. Figure 2 illustrates the connected nature of a continuum.

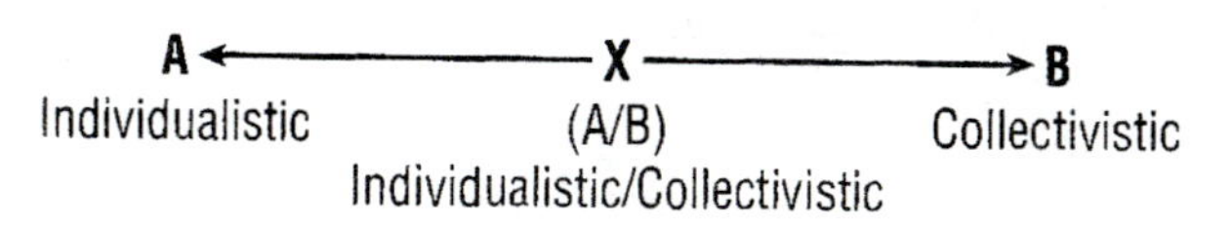

FIGURE 2

The concept of a continuum allows us to stop seeing the world in terms of only two separate entities, providing us with a more complex vision. This vision makes it possible for us to see both sides of the picture, as illustrated in Figure 3.

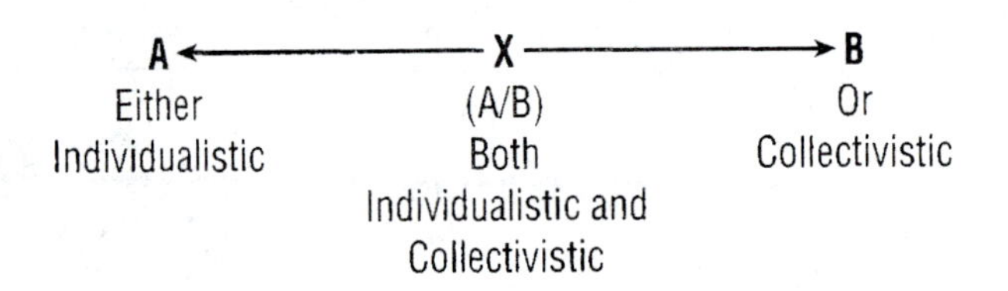

FIGURE 3

Thus, a continuum as a topological space consists of parts, each of which contains other parts; it is a continuous succession of points, or one whole meaning. It is tempting to argue that, because no part can be distinguished from neighboring parts except by arbitrary division, there is little difference among the various points along a continuum. This argument is sometimes called the Bald Man Fallacy. Advocates for the legalization of drugs employ this approach when they argue that many drugs are already legally consumed (e.g., caffeine and alcohol), and it is absolutely arbitrary to legalize some drugs but not others. The fallacy behind this argument (see Ramey, 2002) is that, although it may be impossible to find the exact dividing line between legitimate and illegitimate drug usage, this does not mean that there is no difference between drinking coffee and using LSD. Similarly, we cannot specify exactly when a man goes from not bald to bald, but we can tell the difference between a bald and a nonbald man.

In intercultural communication we can generally avoid falling into the trap of applying this fallacy because we can usually tell the difference between such cultural behaviors as "sticking one's neck out for nobody" and "going an extra mile for people." The first behavior is definitely closer to the individualistic part of the continuum, while the second behavior is closer to its collectivistic part. Figure 4 shows where these two behaviors can be placed (approximately) on the individualistic/collectivistic continuum. It must be emphasized that each of these be-

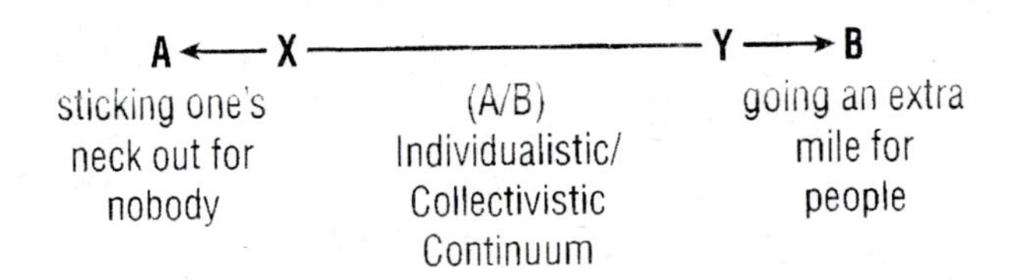

FIGURE 4

haviors, designated as new points X and Y on the continuum, contains *both* parts A *and* B (individualism and collectivism). The two behaviors X and Y are unique only as different points (positions) along the same continuum representing the global meaning of individualism/collectivism. It is appropriate, therefore, to discuss cultural behavior not in terms of "either/or" (e.g., either individualistic or collectivistic), but in terms of "both/and" and "more/less." For instance, "sticking one's neck out for nobody" is more individualistic and less collectivistic, and "going an extra mile for people" is more collectivistic and less individualistic. Notice, however, that each behavior contains *both* individualistic *and* collectivistic features; the difference between them is just a matter of distance or degree. Thus, rather than saying that France is individualistic and Brazil is collectivistic, it is more accurate to say that France has a more individualistic (and less collectivistic) culture than Brazil, while Brazil has a more collectivistic (and less individualistic) culture than France. A continuum is formed by two ultimate parts together.

Connectedness is only one characteristic of a continuum. The other important characteristic of a continuum is compactness. A continuum is not simply a space whose points are all connected; this space must be compact, or bounded. Compactness means that a continuum is a closed space. An infinite straight line is an example of a continuum that is connected, but not closed (compact). "It is, however, possible to compactify an infinite straight line by adding a point at infinity" (Johanson, 2001: 2); this way, a straight line returns on itself and creates a circle. Figure 5 shows the individualistic/collectivistic continuum as a circle.

The continuum in Figure 5 is both connected and compact (bounded). It represents a space that is infinitely divisible into parts. Figure 6 shows the bounded continuum divided into two ultimate parts that have a point of intersection, forming a shape much like that of an infinity symbol.

Thus, the continuum was transformed from a straight line into a circle, which was then divided into two ultimate parts represented by the infinity symbol. What could be more continuous than infinity?

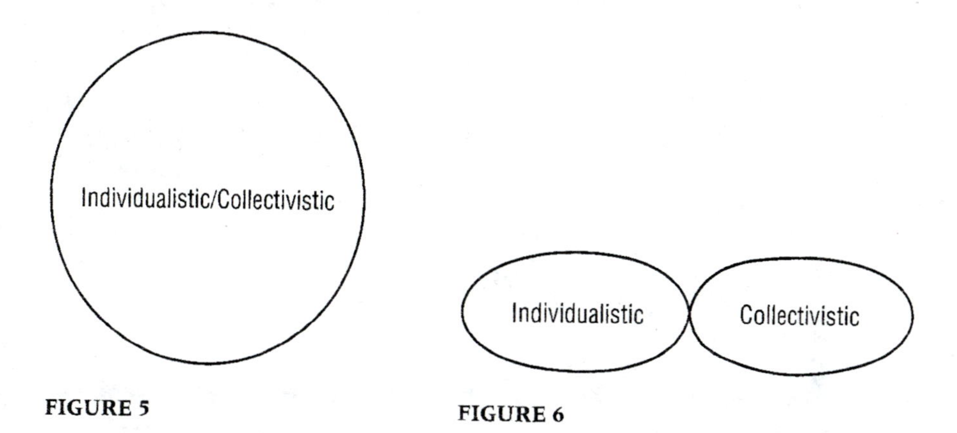

FIGURE 5

FIGURE 6

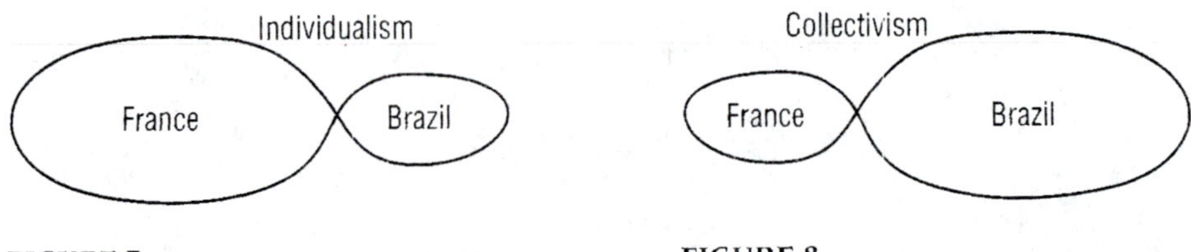

FIGURE 7

FIGURE 8

If we want, for example, to compare France and Brazil on the individualistic/collectivistic continuum, we need to address both these concepts. First, France must be shown as a more individualistic culture and Brazil as a less individualistic culture, as in Figure 7. But Figure 7 does not take into account the other half of the concept—the collectivistic part. So, second, Brazil must be shown as a more collectivistic culture and France as a less collectivistic culture, as in Figure 8. The complete picture of the comparison between France and Brazil along the individualistic/collectivistic continuum must contain both these parts, as shown in Figure 9.

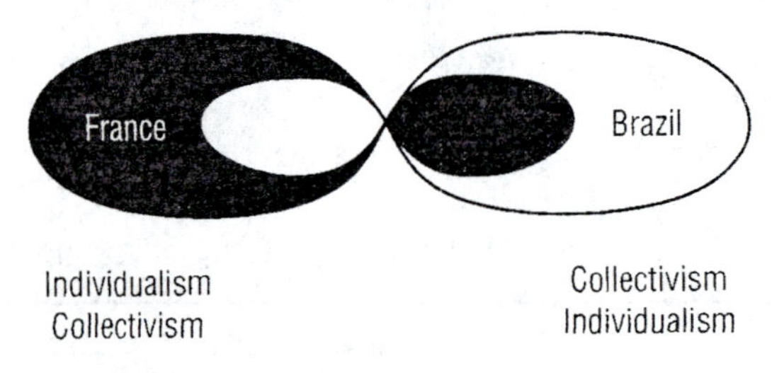

FIGURE 9

Does Figure 9 remind you of the famous Taoistic Yin and Yang symbol shown in Figure 10? Like the picture in Figure 9, the Yin and Yang symbol shows two different sides changing over to each other and sharing qualities. In the next chapter, we will learn more about what makes the sides change over to each other and the intercultural communication spiral move in both directions. Then our understanding of intercultural communication will become more dynamic. Right now, let's return to our discussion of the Continuum Principle.

FIGURE 10

Intercultural Continuum and Digital Communication

Human communication messages "can either be represented by a likeness, such as a drawing, or they can be referred to by a name. . . . These two types of communication . . . are . . . equivalent to the concepts of the analogic and the digital respectively" (Watzlawick et al., 1967: 61–62).

Digital communication can be equated with a system of distinct and separate symbols (digits) that point to meaning. Each such symbol can be viewed as a name representing a certain meaning. A good representation of this form of communication is a digital clock (Figure 11). Each digit has a certain conventional meaning—for example, 3:00 stands for a certain point in time (three o'clock). In this sense, "words are similar to digits; they have specific beginning and ending points and arbitrarily represent something else" (Neuliep, 1996: 296).

Let's look at intercultural communication from this digital perspective, to see what separate symbols (digits) can represent the meanings of our attitudes toward the Other. As you may remember from Chapter 4, an attitude is an evaluative response to something—negative, positive, or neutral (Davidson & Thompson, 1980; Peng, 1974). In the process of intercultural communication, we all respond to the Other's actions, developing certain attitudes.

One of the negative attitudes toward the Other is found in **discrimination** —a distinct symbol that refers to a biased action whereby people from another culture are treated disadvantageously. Unfortunately, we know too many examples of discrimination—racism, sexism, ageism, and so forth. Another negative attitude is represented by **disparagement**—derogating or discrediting the Other. People who have such negative attitudes often do not want to admit it, even to themselves (let alone the Other!). As a result, they engage in relatively effortless behaviors such as donating a small amount of money to persuade the Other (and themselves!) that their attitude is not negative. Such behaviors are considered to be a form of **tokenism** (Brislin, 1993: 189); usually, they fail to conceal the fact that the attitude toward the Other is still negative. Also, a negative attitude can be represented by **avoidance,** which involves simply staying away from the Other. This attitude is still negative because it does not reduce the distance between Self and the Other. Often, such an attitude is manifested in so-called **arm's-length prejudice**—engaging in positive behaviors toward people from other cultures only in certain settings (Brislin, 1993: 191). This term speaks for itself: One draws a negative line between one's culture and the Other, holding the Other at arm's length.

FIGURE 11

One of the positive attitudes toward the Other is found in **sensitivity**—being susceptible to the circumstances of the Other. At this point, one is capable of receiving or admitting the Other into one's world. If our attitude is that of sensitivity, intercultural interaction has a much better chance of success because differences are discussed openly and not avoided; they do not cause animosity or discrimination. Another positive point is represented by the attitude of **acceptance,** which can be identified with reception and approval of the Other. There is an important difference between sensitivity and acceptance; we may be sensitive to another culture while not approving of some of its practices (e.g., eating dogs). Also, a positive attitude toward the Other can be represented by **empathy**—"understanding so intimate that feelings, thoughts, and motives of one are readily comprehended by another" (Morris, 1982: 428). At this point, we are not simply sensitive to and accepting of the Other; we fully relate to the Other's culture.

Such negative attitudes as discrimination, disparagement, and avoidance lead to breakdowns in intercultural communication, and both the Other's and Self's cultures suffer. It is very difficult to find common ground when one person has an attitude of discrimination and the other person has an attitude of empathy. We will discuss the destructive nature of prejudice in more detail later, in Chapter 9. Right now, it is necessary to emphasize that all these attitudes—discrimination, disparagement, avoidance, sensitivity, acceptance, empathy—are names, or digits, that represent, or point to, the meanings of our attitudes toward the Other. Intercultural communication, however, can be viewed not only digitally but also analogically.

Intercultural Continuum and Analogic Communication

Analogic communication can be equated with constructs that are similar to something else—that is, relate to meaning. In this form of communication, meaning is always represented by a likeness to something else.

A good representation of this form of communication is an analog clock (see Figure 12). An analog clock represents meaning through a likeness of the movement of the hands on the face of the clock to the movement of the sun, so the same point in time that was represented digitally earlier (3:00) is now represented by the positions of the two hands.

FIGURE 12

Do you remember the two different ways of perceiving time discussed in Chapter 5? The first (teleological) view is based on perceiving time as a separate entity—as a figure carved out of the world. According to this view, time can be represented in the form of digits, such as 3:00. The second (organic) view is based on perceiving time as part of the world—not as a figure separate from this world. According to this analogic view, time can be represented in the form of a likeness—for example, between the passage of time and the movement of hands on a clock, clouds, or crops. In this sense, "analogic messages are connected more fundamentally to the actualities of communicating and, therefore, they are said to be more immediate than digital messages" (Anderson & Ross, 2002: 148).

Now let's look at intercultural communication from this analogic perspective, returning to the symbols used earlier to represent the meanings of our attitudes toward the Other. We isolated six such symbols: discrimination, disparagement, avoidance, sensitivity, acceptance, and empathy. Each of these names points to the meaning of our attitudes toward the Other from a certain direction, as it were. But all these symbols (digits) relate to the same meaning, so they are similar to one another; the only real difference among them is a matter of distance. It is clear, for example, that discrimination is closer to disparagement than to sensitivity. Based on distances between these symbols, we can construct the continuum shown in Figure 13.

We isolated six names on our attitudes-toward-the-Other continuum. In other research, you may find a different picture of this continuum with different names or a different number of names. For example, Bennet (1986) isolates the following stages: denial, defense, minimization, acceptance, adaptation, and integration. Can you think of some attitudes that are missing from our continuum? Animosity? Awareness? Perhaps you will be the next researcher to present a more complex picture of the attitudes-toward-the-Other continuum. No matter how complex, the picture of a continuum is never complete because new names can always be created; a continuum is infinitely divisible into parts. We will never know all the points that can exist on a continuum, just as we will never determine the exact position of a cultural meaning once and for all (as discussed in Chapter 2).

Thus, a continuum is a space made up of points representing different degrees of the same meaning. All these meanings, therefore, are related; they are, to some degree, like one another. The Continuum Principle builds on the ideas expressed by the Commensurability Principle, showing that intercultural communication is literally commensurable (measurable in terms of distances between points).

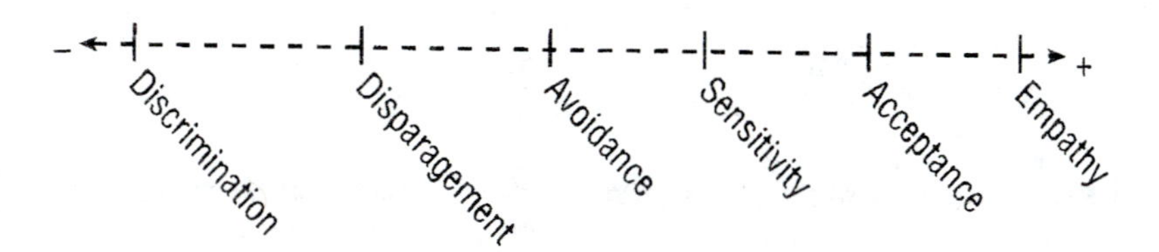

FIGURE 13 Attitudes-Toward-the-Other Continuum

Every meaning can be represented by a certain score (digit), which relates to other scores (digits). For example, it is possible to look at a representative number of similar behaviors and calculate a collective cultural score. Hofstede's research, mentioned earlier, did exactly that, using the data from multiple questionnaires on people's basic values and beliefs.

> [Questionnaires] included such questions as "How important are each of the following to you in an ideal job?" followed by a list of 14 job characteristics such as earnings, job security, challenge, freedom, cooperation, and so forth. In addition, . . . judgments were asked about general issues at work, such as "Competition among employees usually does more harm than good." Employees were asked to rate their responses from "strongly agree" to "strongly disagree." (Hofstede & Bond, 2001: 36)

Average scores were calculated for 53 countries on the four global dimensions, which we discussed earlier. Thus, it became possible to position cultures in accordance with their scores. France received an Individualism score of 71, while Brazil's Individualism score was 38. Figure 14 shows the positions of the two countries, based on their average cultural scores, on a continuum. The continuum ranges from 0 percent to 100 percent. The individualistic part of the continuum is shown below the line, and the collectivistic part of the continuum is shown above the line; this is one way to illustrate both parts of the continuum on a flat surface.

As you can see, France's position is characterized by its scores of 71 on Individualism and 29 on Collectivism, while Brazil's position is characterized by its scores of 38 on Individualism and 62 on Collectivism. In other words, France is a more individualistic culture, while Brazil is a more collectivistic culture. So, the intercultural continuum appears as a series of digits, each representing a certain meaning; for example, 71 represents France's individualism, and 62 represents Brazil's collectivism.

All these points (as scores or names) "are discernible . . . by their distance from each other or by the fact that they have different neighborhoods" (Johanson, 2001: 3). The concept of neighborhood, even though it comes from the field of topology, has a special ring when applied to intercultural communication. Just think about it: We tend to treat those whose meanings are close to ours as our neighbors, and our communication with them is usually more successful. Meaning in analogic communication is represented by a likeness (note the double meaning of the term), and we tend to like those who are similar to us—who live in our neighborhood, so to speak.

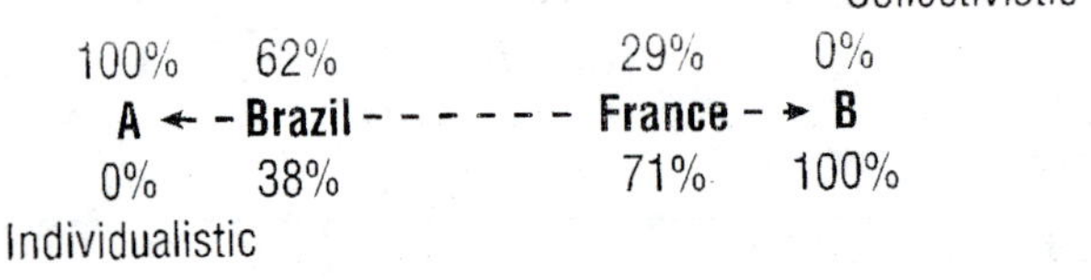

Collectivistic

100% 62% 29% 0%

A ← - Brazil - - - - - - France - → B

0% 38% 71% 100%

Individualistic

FIGURE 14

Of course, some points may be so close that they merge in our perception. In technical terms, "two points merge if they cannot be distinguished by their neighborhood" (Johanson, 2001: 4). For instance, many South and East Asian countries are sometimes treated in the West as one (point)—"Asian culture." This misperception can be an obstacle to successful communication because the cultural spaces of 3.5 billion people cannot be represented by a single point (Emmerson, 1995). Instead, different Asian cultures must be positioned on a continuum as points discernible by their distance from each other (and from the Western culture that is interacting with them).

It is more difficult to treat as our neighbors those people whose meanings are further away from ours. We tend to dislike such people because they are unlike us. In fact, when another culture is *not* perceived as a neighbor, it is tempting to ignore the Other or to reduce the Other to our own culture. We discussed these ethnocentric dangers in Chapter 4—ethnographic reduction (reducing the Other to our culture) and ethnographic negation (ignoring the Other altogether). But these attitudes (and actions) are not constructive. We must learn to treat the Other as our neighbor no matter how far its meanings may be placed from ours, as long as they are still positioned on the same continuum. We may not always bond together, but we are still part of the same intercultural space because we are all connected and bounded; in some way, we all are like one another.

Naturally, when the distance between our culture and the Other is large, intercultural communication requires a large amount of effort. After all, intercultural communication is no different from any other travel: The larger the distance you cover in going from point A to point B, the more challenging the travel. But quite often it is the most challenging journey that is most rewarding!

Intercultural communication is a continuous space, shared by all interacting cultures; its points are analogous to one another and discernible only by distances from one another. If the points, representing cultural meanings, get too close to each other, they merge and cease to be discernible (remember the example of South and East Asian countries merged into one "Asian" culture?). When this happens, intercultural communication ceases (is discontinued).

It seems as if the nature of a continuum is continually slipping from our grasp. At one moment it is a line, then points, then a circle. It is a space, yet it has two parts; no, many parts; in fact, it is infinitely divisible into parts! But a continuum is all of these things because it is a continuous succession of points. Being continuous by nature, intercultural communication can continue only so long as there is a constant transition from point to point. Like a dance, it exists only in transition—as it happens. It is important to realize that cultures remain stable (invariant) only by carrying on this dance. Now you can understand why intercultural communication is a topological space. Not only does it remain invariant under change; it requires change to remain invariant.

So, is intercultural communication digital or analogic in nature? This, of course, is a trick question; the purpose of this chapter is to help you overcome binary thinking. Intercultural communication is *both* digital *and* analogic. It is digital because communication can be viewed as distinct and separate points (digits), each representing a certain meaning. At the same time, it is analogic because all such points represent different degrees of the same meaning. In other words, all meanings are related to one another—they are, to some degree, like one another. Thus, intercultural communication must be viewed in terms of a number of points representing the *same* meaning positioned at *different* distances from one another.

In the previous two chapters, we looked at intercultural communication from two perspectives. In Chapter 4, we presented intercultural communication in more digital terms—that is, as a number of different and specific (separate) positions in the world. In Chapter 5, we presented intercultural communication in more analogic terms, showing how people from different cultures are, in general, alike (analogous to each other, or commensurable). At the beginning of this chapter, we wondered whether unique and same meanings can coexist in intercultural communication. Now we know that specificity and generalness not only can, but must, coexist; otherwise, intercultural communication will not continue. In the remaining chapters, we will have more to say about the dynamic nature of intercultural communication. We will find what drives the intercultural dance, what carries its flow.

The Continuum Principle Defined

Let's now give a more concise formulation of the Continuum Principle, based on the above discussion of its three parts.

First, intercultural communication must be seen as a connected and compact space; its meanings are formed by all cultures engaged in interaction. As a result, meaning in intercultural communication is viewed as a continuous succession of points, or one whole meaning. Such a view allows us to overcome the binary vision of intercultural communication ("either/or") and treat every act of intercultural communication in terms of "both/and" and "more/less."

Second, intercultural communication has a digital nature; its meanings can be represented by distinct symbols or points (digits).

Third, intercultural communication has an analogic nature; its meanings can be represented by their likeness to one another. In other words, all meanings are related to one another—they are, to some degree, like one another. In this sense, meanings are discernible by their distance from each other. Hence, cultural differences are only a matter of distance or degree.

In a nutshell, the Continuum Principle can be formulated as follows:

Intercultural communication is a process whereby people from different cultures continuously construct a shared space where meanings are discernible by their distance from each other.

The Continuum Principle is important because it teaches us to overcome binary thinking. This view of intercultural communication is more complex because it shows how people from different cultures construct a shared and continuous universe while maintaining their different positions.

At the beginning of the chapter, we discussed a contradiction: On the one hand, cultural meanings are presented as unique and relative to a cultural position; on the other hand, common (universal) cultural meanings are presented as ensuring the commensurability of intercultural communication. The Continuum Principle solves this seeming contradiction by showing that intercultural communication is a complex space shared by interacting cultures, where meanings exist as *different* positions along the *same* continua.

Summary

We began this chapter by asking whether we could prove that intercultural communication combines both uniqueness and sameness of meaning. To answer that question, we looked at a number of global cultural dimensions concerned with how people accomplish different tasks. Specifically, we focused on the dimensions of Individualism/Collectivism, Power Distance, Masculinity/Femininity, Uncertainty Avoidance, and High-Context/Low-Context Communication. We showed that each of these dimensions is formed by two concepts that exist together at the same time. Thus, we replaced the binary ("either/or") view of intercultural communication with a more complex "both/and" view.

Based on that view, we approached intercultural communication in terms of a continuum. We showed that, when people from different cultures interact with each other, they form a connected and bounded space—a continuum. Each cultural dimension (e.g., Masculinity/Femininity) is a continuum; the more dimensions (continua) involved in intercultural communication, the more complex it is.

Next, we demonstrated that intercultural communication is both digital and analogic in nature. Communication is digital because meaning can be represented by distinct points (names). Communication is analogic because meaning can be represented by likeness to something else. Overall, intercultural communication was presented in terms of continua, with a number of points representing the *same* meaning positioned at *different* distances from one another.

Based on these ideas, the Continuum Principle was formulated.

So, a continuum is a shared intercultural space made up of points, each representing a different degree of the same meaning. Each global cultural dimension discussed earlier can be seen as a continuum; for instance, Individualism and Collectivism form one continuum, and Masculinity and Femininity form another continuum. The more continua involved in communication between cultures, the more complex their interactions. It is important to remember that a culture moves along a continuum as, for example, attitudes toward the Other change. Thus, it is possible to say that intercultural communication is driven by change. But why exactly do cultures change? If change is the driving force behind the flow of intercultural communication, what drives the change itself? We will make this our next problem question.

CASE STUDY
THE 1999 COCA-COLA SCARE IN EUROPE

This case study is based on an article entitled "Cultural Variability as a Challenge to Global Public Relations: A Case Study of the Coca-Cola Scare in Europe," by Maureen Taylor (2000). As usual, it is recommended that you read the article in its entirety; below is a summary of the article.

Be ready to identify and then discuss the following topics:

1. Intercultural communication as a shared space
2. Reasons for different cultural responses to the crisis
3. Continuous nature of intercultural communication

The article discusses the so-called Coca-Cola tainting crisis, which occurred in Western Europe during the summer of 1999. This crisis was considered the worst health scare in Coke's 113-year history and a public relations disaster.

The crisis broke out in June 1999, when school children in Belgium reported feeling ill after drinking Coca-Cola soft drinks. The Belgian government ordered Coca-Cola to immediately recall all its products in the country. The company complied, but maintained that independent laboratory tests did not show any harmful substances in its products. The next day, France and Spain accused the company of selling tainted products. Coca-Cola pulled all its products from the shelves in those two countries as well. Other European nations, such as Sweden, Norway, and Denmark, reacted differently to the tainting scare and did not recall Coca-Cola products. The Coca-Cola company did not accept any responsibility for the incident, suggesting it was a case of a mass hysteria. Tainting might have been caused by other factors—for instance, the low quality of carbon dioxide in the "fizz" in the products bottled at the Belgian Coca-Cola factory. Not until nine days later did M. Douglas Ivester, CEO of the organization, acknowledge the problem and fly over to the region to deal with the crisis. On June 22, 1999, he apologized to the Belgian people in an open letter published in 15 Flemish and French papers in Belgium.

The article documents in detail the different responses of six West European countries to the scare, as well as Coca-Cola's communication strategy during and after the incident. Belgian, French, and Spanish consumers not only stopped drinking traditional Coke products but also stopped buying related Coca-Cola products such as Fanta and Nestea. In France, the Dunkirk plant manufacturing Coca-Cola products was closed down. In Spain, where most of the Coca-Cola products are manufactured by Coca-Cola Espana, the Health Ministry pulled all imported bottles of Coca-Cola, regardless of place of origin. In Sweden, Denmark, and Norway, however, no actions (e.g., bans or boycotts) were taken against Coca-Cola. Their governments seemed to be less worried that tainting would endanger their populations.

Following the incident, the relations between the organization and its Western European publics were visibly damaged. On December 7, 1999, Ivester, who had been widely criticized for his perceived arrogance after school children in Belgium became sick, announced his resignation. He was replaced by Douglas Draft, an Australian with extensive intercultural expertise. A new "Coke's Back" advertising campaign was carried out in the region. Coca-Cola began to implement a new marketing strategy, trying to better understand cultural differences around the world. As the company learned, the "one market, one strategy" approach did not work. On January 29, 2000, Coca-Cola issued a news release describing its new realignment strategy. Among other things, it said, "Our success depends on our ability to make billions of individual connections each day in every community around the world."

DISCUSSION

Now let's see how this case study can be an illustration of the Continuum Principle of intercultural communication.

1. Intercultural communication as a shared space. Intercultural communication in this chapter is discussed as a space, no part of which can be distinguished from neighboring parts. The interactions between Coca-Cola and the six European cultures can definitely be understood in terms of continua. There would be no interaction between them if they were not connected by lines made up of some ultimate parts. In this particular case, these continua can be represented by such global cultural dimensions as Power Distance and Uncertainty Avoidance. Thus, intercultural communication between Coca-Cola and the six European cultures can be seen as a shared space formed by (at least) two continua—High Power Distance/Low Power Distance and Uncertainty Avoidance/Uncertainty Acceptance. These dimensions apply to all the interacting cultures, such as American Coca-Cola and Belgium. In other words, intercultural communication must be viewed as a process of constructing a shared space.

As we saw, this process, as described in the article, was not successful in some cases and was more successful in others. Why was that? Why did the various European cultures react to the crisis differently?

2. Reasons for different cultural responses to the crisis. Now that we have identified the global cultural dimensions that form the continua, we can take a closer look at the positions that different cultures occupy along the continua. Not surprisingly, the countries that showed a lower tolerance for the crisis (Belgium, France, and Spain) have higher scores on both the Uncertainty Avoidance index and the Power Distance index. According to Hofstede's research, Uncertainty Avoidance scores are as follows: United States, 46; France/Spain, 86; Belgium, 94. Power Distance scores are as follows: United States, 40; Spain, 57; Belgium, 65; and France, 68. These scores explain why Belgium, France, and Spain were so displeased with Coca-Cola. First, because those countries have a low tolerance for uncertainty, they dislike the entry of any global product into their cultures. It might be said that the Coca-Cola company was condemned not so much for the tainting situation as for its silence for over a week after the first illnesses. Second, those countries were not happy with Coca-Cola's response to the crisis because Coca-Cola's claim that its products were safe challenged their authority. In addition, no formal apologies were made to the French public, ignoring a large distance between low power distance United States (40) and high power distance France (68).

The scores of the three Scandinavian nations on the two continua described above are more similar to those of the United States. According to Hofstede's research, Uncertainty Avoidance scores are as follows: United States, 46; Denmark, 23; Sweden, 29; and Norway 50. Power Distance scores are as follows: United States, 40; Denmark, 18; Sweden, 31; and Norway, 31. Thus, more successful communication between Coca-Cola and these cultures may be attributed to their similar attitudes toward risk and authority.

(continued)

THE 1999 COCA-COLA SCARE IN EUROPE CONTINUED

3. Continuous nature of intercultural communication. In this case, communication can continue only because of the distances between Coca-Cola and the European nations, described in the article. In capturing the interactions that took place during the summer of 1999, the article tries to stop the (analogic) flow of communication and present it as a (digital) snapshot.

Coca-Cola, of course, failed to perceive the distances between the countries and draw the distinctions in various continua that formed the intercultural space. As a result, the company had to drop its "one market, one strategy" approach and vow to pay more attention to cultural differences in order to connect with various communities around the world. To its credit, Coca-Cola chose to expand its intercultural horizons. In order to maintain its continuity as one of the leading American companies, Coca-Cola had to change. Appointing a new CEO with extensive intercultural expertise was one of the first steps in that direction.

SIDE TRIPS

1. In an article entitled "The Relationship Between Psychic Distance and Foreign Direct Investment Decisions: A Korean Study," Jai-Beom Kim and Dongkee Rhee (2001) argue that the greater the distance between the home and host cultures, the greater the probability that companies will choose a joint venture over an acquisition. Do you agree with this argument? What global cultural dimensions do you think might affect such business decisions? What culture would you choose to do business with, and in what form?
2. According to Emiko S. Kashima and Yoshihisa Kashima (1998), personal pronouns provide a window through which cultural practices can be investigated. They examine the relationship between culture and language across 39 languages spoken in 71 cultures. More specifically, they compute correlations between the use of first- and second-person singular pronouns (e.g., *I* and *you*) and Hofstede's global cultural dimensions. The personal pronouns are analyzed in terms of the number of first- and second-person singular pronouns and whether these pronouns can be dropped when used as the subject of a sentence in speech. Can you guess some dimensions that characterize cultures with pronoun drop and those with a higher number of personal pronouns? Here are some hints. First, the article focuses on the use of pronouns as they map onto the Self-Other relationship, a basic unit of social process. Second, the authors believe that speakers of pronoun-drop languages face a constant choice between mentioning and not mentioning the subject of the sentence, which adds decisional stress to interaction. What difficulties can arise in interaction between speakers of languages with different pronoun usage?
3. Hon and Brunner (2000) explore the implications of diversity for public relations. Based on interviews with practitioners and executives, they discuss a continuum ranging from organizations with no commitment to diversity to those that treat diversity as a social responsibility—the point where public relations and diversity are linked most meaningfully. Can you think of some other points that might exist on this diversity management continuum? Try to name and define each point.

CHECK YOURSELF

Individualism/Collectivism
Power Distance
Masculinity/Femininity
Uncertainty Avoidance
High-Context/Low-Context Communication
Binary thinking
Continuum
Topology
Digital communication

Discrimination
Disparagement
Tokenism
Avoidance
Arm's-length prejudice
Sensitivity
Acceptance
Empathy
Analogic communication

REFERENCES

Albers-Miller, N., & Gelb, B. (1996). Business advertising appeals as a mirror of cultural dimensions: A study of eleven countries. *Journal of Advertising*, Vol. 25, No. 4, pp. 57–71.
Anderson, R., & Ross, V. (2002). *Questions of communication: A practical introduction to theory*. Boston: Bedford/St. Martin's.

Bennet, M. (1986). A developmental approach to training for intercultural sensitivity. *International Journal of Intercultural Relations*, Vol. 10, No. 2, pp. 179–196.

Brislin, R. (1993). *Understanding culture's influence on behavior*. Fort Worth, TX: Harcourt Brace.

Calori, R. (1994). The diversity of management systems. In Calori, R., & P. de Woot (Eds.), *A European management model: Beyond diversity* (pp. 11–30). New York: Prentice-Hall.

Crosstalk at work: cross cultural communication in the workplace. (1991). Part 1: Performance appraising across cultures. London: BBC Production.

Davidson, A., & Thompson, E. (1980). Cross-cultural studies of attitudes and beliefs. In Triandis, H., & R. Brislin (Eds.), *Handbook of cross-cultural psychology* (Vol. 5). Boston: Allyn and Bacon.

Degabriele, M. (2000). Business as usual: How business studies thinks culture. *M/C: A Journal of Media and Culture*, Vol. 3, No. 2, http://www.media-culture.org.au/0005/business1.html.

Emmerson, D. (1995). Singapore and the "Asian values" debate. *Journal of Democracy*, Vol. 6, pp. 95–105.

Gannon, M. (2001). *Cultural metaphors: Readings, research translations, and commentary*. Thousand Oaks, CA: Sage.

Hall, E. (1976). *Beyond culture*. Garden City, NY: Doubleday.

Hampden-Turner, C., & Trompenaars, F. (2000). *Building cross-cultural competence: How to create wealth from conflicting values*. New Haven, CT: Yale University Press.

Hofstede, G. (1980). *Culture's consequences: International differences in work related values*. London: Sage.

Hofstede, G. (1991). *Cultures and organizations. Software of the mind*. London: McGraw-Hill.

Hofstede, G., & Bond, M. (2001). The Confucius connection: From cultural roots to economic growth. In Gannon, M. (Ed.), *Cultural metaphors: Readings, research translations, and commentary* (pp. 31–50). Thousand Oaks, CA: Sage.

Hon, L. C., & Brunner, B. (2000). Diversity issues and public relations. *Journal of Public Relations*, Vol. 12, No. 4, pp. 309–340.

Hermans, H., & Kempen, H. (1998). Moving cultures: The perilous problems of cultural dichotomies in a globalizing society. *American Psychologist*, Vol. 53, No. 10, pp. 1111–1120.

Johanson, A. (2001). Modern topology and Peirce's theory of continuum. *Transactions of the Charles S. Peirce Society*, Vol. 37, No. 1, pp. 1–12.

Kashima, E. S., & Kashima, Y. (1998). Culture and language: The case of cultural dimensions. *Journal of Cross-Cultural Psychology*, Vol. 29, No. 3, pp. 461–486.

Keating, M. A., Martin, G., & Szabo, E. (2002). Do managers and students share the same perceptions of societal culture? *International Journal of Intercultural Relations*, Vol. 26, pp. 633–652.

Kim, J.-B., & Rhee, D. (2001). The relationship between psychic distance and foreign direct investment decisions: A Korean study. *International Journal of Management*, Vol. 18, No. 3, pp. 286–293.

Marchese, M. (2001). Matching management practices to national culture in India, Mexico, Poland, and the U.S. *The Academy of Management Executive*, Vol. 15, No. 2, pp. 130–132.

Marsella, A., Dubanoski, J., Hamada, W., & Morse, H. (2000). The measurement of personality across cultures. *American Behavioral Scientist*, Vol. 44, No. 1, pp. 41–62.

Morris, E. (Ed.). (1982). *The American Heritage dictionary of the English language*. Boston: Houghton Mifflin.

Neuliep. J. (1996). *Human communication theory: Applications and case studies*. Needham Heights, MA: Allyn and Bacon.

Peng, F. (1974). Communicative distance. *Language Sciences*, Vol. 31, pp. 32–38.

Ramey, B. (2002). The continuum argument for evolution: A critique, http://ourworld.compuserve.com/homepages/billramey/continuum.htm.

Riahi-Belkaoui, A. (1998). Cultural determinism and systematic risk of global stock exchanges. *International Journal of Commerce & Management*, Vol. 8, No. 3/4, pp. 102–108.

Schwartz, S. (1994). Beyond individualism/collectivism: New cultural dimensions of values. In Kim, U., H. C. Triandis, S. C. Choi, & G. Yoon (Eds.), *Individualism and collectivism: Theory, method and applications* (pp. 85–119). Thousand Oaks, CA: Sage.

Taylor, M. (2000). Cultural variability as a challenge to global public relations: A case study of the Coca-Cola scare in Europe. *Public Relations Review*, Vol. 26, No. 3, pp. 277–293.

Triandis, H. (1995). *Individualism and collectivism*. Boulder, CO: Westview.

Watzlawick, P., Bavelas, J. B., & Jackson, D. D. (1967). *Pragmatics of human communication: A study of interactional patterns, pathologies, and paradoxes*. New York: Norton.

Wong, I. (2000). Chinese cultural values and performance at job interviews: A Singapore perspective. *Business Communication Quarterly*, Vol. 63, No. 1, pp. 9–22.

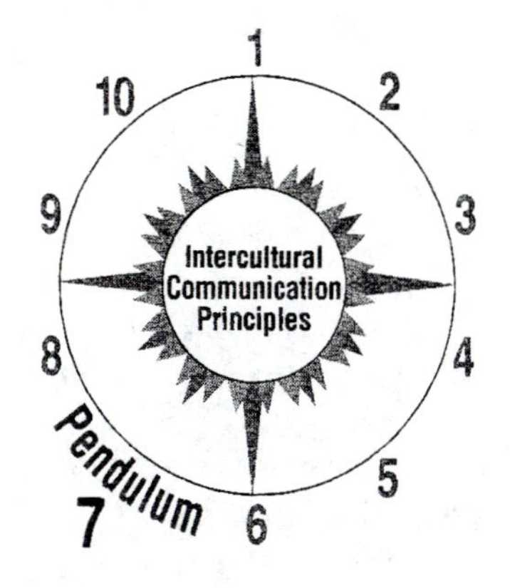

CHAPTER SEVEN

DYNAMICS OF INTERCULTURAL COMMUNICATION: PENDULUM PRINCIPLE

Panta Rhei.

- *Key Theme:* Tension
- *Key Objective:* To help you understand the contradictory nature of intercultural communication

INTRODUCING THE PROBLEM QUESTION

TENSIONS IN INTERCULTURAL COMMUNICATION: CULTURAL NEEDS

INTERCULTURAL COMMUNICATION AND ETHNOLINGUISTIC VITALITY

"VOICE" IN INTERCULTURAL COMMUNICATION

INTRODUCING THE PENDULUM PRINCIPLE

The Contradictory Nature of Intercultural Communication

Intercultural Communication as Praxis

Intercultural Communication and Change

THE PENDULUM PRINCIPLE DEFINED

SUMMARY

CASE STUDY: DIALECTICS OF COLONIAL ENCOUNTER: INTERACTING WITH THE KOBON

SIDE TRIPS

CHECK YOURSELF

REFERENCES

Introducing the Problem Question

In the previous chapter, we saw how cultures in their interactions create a shared space (continuum) that continually changes yet remains stable. It is possible to say that intercultural communication is driven by change. But why exactly do cultures change?

So, our problem question for this chapter is this: *If change is the driving force behind the flow of intercultural communication, what drives the change itself?*

The expression in the subtitle of this chapter—Panta Rhei—belongs to Heraclitus (500 BC) and means "all things are in constant flux." This chapter, more than any other, is about the dynamic nature of intercultural interactions. It might at first be somewhat unsettling to think of intercultural communication in such terms; in this chapter and the following ones, you might be especially tempted to reach for firm ground—only to discover that the way to keep it under your feet is to keep moving.

In this chapter we will

- Emphasize the role of cultural needs in the creation of tensions
- Show the relationship between intercultural communication and vitality
- Discuss the concept of "voice" in intercultural communication
- Analyze the contradictory nature of intercultural interactions
- Highlight the importance of change in intercultural interactions.

Tensions in Intercultural Communication: Cultural Needs

We will begin by looking at three examples of intercultural interactions. As you read the descriptions below, try to think about what these situations have in common.

Our first example is borrowed from Mattson, who presents the situation confronted by a Thai manager working in an American subsidiary in Thailand:

> At New Year's, Thais give presents to customers, but this organization can't. They say it is illegal. If they do give things, they buy one thing in bulk and give it to everybody. In Thai culture, the gifts need to reflect the relationship or the amount of business. (2001: 109)

How should this manager interact with his co-workers, who expect gifts to be bought "in bulk," and his clients, who expect specialized gifts?

The next example describes relations between the white inhabitants of Snow Low, Arizona, and the members of the White Mountain Apache tribe living in the same area (Fire arrest, 2002). One of the members of the Apache tribe was arrested and charged with starting a fire that grew into the largest fire in Arizona history. As a result, the Native Americans began to keep to themselves, fearing retribution, and in the white communities the feeling of resentment was high.

Should the Apaches stop going to their favorite bars and dance halls? Should the white communities stop welcoming the members of the White Mountain Apache tribe?

The last example relates to interactions between the two main ethnic cultures in Fiji: the indigenous Fijians and the Indo-Fijians (for more information, see de Vries, 2002). Fiji is a South Pacific country split into two main cultural groups—the native population and the inhabitants of Indian descent. These two ethnic groups, almost equal in size, have very different positions on most issues, including the land. The indigenous Fijians own most of the land and feel a strong attachment to it, but most of the economic activity is carried out by the Indo-Fijians, many of whom have long-term land leases that are expiring. Not surprisingly, the land issue is a very emotionally charged one on the country's agenda. How can the issue of land proprietorship and use be resolved?

These three scenarios have at least three things in common. First, in each situation a certain tension exists between the interacting cultures. In the first case, the situation is only slightly tenuous, with the manager positioned between the expectations of the organizational and host cultures. In the second case, the tensions between the white communities and the Apache are quite high and may easily turn into violence. In the third case, the situation is truly explosive; the tensions between the indigenous Fijians and the Indo-Fijians may result in a coup and the overthrow of the government, as has already happened in the past.

Second, in all these situations, as a result of tensions, the interacting cultures face a dilemma. You might have noticed that we ended the description of each scenario with a question; these questions are in fact the choices that the cultures must make. In the first case, does the manager go with the bulk-purchase gifts, possibly losing some clients, or with the specialized gifts, possibly alienating himself in the organization? And how should the company deal with this manager? In the second case, should the members of the Apache culture stop going to their favorite bars and dance halls, and should the white communities lash back at them with a vengeance? In the third case, should the indigenous Fijians allow the Indo-Fijians to use their land and on what conditions? And should the Indo-Fijians take to arms or perhaps leave the country if not allowed to renew their leases on the land?

Third, each dilemma calls for resolution; that is, the existing situation of intercultural interaction must be managed. Of course, the need for change varies with the scenario; in the first case the need is not as pressing as it is in the second and, especially, the third case. But in all these scenarios something must change; otherwise, the tensions will grow and the situation may get out of control.

Why do tensions arise between cultures in the first place? Why do people constantly find themselves facing dilemmas—some small, some quite significant? A preliminary answer to these questions can be found in Chapter 4 (the Positionality Principle): Different cultures have different positions on the same issue. But why? For instance, why does the Thai manager in the example above feel he ought to give his clients specialized gifts, while the American company that he works for thinks he should buy one thing in bulk and give it to everybody? To understand why this happens, we must differentiate between *positions,* the explicit claims that cultures make, and *needs,* the inner strivings underlying cultural behaviors. **Positions** are equated with a stance one takes on a certain issue, emphasizing *what* people in a certain culture want—for instance, to buy gifts in bulk and give them to clients. **Needs** are inner strivings, emphasizing *why* people in a certain culture want something—for instance, to avoid preferential treatment and possible lawsuits. It is needs that motivate people to behave in a certain way and take a particular position. Needs give rise to tensions, motivating people to overcome those tensions and reach their goal. The term *motivation* is derived from the Latin *movere* and means to move. People from different cultures can satisfy their needs only if they move—that is, keep doing something.

There are many theories that try to explain and classify human needs. One of the best-known theories, developed by Abraham Maslow (1954), takes the form of a hierarchy of needs. According to this theory, five types of needs influence human behavior: physiological (e.g., oxygen, food), safety (e.g., avoiding harm and disease), love (affection of others), esteem (respect of others), and self-actualization (reaching whatever goal we may have). These five types of needs form a hierarchy because we cannot be motivated to satisfy higher level needs until the lower level needs have been satisfied.

When people from different cultures come into contact, tensions arise because their needs are different. For instance, the indigenous Fijians in the example above feel a strong attachment to the land (love need), while the Indo-Fijians want to use it for their economic projects (self-actualization need). As a result, the land issue is characterized by a lot of tension between these two ethnic cultures. The twist here is that the tension is created by the people from *both* cultures; they exist on the same land, so the land issue is their common dilemma. There is no intercultural communication without this twist, or difference in needs. Do you remember the figure of a circle in Chapter 6, representing a shared space (continuum) formed by two cultures? Well, this figure looks flat and static, but in reality it is not! Imagine this circle on a strip of paper; it ceases to be flat the moment we give the edges a half-twist. The figure comes to life and appears as a dynamic infinity symbol, with tension between the two parts (see Figure 1). It is the tension that motivates the two parts (the people from cultures A and B), making them move.

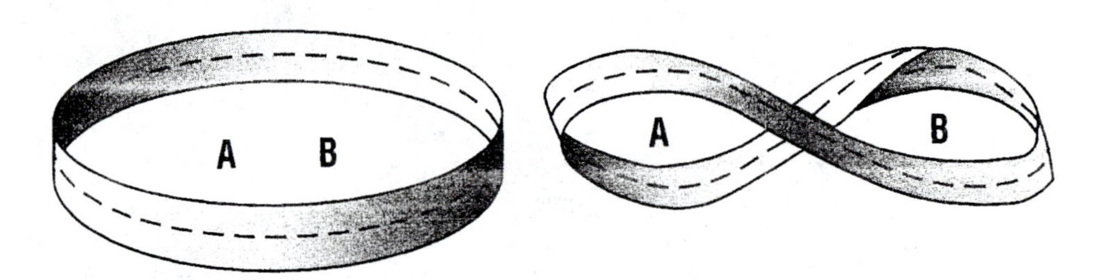

FIGURE 1

Thus, intercultural communication is driven by tensions arising from different cultural needs. Tensions create the potential for change and allow people from different cultures to reach their goals. Zero tension means no potential for change—and no communication.

Intercultural Communication and Ethnolinguistic Vitality

Now we know what makes the world go around: tensions, which are created by different cultural needs. People from all cultures are motivated by their needs, ranging from basic physiological drives to complex desires for self-actualization. Satisfaction of needs is vital to the very existence of any culture. It is no exaggeration to say that the overriding motivation of people is to make sure their culture continues to function. In this sense, realization of needs is vital for people from every culture because it is necessary for the continuation of a culture's life.

The concept of vitality as it applies to culture was introduced by Giles et al. (1977) in the form of the Vitality Theory. This theory aims to assess a culture's strength (vitality) by focusing on a certain aspect of cultural expression. Not surprisingly, attention is usually focused on language as the main means of cultural expression. Thus, a culture's strength is investigated using the concept of **ethnolinguistic vitality**—the extent to which the culture can function as a collective entity because of the range and importance of its language usage. In this sense, "a language group with high vitality is more likely to survive and flourish as a collective entity in an intergroup context. By contrast, groups with low vitality are likely to disappear as discrete linguistic entities in intergroup settings" (Barker et al., 2001: 6).

Two types of ethnolinguistic vitality are isolated: objective and subjective (Giles et al., 1977). **Objective ethnolinguistic vitality** is identified with a culture's position based on available "hard" data such as demographics—for example, the number of people speaking a certain language. **Subjective ethnolinguistic vitality** is identified with a culture's position as perceived by its members. When members of a culture "sense that their vitality is low, or when another language group threatens it, group members may feel their social identity to be negatively valued and act to change their situation" (Barker et al., 2001: 7). So, ethnolinguistic vitality is always a matter of comparison; it can be determined and changed only in the process of intercultural interactions.

Earlier we saw how tensions can arise between people from different cultures over such issues as giving gifts or using land. Now we see that language itself may become a focal point for disagreement, creating tensions between cultures. In many cases, language usage is an explosive issue, and people fight ferocious battles across cultural barricades. Below are several examples of such battles.

In Latvia, a former Soviet republic, the law requires that Latvian be used at public events and in the workplace. It also requires that 75 percent of all radio commercials and chat be in Latvian (Johnson, 2001). Such language policies are a reaction to the use of Russian as the official language in Latvia from 1940, when the country was annexed by the Soviet Union, to 1991, when the Soviet Union ceased to exist. With the dissolution of the Soviet Union, Latvia began reasserting its cultural identity, and the first steps in that direction were aimed at increasing its ethnolinguistic vitality. As a result, Latvian-only signs went up; everyone from doctors to bus drivers was required to speak enough Latvian to do his or her job. However, nearly 40 percent of Latvia's 2.5 million people still use Russian as their main language; naturally, they find many of the language policies of the Latvian government too aggressive or even biased. Tensions between people from these two cultures (Latvian and Russian) are still high, and the language struggle continues.

As another example, consider the negative attitude of people from many cultures to the use of English, whose global spread is sometimes labeled **linguistic imperialism** (Phillipson, 1992). Many people try to strengthen their culture by promoting their own language(s) and discouraging the use of anglicisms. France and Switzerland, for instance, have provided a special vocabulary designed to replace anglicisms with phrases from their own language(s), especially in the areas of computing, business, and entertainment. Instead of *spam*, for example, the Swiss are encouraged to use *courier de masse non sollicité* (unsolicited bulk mail); the French are urged to replace *public speaking* with *l'art oratoire*.

In the United States, the language situation is also far from perfect. One quick look at the **linguistic landscape**—"the language of public signs and symbols, billboards, street names, mail advertising, government information, and notifications" (Barker et al., 2001: 8)—reveals that many other languages are used along with or in place of English in such domains as public administration, business, and education. "According to census data, the top six languages other than English in the U.S. are Spanish, French, German, Italian, Chinese, and Tagalog, with Spanish speakers outnumbering all other minority languages" (Barker et al., 2001: 5). It is not surprising, then, to witness a large number of English-only initiatives, including English-only SAT tests, English-only ballots, English-only driving tests, and English-only advertising.

As a communicative strategy, the English-only movement is, by and large, "the response of the dominant English-speaking majority to what is perceived as the increasing vitality of Spanish-speaking groups" (Barker et al., 2001: 4). However, other cultural voices in the United States should not be ignored or underestimated. For example, in many parts of the country, school instruction is bilingual—it is conducted in English and some other language. Supporters of bilingual education argue that it not only helps different groups to maintain their culture but also allows for stronger integration into the mainstream culture of the United States; they see bilingual education as unifying rather than alienating. Supporters of the English-only movement, in turn, argue that bilingual education (along with other bilingual policies) undermines national unity, resulting in "linguistic separation" of the United States. The issue of bilingual education is a major battleground in the official language debate, which "continues to be a divisive issue in the United States" (Sullivan & Schatz, 1999: 261).

Let's take as an example the battle over Proposition 227, the anti–bilingual education measure put forward in 1998 in California, where about 700,000 children had been taught entirely or partly in their first language (mostly Spanish). This proposition proposed to outlaw nearly all language classes taught in languages besides English, replacing them with an English-language class lasting one school year. Bilingual classes were to be prohibited for children under the age of 10, unless parents of 20 students in the same grade made a request in person each year. Proposition 227 was to let parents sue any teacher who violated its English-only provisions. Districts failing to comply were to be fined about $175 per pupil, with that money given to districts that did comply. The passage of Proposition 227 was expected to distribute $61 million in federal bilingual education money to the state of California. This, of course, is not the complete description of Proposition 227, but it gives you a very good idea of its thrust. How would you vote if you could go to the ballot box—for or against the proposition?

For the sake of the example, suppose 70 percent of California voters vote for the proposition and 30 percent vote against it. These ballots represent two cultural positions: position A (English-only, or Anglo-Saxon) and position B (bilingual, or Hispanic). Naturally, not all Anglo-Saxon people voted for the proposition, and not all Hispanic people voted against it; "Anglo-Saxon" and "Hispanic" are simply labels for the two cultural positions. It is easy to see how one position is stronger than the other—or, put another way, how Anglo-Saxon ethnolinguistic vitality is higher than Hispanic ethnolinguistic vitality (see Figure 2).

As we saw in the previous chapter, when people from different cultures are brought together by a certain issue (in this case, Bilingual Education Measure 227), their interaction forms a shared continuous space. Therefore, Figure 2 can be modified, as shown in Figure 3, to represent the continuous nature of intercultural communication.

In reality, Proposition 227, the anti–bilingual education measure, won overwhelmingly in California (Asimov, 1998). Many bilingual teachers, however, said they would not comply with the English-only rule, despite the threat of lawsuits. They vowed to go to court to fight the measure, and tensions between the two cultures remain high.

FIGURE 2

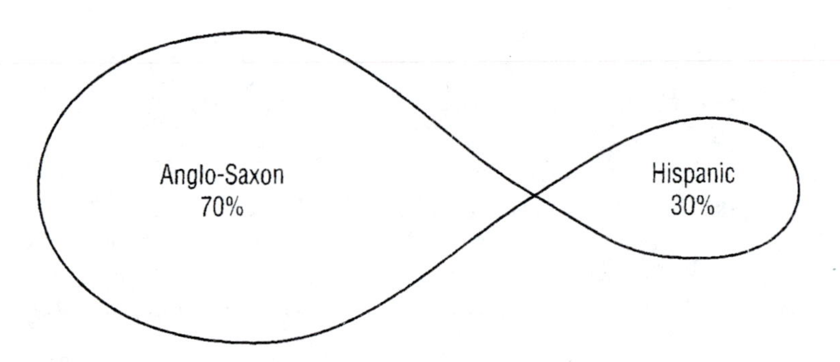

FIGURE 3

To overcome tensions, people from different cultures must voice their positions; in other words, people must express themselves as well as they can, making sure their voice is heard. High ethnolinguistic vitality can be equated with a strong cultural voice, and low ethnolinguistic vitality with a weak cultural voice. The concept of "voice" is very important for our understanding of intercultural communication.

"Voice" in Intercultural Communication

We usually identify voice with sounds produced by the vocal organs—that is, with speech. But **voice** is also a powerful metaphor for "a stance or a position from which to speak. . . . It embodies who can speak, when, and in what ways" (Putnam, 2001: 41). Actually, these two interpretations of voice (literal and figurative) are similar. In both cases, we use voice to recognize or identify people, whether individuals or an entire culture. There can be no identity or recognition (including self-recognition) without voice. It is not surprising, therefore, to find the construct of voice used widely in the practice and study of intercultural communication. For example, we find *Indian Voices,* a monthly publication that pays homage to Native Americans and promotes harmony among the indigenous peoples of the world. Along the same lines, we find an article entitled "Whose Voices Count? Oral Sources and Twentieth-century American Indian History" (LeGrand, 1997), showing how difficult yet critical the study of Native American culture is because its voice sometimes exists only in oral narratives.

The concept of voice is often invoked in relation to people whose cultural positions are not well known or not known at all, calling our attention to "unique perspectives that are often ignored, silenced, or misunderstood" (Putnam, 2001: 41). For example, how much do we know about the views of the Australian Aboriginal culture on music (Dennis, 2003) or the position of non-Western cultures on bioethics (Alora & Lumitao, 2002)? Such unique cultural voices were often ignored or silenced as a result of **colonialism,** a policy by which one culture maintains or extends its control over other cultures that depend on it. As a result of colonialism, powerful cultures like Britain established control over other groups, such as the cultures of Oceania. In this connection, Irwin notes that "the academic field of intercultural communication cannot escape its links to colonialism" (1996: 25). Today, many cultural voices are still silenced or misunderstood. From a Western point of view, many parts of the world are in effect excluded from genuine intercultural interactions:

> We can travel and see them. They cannot travel and see us. They may watch our soaps; we don't see their films. We "see," by and large, only Third World disasters, hunger, and corruption. They mainly see our success stories, the political leadership, the multinationals, the American way. (Oonk, 2002: 535)

In other words, people from many cultures do not hear one another's voices, or they hear the wrong voices. The experience of people in Third World cultures cannot be limited to hunger and disasters, while the experience of people in Western cultures cannot be limited only to soap operas and business corporations. So, the field of intercultural communication still faces this specter of colonialism and has the task of showing how people should interact so that they can hear one another's true voice.

The concept of voice is central to the Theory of the Dialogical Self (Holquist, 1990). According to this theory, everything we say exists only as it relates to something said by someone else (the Other). In other words, our voice exists only as a dialogue with other voices. The word *dialogue* is made up of two concepts—"dia" (one with another) and "legein" (to talk). So, whether we support or criticize someone, we "dialogue" with another position. Our voice, while it is certainly ours, at the same time embodies someone else's voice. The Other enters into our speech not simply as an audience, but as part of our voice, part of our culture. In this sense, our interactions are always characterized by polyphony, or multivoicedness (Bakhtin, 1981). **Polyphony** refers to the human capacity for conducting a dialogue—that is, engaging one's own voice with other voices. It is impossible to understand intercultural communication without understanding its inherently polyphonic nature. Intercultural communication is polyphonic by definition because it is always a conversation between people from different cultures.

Introducing the Pendulum Principle

Based on the discussion above, we will now formulate the seventh principle underlying intercultural communication: the Pendulum Principle. As with the previous principles, we will isolate three parts that make up this principle. Each part deals with the dynamic nature of intercultural interactions. First, we will look at the contradictory nature of intercultural communication. Then we will discuss intercultural interactions in terms of praxis. Finally, we will emphasize the role of change in intercultural communication. We will discuss each part separately and then formulate the Pendulum Principle as a whole.

The Contradictory Nature of Intercultural Communication

We often think of the term *contradiction* as referring to something negative—an inconsistency. However, as we saw in the previous chapter, every meaning presupposes the existence of something contrary to it. In this way, cultural dimensions are formed; for example, individualism is contrary to, yet linked with, collectivism. In this view, our life is nothing but a **contradiction**—an interplay between opposing tendencies. This view of an interplay between unified oppositions is part of the Dialectical Theory of communication, emphasizing its contradictory and dynamic character (cf. Martin & Nakayama, 1999; Martin & Nakayama, 2004: 62–68).

The word **dialectics** means the art of discussion or debate and has its roots in ancient Greek. Such Greek philosophers as Socrates and Plato, regarding dialectics as a search for truth, showed that every issue has two opposing lines of argument. Only through discussion or debate can contradictory arguments be resolved and the truth found.

Thus, everything is driven by contradictions, and intercultural communication is no exception. Take another look at the examples of intercultural interactions discussed earlier in this chapter. You cannot help noticing the contradictory nature of these interactions. More specifically, three things must be emphasized about these interactions.

First of all, in every situation some *opposing forces* can be identified. For instance, in the example of Proposition 227, some people want English to be the only language used in U.S. schools, while other people want instruction to be provided in other languages as well.

Second, in each case oppositions are unified, forming an interactive *unity*. Naturally, both supporters and opponents of Proposition 227 would like to have their own way on the issue of bilingual education in California schools. At the same time, both groups cannot ignore being connected to each other. Thus, in every act of intercultural communication we find both the need for independence and the need for interdependence.

Third, the unified oppositions are not static; in each situation the opposing forces are engaged in *ongoing interplay*. If the opposing force is seen as a static and isolated object, we cannot say that intercultural communication really takes place in the dialectic sense of the word. Recall the examples of ethnocentric reduction and ethnocentric negation from Chapter 4; in both cases, there is no true interaction. In the first case, people from one culture treat the other culture as an object, reducing the second culture to a shadow of the first culture. In the second case, people from one culture simply ignore the other culture. It is as if people from these cultures existed in two parallel worlds that did not cross; here, we deal with dualism, not dialectics. The nature of intercultural communication is always contradictory (dialectical) in the sense that there is an ongoing interplay between opposing forces; it is through discussion, or dialogue, that cultures debate an issue and reach common ground—that is, find the truth.

So, contradictions, as the interplay between unified oppositions, are the driving force of intercultural communication. In this dynamic interplay, tensions are continually created and overcome. The dialectic of tensions presupposes both stretching out and drawing in. If a culture stretches out too far and fails to draw in (i.e., remain itself), it breaks, and tension ceases to exist. If a culture stays drawn in and refuses to stretch out, no tension arises, and therefore no interaction takes place. Tension exists only insofar as something stretches out and draws in at the same time. We can demonstrate the contradictory nature of intercultural communication by returning to the example of Proposition 227, discussed above.

In the case of Proposition 227, the people who support it and those who are against it constitute two contradictory forces. Supporters of the English-only movement argue that bilingual education (along with other bilingual policies) undermines national unity, resulting in linguistic separation within the United States. Supporters of bilingual education argue that it not only helps different groups to maintain their culture but also allows their integration into the mainstream culture of the United States, making it stronger. Thus, the voices of these two groups are clearly divergent; each one pulls out and away from the other one, trying to draw in as many votes as it can. **Divergence,** then, is the act of moving in different directions from a common point—in our case, the common point is the issue of the bilingual education measure. The arrows in Figure 4 show how these two groups take up the issue of the bilingual education measure, pulling out in different directions.

As people in each group "grab" the issue of the bilingual education measure and draw votes in, trying to remain separate, the action of people from the other group creates the opposite movement—that of pulling back. This movement can be seen as the counterpoint to the divergence of the two groups, making them move toward each other, or converge. **Convergence,** then, is the act of approaching the same point from different directions. The arrows in Figure 5 show how the two groups approach the issue of the bilingual education measure, pulling in from different directions.

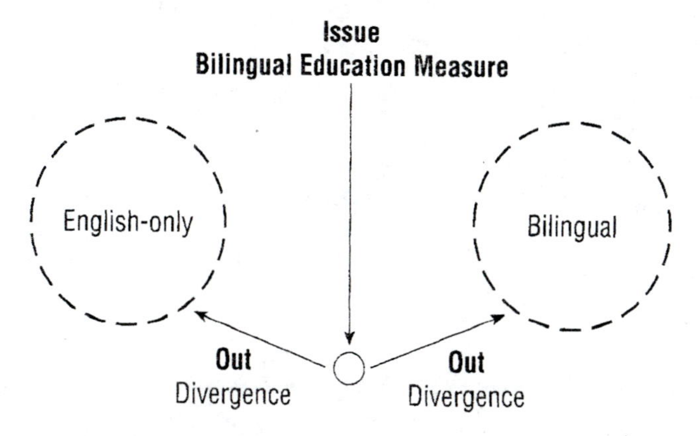

FIGURE 4

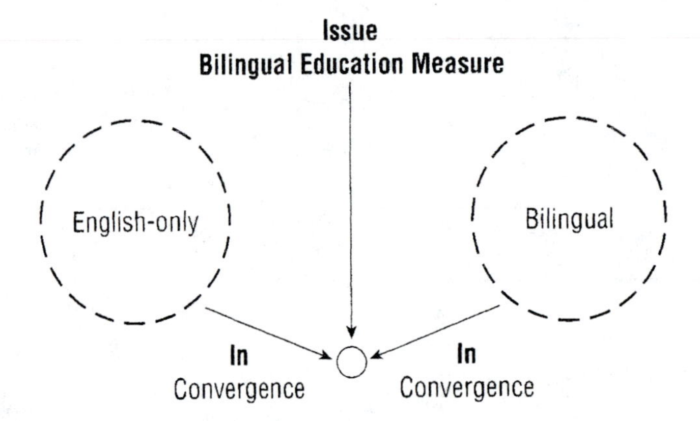

FIGURE 5

The actions of divergence and convergence, represented separately in Figure 4 and Figure 5, are shown in Figure 6 as two sides of the same process, taking place simultaneously. As you can see, the interaction between people from these two groups is one movement that *simultaneously* connects them and keeps them apart. It is but one movement of a pendulum representing an issue being discussed at the moment; in our example, the pendulum represents the issue of Bilingual Education Measure 227. Because the voice of those who support the proposition is stronger at the moment (70 percent of the vote), Figure 7 shows the pendulum of intercultural communication swinging in their direction.

To be consistent with our previous discussion and to emphasize intercultural communication as a continuum (shared space), the intercultural dynamics should be represented as shown in Figure 8. As you can see, the people who voted against the proposition now must reach out (stretch) further to take up the issue of bilingual education, which requires more effort. You might remember that many bilingual

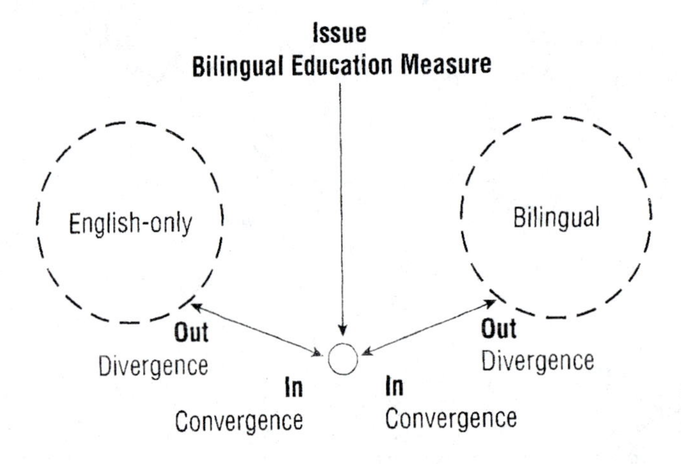

FIGURE 6

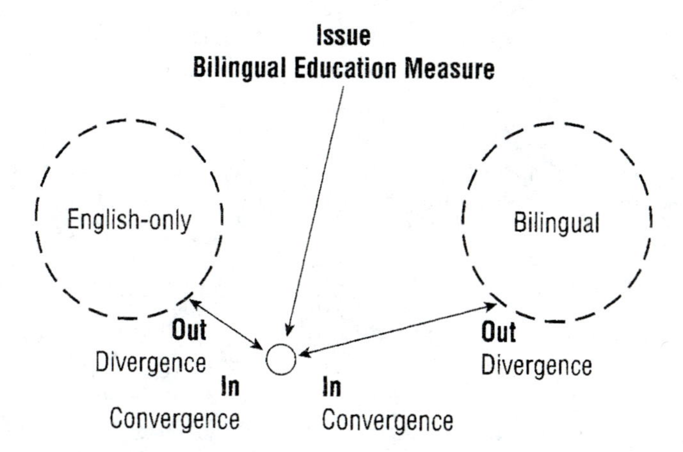

FIGURE 7

teachers said they would not comply with the English-only rule, despite the threat of lawsuits; they vowed to go to court and fight the measure. The situation is still characterized by tensions; in other words, intercultural communication continues.

Intercultural communication will continue as long as two dangers are avoided: overdivergence and overconvergence. Overdivergence means cultural isolation and no dialogue between people from different cultures. Overconvergence means complete submersion of one (weaker) culture by another (stronger) culture. In both cases, the pendulum of intercultural communication stops because there is no Other to provide a countermovement.

So, the contradictory nature of intercultural communication can be revealed using dialectics, a "sensible way to study a world composed of mutually dependent processes in constant evolution" (Ollman, 1998: 342). With the help of dialectics,

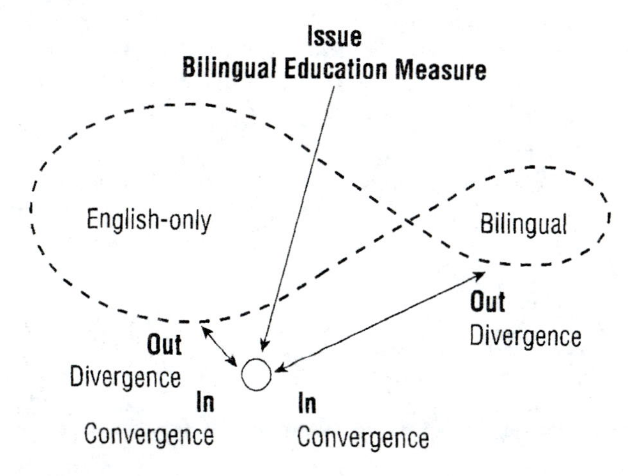

FIGURE 8

we can see that a culture maintains its identity and remains stable only through a process of interaction with other people. There is only one constant, and that is flux, visualized as a pendulum's movement. This view of reality was captured by Heraclitus of ancient Greece in the expression you find in the subtitle of this chapter. *Panta rhei* means that reality is constantly in a state of flux as the unity of opposing (creative and destructive) forces; being in reality is a condition of coming to be and ceasing to be—at the same time! Or, as is stated in an article on intercultural communication in which the identity of Jewish culture is discussed, "To be and not to be, that is the answer" (To be and not to be, 1996).

Intercultural tensions are created and overcome through concrete practices of real people in real situations. Through such practices, people from different cultures acting as opposing forces gain or lose voice, increasing or decreasing their vitality. This brings up another important aspect of the Pendulum Principle—praxis.

Intercultural Communication as Praxis

In Chapter 3, we saw that intercultural communication is performed. When people enact meaning, they must, at every moment of their interactions, decide how to deal with various tensions, such as the needs for connection and autonomy, expression and privacy, predictability and novelty (Baxter & Montgomery, 1996). Intercultural communication, then, must be viewed as **praxis**—concrete practices by which people choose how to resolve the tensions of the moment.

When people make choices, they establish new boundaries for intercultural interactions. At the same time, these new boundaries begin to function as normative practices, affecting people's choices. In other words, people give "communicative life to the contradictions that organize their social life, but these contradictions in turn affect their subsequent communicative actions" (Baxter & Montgomery, 1996: 13–14). New contradictions create new tensions that need to be resolved, so praxis is an inherent part of intercultural communication. Below is a real-life example of how intercultural praxis is manifested.

Trompenaars and Hampden-Turner describe a recent incident at one of Motorola's branches in East Asia. As part of its operation, the corporation had established a practice regulating its interactions with East Asian engineers, who

> were given a $2,000 housing allowance so that they could live comfortably adjacent to the plant. One day a senior engineer had to be contacted urgently at home and was found to be living in a shack. He had spent his housing allowance on putting his siblings through school. (2002: 26)

It was clear that the established boundaries had failed to be effective, creating a tense situation. In other words, the tables had been turned on the very people who had established those boundaries; as a result, the people had to react to the new situation. The corporation could have fired the engineer, of course, as he had misallocated the funds. To its credit, the corporation decided that the engineer

> had put the money to better use than he would have by isolating himself in relative luxury as the "kept man" of a foreign corporation. Was thinking of one's own family an "offence"? The rules were changed. Today you can use the allowance for your own purpose and to implement local values. (2002: 26)

This intercultural scenario can be understood, in terms of praxis, as creating a meaningful rule (money is to be used as housing allowance), which leads to new tensions (misallocation of funds), which are resolved by establishing another rule (money can be used for one's own purposes in accordance with cultural needs).

Specific forms of praxis in intercultural interactions vary from situation to situation. They range from negotiations, one of the most constructive forms of intercultural communication, to discriminatory laws and violence, as the most destructive forms. One of the most important forms of praxis is a **ritual,** "a structured sequence of actions the correct performance of which pays homage to a sacred object" (Philipsen, 1987: 250). Perhaps you think of a ritual as something once important but now reduced to simply "going through the motions"—obsolete and meaningless. Do we really pay homage to any sacred objects these days? Yes, we do, and rituals are an important part of communication today, just as they were in the past. What is held sacred changes with time, but people from every culture pay homage to its sacred objects through a structured sequence of actions. In fact, it is the repeated nature of rituals that shows their importance; rituals are so natural to our culture that we do not think much about them. (Using the terminology from Chapter 3, we can say that rituals are forms of operationalized communication.) Any actions that are repeated over and over again take on the form of cultural rituals; there are eating and drinking rituals and rituals associated with birth and death. The tea ceremony in Japan is a ritual where homage is paid to such sacred objects as purity, reverence of nature, and the uniqueness of every human encounter. Because rituals are so engrained in the fabric of one's culture, it is easy for people from another culture to fail to carry out the sequence of actions correctly; if you, as a guest taking part in the tea ceremony, make a wrong movement or eye contact, the intercultural dance falters. Shared rituals are very important for effective intercultural communication. For instance, successful intercultural mergers and acquisitions are often based on such rituals as introduction programs, training, cross-visits, retreats, celebrations, and similar activities (Larson & Lubatkin, 2001).

When people from different cultures share common rituals as a form of praxis, they decide together which practices to use to resolve tensions, establishing new boundaries and improving their interactions. For example, the issue of English-only versus bilingual education had been dealt with through a number of concrete practices, ranging from conversations at dinner tables to political campaigns. Eventually, the issue took the form of a proposition that was voted upon at the ballot box. Voting is an important ritual that allows people from two groups to resolve an issue and decrease tensions. When people go to the ballot box and cast their votes, they give voice to their support of or opposition to a certain issue. By following a structured sequence of actions, they pay homage to a sacred object—in this case, the ideas of democracy and freedom of expression as they understand them. Voting and negotiations are perhaps two of the most effective intercultural rituals.

Thus, every form of praxis can be seen as a jointly enacted communicative choice. Through such choices, people from different cultures change the dialectical situation present at the moment, creating a new situation and therefore a new choice. In a way, praxis can be seen as the mechanism of the pendulum of intercultural communication—it keeps the pendulum swinging as long as people from different cultures act together. The pendulum of intercultural communication does not swing because of some mysterious outside force; it is set and kept in motion by the people themselves. Intercultural communication requires a constant effort. If intercultural communication works "like a clock," it is because there is a lot of work going on behind the scenes. The movement of the pendulum is not always smooth, of course, and we will discuss what makes this movement more or less smooth in the next chapters. Right now, it is important to understand that cultures can keep their identities (remain stable) only by interacting—continually creating and changing their relationships.

Intercultural Communication and Change

Change is one of the core concepts of dialectics. It is impossible to understand the true (contradictory) nature of intercultural communication without emphasizing its dynamic character. Intercultural communication exists only insofar as people from different cultures continue to interact and change, resolving their contradictions and looking for the true meaning of every communicative practice. Consider the different cultural views on the practice of drinking (Room & Makela, 2000): In "abstinent cultures" (some Islamic societies), drinking is religiously and legally forbidden; in "strained ritual drinking cultures" (Orthodox Jews), a small amount is drunk only on certain occasions; in "banalized drinking cultures" (e.g., Southern European societies), drinking is more accepted. However, none of these cultures can claim that their view on drinking is the only true one. Their cultural voice can exist only because there are other voices—contrary to it—on the same issue. People from every culture can express themselves and maintain their identity as long as they carry out an ongoing dialogue with other people, simultaneously diverging and converging. No culture owns the truth, and the search for knowledge is a joint enterprise.

So, change is vital to every culture engaged in interactions. That is why it is especially important to be able to predict change and its consequences, or—to use the metaphor from this chapter—to see which way the pendulum is swinging and what its movement may entail. In a recent study that compared perceptions of change in Eastern and Western thinking patterns, Ji et al. (2001) found that Chinese were more likely than Americans to predict change in events. Also, Chinese were found to anticipate more alteration in the direction of trends and more variation in the rate of change, and they were more likely than Americans to regard people who predict changes as wise. Not surprisingly, parallels are often drawn between dialectics and wisdom (Gollobin, 1998). Successful intercultural communication requires that people from different cultures listen to one another's voices predicting change; this way, they can make better (wiser) decisions about how to act in this or that situation.

So, intercultural communication is based on the assumption that cultures can, and do, change. Every movement of the pendulum of intercultural communication brings about change—sometimes dramatic, sometimes quite subtle. The two dangers of ethnocentrism discussed in Chapter 4 lead to breakdowns in intercultural communication precisely because they do not incorporate this assumption. On the contrary, the Other (culture) is viewed as a passive object that cannot change and must be reduced to Self or ignored. As a result, interaction either does not take place (ethnocentric negation) or is replaced by action of one culture on another, whereby the Other is reduced to Self (ethnocentric reduction). In both cases, the Other remains an outside object whose voice is not heard. In both cases, no real tension exists between Self and the Other, and no interplay of opposing tendencies takes place. Self can develop and maintain its identity only through interaction with the Other. Once the Other is ignored or reduced to Self, intercultural communication breaks down: The pendulum of intercultural communication stops. Now Self has no Other to interact with; Self has undermined its own stability by refusing to change. Therefore, the very existence of cultures depends on their ongoing interplay. Stability is the result of change, which is the only true constant—that is, the overall truth. Remember: *Panta rhei*—All is flux.

The Pendulum Principle Defined

Let's now give a more concise formulation of the Pendulum Principle, based on the above discussion of its three parts.

We noted the contradictory nature of intercultural communication. In every intercultural interaction there are opposing tendencies at work, and in each case these oppositions are unified, forming an interactive unity. Thus, the contradictory nature of intercultural communication lies in the ongoing interplay of opposing forces.

Tensions between cultures are created and resolved through concrete practices, or praxis. People always function as subjects, establishing new boundaries for intercultural interactions. At the same time, these new boundaries begin to function as normative practices, affecting people's choices. Thus, every form of praxis is a jointly enacted communicative choice. This joint effort is what keeps the pendulum of intercultural communication swinging.

We also showed that it is impossible to understand intercultural communication without emphasizing its continually changing nature. Intercultural communication continues only insofar as cultures keep interacting, and every movement of the pendulum affects and is affected by their positions in the overall continuum. Every cultural position can be seen as a "voice," or a stance from which the culture collectively speaks. Intercultural communication is polyphonic by nature because it is always a conversation (dialogue) between people from different cultures. Thus, in the ongoing interplay of opposing tendencies, multiple voices are produced.

In a nutshell, the Pendulum Principle can be formulated as follows:

Intercultural communication is an ongoing and interactive process that simultaneously connects and keeps apart people from different cultures, producing multiple voices.

It is important to emphasize that these two processes—the centrifugal force of divergence and the centripetal force of convergence—take place at the same time.

Summary

We started this chapter by looking at the tensions that continually arise between cultures. We saw that tensions exist between people from interacting cultures because their needs are different. Without differences, there would be no tensions and therefore no intercultural communication. Thus, we determined that motivation to satisfy needs is vital to the very existence of intercultural communication in general and each culture in particular.

In connection with the satisfaction of cultural needs, we looked at the concept of ethnolinguistic vitality—a measure of a culture's strength based on the importance of its language. High ethnolinguistic vitality was equated with a strong cultural voice, and low ethnolinguistic vitality with a weak cultural voice. A cultural voice was defined as a stance or position from which a culture collectively speaks. We showed how every cultural voice embodies other voices—that is, how our voice exists as part of a dialogue with other voices. Thus, our intercultural interactions are characterized by polyphony, or multivoicedness. Intercultural communication is polyphonic by definition because it is always a conversation between people from different cultures.

We then emphasized that the contradictory nature of intercultural communication lies in the ongoing interplay of opposing forces. We showed how tensions between cultures are created and resolved through concrete practices, or praxis. As a result of such practices, multiple cultural voices are produced. Thus, intercultural communication was presented as an ongoing and interactive process that simultaneously connects and keeps apart people from different cultures, producing multiple voices.

Based on these ideas, the Pendulum Principle was formulated.

In this chapter, intercultural communication was compared to the movement of a pendulum—a process encompassing difference and unity simultaneously. In this process, people must continually decide how to make sure the pendulum swings in such a way that their voices are heard and accepted by others. What are some specific ways to keep the pendulum of intercultural communication swinging? In other words, how do people from different cultures resolve their tensions so that the pendulum can swing? We will answer this question in the next chapter.

CASE STUDY

DIALECTICS OF COLONIAL ENCOUNTER: INTERACTING WITH THE KOBON

This case study is based on "The Transformation of Violence in the Colonial Encounter: Intercultural Discourse and Practices in Papua New Guinea," by Joachim Görlich (1999). As usual, it is recommended that you read the article in its entirety; below is a summary of the article.

Be ready to identify and then discuss the following topics:

1. The contradictory nature of the colonial encounter
2. The strategies employed in the interactions
3. The transformations that emerged from the interactions

This article analyzes the dialectics of the interactions between the Australian administration and the Kobon culture in the Northern Highlands of Papua New Guinea between 1953 and 1975. The article begins by describing the precolonial social order among the Kobon as based on reciprocity and characterized by such activities as the exchange of material goods, women, and services—including violent acts of vengeance. For example, when someone died, the person thought to be responsible for that death had to be found and killed in revenge; this act was justified by attributing the death to witchcraft. The witch was killed through a surprise attack; afterwards, everyone involved in the vengeance received a compensation payment from the relatives of the avenged person. If the surprise attack was not successful, a ritualized battle took place with up to a hundred people on each side. The battle continued until the first lives were lost, causing one side to retreat. A peace ceremony after the battle did not exclude future acts of vengeance. Violence therefore was not regarded by the Kobon as something negative, and this was a major obstacle for the Australian culture to overcome.

The very first contacts between the Kobon and Australian officers made it clear that the two radically different cultural concepts—"law and order" and "state of nature"—clashed. These contacts were characterized by a lot of uncertainty and tension: The Kobon associated the white people with spirits, while the officers could not help but feel a real danger of violence emanating from the opposite party. In this risky situation, the Australian patrols communicated their peaceful intentions by offering gifts, engaging in barter, and, where possible, communicating orally through bilingual speakers. Insofar as the Kobon willingly participated in exchange transactions, they saw the white people not only as a threat but also as a potential ally that could be mobilized to help in the realization of their own goals. At the same time, the colonial message was clear: The Australians had a desire to cooperate but were willing to use violence if the Kobon continued their vengeance killings. The Australian administration communicated this message through oral orders to refrain from violence and through demonstration of their firearms. Also, they would set up a large camp at the spot where a vengeance killing had taken place and talk to the Kobon, explaining their purpose and intentions. They also exploited the importance of the Kobon ritual of *parom*—a dance festival where extensive exchanges took place. During this festival, the officers displayed their superior weapons, threatened to use them, and announced prison sentences as a sanction for vengeance killings. The Kobon soon became familiar with the concepts of court proceedings and prison. Some of the former Kobon prisoners were later re-educated and appointed as assistants to the patrol officers.

Step by step, the Australians made the new state of affairs more acceptable to the Kobon people. Patrols began carrying out such new activities as taking a census, collecting taxes, and organizing elections. Görlich notes that, in describing their experiences to him, the Kobon repeatedly mentioned the importance in their interactions with the Australians of such new rituals as the daily morning and evening roll calls, hoisting the flag, and census patrols, at which they were ordered to stand in line in front of the officer.

Gradually, a number of significant changes took place in the interactions between the Kobon and the Australians. For example, the Kobon stopped using direct physical violence against those suspected of witchcraft; instead, they began to use symbolic violence in the form of counter-witchcraft. As before, the participants in a counter-witchcraft action received compensation payments in return for their service. Their attitude toward witchcraft changed, too. It was no longer seen as the embodiment of antisocial behavior, undermining the cultural order; some people even spoke openly about their skills in witchcraft, as if advertising their services and hoping for compensation payments. Thus, the concept of witchcraft now included the idea of its manipulation. Naturally, once the risk of violent conflicts had been reduced, it became possible for the Australian administration to build more cooperative relationships with the Kobon people.

DISCUSSION

Now, let's see how this case study can be an illustration of the Pendulum Principle of intercultural communication.

1. The contradictory nature of the colonial encounter. The intercultural encounter described in the article is clearly characterized by two opposing forces—the Kobon people and the Australian administration (the colonized and the colonizers). In this encounter, two cultural concepts—"law and order" and "state of nature"—give rise to tensions and a lot of uncertainty. The Kobon at first see the white people as spirits that may or may not be peaceful, while the officers find themselves in a highly risky situation, facing the possibility of unjustified violence. Thus, the centrifugal forces of divergence are strong, as the people from each culture are motivated to preserve their own order. At the same time, the encounter brings the two cultures together and forces them to interact. The first steps taken by the administration include giving gifts, and the Kobon take part in exchange transactions. As a result, the centripetal forces of convergence begin to operate in their transactions as well. So the nature of this colonial encounter is truly contradictory, showing the interplay between two opposing forces. The Kobon people often had no choice other than to submit to the force of the Australian administration; hence, their interaction is labeled "a colonial encounter." At the same time, the white officers could not but listen to the Kobon collective voice too; that dialogue was carried out through a number of strategies of praxis.

2. The strategies employed in the interactions. Initially, intercultural communication was carried out mostly through simple barter transaction—for example, the exchange of gifts. The nonverbal strategy of the firearms display was used

(continued)

DIALECTICS OF COLONIAL ENCOUNTER: INTERACTING WITH THE KOBON CONTINUED

along with such exchanges. At the same time, verbal communication, made possible by bilingual speakers, was employed from the start, in the form of orders, threats, and explanations. For instance, explanation (of the purpose and intentions of the Australian administration) was the main rationale for conducting camps at the spot where a vengeance killing had taken place. Later, the strategy of political instruction made it possible for the people from the two cultures to start using more complex forms of praxis, such as court proceedings and elections.

Of special importance was the use of rituals. For example, the Australian patrols were able to exploit the Kobon ritual of *parom,* preserving its original nature as a dance festival where extensive exchanges took place and, at the same time, introducing the new message that physical violence in acts of vengeance was prohibited. The Kobon themselves mentioned the importance in their interactions with the Australians of such new rituals as the daily morning and evening roll calls, hoisting the flag, and census patrols. All these strategies transformed the interactions between the Australians and the Kobon.

3. The transformations that emerged from the interactions. First of all, violence is no longer viewed by the Kobons as an integral part of their culture; this perhaps is the most significant transformation. The Kobon stopped using direct physical violence against those suspected of witchcraft and began to use symbolic violence in the form of counter-witchcraft. Another transformation was the change in attitude toward witchcraft in general. It is no longer seen as the embodiment of antisocial behavior, undermining the cultural order, and some people even advertise their services, looking for compensation payments. Thus, the concept of witchcraft has been transformed to include the idea of its manipulation. The risk of violent conflicts between the Australians and the Kobon has been reduced, and it is now possible for the two cultures to build more cooperative relationships with each other. This is not to say, however, that the interactions between these two cultures have lost their contradictory nature. Newly established boundaries simply create new tensions that need to be resolved, so every intercultural interaction is an ongoing encounter.

SIDE TRIPS

1. An article entitled "Tribe Tries to Breathe Life into Language" (Rivera, 1998) talks about the culture of the Cochiti, a New Mexico pueblo tribe that introduced an aggressive program to promote its native language of Keres. After a small Cochiti pueblo village located in the Jemez Mountains south of Santa Fe found out that only one-third of the 700 residents still spoke Keres, they offered adult Keres classes, began working with the local schools, and started a youth program in the summer. The Cochiti developed their total immersion program with three rules: All teaching would be done in Keres, the traditional calendar would be used as a guide for learning, and all lessons would be based on Cochiti culture. Using the concept of ethnolinguistic vitality, how would you evaluate the Keres revitalization program?
2. An article entitled "Quebec Seeking to End Its Old Cultural Divide" (Krauss, 2003) talks about the growing acceptance by English-speaking Canadians of the Quebecois culture. While in the past Quebec tried to separate from Canada, holding two very close referendums on the issue, today the signs of mutual acceptance are everywhere. For example, conversations in cafes go back and forth in English and French, and more of Quebec's English speakers are now marrying French speakers. More French-speaking students are now enrolling at McGill University and writing their papers in French, while English-speaking students are enrolling in large numbers at the University of Montreal and writing their papers in English. The *Montreal Gazette*, the English-language daily, has begun to advertise in the French-language news outlets and promote itself on billboards in French. And employees of department stores, once considered the domain of the English elite, now welcome all customers with "Bonjour." What forms of intercultural praxis can you identify in the interactions between the French-speaking Quebecois culture and the English-speaking Canadian culture?
3. During the spring of 2001, in McMinnville, Tennessee, a number of police officers and Warren County sheriff's deputies spent Thursday nights in a Spanish class designed for law enforcement officers (see Sack, 2001). Through role-play and repetition, the 30-hour course is designed to teach the officers how to make an arrest, conduct a basic interrogation, calm a victim, read a Miranda warning, and recognize swear words, all in Spanish. Some Latinos question whether such training will be effective, especially in high-pressure situations. Do you think such an attempt at intercultural convergence is necessary? Do you believe it can be effective?

CHECK YOURSELF

Positions
Needs
Ethnolinguistic vitality
Objective ethnolinguistic vitality
Subjective ethnolinguistic vitality
Linguistic imperialism
Linguistic landscape
Voice

Colonialism
Polyphony
Contradiction
Dialectics
Divergence
Convergence
Praxis
Ritual

REFERENCES

Alora, A., & Lumitao, J. (2002). Beyond a Western bioethics: Voices from the developing world. *Perspectives in Biology and Medicine,* Vol. 45, No. 4, pp. 627–628.

Asimov, N. (1998). Big victory for measure to end bilingual education. *San Francisco Chronicle,* June 3, p. A1.

Bakhtin, M. (1981). *The dialogic imagination: Four essays by M. M. Bakhtin.* M. Holquist (Ed.). Austin: University of Texas Press.

Barker, V., Giles, H., Noels, K., Duck, J., Hecht, M., & Clément, R. (2001). The English-only movement: A communication analysis of changing perceptions of language vitality. *Journal of Communication,* Vol. 51, No. 1, pp. 3–37.

Baxter, L., & Montgomery, B. (1996). *Relating: Dialogues and dialectics.* New York: Guilford.

Dennis, L. (2003). Aboriginal voices in textual spaces, http://www.fl.net.au/~lyndenal/204essay.htm.

de Vries, R. E. (2002). Ethnic tension in paradise: Explaining ethnic supremacy aspirations in Fiji. *International Journal of Intercultural Relations,* Vol. 26, pp. 311–327.

Fire arrest increases race tension. (2002). *The Spokesman-Review,* July 2, p. A3.

Giles, H., Bourhis, R. Y., & Taylor, D. M. (1977). Towards a theory of language in ethnic group relations. In Giles, H. (Ed.), *Language, ethnicity and intergroup relations* (pp. 307–349). London: Academic.

Gollobin, I. (1998). Dialectics and wisdom. *Science and Society,* Vol. 62, No. 3, pp. 483–496.

Görlich, J. (1999). The transformation of violence in the colonial encounter: Intercultural discourse and practices in Papua New Guinea. *Ethnology,* Vol. 38, No. 2, pp. 151–162.

Holquist, M. (1990). *Dialogism: Bakhtin and his world.* London: Routledge.

Irwin, H. (1996). *Communicating with Asia: Understanding people and customs.* Sydney: Allen & Unwin.

Ji, L.-J., et al. (2001). Culture, change, and prediction. *Psychological Science,* Vol. 12, No. 6, pp. 450–456.

Johnson, S. (2001). Language police called out to rescue Latvian. *The Los Angeles Times,* January 28, p. A6.

Krauss, C. (2003). Quebec seeking to end its old cultural divide. *The New York Times,* April 13, p. A6.

Larson, R., & Lubatkin, M. (2001). Achieving acculturation in mergers and acquisitions: An international case survey. *Human Relations,* Vol. 54, No. 12, pp. 1572–1607.

LeGrand, J. (1997). Whose voices count? Oral sources and twentieth-century American Indian history. *American Indian Culture and Research Journal,* Vol. 21, No. 1, pp. 73–105.

Martin, J., & Nakayama, T. (1999). Thinking dialectically about culture and communication. *Communication Theory,* Vol. 9, pp. 1–25.

Martin, J., & Nakayama, T. (2004). *Intercultural communication in contexts.* Boston: McGraw-Hill.

Maslow, A. (1954). *Motivation and personality.* New York: Harper.

Mattson, M., & Stage, C. (2001). Toward an understanding of intercultural ethical dilemmas as opportunities for engagement in new millennium global organizations. *Management Communication Quarterly,* Vol. 15, No. 1, pp. 103–109.

Ollman, B. (1998). Why dialectics? Why now? *Science and Society,* Vol. 62, No. 3, pp. 338–357.

Oonk, G. (2002). Globalization and culture/globalization and identity: Dialectics of flow and closure. *Journal of World History,* Vol. 13, No. 2, pp. 532–537.

Philipsen, G. (1987). The prospect for cultural communication. In Kincaid, D. L. (Ed.), *Communication theory: Eastern and Western perspectives* (pp. 245–254). San Diego, CA: Academic.

Phillipson, R. (1992). *Linguistic imperialism.* Oxford, UK: Oxford University Press.

Putnam, L. (2001). 2000 ICA presidential address: Shifting voices, oppositional discourse, and new visions for communication studies. *Journal of Communication,* Vol. 51, No. 1, pp. 38–51.

Rivera, R. (1998). Tribe tries to breathe life into language. *Denver Post,* June 26, p. A24.

Room, R., & Makela, L. (2000). Typologies of the cultural position of drinking. *Journal of Studies on Alcohol,* May, pp. 475–483.

Sack, K. (2001). Police learning Spanish as Latino population grows. *The New York Times,* March 4, p. A16.

Sullivan, N., & Schatz, R. (1999). When cultures collide: The official language debate. *Language and Communication,* Vol. 19, pp. 261–275.

To be and not to be, that is the answer. (1996). *The Economist,* Vol. 341, pp. 91–92.

Trompenaars, F., & Hampden-Turner, C. (2002). *21 leaders for the 21st century: How innovative leaders manage in the digital age.* New York: McGraw-Hill.

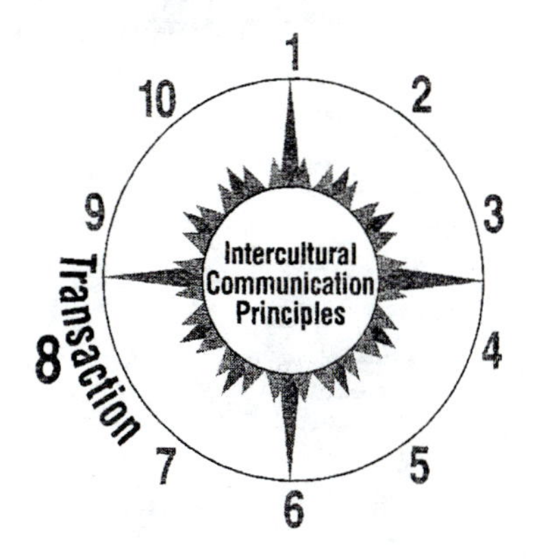

CHAPTER EIGHT

RESOLVING INTERCULTURAL TENSIONS: TRANSACTION PRINCIPLE

It Is Not a Game!

- *Key Theme:* Resolution
- *Key Objective:* To help you understand the importance of managing intercultural tensions

INTRODUCING THE PROBLEM QUESTION

APPROACHING CONFLICT
- Roots
- Routes

INTRODUCING THE TRANSACTION PRINCIPLE
- Intercultural Transactions: Perception and Reality
- Intercultural Communication as a Negotiation Zone
- Back to the Future: From Positions to Interests

THE TRANSACTION PRINCIPLE DEFINED

SUMMARY

CASE STUDY: "THE WALL OF DEATH": A CONFLICT BETWEEN JAPANESE AND WESTERN CULTURES

SIDE TRIPS

CHECK YOURSELF

REFERENCES

Introducing the Problem Question

In Chapter 7, intercultural communication was presented as a pendulum kept in motion by tensions. Now we need to take a closer look at how people from different cultures strive to maintain their vitality—how they make sure the pendulum swings in such a way that their voices are heard.

In other words, the problem question is this: *How do people from different cultures manage to resolve their tensions?*

In this chapter we will

- Define conflict in intercultural communication and identify its roots
- Discuss the main ways of managing intercultural conflict
- Show how our perception of reality affects the way conflict is managed
- Present intercultural conflict as a transaction
- Show how conflict is managed within a negotiation zone
- Emphasize the role of interests in managing intercultural conflict.

Approaching Conflict

Roots

The United Nations proclaimed the year 2001 the Year of Dialogue among Civilizations. In an address given on February 5 at Seton Hall University, Kofi Annan, U.N. Secretary-General, noted that cultural diversity is both the basis for this dialogue and the reality that makes the dialogue necessary. He expressed the hope that, through such dialogue, people from all cultures could flourish and bear fruit in every field of human endeavor. At the same time, he could not help but mention the dark side of this dialogue—for example, the conflicts between the Israelis and Palestinians in the Middle East and the Muslims and Christians in the Balkans. He called for understanding the grievances that lie at the roots of conflict; these grievances must be addressed if conflict is to be resolved. So what *are* the roots of intercultural conflict?

Intercultural Conflict Defined. Most people understand conflict as a clash or disagreement, which is quite correct. Suppose two friends are discussing their favorite ethnic food, and one likes Thai while the other likes Mexican. Is there a conflict here? Yes; this disagreement is called a conflict of opinion (cf. Thompson, 2000). Two friends have different opinions as to which ethnic food is better; they might argue for a while and then call the whole thing off, going their separate ways. But suppose the same two friends want to eat out and need to decide which kind of restaurant to go to—Thai or Mexican. Is there a conflict here? Yes, but this disagreement is a different kind of conflict, which is called a conflict of interest (cf. Thompson, 2000). A conflict of interest requires that something be done; that is, it requires resolution. Now there is more at stake than just opinions; neither friend is interested in spending time and money on food that he or she does not like. Yet both want to eat out together, so they need to resolve their tensions together. They may decide to try Thai one night and Mexican another night or to compromise on an Italian restaurant. Whatever they decide to do results in resource allocation; in other words, they make a decision as to how to spend their resources of time and money. So, **conflict** can be defined as a perceived disagreement over resource allocations.

That this definition of conflict is widely accepted (Faure & Rubin, 1993; Thompson, 2000) should not be surprising to you, since, in the introduction to this book, *culture* was defined as a system of symbolic resources. As you may remember, a resource is anything that can be drawn upon when needed by people from different cultures and used to their advantage. When people cannot agree on how to use resources claimed by interacting cultures, a conflict arises. In Chapter 7, we saw that language is one such resource because it is crucial for cultures' vitality. Also, people from every culture need natural resources for their support; such tangible resources as land, water, and oil are often a cause of intercultural conflict. For example, in 1979, Egyptian President Anwar Sadat announced that the only issue that would prompt Egypt to declare war would be water; his threats were directed at Ethiopia, where the majority of Egypt's Nile waters originate. In the 1990s, King Hussein of Jordan issued a similar declaration targeted at Israel. "While Egypt and Jordan have not yet found it necessary to act on their threats, these examples illustrate the conflict potential of a scarce resource like freshwater" (Dinar, 2002: 229). A conflict over natural resources did take place in 1997 between the U.S. company Occidental Petroleum and the U'wa Indians of Colombia. At issue was a field with oil resources believed to be worth billions of dollars. The U'wa Indians, who consider oil the "blood of mother Earth," refused repeated efforts by Occidental to make a deal (Drilling blocked, 1997).

We must not think of cultural resources only in terms of tangible supplies like water or oil, however; resources have their intangible side as well. Before the 2003 war in Iraq, a 16-year-old student in Dearborn, Michigan, came to school wearing a T-shirt on which were printed the words *International Terrorist* and a picture of President Bush. He was asked by school officials to go home because they were worried that the T-shirt would inflame passions at the school, where the majority of students were Arab-American. This conflict was not just about a tangible resource (a T-shirt); it was about such intangible resources as freedom of expression (for the student) and safety (for school officials). Similarly, in the examples discussed earlier, people from different cultures clashed not simply over water or oil, but over less tangible resources such as security and sacredness of land. Intangible resources are, for example, "safety, attention, affection, understanding, respect, support, self-esteem, and power" (Ting-Toomey, 1999: 197).

So, an intercultural conflict is not just a disagreement; it is a clash over allocation of resources that have tangible and intangible sides. Although the intangible side of resources in an intercultural conflict may be hidden from view, it is generally more important, just like any other roots. These two sides of resources—tangible and intangible—make up a cultural identity; in the end, every conflict is a conflict of different cultural identities. For example, when an interfaith couple argue about what religious faith they want to instill in their child, they clash over such resources as their time or power. Overall, however, they clash over the worthiness of their beliefs and values—everything they identify with. Each spouse wants the child to choose his or her own religion, thus reinforcing her or his own identity. Suppose a Jewish husband disagrees with his Catholic wife's choice of religion for their child and instead wants to resort to his Jewish identity and raise their child in that faith—a desire his wife does not share. Both husband and wife find their identities challenged or even threatened, as they cannot draw on their beliefs and values to reinforce their cultural identities. Thus, whatever they decide, their identities affect and are affected by their decision.

Or consider the real-life example of a teacher at Amelia County High School in Virginia, who was told not to wear African headdresses after some parents complained when she wore them during Black History Month (Teacher may not wear African hats, 1995). The school had a policy against hats unless they were related to religious customs. The teacher said she would stop wearing the headdresses but felt very strongly about how they represented her appreciation of her heritage. Was this conflict about tangible resources (headdresses) or intangible resources (freedom of expression vs. adherence to rules)? Both. In the end, it was a clash over cultural identities: The teacher identified with the African American culture, while school officials identified with the dominant Anglo-Saxon culture, one of whose rules prohibits wearing hats in school. Again, whatever decision the two sides make in the future is going to be affected by and affect their identities. In intercultural conflict, therefore, we must learn how to "allocate" our very identities.

Because an intercultural conflict is a perceived disagreement over resource allocation, achieving a deep understanding of an intercultural conflict requires that we identify its roots. Such identification becomes more difficult as resources get more intangible. Yet only this way can we find out what is really at stake in a conflict. Otherwise, we run the risk of identifying a conflict with only its most tangible resources, such as water, oil, a T-shirt, or a headdress.

Two Sides of Conflict. The nature of conflict is dialectic, as every conflict has two contradictory sides—destructive and constructive. Let's look first at the destructive side of an intercultural conflict.

1. A conflict often intensifies blurred perceptions of the other culture and our own; it seems that our culture and the other culture are polar opposites.
2. As a result of magnifying differences and minimizing similarities, people often become locked into their positions. Such inflexibility often results in an impasse or violence.
3. As a result of an impasse or violence, the relationship between people may be spoiled or completely ruined.
4. As a result of a ruined relationship, we come to view conflict negatively—as an emotionally draining experience charged with animosity, anger, and frustration.

Now let's look at the constructive side of an intercultural conflict.

1. A conflict can help us to become more aware of the other culture and our own. Through conflict, we get a clearer picture of the identity of people from the other culture and our own cultural identity.
2. As a result of such awareness, we are able to see and articulate our positions, finding out that we share a lot of interests with other people. Thus, we overcome an impasse and avoid violence.
3. As a result of finding shared interests, we manage to solve conflict and grow stronger; the relationship between us and people from the other culture grows stronger.
4. As a result of our strengthened relationship, we come to view conflict positively—as an emotionally stimulating and enjoyable experience.

It might seem that we have just described two different conflict situations. However, we have simply looked at one and the same conflict situation from two different sides! You might have noticed that each destructive feature of conflict, as if reflected in a mirror, has its constructive counterpart. Table 1 summarizes the dual nature of conflict.

In every conflict situation, these two sides—destructive and constructive—exist together. The goal of intercultural communication is not to *eliminate* conflict, for its constructive side with all its transformative potential would be eliminated as well. In intercultural communication, the goal is to *manage* conflict. In other words, people must learn how to control its destructive side while making the most of its constructive side. A conflict is like growing pains; people from different cultures must learn how to handle it, avoiding pathological processes and promoting healthy growth. The Japanese use the metaphor of **nemawashi**—cutting around the roots of a tree before transplanting it, enabling the tree to bear better fruit. Gently working around the roots of a conflict helps people to adjust to differences and make their relationships more harmonious. It is important to emphasize that in the process of nemawashi we cut around the roots of a tree not in order to pull it out, but in order to transplant it and help it grow better. Similarly,

TABLE 1 Conflict

DESTRUCTIVE SIDE	CONSTRUCTIVE SIDE
Blurred perceptions of another culture and our own culture	Increased awareness of another culture and our own culture
Inflexibility of positions without a productive outcome	Flexibility to look for shared interest and a productive outcome
Ruined relationship	Strengthened relationship
Negative view of conflict	Positive view of conflict

we cannot manage a conflict unless we can work around its roots before "transplanting" (resolving) it in order to enjoy better "fruit" (potential). So, once again we see that a deep understanding of an intercultural conflict requires that we identify its roots. How we manage the conflict after we identify its roots depends on our approach to conflict, or what route we take.

Routes

A number of different approaches to conflict resolution have been suggested. All these approaches, however, begin with the same **dual concern model** (Pruitt & Rubin, 1986). This model is fundamental because it provides a foundation for analyzing conflict in terms of two main concerns—our own culture's outcomes and the other culture's outcomes. Often, this model is represented in the form of a table with two dimensions; in Figure 1, Self (our culture) is shown on the vertical axis, and the Other (the other culture) is shown on the horizontal axis. Theoretically, within the space of these two dimensions, we could identify an infinite number of ways of resolving conflict. However, several main approaches can be isolated. Let's look at these main ways of managing intercultural conflict.

As an example, we will use the incident that took place at one of Motorola's branches in East Asia, discussed in Chapter 7 as a form of intercultural praxis. As you may recall, one day a senior East Asian engineer had to be contacted urgently at home and was found to be living in a shack, even though Motorola had given all the engineers a $2,000 housing allowance so that they could live adjacent to

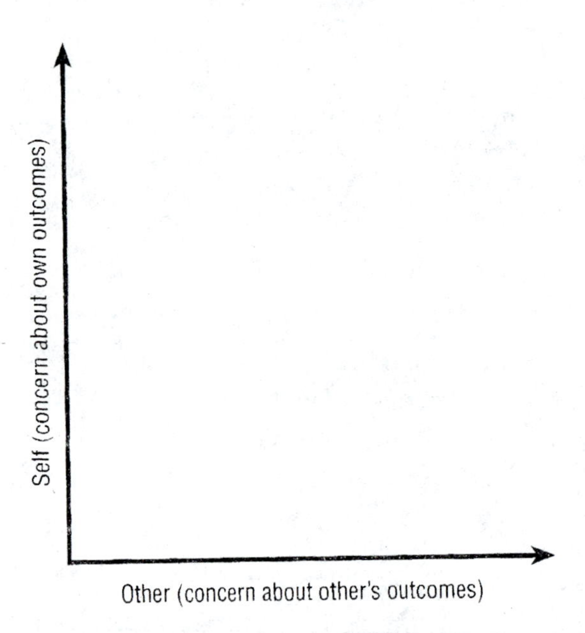

FIGURE 1 Dual Concern Model

the plant. It turned out that the engineer had spent his housing allowance on putting his siblings through school. It was clearly a tense situation for both sides, and it could be handled in several ways.

Avoidance. The easiest option for both sides in this situation is to do nothing. Neither side might really be too concerned about the outcome of the incident; the East Asian engineer might think he had not done anything wrong, and Motorola management might not be worried about such a small (for the corporation) sum of money. Yet the funds have clearly been misallocated, emphasizing the contradictory desires of the two sides. To ignore this fact might not be the best approach, because the root of the conflict would not be addressed. As a result, the conflict might turn into a more explosive situation later on. For example, the same engineer might need to be contacted in another emergency situation and not be found; then the corporation might lose time, money, or even lives. Or Motorola management might decide to confront the engineer after he keeps misusing the money, and his reaction might be one of rightful surprise or indignation since nothing had ever been said to him about past incidents. This confrontation could create bad blood between the engineer and the company or perhaps even a lawsuit. Left unattended, this small conflict might go away, but it might also turn into a much bigger one.

This approach to conflict can be called **avoidance;** it consists of not managing tensions at all. This approach of inaction shows no concern for the outcome of the interaction on the part of people from either culture. It can be illustrated as shown in Figure 2.

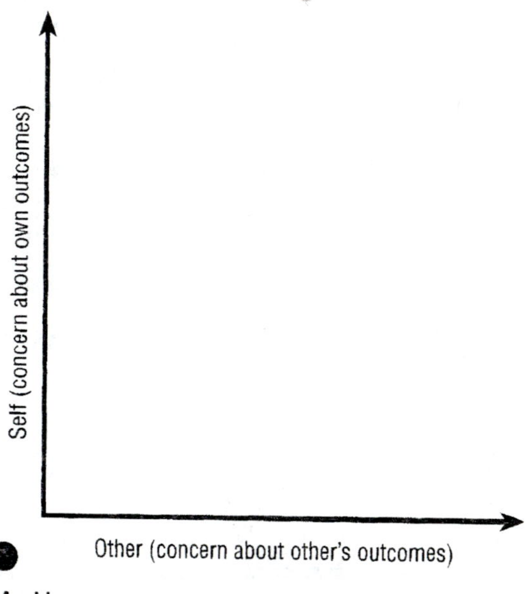

FIGURE 2

Polarization. Quite likely, the two sides in this conflict will take some action rather than avoid the tensions. Each side might naturally be concerned about the outcome of the situation for itself, but show little or no concern for the Other. For example, Motorola managers might not want to tolerate any violation of the rules, no matter how small, so their resolution might be to fire the engineer on the spot. In the same vein, the engineer, because of hurt feelings or stubbornness, might decide to leave the corporation. Such a response by Motorola would show little concern about losing the engineer; such a response by the engineer would show little concern about working for the company. These two positions are clearly at odds; in fact, they are diametrically opposite.

This competing or dominating approach to intercultural tensions can be called **polarization;** it shows high concern on the part of each culture for Self and little concern for the Other, as is illustrated in Figure 3.

Compromise. If the two sides take time to cool off, they might choose another route to resolving their tensions. Both sides might realize that they cannot achieve their goals without each other. Motorola values the engineer as a well-trained specialist, while the engineer values the corporation and his job—without this job, his siblings' education would be at risk. At the same time, Motorola management is reluctant to let the engineer have his way with the funds; after all, the engineer had been given the money to rent a place near the plant so as to be readily available when necessary. And the engineer might be reluctant to continue working for Motorola if forced to use the $2,000 allowance only for housing. With these realizations, the two sides show a moderate degree of concern for Self and the Other.

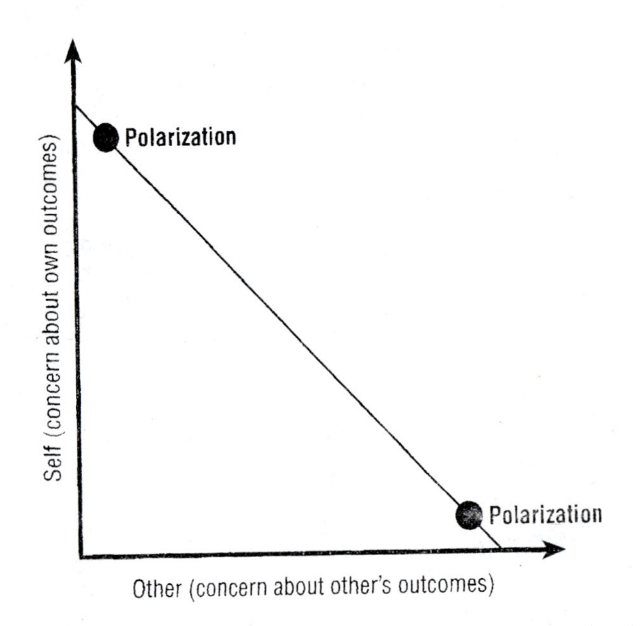

FIGURE 3

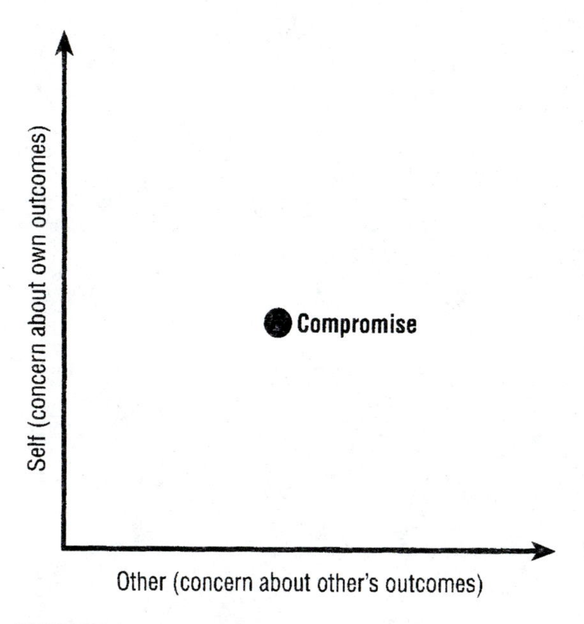

FIGURE 4

It is therefore only natural for the two sides to meet each other halfway. Thus, the decision might be for the engineer to spend half of the allowance ($1,000) on housing and the other half ($1,000) on education. Motorola's goal had been to have the engineer spend $2,000 (not $1,000) on housing, and the engineer's goal had been to spend $2,000 (not $1,000) on his children's education, so neither's goal would be *completely* met.

This approach to intercultural tensions can be called **compromise;** it often involves a classic 50/50 split, acceptable to both sides because each side gets (or does not get) the "same." The compromise approach to conflict can be illustrated as shown in Figure 4.

Integration. It is common to consider compromise the ultimate resolution of intercultural tensions; for instance, one hears such expressions as "a compromise has finally been reached." Yet another approach to conflict is possible, exhibiting a higher concern for people from both cultures (Self and the Other) than is shown by compromise. In our example, managers at Motorola are obviously concerned about the success of their own operation, which involves rules being followed and funds being used appropriately. At the same time, they might be equally concerned about the engineer because he has put the money to good use based on the local values. By the same token, the engineer is obviously concerned about his siblings' education, but he might be equally concerned about the successful operation of the corporation. If the two sides spend enough time discussing the situation and openly sharing their needs and desires, they might find a solution that satisfies their goals more fully than compromise. For example, one decision might be that

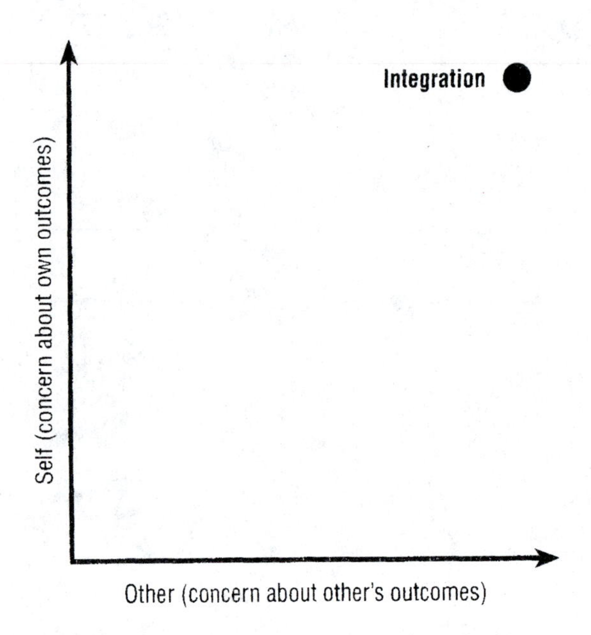

FIGURE 5

the corporation would provide education for the engineer's siblings as long as the engineer promised to be readily available at all times. This might prove easier and cheaper for the corporation than the proposed compromise, and the engineer's motivation and loyalty might increase. The corporation's real-life decision—changing the rule and letting its engineers use the allowance for their own purposes as long as they remained available and local values were implemented—fits into this approach.

This collaborative approach to intercultural tensions, which shows high concern for people from both cultures, can be called **integration.** It can be represented as shown in Figure 5.

Thus, four main approaches to managing intercultural conflict are possible:

1. Avoidance, with no concern for Self or the Other
2. Polarization, with high concern for Self and low concern for the Other
3. Compromise, with moderate concern for both Self and the Other
4. Integration, with high concern for both Self and the Other

Each of these approaches can be seen as a mechanism behind the pendulum of intercultural communication. These four main approaches are depicted together in Figure 6.

Transactions. Notice that in each of the four approaches we have discussed, a decision is made *by* the people from the different cultures. There are situations, however, when a decision is made *for* the two sides by a third party. This may hap-

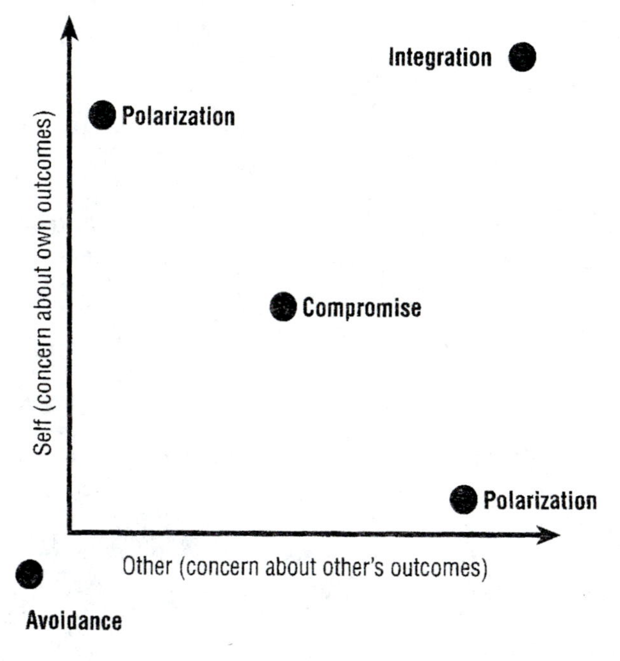

FIGURE 6

pen when the situation is extremely volatile, prompting third-party involvement in the conflict. There are two main approaches to resolving conflict when a third party is involved: **arbitration** and **mediation** (for more information, see Brett, 2001). Arbitrators are authorized to make a decision for the parties in conflict but not to control the process of their interaction. Mediators are authorized to control the process of interaction of the parties in conflict but not to impose a decision upon them.

In the end, people from different cultures find the best and most lasting solution to their tensions when they themselves control both the process of their interaction and its outcome. The two sides have to come to the realization that they must open up channels of communication and manage conflict together. In this sense, intercultural interaction is always a transaction. We usually think of transactions in a business setting; however, any interaction that affects both sides and results in some kind of resolution is a **transaction.** Even such a simple act of communication as saying "Hello!" or smiling at someone is an example of a transaction. During transactions, people try to negotiate with each other and reach an agreement. The word *negotiation* comes from the Latin *negotium, neg* meaning not and *otium* meaning leisure. Communication as a transaction is "not leisure"—that is, it is serious business. And it is certainly not a game! Just think of all the examples discussed in this chapter and earlier in the book. Are the Greeks and Turks in Cyprus amused by trying to solve their dilemma? Is the battle between the U'wa Indians of Colombia and Occidental Petroleum a harmless game? And was any fun had by the relatives and friends of Yoshihiro Hattori, a Japanese exchange student who was shot and killed in Baton Rouge, Louisiana, after he went to the wrong door when looking for a Halloween party and apparently did not understand the command "Freeze!"?

We must not think of transactions only as two or more parties sitting around a table and conducting rounds of formal business negotiations. Whenever we come into contact with people from other cultures, our goal is to carry interaction through and reach an agreement; this resolution affects both us and other people. The transactional nature of intercultural communication becomes especially clear when tensions intensify; then finding a resolution becomes crucial.

Introducing the Transaction Principle

The discussion above has laid the groundwork for the eighth principle underlying intercultural communication—the Transaction Principle. As with the previous principles, we will isolate three parts that make up this principle. Each part deals with intercultural communication as a transaction. First, we will discuss how our perception affects the outcome of intercultural transactions. Next, we will look at intercultural transactions in terms of negotiation zones. Finally, we will discuss intercultural transactions as a process of moving from positions to interests. We will discuss each part separately and then formulate the Transaction Principle as a whole.

Intercultural Transactions: Perception and Reality

As we saw earlier, perception is very important in approaching intercultural communication. Resolution of intercultural tensions depends on how intercultural transactions are perceived.

There are three main patterns of perception that determine the outcome of intercultural transactions: zero-sum, fixed-sum, and flexible-sum (cf. Thompson, 2000). The word *sum* here refers to the amount of value (resources) perceived to exist in the situation of intercultural interaction.

Zero-Sum Perception. The zero-sum pattern implies that there is no (zero) value in interacting; each side believes that it can create value on its own, without any help from the Other. Thus, with the **zero-sum perception,** value in intercultural transaction is ignored.

In this case, people do not perceive any tension between them and are not concerned about what may happen as a result of non-interaction. It is easy to see that the zero-sum perception is the basis for the avoidance approach to intercultural communication.

With two circles, Figure 7 illustrates how people from two different cultures seem to exist separately; yet the dashed lines between them indicate that the two circles still can, and must, be connected. In other words, potential can, and must, be realized for mutual benefit.

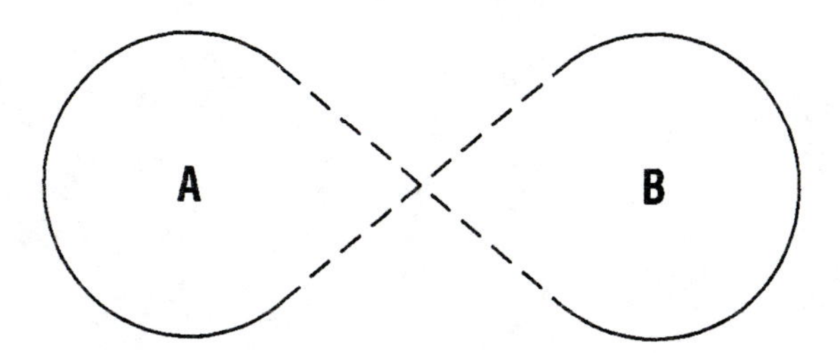

FIGURE 7

Fixed-Sum Perception. According to the fixed-sum pattern, value is fixed; sometimes the **fixed-sum perception** is called a fixed pie perception (Lewicki et al., 1997: 74). When it comes to dividing the pie, anything one culture gets, the other does not; hence, people from every culture try to distribute the pie in such a way that they can have a bigger piece (more resources). The fixed-sum pattern of perception is about claiming or distributing resources; as a result, value in intercultural transaction is claimed or distributed.

People subscribing to the fixed-sum pattern may perceive each other as polar opposites (enemies). Such a perception leads to the idea that the right way to manage tensions is "my" way—if other people do not share my views, their culture must be conquered and eliminated; otherwise, they will conquer and eliminate my culture. This is an "either/or" mentality, leading to cultural aggression and domination. Only one culture can emerge as the winner of this intercultural interaction: the one that claims more resources—ideally, all of them. It is easy to see that the fixed-sum perception is the basis for the polarization approach to intercultural communication. Perceiving interaction in terms of polarization is not a constructive approach to managing intercultural tensions. By destroying what we perceive to be our enemy, we deprive ourselves of the possibility of interacting with the Other; in essence, we destroy ourselves. That is why cultural domination is not only destructive of other cultures, but also self-destructive. If we completely eliminate our "enemy," we have no one to interact with. It is said that the next worst thing to losing a war is winning it.

Figure 8 depicts the result of a battle between people from two cultures over resources, in which culture A is clearly the "winner." When the ultimate "victory" is proclaimed—that is, when culture B disappears—intercultural communication will stop.

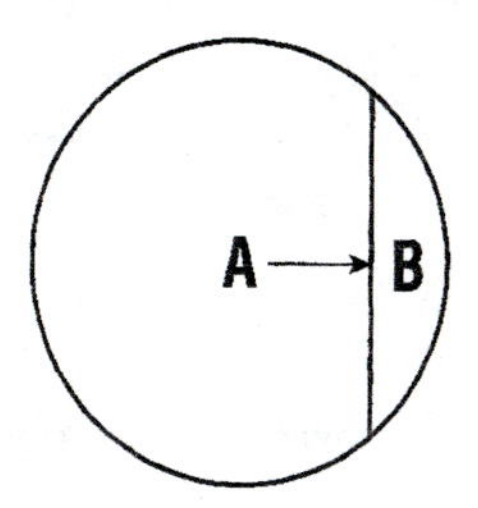

FIGURE 8

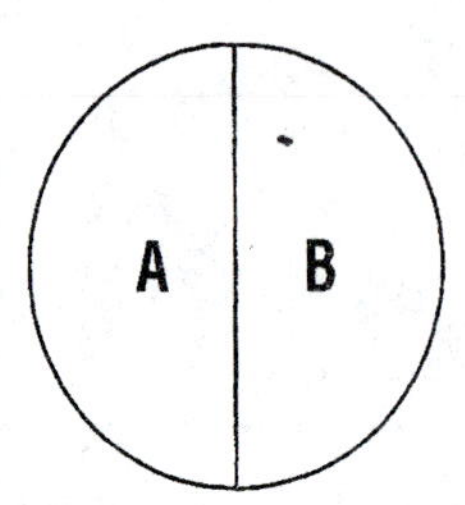

FIGURE 9

If people do not perceive each other as polar opposites but yet do not perceive each other as friends, willing to cooperate and share their resources, the outcome of an intercultural transaction may be agreeing to disagree. The optimal way to reach such an agreement is by dividing all available resources in half. Thus, it is easy to see that the fixed-sum perception is also the basis for the compromise approach to intercultural communication; here, the sum is distributed equally so that each culture gets 50 percent of the value.

Figure 9 shows people from two cultures splitting the value in half. Obviously, this outcome is not as destructive as the one based on polarization; after all, your culture claims half of all available resources. But this outcome is not constructive either, because it does not help people to construct their collective identity.

Flexible-Sum Perception. According to the flexible-sum pattern, the sum is flexible: Any situation of intercultural communication is perceived as dynamic and subject to change. Here, the objective of an intercultural transaction is not to ignore or to claim value, but to create value together to enlarge the pie so that all people can have a bigger piece. The **flexible-sum perception** implies that value cannot be created unilaterally, because people can create and sustain their resources only in dynamic interaction with each other; as a result, value in intercultural communication is created and shared.

People subscribing to the flexible-sum pattern perceive each other as friends, willing to cooperate and share their resources. You might wonder how this sharing can be accomplished. With compromise, we seem to have reached the optimal outcome, as 50/50 appears to be the most acceptable and fair way to divide value. Well, not if we base our view of intercultural communication on the flexible-sum perception! If we view any intercultural situation as dynamic and subject to change, we can move *beyond* that separating line and into the space occupied by the Other. Naturally, this might be perceived by the Other as a dangerous move because we claim its resources. But if we allow the Other to move into our space and share some of our resources, then both cultures win. And reaching out and allowing the Other to use our resources changes both cultures. Another culture becomes part of ours, and vice versa. Thus, both cultures join forces, integrating their resources, yet still remain distinct cultures with their own values. It is easy to see that the flexible-sum perception is the basis for the integration approach to intercultural communication.

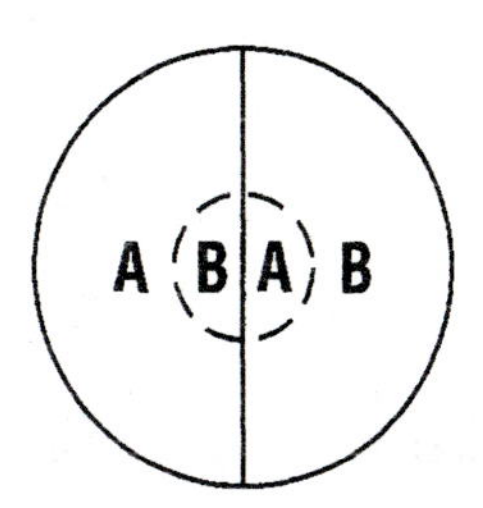

FIGURE 10

Figure 10 shows the integration of two cultures—part of culture A exists within culture B, and vice versa.

Figure 10 might remind you of the famous Taoistic Yin and Yang symbol discussed in Chapter 6, which represents the type of integration in which two different sides change into each other and share the other's qualities. Similarly, as people from two different cultures share their resources, they flow into each other and form a shared space.

Reality. As was said earlier, perception determines the outcome of intercultural transactions. Table 2 presents the three main patterns of perception and the four approaches to intercultural transactions based on these patterns, along with the resultant treatment of value.

Our perception of intercultural communication becomes reality, as we ourselves create the outcomes of our transactions. Our cultural resources are at the mercy of our perception. We might be unaware of their existence or potential (zero-sum perception), we might fight for them and squander them in the process or sit on them stingily like a dog in the manger (fixed-sum), or we might share them and allow them to grow (flexible-sum perception). It is clear that for a transaction to be successful, people from different cultures must move from avoiding each other to integrating their potential. Without a doubt, this is a difficult task; it is easier to ignore each other or perceive each other as enemies. Working out a compromise is more challenging, but even then people generate no new knowledge of each other because no real exchange of meanings takes place. Compromise should be described as conciliatory because it "results in no genuine resolution and hence no new understanding at all" (Ho, 2000: 1065). Only with

TABLE 2

PATTERN OF PERCEPTION	APPROACH	VALUE
Zero-sum	Avoidance	Ignored
Fixed-sum	Polarization	Claimed/Distributed
	Compromise	
Flexible-sum	Integration	Created/Shared

integration do people share their resources and create a shared space, which allows them to sustain and develop their unique identities. This shared space is a special zone where they carry out their transactions—that is, where intercultural communication takes place.

Intercultural Communication as a Negotiation Zone

When people engage in a transaction, each side must make two important decisions. First, each side must set a clear goal (i.e., what it wants to achieve); this goal is called the **target point.** Second, each side must set a stopping point beyond which the side will not go, preferring to break off interaction; this stopping point is called the **resistance point.** A resistance point cannot be determined without thinking of a back-up plan, called the **BATNA** (Best Alternative To Negotiated Agreement). In other words, each side must think about what can be done if the desired goal is not achieved.

Let's take a typical case of intercultural transaction. Suppose you go to a market in Tunisia and see a man selling beautiful Berber jewelry that incorporates silver and amber in complicated forms. He wants 25 dinars for each piece of his jewelry (target point); in his mind, however, he is willing to go as low as 10 dinars (resistance point). The seller has set this resistance point based on his BATNA, which might be selling his merchandise wholesale later in the day. You want to buy one piece of jewelry from him for 5 dinars (target point), but you are willing to go as high as 15 dinars (resistance point). You will not pay more than 15 dinars because of your own BATNA—you might have seen a similar piece elsewhere for about the same price. So, you start bargaining with the man. Does the intercultural transaction between you as a buyer and the man as a seller have potential for being successful? Yes; this potential exists in the form of a negotiation zone, also known as a bargaining range, settlement range, or zone of potential agreement (Lewicki et al., 1997: 33). The **negotiation zone** is the spread between the two resistance points; in our example, this spread is 5 dinars—the difference between 10 and 15 dinars. It is within this zone that you and the man should carry out your transaction, trying to find a resolution.

Let's see how this intercultural transaction can be represented graphically. Figure 11 shows the seller's target and resistance points. Figure 12 shows the buyer's target and resistance points. Finally, Figure 13 depicts the actual transaction between the seller and the buyer. The negotiation zone is the overlapping range in the middle; herein lies potential for a productive intercultural resolution.

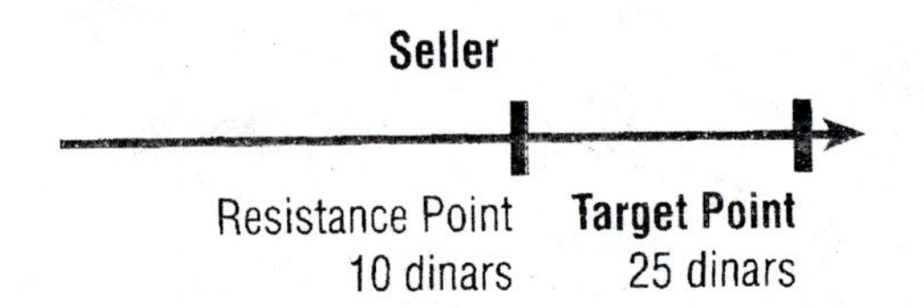

FIGURE 11

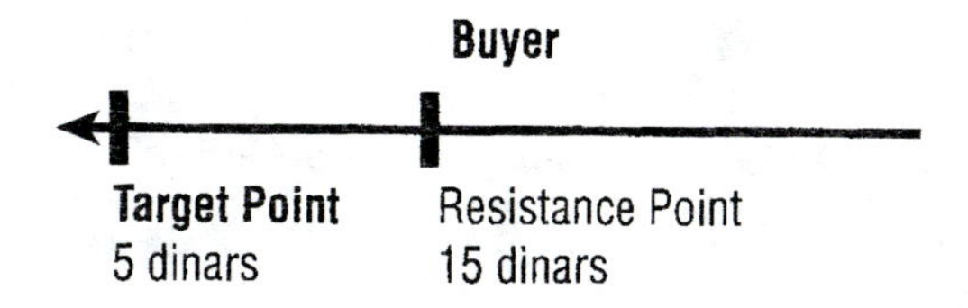

FIGURE 12

In real-life situations, of course, it is very difficult to determine one's target and resistance points with mathematical precision. As you may remember, intercultural conflict is a disagreement over resource allocations, and resources are not always as tangible as a manufactured product with a price tag. How is it possible to calculate the value of such resources as reputation, power, and affection? However, even such intangible resources must be evaluated and represented in the form of target and resistance points; unless people do this homework, they may never figure out whether a negotiation zone exists and what this zone is. People may waste a lot of time and effort trying to find a resolution when no negotiation zone exists. Or, on the other hand, people may think that there is no negotiation zone in a situation when in fact such a zone exists and they are simply unable to find it. As a result, the potential of the negotiation zone is not realized, and people miss their opportunity to benefit from it. In the summer of 1990, the cultures of Quebec and the Mohawk tribe clashed over extending a golf course into land that the Mohawk felt was sacred (Friesen, 1991). The Mohawk wanted to talk about their sovereignty, land claims, and preservation of natural resources. The Quebec officials perceived the Mohawk tribe as warriors and criminals. In the end, the Mohawk tribe erected barricades and the Quebec police took them down. The golf course was not extended, but the tensions were not resolved, because no negotiation zone was ever found or created by the conflicting sides.

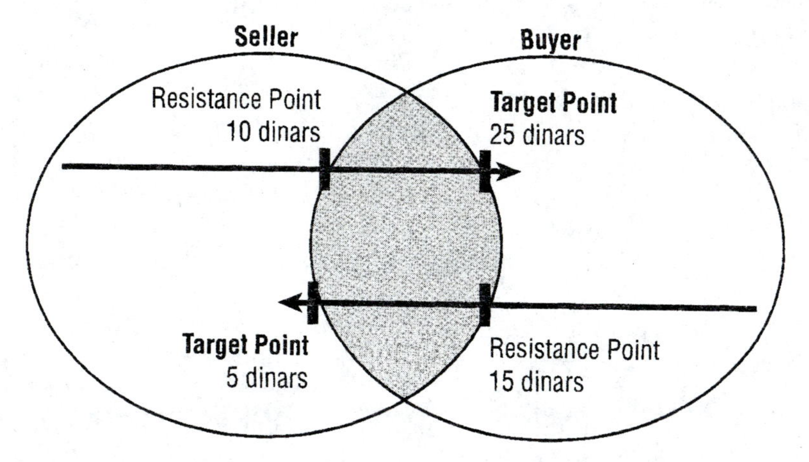

FIGURE 13 Negotiation Zone in an Intercultural Transaction

If a negotiation zone is perceived as nonexistent or small, then potential for a constructive intercultural resolution is also nonexistent or small. Let's see how a negotiation zone with potential can be created or expanded to facilitate intercultural transactions.

Back to the Future: From Positions to Interests

As you know, every intercultural transaction involves a clash of cultural identities. In concrete situations, cultural identities are manifested in the form of specific resources, tangible or intangible, and each resource might become an issue of conflict. Every intercultural conflict is characterized by one or more issues; naturally, the more issues involved, the more complex a transaction is. Therefore, in every conflict, the main issues (resources) must be identified. For example, in the Motorola case discussed earlier, the main issues are the amount of money, education for the engineer's siblings, and the availability of the engineer. In the case of the 16-year-old student and school officials in Dearborn, Michigan, the main issues are the T-shirt, freedom of expression, and safety.

On every issue, people from different cultures take a stand, expressing a certain **position.** In other words, each side states what it wants. For example, in the Dearborn, Michigan, situation, the student wanted to wear the T-shirt, while school officials did not want him to wear it to school. In Chapter 4, we discussed in more detail how each culture positions itself and claims its vision of the world. Often, positions that different cultures take in a conflict situation appear in complete opposition; as a result, no negotiation zone seems to exist, and reaching a resolution seems impossible. Focusing only on positions often leads to an impasse in intercultural transactions or even physical violence. That is why people must look beyond their positions and identify the interests that underlie each situation.

As you remember from Chapter 6, **interests** are underlying needs and desires that motivate people from a culture to take a certain position. Identifying interests is more difficult than identifying positions because interests are grounded in resources that are less tangible. And yet this is the best way to make sure common ground is identified and a productive resolution is worked out. Instead of looking only at their positions, which are usually divergent and often appear to be in complete opposition, people must look for shared interests and build decisions on their solid foundation. Consider the situation in India, where the conflict between Sikhs and Hindus had been escalating for a long time (see Fisher et al., 1994). Their positions appeared to be in opposition: Sikhs wanted independence and more access to water resources, while Hindus wanted India to be unified and water resources to be distributed equally. In spite of these different positions, three shared interests were found. First, both sides wanted economic prosperity for Punjab. Second, both sides wanted a reduction in ethnic fighting. Third, both sides wanted Sikhs to regain confidence in the Indian government.

Let's take a quick look at some examples discussed in this chapter and see how shared interests can be identified, helping the interacting sides to reach a more constructive resolution of their tensions.

With the two friends who must decide on an ethnic restaurant (the very first example in this chapter), identifying shared interests is relatively simple. Most likely, they still want to remain friends. As a result, they should find it easy to work out a mutually acceptable solution. For example, as was mentioned, they might decide to try Thai one night and Mexican another night or to compromise on an Italian restaurant.

In the situation of the 16-year-old student in Dearborn, the tensions are higher and the transaction more complex. The positions of the student and school officials appear in complete opposition, which only makes it more crucial to look for shared interests; otherwise, a constructive resolution can hardly be found. It is quite likely that both sides (student and school officials) want their school to be a nurturing learning environment with a good reputation. If they focus less on their positions and more on shared interests, or common ground, the two sides have a better chance of reaching a mutually acceptable resolution—that is, of conducting their intercultural transaction successfully.

Thus, in every transaction, people from different cultural groups must move from battling over positions to a "collaborative focus on shared and underlying interests (each side's needs, concerns, hopes, and fears that lay beneath their positions)" (Rothman & Olson, 2001: 294). As people move from identifying positions to identifying common interests, they work toward a resolution acceptable to both sides, through which each side is able to realize its own goals more successfully. In a way, it is necessary to go back to the root of conflict; however, this backward movement is the only way to move forward toward a successful resolution.

The Transaction Principle Defined

Now we can give a more concise formulation of the Transaction Principle, based on the above discussion of its three parts.

First, our perception determines the outcome of an intercultural transaction. We saw how the three main patterns of perception are related to the four approaches to intercultural interactions. For their interactions to be successful, cultures must move from avoiding each other to integrating their resources. Then they can reach a constructive resolution of their tensions.

Second, intercultural transactions take place within a special zone known as a negotiation zone, bargaining range, settlement range, or zone of potential agreement. In this zone lies the potential for a productive intercultural resolution. Thus, such a zone must be created or expanded to its optimal potential for both sides.

Third, every intercultural situation is manifested in the form of specific resources, tangible or intangible, and each resource may become an issue. People take a stand on each issue, expressing a certain position. Positions might appear to be in complete opposition, and no negotiation zone might appear to exist. That is why it is important to look beyond positions and identify interests that motivate people to take a certain position. By moving from identifying positions to identifying shared interests, parties are more likely to reach a mutually acceptable resolution.

In a nutshell, the Transaction Principle can be formulated as follows:

Intercultural communication is a process whereby people from different cultures move within a negotiation zone from positions to interests, in search of an acceptable resolution.

This principle teaches us that intercultural communication is always a transaction. When cultures come into contact, both sides are affected by how their transaction is resolved. Intercultural communication cannot be considered effective without a resolution of tensions.

Summary

We started this chapter by defining intercultural conflict as a perceived disagreement over allocation of resources. We emphasized that resources have two sides, tangible and intangible, making up a cultural identity. In the end, every intercultural conflict is a disagreement over different identities. Achieving deep understanding of an intercultural conflict requires that we identify its resources, which becomes more difficult to do as resources become more intangible.

Next, we discussed the destructive and constructive sides of intercultural conflict. We emphasized that these two sides exist together in every situation; that is why conflict cannot be eliminated but must be managed. In other words, the destructive side of conflict must be kept under control, while the constructive side of conflict must be enhanced. Every intercultural conflict has transformative potential that must be realized.

Next, we showed how intercultural conflict can be managed, following four different routes: avoidance, polarization, compromise, and integration. These approaches to conflict are based on our perception of intercultural communication as a transaction. We showed how the three main patterns of perception (zero-sum, fixed-sum, and flexible-sum) are related to the four routes identified above. We emphasized that our perception of intercultural communication becomes reality as we ourselves create the outcomes of intercultural transactions.

We noted that intercultural communication is more effective when people perceive their transaction as flexible-sum and are willing to integrate their resources. Then a shared space is created where people can carry out their transactions. We looked at this space as a negotiation zone. It was pointed out that if this zone is perceived as nonexistent or small, potential for a constructive resolution of intercultural tensions is also nonexistent or small. Thus, it was concluded that a negotiation zone with potential must be created or expanded to facilitate intercultural transactions.

We showed that an intercultural transaction is more likely to be effective when the parties from different cultures move from staking out positions to taking an interest in trying to find a resolution to their tensions. Positions of the conflicting sides often appear to be in complete opposition, but common interests can, and must, be found for a constructive resolution. Thus, we essentially need to go back to the root of conflict to move forward toward resolution.

Based on these ideas, the Transaction Principle was formulated.

It is clearly important for people from different cultures to move from positions to interests and make the most of the negotiation zone. It is likewise important for people to be flexible and integrate their resources. But why, exactly, is intercultural integration so important? And what *is* integration, anyway? We will discuss this in the next chapter.

CASE STUDY

"THE WALL OF DEATH": A CONFLICT BETWEEN JAPANESE AND WESTERN CULTURES

This case study is based on an article entitled "Intercultural Conflict: A Case Study" by Bradford 'J' Hall and Mutsumi Noguchi (1993). As usual, it is recommended that you read the article in its entirety; below is a summary of the article.

Be ready to identify and then discuss the following topics:

1. The issues in this conflict
2. The positions and interests of the two conflicting sides
3. The success of the resolution of the intercultural transaction

In the spring of 1978, the fishermen of Iki Island in Japan invited Japanese TV reporters to cover the story of dolphins versus drift-net fishing. The fishermen's catch was on the decline, and they attributed the problem to an increasing dolphin presence. The Japanese fishermen hoped that media coverage would bring them assistance in their battle with the dolphins. However, the coverage reached around the world and, instead of sympathy, the fishermen's practice was met with outrage in many Western cultures, especially the United States. (The authors of the article note that they chose the gloss "Western" because a number of Western cultures had a reaction similar to that of the United States.)

Following the media coverage of more than one thousand dolphin deaths, Western conservationists came to Japan to discuss the problem. They tried to explain to the fishermen that dolphins were not responsible for the declining catch, but they failed to change the Iki fishermen's attitude. Under cover of night, several of the conservationists freed hundreds of dolphins.

In 1982, the issue was partially resolved by a compromise: The Japanese fishermen promised to stop capturing and killing dolphins en masse, while the Western conservationists promised not to come to the island again in order to free dolphins. However, this compromise had not resolved the conflict, and drift-net fishing practices continued. By the end of 1991, a variety of wildlife, including many dolphins, had died in a string of nets that stretched for miles; *Time* magazine described this string as the "Wall of Death." Disagreements continued, revealing a clash of cultural worlds.

The authors of the article discuss in detail how the Western symbol *dolphin* and its Japanese equivalent *iruka,* while referring to the same mammal, evoke different cultural interpretations. In the Japanese culture, a dolphin (*iruka*) is perceived as either food or an evil creature of the sea. Today, few Japanese eat dolphin, and the dolphins killed by the Iki fishermen were not killed for human consumption. However, dolphins are widely used as fertilizer and pig food. Since dolphins are known to gobble up large quantities of fish, Japanese fishermen perceive them as direct competitors. Dolphins are viewed as enemies, or "gangsters," threatening the livelihood of the fishermen. The term *iruka* evokes such associations in Japan as "evil," "damage," and "threat." Those who fight against such evil creatures are seen as heroic warriors. Naturally, when Western conservationists tried to convince the Japanese fishermen to stop killing dolphins, their arguments failed, and they were perceived by the fishermen as lacking compassion. The fishermen tried to accommodate the Western conservationists who came to Japan, but became frustrated and uncooperative faced with the conservationists' bossy attitude and lack of recognition of the seriousness of the fishermen's plight.

In Western cultures, dolphins are seen as highly intelligent and friendly mammals. A special bond is perceived to exist between humans and dolphins, as evidenced by tales of rescue and dolphins' seeming efforts to communicate with humans. Thus, humans identify with dolphins, and this affinity explains why the Western conservationists were shocked by the slaughter. The Western conservationists tried to convince the Japanese fishermen that their own practices were more to blame for their problem than the dolphins were, but they had little success. Those Western conservationists who freed hundreds of dolphins under cover of night were perceived by their cultures as heroes.

Finally, Japan's Prime Minister announced that Japanese fishermen would stop using drift-net fishing practices by the end of 1992. In making that announcement, the Japanese side gave no indication of ever having been in the wrong. The Western conservationists were happy with this resolution, while the Japanese fishermen found it not particularly satisfying. The authors of the article quote one of the fishermen as saying that their future is pitch black.

DISCUSSION

Now, let's see how this case study can be an illustration of the Transaction Principle of intercultural communication.

1. The issues in this conflict. We have discussed how intercultural conflict is a clash of identities. In concrete situations, cultural identities are manifested in the form of specific resources, tangible and intangible, and each resource might become an issue of conflict.

In this case, the tangible resource is obvious: the dolphins. However, another issue, equally important, is found in the intangible resources: the symbolic meanings associated with *dolphin* (in the West) and *iruka* (in Japan).

In the Japanese culture, the *iruka* is viewed as an evil creature, threatening the livelihood of the fishermen. Those people who fight against such evil creatures are seen as heroic warriors. In Western cultures, the dolphin is perceived as a highly intelligent and friendly mammal. Therefore, people feel strongly about protecting the dolphin's special status. In short, there are (at least) two main issues in this conflict: dealing with the mammals and dealing with the people's perceptions of the dolphin and the *iruka*, including their self-perception in relation to this mammal. It is impossible to ignore either of these issues while trying to resolve this situation.

2. The positions and interests of the two conflicting sides. The positions of the two conflicting sides are clear: The Japanese fishermen want to continue catching and killing dolphins, while the Western conservationists want to put an end to such practices. Identifying interests is more difficult; as you remember, interests are the underlying needs and desires that motivate people from different cultures to take certain positions. In this case, the Japanese fishermen's actions are driven by their desire to protect their livelihood. Thus, their main interests are grounded in physiological and safety needs. The Western conservationists' actions are driven by a more complex desire to protect their special bond with dolphins; in essence, by defending dolphins' rights, the Western conservationists are defending their own identity. To kill such a mammal is to kill a friend; it means giving up some of the values that make up

(continued)

"THE WALL OF DEATH": A CONFLICT BETWEEN JAPANESE AND WESTERN CULTURES CONTINUED

the Western conservationists' cultural identity. Thus, their main interests are grounded in self-realization needs.

From the Japanese fishermen's perspective, the Western conservationists failed to understand their interests, displaying a bossy attitude and a lack of recognition of the seriousness of the fishermen's plight. From the Western conservationists' perspective, the Japanese fishermen failed to understand their interests, continuing to blame the dolphins for their problem. So the two sides did not really move from positions to interests, which affected the resolution of this intercultural transaction.

3. The success of the resolution of the intercultural transaction. The first time (in 1982), the conflict was partially resolved by a compromise: The Japanese fishermen promised to stop capturing and killing dolphins en masse, and the Western conservationists promised not to come to the island again in order to free dolphins. However, the tensions continued, and ten years later Japan's Prime Minister announced that Japanese fishermen would stop using drift-net fishing practices. The Western conservationists were happy with this resolution, but the Japanese fishermen found it not particularly satisfying; as one of the fishermen put it, their future was pitch black. This resolution fits the polarization approach—a lopsided solution that is not very stable because one side (Japan) is less happy than the other with the outcome and is more likely to try to change it.

What is most important, the transaction was not very successful because no genuine communication, in the form of an exchange of different points of view between the two sides, took place. The two sides failed to see the conflict through each other's eyes and change. For example, the Japanese side gave no indication of ever having been in the wrong; thus, their attitude toward dolphins and the whole situation had not changed. By the same token, the Western conservationists did not change their bossy attitude and failed to exhibit recognition of the seriousness of the fishermen's plight.

It is clear that the Japanese fishermen wanted to kill the dolphins not out of some cruel intentions, but for self-protection. By the same token, it is clear that the Western conservationists wanted to save the dolphins not at the expense of the fishermen's lives, but because of their special bond with the mammals. So saving lives (both human and dolphin) could have become a foundation of shared interests. Had such shared interests (or perhaps some others) been identified and had the two sides been willing to change, a more productive resolution could have been worked out.

SIDE TRIPS

1. The description below of tragic events in Ecuador is based on a bulletin from the World Rainforest Movement (2002).

> Recently, clashes took place between the Tagae people who live in the Amazon basin and Ecuadorian loggers; as a result of the conflict, an indigenous Tagaeri and three loggers are dead. The Tagaeris felt the loggers had invaded their territory, making excessive noise in their forest habitat and showing no respect toward their land and ancestors. According to the ancestral customs of the Tagae culture, anyone who violates their territory deserves death. The loggers knew of the Tagaeris' concern over their constant presence in the zone the Tagaeris felt belonged to them; however, they did not take notice and continued with their work. One day the Tagaeris attacked the loggers, who fired back, killing one of the members of the Tagae family. A few days later, the loggers were again attacked and three of them killed by the Tagaeris' lethal chonta lances.

   Identify the approach chosen by the people from the two different cultures to resolve their conflict.
2. When India's "garden city"—Bangalore—was chosen as a site for the Miss World beauty pageant, the plan was labeled a merchandising device for the decadent cultural imperialism of the West. The conflict over the beauty pageant turned into a fight over India's soul. According to Hinduism, a woman's beauty must be natural and not affected by cosmetics; also, opposition to the swimsuit contest was very strong. In addition, farmers in India were afraid that a wave of big agricultural interests would force them from their land. Many people in India also felt that the country had become a dumping ground for the West's rejects, and the Miss World beauty pageant was perceived as fitting the bill. Identify the main resources involved in this intercultural conflict.
3. The Amish culture is known to resist what Amish call the "English" culture of the outside world. Yet the Amish and the English have been able to manage their tensions quite well. For example, one can see Amish riding in cars and trucks or hiring outsiders to drive their produce to market, even though the Amish cannot own cars or trucks because they allow for too much contact with the outside world. Similarly, the Amish cannot use 110-volt electricity, because power lines would connect their culture with the English world; yet the Amish often use 12-volt batteries to generate electricity for their farms or shops. Identify the Amish approach to managing the conflict.

CHECK YOURSELF

Conflict
Nemawashi
Dual concern model
Avoidance
Polarization
Compromise
Integration
Arbitration
Mediation
Transaction
Zero-sum perception
Fixed-sum perception
Flexible-sum perception
Target point
Resistance point
BATNA
Negotiation zone
Positions
Interests

REFERENCES

Brett, J. (2001). *Negotiating globally: How to negotiate deals, resolve disputes, and make concessions across cultural boundaries.* San Francisco: Jossey-Bass.

Dinar, S. (2002). Water, security, conflict, and cooperation. *SAIS Review,* Vol. 22, No. 2, pp. 229–253.

Drilling blocked after tribe threatens suicide. (1997). *The Spokesman-Review,* February 4, p. A9.

Faure, G., & Rubin, J. (Eds.). (1993). *Culture and negotiation.* Thousand Oaks, CA: Sage.

Fisher, R., Kopelman, E., & Schneider, A. K. (1994). *Beyond Machiavelli: Tools for coping with conflict.* Cambridge, MA: Harvard University Press.

Friesen, R. (1991). Reflections on Oka: The Mohawk confrontation. *Conflict Resolution Notes,* Vol. 8, No. 4, pp. 36–38.

Hall, B., & Noguchi, M. (1993). Intercultural conflict: A case study. *International Journal of Intercultural Relations,* Vol. 17, pp. 399–413.

Ho, D. (2000). Dialectical thinking: Neither Eastern nor Western. *American Psychologist,* September, pp. 1062–1063.

Lewicki, R., Barry, B., Saunders, D. M., & Minton, J. W. (1997). *Essentials of negotiation.* New York: McGraw-Hill.

Pruitt, D. G., & Rubin, J. Z. (1986). *Social conflict: Escalation, stalemate and settlement.* New York: Random House.

Rothman, J., & Olson, M. (2001). From interests to identities: Towards a new emphasis in interactive conflict resolution. *Journal of Peace Research,* Vol. 38, No. 3, pp. 289–305.

Teacher may not wear African hats. (1995). *The Spokesman-Review,* March 1, p. A6.

Thompson, L. (2000). *The mind and the heart of the negotiator.* Englewood Cliffs, NJ: Prentice-Hall.

Ting-Toomey, S. (1999). *Communicating across cultures.* New York: Guilford.

World Rainforest Movement. (2002). Ecuador: clashes between indigenous group and loggers in the Amazon. *WRM Bulletin,* No. 58, May, http://www.wrm.org.uy/bulletin/58/Ecuador.html.

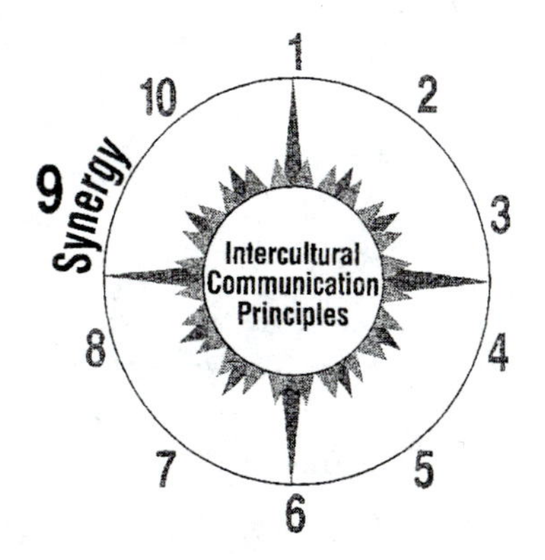

CHAPTER NINE

COOPERATION BETWEEN CULTURES: SYNERGY PRINCIPLE

2 + 2 = 5 (or more!)

- *Key Theme:* Cooperation
- *Key Objective:* To help you understand the nature and importance of intercultural collaboration

INTRODUCING THE PROBLEM QUESTION

PERCEPTION: SEIZING THE WORLD

Stereotype: Not All Swans Are White

Prejudice: The U.S. and the Rest-of-the-World Soccer Cup

INTERCULTURAL INTEGRATION: BREAKING DOWN THE WALL

INTRODUCING THE SYNERGY PRINCIPLE

Intercultural Synergy and Flow Dynamics

Intercultural Synergy and Nonsummativity

Toward Pareto Optimality

THE SYNERGY PRINCIPLE DEFINED

SUMMARY

CASE STUDY: THE CASE OF AMD: UNLEASHING INTERCULTURAL POTENTIAL

SIDE TRIPS

CHECK YOURSELF

REFERENCES

Introducing the Problem Question

In Chapter 8, we talked about intercultural communication as a transaction. We saw that an intercultural transaction takes place in a negotiation zone. Based on how this zone is viewed, a number of approaches to an intercultural transaction are possible. We noted that only with the integration approach do people perceive their transaction as having potential for mutual benefit. Even when no negotiation zone seems to exist, one can be created; it is as if people knew some secret for making a negotiation zone appear out of nowhere and finding a resolution for their tensions!

So, in this chapter we take up the following problem question: *What is this magic approach of integration?*

In this chapter we will

- Draw a distinction between stereotyping and generalization
- Draw a distinction between prejudice and conviction
- Show what stereotype and prejudice have in common as forms of perception
- Emphasize the importance of cooperation between different cultures
- Show why intercultural cooperation is the optimal way for people to interact.

Perception: Seizing the World

As we saw earlier, perception is a crucial part of communication. When we perceive reality, we try to conceptualize and evaluate our experiences. For instance, if we come across a large elevation of the earth's surface with steep sides and then another large elevation of the earth's surface with steep sides, we conceptualize this part of reality as "mountains." When we conceptualize our experiences, we assign them to general types—for instance, the type "mountains." **Conceptualization,** then, is a process of generalizing or typifying. Also, we evaluate our experiences; in our judgment, for instance, mountains may be seen as a source of beauty and inspiration or as a challenge. **Evaluation,** then, is a process of appraising or judging.

You might be wondering what all this has to do with intercultural communication. The fact is, that when we come into contact with people from another culture, we also conceptualize and evaluate our experiences. Suppose you planned to go to Spain, and in one of your travel guides you came across a picture of bullfighting; you might decide that all Spaniards like bullfighting and thus put Spaniards into the general type "like bullfighting." Or, if you happened to see an awkward person from the United States trying to dribble a soccer ball, you might make the judgment "Soccer in the United States is a joke." However, it so happens that your perceptions in these two cases would be flawed; your conceptualization is too general (oversimplified), and your appraisal is too biased. It is as if perception had played two tricks on you called stereotype and prejudice.

Stereotype: Not All Swans Are White

Definition. The term *stereotype* was introduced in 1824 to describe a printing duplication process "in which the original is preserved and in which there is no opportunity for change or deviation in the reduplications" (Rudmin, 1989: 8). The meaning of the term has changed somewhat, but the basic idea is still the same: You take an original conception, just like a metal printing plate, and start using it in different situations, expecting the original conception to be preserved. That is, you expect the meaning to be the same in every situation of its use. So a **stereotype** is an overgeneralization or fixed perception, which may be applied to people from another culture. Through such fixed overgeneralizations we come to perceive each and every individual from that culture.

Origins. Two kinds of stereotypes are usually isolated—normative and nonnormative (see Gudykunst & Kim, 2003: 129). **Normative stereotypes** are overgeneralizations that are based on limited information, such as the travel guide mentioned above. The normative stereotype of Muslims, based on media news accounts, usually involves bombings, violence, and terrorism. So when a group of Muslims on a holy pilgrimage wandered through Harrington, Washington, leaving a trail of good will and friendliness (Clark, 1995), the intercultural encounter was quite surprising to the people of that small town. **Nonnormative stereotypes** are overgeneralizations that are purely self-projective; we project concepts from our own culture onto people of another culture. For example, Italians might think that the French also love pasta. Regardless of its origin, every stereotype is a firm conception (*stereo* means solid or firm) that we use over and over again with the assumption that it reflects the same reality—that is, has the same meaning—whenever we use it. But how does such conceptualization of experiences affect intercultural communication?

Communication is successful when our conceptualization reflects reality and can be duplicated. If we use the word *mountain* each time we come across a large elevation of the earth's surface with steep sides, our communication is likely to be successful. If, all of a sudden, we are faced with a large elevation of the earth's surface with steep sides and call it a *tree*, communication is likely to break down. By the same token, conceptualization of our experiences in dealing with people from another culture must reflect that culture.

Generalization versus Stereotyping. We can look at the process of conceptualization in terms of a cultural gaze (discussed in Chapter 4)—a projection beam aimed at our experiences of interaction with people from another culture and reflecting back everything it observes in the form of more or less general types. Conceptualization as a dynamic process takes place somewhere between individualization (individual cases) and generalization (see Figure 1).

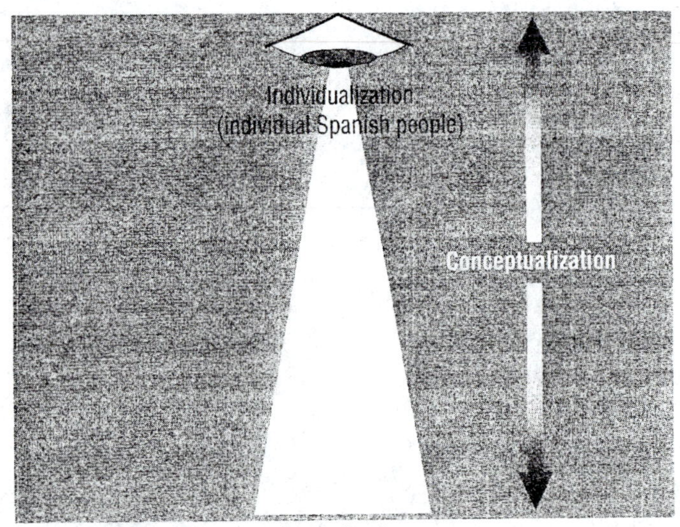

FIGURE 1

When we approach people from another culture, we tend to resort to **generalization,** putting our experiences in general categories, or types. A number of different general conceptualizations of Spaniards in relation to bullfighting can be created on the basis of the travel guide mentioned earlier. For example, we might decide that few (e.g., 10 percent), some (e.g., 20 percent), many (e.g., 40 percent), most (e.g., 80 percent), or all (100 percent) Spaniards like bullfighting (see Figure 2).

Each consecutive conceptualization covers more ground, reflecting more of Spanish culture. The more ground covered and reflected, the more a conceptualization functions as a generalization and the more we can rely on it in carrying out our intercultural interactions. For example, we might bring up bullfighting more and more often as a way of starting a conversation and building a relationship. However, for our communication with Spaniards to be as effective as possible, we must make sure that our conceptualization is as accurate as possible. According to *Let's Go City Guides: Barcelona, 2002,* 87 percent of Spaniards believe that it is wrong to make animals suffer for public entertainment; 60 percent think Spain has a bad reputation for its treatment of animals; and 80 percent of Spaniards had not been to a bullfight even once in the previous year. The more individual cases (Spanish people who have different opinions of bullfighting) that remain outside our conceptualization, the more stereotypical, and therefore less reliable, the conceptualization becomes. Similarly, the more accurate the observations we are able to make of individual cases, the more a conceptualization constitutes a generalization rather than a stereotype (see Figure 3). So our general conceptualization of Spaniards in relation to bullfighting might take the following form: "Some Spaniards like bullfighting." As a result, we will perhaps be careful about bringing up bullfighting as a topic when we want to strike up a conversation and build relationships with Spaniards.

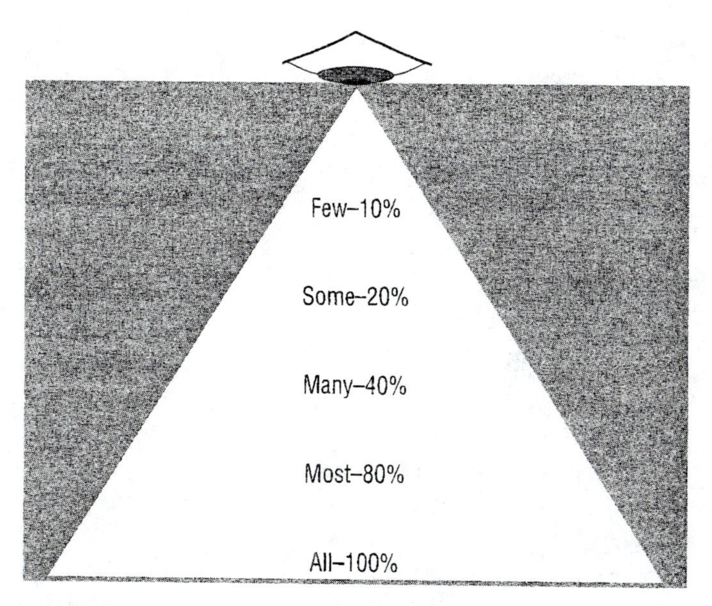

FIGURE 2

The more stereotypical our perception of the Spanish culture, the less effective our interactions with Spaniards will be. For example, if we believe that all (100 percent) Spaniards like bullfighting when in fact only a few (10 percent) do, our stereotyping is very significant (90 percent of individual cases left out). If we believe that most (80 percent) Spaniards like bullfighting when in fact only some

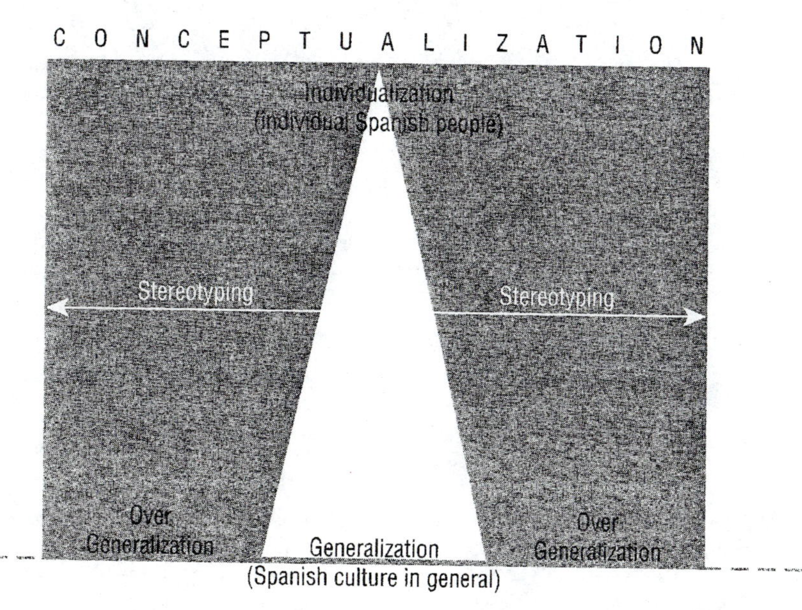

FIGURE 3

(20 percent) do, our stereotyping is still quite significant (60 percent), and so on. Thus, the degree of stereotyping can be seen in the difference between the total percentage of cases included in the overgeneralization and the percentage of cases included in the more accurate generalization. For instance, in the situation depicted in Figure 4, 100% – 20% = 80% stereotype. Naturally, the smaller this difference, the more reliable our conceptualization and the more effective our intercultural communication.

It is obvious that intercultural communication becomes more effective as we overcome stereotyping and increase the accuracy of our generalization. Then stereotyping gives way to generalization (typifying), or generalization (typifying) pushes stereotyping out. Suppose we spend more time in Spain and meet more and more individuals there who refuse to talk about bullfighting. Then our conceptualization might take the following form: "Most Spaniards dislike bullfighting." By moving further away from such overgeneralizations (stereotypes) as "All Spaniards like bullfighting" and "Most Spaniards like bullfighting," our conceptualization functions more as a generalization (typifying), leaving less room for overgeneralization (stereotyping). But stereotyping is always possible.

Karl Popper (1902–1994), a famous philosopher, gave the example of Europeans who, over a thousand years, had observed millions of white swans. Naturally, their conceptualization was that all swans are white. However, when

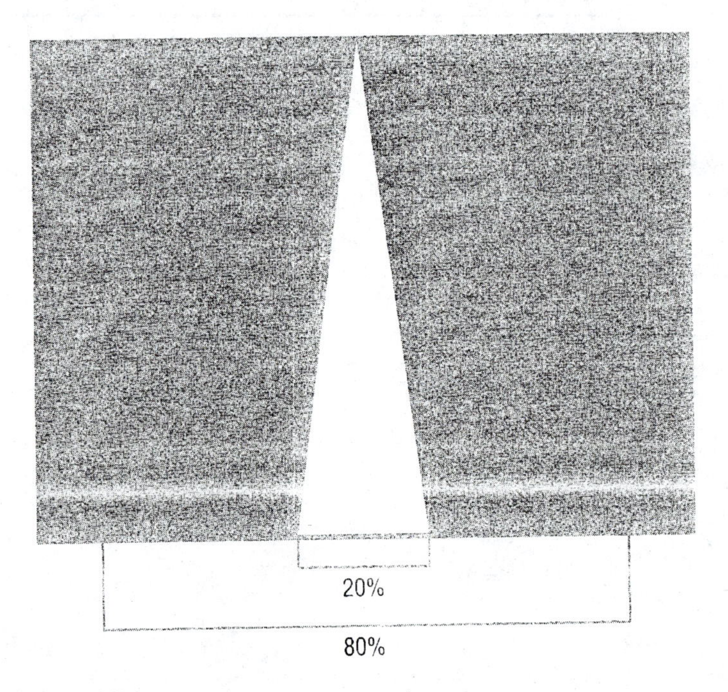

FIGURE 4

exploration of Australasia introduced Europeans to black swans, only one black swan was needed to change the conceptualization that all swans are white. In other words, we can never be certain that we have the final truth, the one and only generalization.

The best we can do is to make sure our generalizations are as accurate as possible and avoid overgeneralizations, especially those beginning with "All." We must be sure to speak of white swans when the swans we observe are white. If we begin to come across black swans but continue to assume that all swans are white, our cultural gaze becomes stereotypical and our interaction with the "culture" of swans less reliable. The more ground covered by the dark forces of stereotyping, the less ground left for generalization. Conversely, the more ground covered by the light forces of generalization, the less ground left for stereotyping. In the struggle between the light and the dark forces, the more we assume that "all swans are white" when in fact we see more and more black swans, the more the forces of darkness win. Like swans, the dark forces of stereotyping spread out their wings, as it were, blocking out the light forces of generalization (see Figure 5).

Intercultural communication is effective when our observations and reflections of people from the other culture are accurate and function as generalizations (typifying). However, we must always be ready to make changes in our conceptualization when new experiences do not fit into our original general types. Our intercultural experiences are always more complex than any generalization, let alone an overgeneralization; one-size-fits-all conceptualization does not work very well for intercultural communication.

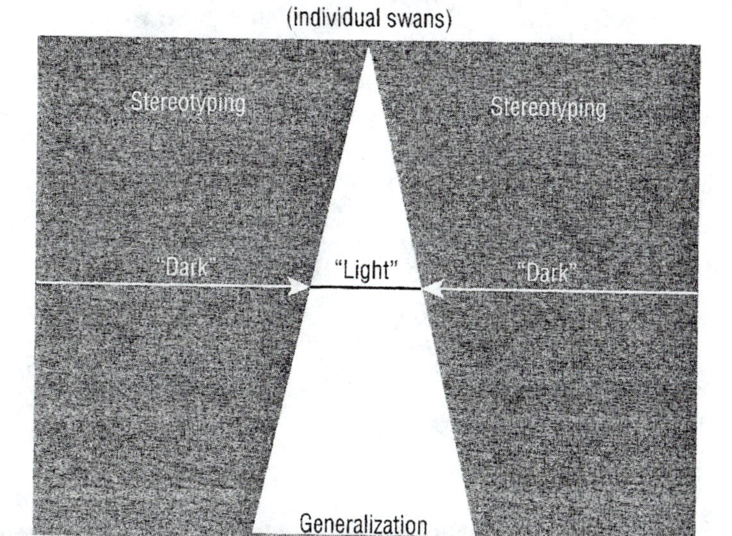

FIGURE 5

So, if you plan to travel to Italy, for example, and someone tells you all Italians are fond of opera, do your homework and try to find out as much as you can about this conceptualization. And be ready to change your conceptualization, if necessary, as you interact with Italians. If only very few Italians (10 percent) love opera, then bringing up opera as a conversation opener might not be a good idea.

Remember: Not all swans are white.

Prejudice: The U.S. and the Rest-of-the-World Soccer Cup

Definition. The word *prejudice* is derived from the Latin *praejudicium*; *prae* means before and *judicium* means judgment. Thus, prejudice is a not very rational and quite emotional judgment made beforehand or without examination of the facts. **Prejudice** is a prejudgment (premature judgment), based on little interaction with people from another culture. Prejudice can be positive or negative, but it usually carries a negative bias toward people from another culture.

Origins. Prejudice develops when people feel insecure about their own identity. They are concerned that others will claim the resources that make up their cultural identity, thus undermining their vitality. So, people develop prejudices through ignorance, fear, apprehension, and so forth. Such feelings are natural. After all, intercultural communication always takes place against a backdrop of uncertainty; we can never be completely certain what the Other wants and plans to do. But how does prejudice affect intercultural communication?

Suppose you come from a culture such as Brazil, where soccer is idolized and almost everyone can play it very well. One day, you come across a person from the United States clumsily dribbling a soccer ball. The next day, you come across this statement in a magazine: "There are just two things about the World Cup that prevent Americans from caring: it involves soccer and the rest of the world" (Stein, 2002: 88). Based on these experiences (and your own passion for soccer), you might decide that soccer in the United States is a joke and make statements to that effect in conversations with your friends and people from the United States.

However, as you interact more with people from the United States, you soon discover that your negative attitude overlooks a number of important facts. For example, the U.S. Soccer Federation, one of the world's first organizations to be affiliated with FIFA (soccer's world governing body), celebrated its 90th anniversary in 2003. According to the 2002 FIFA world ranking, the United States broke into the top ten for the first time in 2002, moving into a tie with Italy for 9th. As for that magazine article mentioned earlier, it happens to be an example of self-satire. It seems that your original (negative) prejudgment ("Soccer in the United States is a joke") can hardly be considered accurate and will not help your intercultural interactions. So, why not correct your appraisal? Well, it is easier said than done. Prejudice is so widespread and enduring because people are quite creative when it comes to protecting their cultural identity at the expense of others—and ultimately at their own expense. People resort to a special form of reasoning called the fundamental attribution error (see Cushner & Brislin, 1996; Heider, 1958). Let's see what form this reasoning takes and why it is so dangerous.

Conviction versus Prejudice. When we interact with other people, we attribute every action to either disposition or situation. Disposition is what we are like, as a personality; for example, we might think of ourselves as smart, outgoing, or capable. Applied to culture, disposition is our collective identity, our "cultural personality." And situation, of course, is circumstances, or what happens to us. If you, as in our example above, see an American awkwardly dribbling a soccer ball and decide that Americans are not good at soccer, you attribute this characteristic ("not good at soccer") to the person's cultural disposition; you reason that the person is not good at soccer because he happens to be from the United States. But what if you see another American dribbling a ball like a professional soccer player? How do you explain that? You attribute this characteristic ("excellent soccer player") to a situation. For example, you might think that the person must have spent some time in Brazil (your country!), making it sound as if you should take credit for that person's success. In other words, you take this person to be an exception and do not change your original appraisal: Soccer in the United States is still a joke.

So, in our perception of people from other cultures we tend to make the **fundamental attribution error,** which is a tendency to attribute negative behaviors to dispositional factors and positive behaviors to situational factors in explaining others' behavior. Needless to say, we perceive people from our own culture in exactly the opposite way: We justify negative behaviors by situational factors, thus underestimating them, and present positive behaviors as part of our cultural disposition, thus overestimating them.

Thus, prejudice serves two important functions: value-expressive and ego-defensive (Brislin, 1993). The value-expressive function helps people to promote their perception of their own culture—to blow their own horn, so to speak. This tends to take place when people from one culture do something better than people from other cultures. For example, people in Brazil might express the value of the way they play soccer (better than most). The value-expressive function is similar to emphasizing a positive cultural disposition. The ego-defensive function helps people to protect their perception of their own culture—to downplay their failures, so to speak. This becomes necessary when people from one culture do not fare well compared to people from other cultures. For example, if a soccer team from Brazil were to lose to a U.S. team, they might defend their defeat by pointing out that many players on their team were tired or sick. The ego-defensive function is similar to emphasizing a negative situational factor. The value-expressive function and ego-defensive function are two sides of the same coin, and this coin is the fundamental attribution error.

People can be quite creative (consciously or unconsciously) with their positive self-presentation and their negative presentation of people from another culture. For example, van Dijk (1984) lists the following strategies for expressing prejudice:

1. Apparent denials ("I have nothing against Blacks, Turks, Jews, but . . .")
2. Apparent admissions ("Of course there are also smart Blacks, Turks, Jews, but . . .")
3. Transfer ("I don't mind so much, but my neighbor, colleagues . . .")
4. Contrast ("We always had to work a lot, but they . . .")

Notice how Self always looks good ("We always had to work a lot") while blame is shifted to the Other (there is a "but" in every statement). We always want to perceive our own culture in a positive light, and the fundamental attribution error allows us to do so by manipulating dispositional and situational factors—always in our favor. With this reasoning, what can go wrong? A lot!

The fundamental attribution error is still an error of perception, and it is truly fundamental. It prevents us from seeing ourselves the way we really are and people different from us the way they really are—a U.S. soccer team stronger than our own team, for example. We can continue to think and say that soccer in the United States is a joke, but this will not help our cultures to interact successfully. By holding a prejudice against soccer in the United States, we refuse to appreciate its positive aspects and admit our own weaknesses. As a result, we fail to replace a weak link in our own culture—for example, to make changes in the way we play soccer. So, prejudice is not only destructive toward another culture; it is also self-destructive.

If you are convinced that your culture is superior at soccer, there is only one way to find out whether that is really the case—to play against teams from other cultures. If your team wins over and over again, you can reasonably argue that your culture is, indeed, superior at soccer. Then other cultures may learn from yours. There is a difference between a firm (inflexible) prejudice and a firm (strong) conviction. Those who hold a prejudice are usually reluctant to discuss their attitude—for instance, stubbornly or blindly insisting that their soccer team is the best, even though it keeps losing, and that soccer in the United States is a joke. Those who hold a conviction are open to discussion and willing or eager to test out their conviction—say, by playing a soccer match. If people from another culture think and say that the way soccer is played in your culture is a joke and you are convinced that this is not true, you should not adopt a negative attitude toward those people for their judgment, but rather try to provide all the facts you have to help them change their judgment. After all, prejudice is a premature judgment, and your task is to help those people see soccer in your culture the way it really is, after they have all the facts at their disposal. Then their attitude toward your culture (as far as soccer is concerned) will change, becoming more mature; they will replace a weak link in their culture and perhaps start playing soccer better. As a result, all of you will be able to enjoy more competitive and rewarding soccer matches, for a win-win situation.

What Stereotype and Prejudice Have in Common. Stereotype and prejudice have one thing in common: They are rigid and inaccurate perceptions of people from another culture. They are based on the assumption that cultures are static objects, like mountains, and that, once our cultural self-concept and our appraisal of people from another culture have been created, they change only at our will and always in our favor. We are reluctant to make adjustments to our conceptualizations and appraisals of another culture when evidence goes against our original conceptualizations and appraisals. But sometimes we have to make adjustments even to conceptualizations of seemingly static objects. In the movie *The Englishman Who Went Up a Hill But Came Down a Mountain,* a group of British cartographers and the townsfolk of a small Welsh town cannot agree on whether a large elevation of the earth's surface with steep sides should be called (categorized as) a "mountain" (which must be at least 1,000 feet tall according to British government regulations) or a "hill." The movie tells a sweet fable, but also makes a serious point: How can we be certain where a hill ends and a mountain begins? So, our perception sometimes changes even when we are dealing with static objects—we might start calling a large elevation of the earth's surface a mountain instead of a hill.

People, of course, are nothing like static objects; they interact, and it is simply impossible to pin them down in fixed general types and fixed appraisals. The word *perception* is derived from the Latin *percipere*—to seize wholly or to see all the way through. It is only natural that we want to see ourselves and other people "all the way through," seizing the whole world. In other words, we want to set our mind once and for all, with the assumption that we can rely on our conceptualizations and appraisals in every intercultural encounter. We create categories and start using those general types as if they were metal plates, expecting them to be reliable in all situations; when we fail to notice that they no longer work because they are too simple or too general, we become victims of stereotypes. For instance, as we said earlier, if most Spaniards change the subject as soon as they hear the word *bullfighting* but we still continue to open conversations with a comment about bullfighting, then we become victims of our stereotype—we fail to notice that our conceptualization is too general and leaves out many individual cases (those Spanish people who have a different opinion about bullfighting). Similarly, we make quick judgments about other people and stick to them no matter what; for example, if our Brazilian soccer team loses to a U.S. team, we explain the loss away to situational factors. We do not think (or do not want to think) that a change has taken place—that our team is not as strong as it once was or that the team that beat us is stronger than before. If we continue to stick to our judgment that we are better at soccer and our losses are just an accident, we become victims of prejudice. Often, overgeneralization (stereotype) and negative appraisal (prejudice) lead to **discrimination**—biased action whereby people from another culture are treated disadvantageously.

In a way, stereotype and prejudice are imperialistic by nature. We want to seize the whole world, as it were, and put it in our system of meanings, resisting (or allowing only positive) change in ourselves and denying (or allowing only negative) change in the Other. For instance, the fact that a number of U.S. colleges use American Indian icons as their mascots has been seen as a manifestation of imperialism, leading to tensions on and off campus. Many examples of such tensions are described in the book *Beyond the Cheers: Race as Spectacle in College Sports* (Springwood & King, 2001a). In an article in *The Chronicle of Higher Education,* Springwood and King quote environmental historian Richard White, who suggests that "White Americans are pious toward Indian peoples, but we don't take them seriously; *we don't credit them with the capacity to make changes*" (Springwood & King, 2001b; italics added). In other words, White Americans fail to accept the fact that American Indians cannot be put into the stereotype (familiar and convenient to White Americans) of "wild and pristine savages" and judged accordingly, because they are now a very different and complicated culture.

Both stereotype and prejudice ignore reality—that is, our interactions with other people. They trick people from one culture into thinking that their conceptualizations and appraisals of people from another culture are accurate and reliable when, in fact, they are not! Stereotype and prejudice go *against* reality: Black swans are called white, and a strong soccer team is considered a joke. It is as if people had blinds on, preventing them from seeing the real Other and the real Self. Stereotype and prejudice are not the best ways to perceive reality; the image that we get is distorted, and it fails us in our intercultural interactions. It is as if a wall existed between people, preventing them from developing reliable conceptualizations and appraisals of each other.

But how can people develop reliable conceptualizations and appraisals of each other? Who is to decide what generalizations are accurate and what judgments are valid? The answer is obvious: Such decisions can be made only by people from the two cultures interacting *together*. Only by acting together is it possible for people to create accurate categories and reasonable judgments of each other. Then we can break down the wall created by uncertainty, insecurity, fear, apprehension, or ignorance.

Intercultural Integration: Breaking Down the Wall

Solving the Prisoner's Dilemma. The study of intercultural communication has a lot in common with game theory (Avenhaus, 2002). Game theory can be used to analyze any situation in which one party's decision depends on another party's decision. In this sense, intercultural communication is an example of a game because the actions of people from one culture depend on the actions of people from the other culture. As we saw in Chapter 8, intercultural communication is always a transaction because its outcome affects all parties involved.

To appreciate the value of intercultural integration, let's look at the game called the **prisoner's dilemma.** In this game,

> two persons suspected of being partners in a crime are arrested and placed in separate cells so that they cannot communicate with each other. Without a confession from at least one suspect, the district attorney does not have sufficient evidence to convict. So he tells each suspect the possible consequences of their actions:
>
> If one confesses and the other does not, the one who confesses goes free but the other gets ten years in jail.

If both confess, each gets five years.
If both remain silent, each gets one year on a lesser charge.

(Avenhaus, 2001: 203–204)

The dilemma is that both persons are better off if they cooperate with each other—that is, if they do not confess. If neither confesses, they will both get 1 year in jail, rather than a bad outcome (5 years) or a terrible outcome (10 years). However, each person fears that the other one will confess, so the best strategy seems to be to defect (confess), thereby either getting a great outcome (freedom) or at least avoiding a terrible outcome (10 years). So they both follow this logic and confess, and each gets 5 years—a bad outcome. By choosing defection over cooperation, each person loses in the end. The prisoner's dilemma is illustrated in Table 1, where the first person is called Self, and the second person the Other.

The main lesson to be learned from the prisoner's dilemma is that mutual cooperation is better than mutual defection. Both sides must realize that it is in their best interests to move from the bottom right-hand cell of mutual defection to the top left-hand cell of mutual cooperation. Then they can leave the prison of mutual suspicion and fear, setting themselves free! The way the prisoner's dilemma is solved depends on how people from different cultures perceive reality. They might perceive an intercultural encounter as a battle between Us and Them, thus going against each other and both losing in the end. Or they might perceive it as an opportunity to escape the walls of uncertainty and fear, cooperating with each other and both benefiting as a result. It is only when people cooperate, integrating their forces, that they can achieve the optimal resolution.

As mentioned earlier, intercultural communication can be viewed as an example of the prisoner's dilemma because the outcome of one side's decision depends on the other side's decision. At the same time, no one can put intercultural communicators into prison, as it were, but the communicators themselves! In other words, unlike the two suspects placed in separate cells, people can communicate unless they themselves put on blinds and refuse to deal with each other. If, through overgeneralization or biased appraisal of each other's cultures, people from different cultures create a wall that prevents them from reaching the optimal

TABLE 1

	THE OTHER	
SELF	*Cooperate*	*Defect*
Cooperate	Better outcomes for both	Best outcome for the Other and worst outcome for Self
Defect	Best outcome for Self and worst outcome for the Other	Worse outcome for both than if both cooperated, but better outcome than if one cooperated while the other did not

outcome for both sides, they must use communication and trust to break down this wall and realize their full potential—a win-win outcome. We will discuss the role of trust in intercultural communication in more detail in Chapter 10.

Thus, the key to reaching the optimal outcome in intercultural communication is for people to work not against, but with, each other. During this process, people from one culture might find out that their positions and interests differ from another culture's. However, clearly stating one's positions and defending one's convictions, based on accurate categorization and judicious reasoning, is not the same as stubbornly sticking to one's stereotypes and prejudices, refusing to change, and failing to accept change in others. Discussion does not make conflict go away, of course, because in every intercultural encounter conceptualizations and appraisals still differ, creating tensions. However, management of intercultural tensions becomes more rational, with a higher chance of success.

So, there is a difference between overgeneralization (stereotyping) and generalization (typifying); all people must be willing and able to explain why they think that Spaniards like bullfighting or that swans are white, changing their original conceptions if necessary. By the same token, there is a difference between prejudices and convictions; all people must be willing and able to defend their argument that their country's soccer team is better, changing their judgment if necessary. Categorization and convictions are natural and necessary parts of effective intercultural communication, allowing differences to be voiced and settled peacefully, and not on a real battlefield.

People from different cultures can create accurate categorizations and appraisals of each other only through a mutual dialogue. If people from one culture set their collective mind once and for all, refusing to change their conceptualizations and judgments and failing to listen to people from the other culture, they fall victim to stereotyping and prejudice.

Thus, stereotyping must give way to generalization (typifying); prejudice must be fought and ideally eliminated; and cultural differences must be respected and managed peacefully through communication. In Chapter 7, we spoke about the importance of voice in intercultural communication. Now it is clear that we must listen very carefully to voices of people from other cultures and our own voices so that we can manage our differences together.

Introducing the Synergy Principle

The discussion above provides the basis for the ninth principle underlying intercultural communication—the Synergy Principle. As with the previous principles, we will isolate three parts that make up this principle. Each part deals with intercultural communication as a process of synergy. First, we will discuss intercultural communication in terms of flow dynamics. Then we will look at intercultural synergy as nonsummativity. Finally, we will present intercultural communication as a search for Pareto optimality. We will discuss each part separately and then formulate the Synergy Principle as a whole.

Intercultural Synergy and Flow Dynamics

The word *synergy* is derived from the Greek *synergos,* which means working together (*syn* meaning together and *ergon* meaning work). You are perhaps more familiar with the word *energy,* which refers to forces of isolated objects; in this sense, it is possible to speak of forces (or energies) of separate cultures. Intercultural **synergy** represents a process whereby people work with each other, integrating their forces (or energies).

As we saw by looking at the prisoner's dilemma, it is better for people to cooperate with each other, integrating interests, than to go against each other. Whenever we look at an example of ineffective intercultural interaction (and we have discussed quite a few in this book), we realize that the interaction was ineffective because people did not see the need or simply refused to work together. They spent a lot of their energy trying to accomplish a task, yet never completely succeeded or completely failed. Somehow, intercultural communication in such cases did not flow. The problem is that a flow is synergistic by definition: It requires that people work together, not without or against each other.

Some of the best-known research in the area of flow dynamics has been done by Mihaly Csikszentmihalyi (1996), who defined and described **flow states**—those peak experiences when people realize their potential and find optimal solutions. Every flow state involves a sense of discovery, a feeling of creating a new reality and moving to a higher level of performance. In such states, a new level of attainment is reached and new strengths are discovered, so whatever we do just "flows." Then a solution becomes a pleasurable and triumphant experience. As Trompenaars and Hampden-Turner note, the word *solution* means, among other things,

> a combination formed by dissolving something into a more fluid medium. When a solution is found to a problem, the hard edges of that problem dissolve and the separate identities of skills and challenges are transcended. The one flows into the other like an onrushing stream of energy. (2002: 116)

This is exactly what takes place when people from different cultures work together, realizing their potential. People may, and often do, put tremendous effort into resolving their intercultural tensions, but the overall flow state is still desirable and enjoyable because everyone is satisfied with this optimal experience.

Thus, intercultural communication can be viewed as a synergistic process directed toward achieving flow states, when people realize their potential and the outcome of their interaction reaches a new level. We should not be deceived by the word *state* into thinking that this is a destination that can be reached once and for all. Every state is part of the overall and never-ending process of intercultural interaction; it is dynamic by nature. Every state is a point in the continuous movement of the intercultural pendulum. If tensions are managed successfully and cultural forces are integrated into flow states, the intercultural pendulum swings smoothly; that is, it flows.

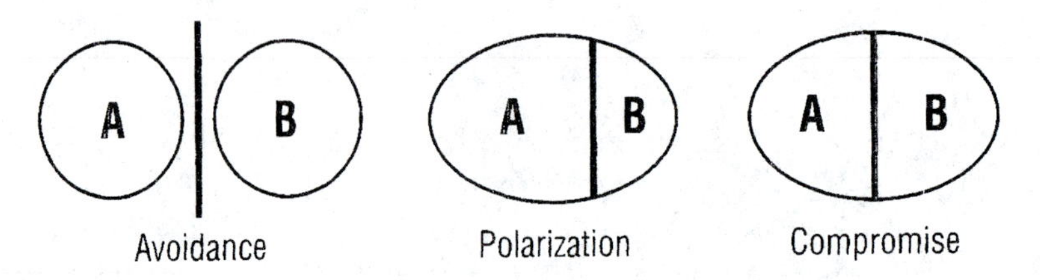

FIGURE 6

When people attempt to work without each other (avoidance approach), against each other (polarization approach), or not quite with each other (compromise approach), their interaction is not effective, because no shared space is created where intercultural communication can flow. Intercultural interaction comes down to one fixed line, as shown in Figure 6. When you have one fixed line, one culture can only move into what the other side considers its own territory. The result is a tug-of-war: distributing but not sharing cultural resources.

With integration, people are able to cross this line in both directions, so we now add two dynamic lines—and an area in between, as shown in Figure 7. In the space thus created, people can move back and forth and exchange meanings—intercultural interaction can flow. This situation can also be represented as shown in Figure 8. The common area can be seen as the shared continuous space (continuum) discussed in Chapter 6, as the pendulum movement discussed in Chapter 7, or as the negotiation zone discussed in Chapter 8. Because this area continually changes, it must be established through a process of transaction by the interacting cultures. People must choose a mutual solution to their tensions and establish lines between themselves. If people agree on where to draw these lines, they establish an effective solution. "An established solution is said to be stable if or to the extent that incentives to defect are absent" (Underdal, 2002: 118). In other words, if people are comfortable with the solution and do not feel any need to defect, or change the situation, we have a win-win situation. With true synergy, the prisoner's dilemma is solved. As long as people from different cultures can manage to continuously redraw the lines between themselves to their mutual satisfaction, their interaction will be successful and their development stable. If their development is stable, they are able to draw on their resources and function freely, without feeling any need to oppress the Other or blame the Other for their own problems.

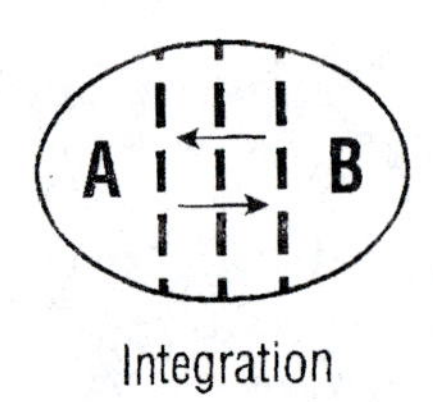

FIGURE 7

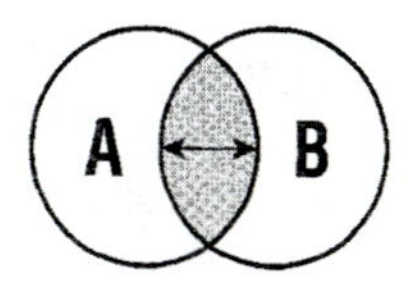

FIGURE 8

Thus, we have come full circle and returned to the importance of the boundary lines discussed in Chapter 1. As we discussed then, every boundary line is an idea. Now we see that the most constructive way to envision a boundary line is in terms of synergy. By crossing over the imaginary dividing line and sharing a space, people from different cultures are able to achieve a result that they cannot achieve on their own.

Intercultural Synergy and Nonsummativity

Intercultural synergy is based on the idea of nonsummativity. The idea of **nonsummativity** is that separate entities working together and integrating their resources can achieve results that none could achieve individually. In simple terms, the whole is greater than the sum of its parts.

People cannot achieve intercultural synergy simply by adding their forces together; they must integrate their forces. The difference between adding and integrating forces is crucial. If we *add* something and something else (say, the numbers 2 and 2), we get their sum (2 + 2 = 4). If we *integrate* something with something else, we get a new entity that does not equal the sum of its parts; it is qualitatively different. In that case, 2 plus 2 does not equal 4; rather, it might be 5 (or more!). If we put flour, eggs, oil, and sugar in a bowl, we get exactly that—flour, eggs, oil, and sugar. However, if we mix them all together, integrating these ingredients, we get batter for a cake—a new entity with a unique taste different from the taste of each individual ingredient.

When people from different cultural groups come into contact but no exchange takes place between them, we cannot speak of intercultural communication as a genuine synergistic process. Their "interaction" is reduced to a tug-of-war, as they push the line between them, each culture trying to get as many resources as it can. At best, people from the interacting cultures might settle on dividing the resources exactly in half, reaching a compromise. But, as you might remember, unless people from different cultures venture—and are allowed—into each other's territory, they do not integrate; thus, they do not really share any ideas, which is to say they do not really communicate. Intercultural communication is an integration of ideas and presupposes a dynamic effort—and change—just like making a cake.

Take as an example an intercultural family: When people from different cultures marry, a new entity is formed with its own beliefs, values, and norms. Or take the example of the acquisition of a U.S. firm by a Swedish manufacturer of high-precision metal products. As engineers from the two firms came to know and trust each other, both sides incorporated elements of the other firm's processes; as a result, the facility's output was significantly boosted (Stauffer, 2003). Thus, by working together, people from different cultures can attain optimal outcomes that cannot be achieved by any one culture individually.

Toward Pareto Optimality

As you remember from Chapter 8, people can take several routes as they manage tensions and strive for resolution.

The first route is one of avoidance, in which cultures choose not to address tensions. This approach can be dangerous because it fails to resolve the source of tensions. People do not know how to set their goals and create a negotiation zone; in a way, they are defeated by the situation. People fail to use its potential for mutual benefit; in other words, they lose an opportunity to change and integrate their potential. In this case, neither culture really wins; this "neither/nor" approach to tensions is a lose-lose situation.

The second route is one of polarization, in which each culture views the Other as the enemy and tries to undermine and eventually destroy its position. Here, the zone of potential agreement turns into a war zone: People from one culture can win only if people from the other culture lose. This approach is dangerous because it may end in eliminating the Other; then Self is left without any culture to interact with. This "either/or" approach to tensions is a win-lose situation.

The third route is one of compromise, in which people from different cultures agree to disagree. Here, the negotiation zone is split 50/50. In the Arabic language, compromise is translated as two words, literally meaning halfway solution (Heggy, 2002); this is a good way to describe the compromise approach to resolving intercultural tensions. Sometimes compromise is even perceived as a negative approach to conflict, associated with defeat, weakness, and capitulation. Compromise is better than no solution at all (avoidance) or a lopsided solution (polarization). However, it is still a halfway solution because people from each culture have to give something up. Here, people from both cultures seem to win, yet neither culture completely reaches its goal; this "both/neither" approach is a no lose–no win situation.

The fourth route is one of integration, in which cultures show a high concern for each other as they strive toward a resolution that benefits both sides. In this case, people from both cultures reach their goals and do not lose; this "both/and" approach is a win-win situation.

Thus, in intercultural communication, people must (1) move from the "neither/nor" approach of avoidance, (2) avoid the trap of the "either/or" approach of polarization, (3) build on the "both/neither" approach of compromise, and (4) strive for the "both/and" approach of integration. People must move toward this upper limit by making the most of their negotiation zone, thereby reaching the optimal agreement.

The term used to denote this upper limit of creative options, or optimal agreement, is *Pareto optimality* (Lax & Sebenius, 1991). In simple terms, **Pareto**

optimality is a solution that cannot be improved on without putting one of the sides in a worse position. After determining and trying all options, people agree on a joint resolution that satisfies all sides and that cannot be improved upon any further without making the position of one of the sides worse. It is easy to see that, of the four routes we have discussed, the approach closest to Pareto optimality is integration; here, a decision is made jointly that satisfies people from all interacting cultures. If this resolution cannot be improved upon any further, people from all interacting cultures have made the most of the zone of potential agreement.

Pareto optimality is not a real point that can be reached; rather, it is an ideal toward which people must strive. That is why Pareto optimality is often called the efficient frontier (Watkins & Rosegrant, 2001) or Pareto frontier (Sebenius, 2002: 237). In Figure 9, the Pareto frontier is shown on the dual concern model, along with the locations of the four approaches to managing intercultural interactions.

The shaded zone in Figure 9, between the two axes and bounded by the frontier, is the negotiation zone, or the zone of possible agreement. Overall, effective intercultural communication as a synergistic process is directed toward Pareto optimality—the frontier that is never really reached but is always out there. It is an idea, an ideal. The more synergistic intercultural communication is, the closer people from different cultures come to this frontier.

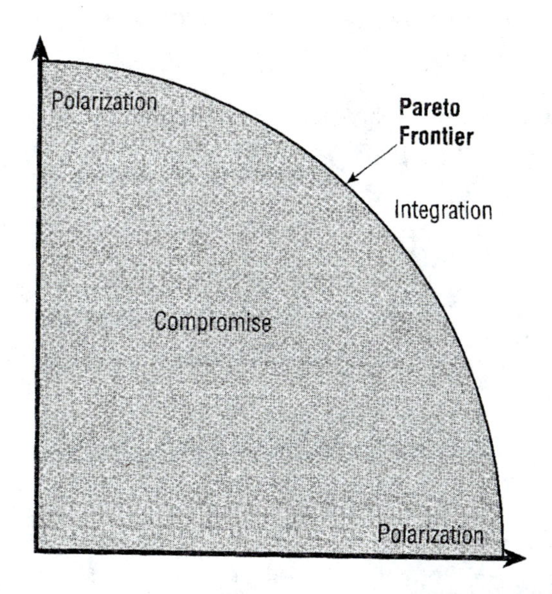

FIGURE 9

But what exactly is this idea, this ideal frontier? The concept of Pareto optimality might seem a bit abstract. Can it be presented in more exact terms? We will discuss this optimal outcome in the next chapter.

The Synergy Principle Defined

Now we can give a more concise formulation of the Synergy Principle, based on the above discussion of its three parts.

First, intercultural communication can be viewed as a synergistic process directed toward achieving flow states, when people from different cultures realize their potential and the outcome of their interaction reaches a new level. For intercultural communication to flow, people must work together, not without or against each other.

Second, as people from different cultures work together and integrate their potential, they are able to achieve an outcome that cannot be achieved by any one culture individually. This idea is known as nonsummativity.

Third, nonsummativity allows people to reach the optimal agreement for all sides. Such an agreement is reached when all options have been tried and the solution cannot be further improved upon without making the position of one of the sides worse. This outcome is known as Pareto optimality, or the efficient frontier.

In a nutshell, the Synergy Principle can be formulated as follows:

> *Intercultural communication is a process whereby people from different cultures integrate their resources, striving toward an optimal result that cannot be achieved by any culture individually.*

The Synergy Principle teaches us that the optimal way for people from different cultures to interact is by cooperating with each other. Collaborating and integrating resources is the right thing to do.

Summary

We started this chapter by looking at the role of perception in intercultural communication. We noted that, when we come into contact with people from another culture, we conceptualize and evaluate our experiences. Naturally, we want to create conceptualizations and evaluations that will work in all situations. However, there are dangers in adopting such inflexible conceptualizations and evaluations—they might prove inaccurate. We looked at two dangers: stereotype and prejudice. We showed that stereotype and prejudice distort our perceptions of interactions with people from another culture. It was emphasized that the best way for people from different cultures to develop reliable conceptualizations and evaluations of each other is through collaboration, or open dialogue. In open dialogue, stereotyping gives way to generalization, and prejudice is replaced with conviction. When people from different cultures work together, relying on generalizations and convictions, they can achieve the optimal outcome, as was demonstrated using the example of the prisoner's dilemma.

Thus, we presented intercultural communication as a synergistic process directed toward achieving flow states, when people from different cultures realize their potential and the outcome of their interaction reaches a new level. We noted that intercultural synergy is based on the idea of nonsummativity: People from different cultures working together and integrating their resources can achieve results that no culture can achieve individually. By working together, people from different cultures can attain the optimal outcome known as Pareto optimality. After determining and trying all options, people from different cultures agree on a joint resolution that satisfies all sides and that cannot be improved upon without making the position of one of the sides worse.

Based on these ideas, the Synergy Principle was formulated.

So, the optimal way for people from different cultures to interact with each other is synergistically. Cooperating and integrating resources is the right thing to do. But, *why* is it the right thing to do? There must be something about intercultural synergy that people in all cultures can benefit from. Why, in the final analysis, is synergy the right approach to intercultural interactions? We will discuss this question in the next chapter.

CASE STUDY
THE CASE OF AMD: UNLEASHING INTERCULTURAL POTENTIAL

This case study is based on Chapter 4, "Creating a Hyperculture: Martin Gillo, Advanced Micro Devices," in *21 Leaders for the 21st Century: How Innovative Leaders Manage in the Digital Age*, by Trompenaars and Hampden-Turner (2002). As usual, it is recommended that you read the chapter in its entirety; below is a summary of the chapter.

Be ready to identify and then discuss the following topics:

1. Some of the perceptual challenges faced by the cultures of AMD
2. How those challenges were overcome
3. The outcome of unleashing the intercultural potential of AMD

In 1995, Advanced Micro Devices (AMD), a large U.S. chip maker, decided to build a mega-factory near Dresden in the former East Germany. AMD wanted to produce state-of-the-art microprocessors equivalent or even superior to those of Intel. The factory would be dedicated to producing the chip that would enter the market under the AMD Athlon brand name. People from three cultures were going to come together there: United States, West Germany, and East Germany. Trompenaars and Hampden-Turner note that, according to their research, cultural differences between East Germany and West Germany are at least as large as those between West Germany and other European countries.

Making a microchip is an extremely complex process that requires the harmonious work of all parties involved. In this sense, the business of AMD depended on fine-tuning communication among people from three different cultures. The operation could become a highly profitable business and a feat of intercultural cooperation, but it could also prove a disaster. Cultural clashes and misperceptions were unavoidable.

There were tensions between the U.S. and West German sides. First of all, the Americans thought of Germany as a country with too many laws and regulations. Also, the Americans believed that the German engineers tried to be too rational and too cerebral, preferring to work individually and avoiding spontaneous group discussions and brainstorming. From the West German perspective, the Americans shot from the hip without taking careful aim; in other words, they did not take time individually to think through their problems and come to rational conclusions. Naturally, there was a language barrier; the American managers preferred to hold brainstorming sessions, where ideas could be developed freely, in English, while the Germans wanted to present their ideas in German and in a more formal setting.

There were tensions between the West German and East German sides, too. Many East Germans perceived the West Germans as arrogant and rejected their tendency toward consumerism and superiority. Also, many East Germans still felt that the West Germans did not honor their East German compatriots enough for their courage during the oppression by the Stasi (secret police). The West Germans, on their part, still sometimes perceived East Germany as a backwater because of its years under a communist regime. However, East German "backwardness" was by no means uniform; in some respects, East Germany was ahead of West Germany. For example, East Germany awarded many technical degrees for highly skilled manual labor, including that of semiconductor technician.

The AMD startup team rejected the approach of cultural colonialism, whereby U.S. cultural practices would be imposed. Instead, they chose the approach of cultural symbiosis, whereby people from the United States, West Germany, and East Germany would combine their preferences and integrate their potential. In this process, each culture's potential would be strengthened through the others'; as a result, the overall intercultural potential of AMD would be unleashed. The so-called systematic experimentation method was endorsed at AMD; the systematic part appealed to German rationality, while the experimentation part appealed to American improvisation.

The AMD startup team first considered alternating German-style formal meetings and American free-form brainstorming sessions. However, such a solution would not be optimal because no real exchange would take place between the two sides; in other words, one side's potential would not be strengthened through the other's. So a different meeting format was designed that opened with an American-style brainstorming session, when input was encouraged from everyone, and concluded with a formal reflective process, when ideas were presented and summarized. Whenever appropriate, ideas were written down and posted on boards during the brainstorming sessions; that way, those not confident of their verbal skills could add ideas more easily. AMD's *lingua franca* was English; however, meetings were held in both English and German, and anyone could express an idea in either language without recrimination. As a result, both sides gradually began to change: The Americans began to learn the skills of more rational deliberation, while the Germans began to learn the more dynamic skills of brainstorming and improvisation. Thus, the sides began to integrate their forces, reaching new states. Reaching each new state was seen as a peak experience that unleashed the integrated intercultural potential of AMD. Suddenly, all the former challenges were overcome, and a level of combined attainment was realized.

Interestingly, Martin Gillo, AMD's CEO, had been fascinated for many years by the research of Mihaly Csikszentmihalyi, especially his description of flow states. Gillo had published his own in-house pamphlets promoting the idea of a stimulating engagement with the task at hand. Such continuous engagement with every task resulted in the overall success of AMD. The Dresden operation was pronounced the most successful startup in the history of the company, while the 0.18-micron copper version of the AMD Athlon microprocessor was the most advanced in AMD's worldwide operations.

DISCUSSION

Now let's see how this case study can be seen as an illustration of the Synergy Principle of intercultural communication.

1. Some of the perceptual challenges faced by the cultures of AMD. It would have been easy for the cultures of AMD to fall into the trap of stereotyping when dealing with one another. For example, the East Germans could have conceptualized their West German colleagues as arrogant and lacking compassion. On their part, the West Germans could have conceptualized East Germany as a backwater because of its years under a communist regime. However, the West Germans turned out to be quite friendly and willing to work together, while the East Germans turned out to be highly skilled.

Also, it would have been easy for the cultures of AMD to fall into the trap of prejudging each other, developing a negative attitude. For example, the U.S. side could have decided that because Germany had numerous laws and regulations and because

(continued)

THE CASE OF AMD: UNLEASHING INTERCULTURAL POTENTIAL CONTINUED

its engineers were too rational and too cerebral, their collaboration would be ineffective. For their part, the West German side could have decided that because Americans were too carefree and never thought through their problems, their collaboration would be ineffective.

Fortunately, such perceptual challenges as overgeneralization (stereotypes) and prejudgment (prejudices), which could have prevented the cultures of AMD from successfully collaborating, were overcome.

2. How those challenges were overcome. These potential challenges were overcome through the approach of cultural symbiosis, whereby people from the United States, West Germany, and East Germany combined their preferences and integrated their potential. In this synergistic process, each culture's potential was strengthened through the others'. For example, the so-called systematic experimentation method was endorsed at AMD, the systematic part appealing to German rationality and the experimentation part appealing to American improvisation.

As one manifestation of this method, the AMD startup team decided not to alternate German-style formal meetings with American-style brainstorming sessions. Such a solution would simply have been a compromise because no real change would have taken place in the two sides; in other words, one side's potential would not have been strengthened through the other's. So a different meeting format was designed, blending American-style brainstorming sessions with a formal reflective process. Also, English and German were integrated, as anyone could express an idea in either language, either orally or by writing it down and posting it on a board during meetings. Thus, all sides changed: The Americans learned the skills of more rational deliberation, while the Germans learned the dynamic skills of brainstorming and improvisation. As a result, the sides moved beyond compromise, integrating their forces to reach a new state.

3. The outcome of unleashing the intercultural potential of AMD. The outcome of unleashing the intercultural potential of AMD was harmonious work among all the sides involved. The business of AMD depended on fine-tuning communication among people from three different cultures; because their interactions flowed smoothly, the operation became a highly profitable business and a feat of intercultural cooperation. Their continuous engagement with every task resulted in the overall success of AMD; the Dresden operation was pronounced the most successful startup in the history of the company, while one of their microprocessors turned out to be the most advanced in AMD's worldwide operations.

SIDE TRIPS

1. Soon after an American high school sophomore started an e-mail exchange with an Egyptian counterpart (see "Valley, Egyptian teens bond," 2003), the Iraqi Freedom military action began, and the American student received a short message written in all capital letters. The Egyptian student described watching bombs striking Baghdad on television, called the war unjust, and said that he was angry with everything American. After that, the American student did not hear from him again. How would you analyze this intercultural exchange in terms of conceptualization and appraisal?
2. Many Anglo-Americans believe that the use of Indian names and images for sports teams is insignificant and inoffensive. However, most Native Americans find such stereotypes misleading and offensive. Dolph Hatfield argues that this is very easy to demonstrate:

   > The easiest way to demonstrate this is to ask whether symbolizing any other minority in the same way or in a similar manner would be acceptable. Certainly blacks, African Americans, Asians, Hispanics, Jews, and Martin Luther King Jr. are comparable names, but Brownman Chewing Tobacco or Martin Luther King Jr. Malt Liquor would never be tolerated. Likewise, although Jeep Cherokee and the Apache helicopter are freely used in society, there would never be a Jeep African, Jeep Mexican, Oriental Helicopter, or Jew Helicopter. (2000: 43–44)

   What do you think of his argument?
3. Dr. Beatrice Fennimore (1994), in the paper "Addressing Prejudiced Statement," suggests that a productive response to a prejudiced statement can be formulated by taking the following steps: (1) pulling the prejudice out of the statement and restating it in a calm and objective way, (2) stating your personal beliefs in a clear and assertive way, (3) making a positive statement about the specific targets of the prejudice, and (4) gently turning the subject to a new direction. Try using this approach in addressing a prejudiced statement and think about what other steps could be added to make your response more effective.

CHECK YOURSELF

Conceptualization
Evaluation
Stereotype
Normative stereotype
Nonnormative stereotype
Generalization
Prejudice
Fundamental attribution error
Discrimination
Prisoner's dilemma
Synergy
Flow states
Nonsummativity
Pareto optimality

REFERENCES

Avenhaus, R. (2002). Game theory. In Kremenyuk, V. (Ed.), *International negotiation: Analysis, approaches, issues* (pp. 202–228). San Francisco: Jossey-Bass.

Brislin, R. (1993). *Understanding culture's influence on behavior.* Fort Worth, TX: Harcourt Brace.

Clark, D. (1995). Muslim pilgrims leave a trail of good will in Harrington. *The Spokesman-Review,* October 12, p. B5.

Csikszentmihalyi, M. (1996). *Creativity: Flow and the psychology of discovery and invention.* New York: HarperCollins.

Cushner, K., & Brislin, R. (1996). *Intercultural interactions: A practical guide.* Thousand Oaks, CA: Sage.

Fennimore, B. (1994). Addressing prejudiced statement: A four-step method that works! *Childhood Education,* Summer, pp. 202–204.

Gudykunst, W., & Kim, Y. (2003). *Communicating with strangers: An approach to intercultural communication.* New York: McGraw-Hill.

Hatfield, D. (2000). The stereotyping of Native Americans. *The Humanist,* Vol. 60, No. 5, pp. 43–44.

Heggy, T. (2002). Our need for "a culture of compromise." *Viewpoints,* October 27.

Heider, F. (1958). *The psychology of interpersonal relations.* New York: Wiley.

Lax, D., & Sebenius, J. (1991). The power of alternatives or the limit to negotiation. In Breslin, J., & J. Rubin (Eds.), *Negotiation theory and practice* (pp. 97–114). Cambridge, MA: Program on Negotiation Books.

Rudmin, F. (1989). The pleasure of serendipity in historical research: On finding "stereotype" in Morier's (1824) Haiji Baba. *Cross-Cultural Psychology Bulletin,* Vol. 23, pp. 8–11.

Sebenius, J. (2002). International negotiation analysis. In Kremenyuk, V. (Ed.), *International negotiation: Analysis, approaches, issues* (pp. 229–255). San Francisco: Jossey-Bass.

Springwood, C., & King, C. (Eds.). (2001a). *Beyond the cheers: Race as spectacle in college sport.* New York: SUNY Press.

Springwood, C., & King, C. (2001b). "Playing Indian": Why Native American mascots must end. *The Chronicle of Higher Education,* Vol. 48, No. 11 (November 9).

Stauffer, D. (2003). The business case: Today diversity is imperative. *Fastforward,* Vol. 2, No. 1, http://sodexhousa.com/pubs_fastforward.htm.

Stein, J. (2002). The rest-of-the-world cup. *Time,* June 17, p. 88.

Trompenaars, F., & Hampden-Turner, C. (2002). *21 leaders for the 21st century: How innovative leaders manage in the digital age.* New York: McGraw-Hill.

Underdal, A. (2002). The outcomes of negotiation. In Kremenyuk, V. (Ed.), *International negotiation: Analysis, approaches, issues* (pp. 110–126). San Francisco: Jossey-Bass.

Valley, Egyptian teens bond. (2003). *The Spokesman-Review,* March 29, p. 1A.

van Dijk, T. (1984). *Prejudice in discourse.* Amsterdam: Benjamins.

Watkins, M., & Rosegrant, S. (2001). *Breakthrough international negotiation: How great negotiators transformed the world's toughest post–Cold War conflicts.* San Francisco: Jossey-Bass.

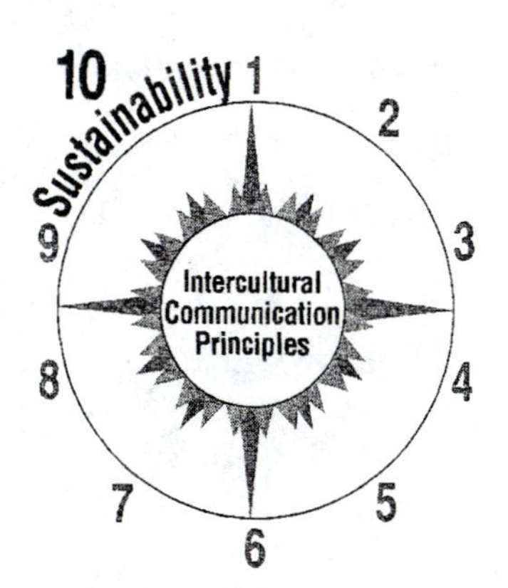

CHAPTER TEN

INTERCULTURAL ETHICS AS RATIONALITY: SUSTAINABILITY PRINCIPLE

All for One, and One for All.

- *Key Theme:* Survival
- *Key Objective:* To help you understand why cooperative behavior is right (ethical) in intercultural communication

INTRODUCING THE PROBLEM QUESTION

ETHICS AND INTERCULTURAL COMMUNICATION: AN OVERVIEW

APPROACHES TO ETHICS IN INTERCULTURAL COMMUNICATION

INTRODUCING THE SUSTAINABILITY PRINCIPLE

Nature of Sustainability: Thinking about Forever
Strategies of Intercultural Sustainability: Tolerance, Trust, and Resistance
Formula for Intercultural Sustainability

THE SUSTAINABILITY PRINCIPLE DEFINED

SUMMARY

CASE STUDY: AN ETHIC OF CULTURAL EXCHANGE

SIDE TRIPS

CHECK YOURSELF

REFERENCES

Introducing the Problem Question

The previous chapter showed that the optimal way for people from different cultures to interact with each other is synergistically. By cooperating with each other and integrating their resources, people can achieve results they cannot achieve separately. With cooperation, something crucial can be accomplished. What is it that different cultures can accomplish by cooperating and integrating their resources?

In other words, we will answer the following problem question: *Why is cooperating the right behavior for people from all cultures?*

In this chapter we will

- Provide an overview of ethics in intercultural communication
- Discuss the main approaches to ethics in intercultural communication
- Emphasize the idea of a relationship between a culture and its environment
- Introduce the concept of sustainability as a metaethic for intercultural communication
- Outline the main strategies of intercultural sustainability
- Present a formula for intercultural sustainability.

Ethics and Intercultural Communication: An Overview

In this book we have discussed numerous examples of intercultural interactions. For instance, in Chapter 4, we talked about the Masai people who offered as a gift to the United States some of their cows—one of their most valuable possessions. The gift was duly appreciated by the U.S. people as an extension of good will, but, because of the difficulty of transporting the cows, the Masai were asked to send beads instead. In Chapter 7, we talked about what happened between the white inhabitants of Snow Low, Arizona, and the members of the White Mountain Apache tribe when one of the members of the Apache tribe was arrested and charged with starting a fire that grew into the largest fire in Arizona history. The Native Americans began to keep to themselves, fearing retribution; among the white communities, the feeling of resentment was high. Another example from that chapter was the reaction of people from many cultures to the global spread of English. We mentioned how France and Switzerland, for instance, resist what is sometimes called the "linguistic imperialism" of English, providing a special vocabulary aimed at replacing anglicisms with words from their own language(s), especially in the areas of computing, business, and entertainment. In Chapter 8, we discussed in detail the decision of Motorola management not to fire a senior East Asian engineer, instead allowing him to use his housing allowance for any purpose as long as local values were implemented. And Chapter 9 showed how people from three different cultures managed to work harmoniously at the AMD mega-factory, unleashing its potential.

In each of these cases, people's actions can, and must, be judged right or wrong, good or bad. For example, was it right for the Masai to offer their cows as a gift, and was it right of the U.S. people not to accept the cows, asking instead for beads? Is it good for the Native Americans in Arizona to keep to themselves, and are the white communities right to resent them? Is it wrong for people in France and Switzerland to resist anglicisms, and can the global spread of English be considered good behavior on the part of the Anglo-Saxon cultures? Was Motorola management right not to fire the East Asian engineer, and was his use of his housing allowance for another purpose good or bad? Finally, was the decision of people from three different cultures to work together at AMD right or wrong? In every situation of intercultural interaction, people make judgments about what ought to be done under the circumstances—that is, what course of action is right and what behaviors are deemed wrong. Such judgments have a moral dimension and are traditionally studied in the domain of ethics.

Ethics and Morality. A distinction is usually made between morality and ethics. **Morality** generally refers to customs and traditions of a given culture, which regulate relationships and prescribe modes of behavior. **Ethics,** in turn, refers to the study of the general nature of modes of behavior and moral choices made by people in relationships with others. Thus,

> ethics most often refers to a domain of inquiry, a discipline, in which matters of right and wrong, good and evil, virtue and vice, are systematically examined. Morality, by contrast, is most often used to refer not to a discipline but to patterns of thought and action that are actually operative in everyday life. In this sense, morality is what the discipline of ethics is about. (Goodpaster, 1992: 111)

Moral patterns of thought and action may collide as people from different cultures enact different views of what it means "to do the right thing" in various situations of interaction. Not surprisingly, ethical issues are addressed in many books on intercultural communication. In these books, ethics is consistently defined as the study of "the means or moral standards by which actions may be judged good or bad, right or wrong" (Hall, 2002: 330), emphasizing that ethical judgments focus "on the degree of rightness and wrongness in human behavior" (Martin & Nakayama, 2000: 19).

As we saw from the examples discussed at the beginning of the chapter, ethical judgments include such decisions as whether to share one's resources (e.g., cows in the Masai example and professional expertise in the AMD example), whether to allow the Other's resources into one's cultural territory or put up resistance (e.g., fighting back against anglicisms in France and Switzerland), and whether to trust people from another culture (e.g., the white and Native American communities in Arizona). As a result of each ethical judgment, a choice is made and meanings are enacted. This way, cultures are formed as shared systems of symbolic resources. Based on its own system of resources, every culture positions itself toward other cultures. Naturally, all people want to make sure that the position of their culture is strong and stable—that their resources allow them to carry out what they want to accomplish. Thus, people from every culture want to determine what behavior is right (good) for them. So, the question that every culture faces is this: What does being moral mean? In this sense, "we must recognize that being moral takes precedence over all other concerns" (Gudykunst & Kim, 2003: 407).

Approaches to Ethics in Intercultural Communication

There is a large amount of literature devoted to ethics, with many opinions about what is right and wrong in intercultural interactions. However, several main approaches can be isolated.

Two Broad Approaches. There are two broad approaches to ethics as it relates to culture—universalism and relativism. The debate between ethical universalists and relativists has been going on for centuries, and both views are still strongly held today (Fleischacker, 1994). Each approach has its own understanding of the relationship between ethics and culture, with certain implications for the study of intercultural communication.

According to the **universalist approach,** people's actions must be applicable to all cultures; that is, there is one correct way for people from all cultures to do something. Ethical universalists try to identify actions that people from all cultures can agree upon as right or wrong. For example, the Ten Commandments are sometimes presented as a universal ethical code of action. Another proposal for a universal code of ethics is one based on the inherent goodness of peace and sacredness of the human spirit (Kale, 1994).

According to the **relativist approach,** people's actions are culture-bound; that is, each culture has its own ideas about what is right and wrong. Hence, people's actions can be judged only in terms of their culture's ethical system. For instance, an ethical judgment about eating dogs can be made only from the point of view of a particular culture; thus, it may be the right behavior in Korea and the wrong behavior in most other cultures. In other words, ethical relativism maintains that "the value of actions and the validity of moral judgments are dependent upon their sociocultural context" (Barnsley, 1972: 327).

Both universalist and relativist approaches have positive and negative aspects.

A universalist ethics is proposed as a desirable moral option for today's multicultural world because it provides a set of moral standards for all cultures to follow. Yet any universal moral standards are formulated by particular cultures—that is, from a certain point of view. For example, even the Ten Commandments present a particular view about what is right and wrong and cannot be considered a universal ethical code.

> The concept of universal ethics, standards of goodness that apply to everyone, everywhere, and at all times, is the very sort of myth people struggle to hold onto. . . . All moral choices flow from the perceptions of the decision maker, and those perceptions are produced by unique experiences in one person's life, in the context in which the choices are made. (Howell, 1982: 187).

In other words, people from each culture naturally want to see as universal their own moral standards of good behavior. Such a view is potentially dangerous because it leads to imposing one's own moral standards on other cultures; the most powerful culture always "defines and dominates the criteria by which ethical behavior is evaluated" (Pedersen, 1997: 154).

Not surprisingly,

> Contemporary critics of universalism argue that such ethics turns out to be a form of cultural chauvinism, a way of imposing culturally specific standards upon societies where they would not be useful or appropriate. Even the most seemingly universalist rules—such as injunctions not to harm or steal from other people—are always created by particular cultures or groups to serve their interests. . . . Universalism is, indeed, always a form of ethnocentrism. (Moscovici, 2001: 289)

Ethical universalism in its extreme form can be identified with ethnocentric reduction, discussed in Chapter 4. One culture is viewed as imposing its system of moral standards on all other cultures, reducing them to Self—that is, to its own moral code of behavior.

A relativist ethics also is proposed as a desirable moral option for today's multicultural world because it allows different moral standards, which preclude various cultures from judging one another. Yet, "such a stand is as potentially dangerous and untenable as the strong universalist stance" (Hall, 2002: 342). Ethical relativism in its extreme form—"anything goes!"—leads to the view that any action is acceptable as long as it is judged morally right by a certain culture; in this sense, ethical relativism can be seen as "a doctrine of ethical indifference" (Hall, 2002: 342). Ethical relativism is dangerous because it discourages "moral discourse and disregards ethical guidelines outside of each cultural context" (Pedersen, 1997: 155).

Ethical relativism in its extreme form is also a form of ethnocentrism and can be identified with ethnocentric negation, discussed in Chapter 4. Each culture claims that its actions cannot be judged by other cultures, disregarding (negating) any other moral standards.

Thus, both universalism and relativism, taken separately, have an ethnocentric bias. A culture with a universalist stance aims to reduce all other cultures to Self (its own system of moral standards), while a culture with a relativist stance aims to negate all other cultures as simply not Self, claiming its own system of moral standards (Self) as the only acceptable ethical code. As a result, both universalism and relativism approach ethics from the perspective of only one culture (Self), without engaging the perspective of people from other cultures (the Other).

At the same time, it is impossible to come up with *the* universal code of behavior without looking at different ways of doing things; for example, what is *the* right way of eating rice—with a spoon, with chopsticks, or with your hands? No universal ethical code can be formulated based only on the moral standards of one culture without including views that exist in other cultures; thus, universalism presupposes relativism. By the same token, it is easy to see that, without some universal ethical foundation, a multicultural world risks plunging into fragmentation and chaos. "Without universal values . . . the very notion of ethics, or morally desirable codes of conduct, risks meaninglessness" (Moscovici, 2001: 290); thus, relativism presupposes universalism.

It seems as if universalism and relativism try to present *the* definitive view of ethics. The view presented by universalism is large, embracing all cultures, while the view presented by relativism is smaller, based on only one culture's code of ethics. Yet both universalism and relativism attempt to own the truth. Universalism and relativism need each other in order to reveal the true nature of ethical behavior. According to Hegel, "The Truth is the Whole" (see Levins, 1998: 382). In our case, the Whole must somehow reconcile the large view on ethics with all smaller views. Thus, intercultural communication can be said to oscillate "between the poles of universalism and relativism, without settling on either" (Moscovici, 2001: 290). In other words,

> Ethics may be viewed as a compound of universalism and relativism. All ethical systems involve a tension between what is universal and what is relative. . . . The challenge, then, is to understand the nature of this compound and its implications in intercultural settings. (Hall, 2002: 343)

Many attempts have been made to understand the nature of this tension. Below, five specific approaches, based on Hall's work (2002: 330–336), are briefly reviewed.

Five Specific Approaches. Hall isolates five golden approaches to ethics—the golden law, the golden purse, the golden consequence, the golden mean, and the golden rule. Each approach has certain implications for intercultural communication.

The **golden law** focuses on the inherent goodness or badness of people's actions. All actions are said to be inherently ethical or unethical, regardless of who performs them. This law applies equally to everyone: What is right or wrong for one person is also right or wrong for all other people. According to Kant's famous discussion of the categorical imperative (Kant, 1959), such laws take on the forms of positive actions (e.g., give aid, show gratitude) and negative actions (e.g., do not lie, do not steal).

The **golden purse** is based on the notion of power, understood as physical strength, wealth, and so forth. This approach to ethics can be summed up by the saying "He rules who has the gold." While this approach is often used by more powerful cultures in intercultural interactions, "it provides an extremely unstable foundation upon which to build mutually beneficial intercultural communities" (Hall, 2002: 332).

The **golden consequence** is grounded in the outcomes of people's actions; ethical decisions are based on what will bring the most good for the most people. In this context, an action generally considered unethical, such as lying, may be deemed the right behavior if it leads to the greater good. This approach allows people to go any way using their ethical reasoning; besides, "humans don't really know what the consequences of certain actions will be" (Hall, 2002: 335).

The **golden mean** can be traced back to the ideas of Aristotle and Confucius, who saw the right behavior as a blending of opposites. For example, neither cowardice nor foolhardiness is right, but courage, as the golden mean between the two, is. Thus, an ethical choice is a happy medium between two extremes.

The **golden rule** states that we should act toward people from other cultures as we would have them act toward us. The golden rule is upheld not only in the West but also in the East, where it is expressed in the Confucian saying "Do not do to others what you do not like others to do to you."

Each of these five specific approaches to ethics tries to resolve the tension between universalism and relativism. It is easy to see that the golden law approach gravitates toward the universal pole of ethics: It claims universality for moral standards. The golden purse and golden consequence approaches, on the contrary, gravitate toward the relativist pole of ethics: They claim that moral standards depend on, or are relative to, power or outcomes of actions. The golden mean and the golden rule are more successful at balancing tensions between universalism and relativism because they are based on the idea that, in making ethical judgments, "we need to focus on the other culture's perspective as well as our own" (Hall, 2002: 336). In other words, these approaches try to reconcile one culture's ethical code (smaller view of ethics) with all other cultures' ethical codes (large view of ethics). These approaches are more successful because they pay attention to both Self (one culture's ethics) and its environment (the Other, or other cultures' ethical codes).

Introducing the Sustainability Principle

The discussion above provides a basis for the tenth (and last) principle underlying intercultural communication—the Sustainability Principle. As with the previous principles, we will isolate three parts that make up this principle. Each part deals with intercultural communication as a process whereby people must make ethical choices. First, we will discuss the general nature of sustainability and how it can be applied to intercultural communication. Then we will present the main strategies of sustainability in intercultural communication. Finally, we will suggest a formula for intercultural sustainability. We will discuss each part separately and then formulate the Sustainability Principle as a whole.

Nature of Sustainability: Thinking about Forever

According to Barnlund,

> The moral issues that attend intercultural encounters are not simply more complicated, they are of an entirely new dimension. Despite the pervasiveness of cross-cultural contact, these complications remain overlooked and unexplored in any systematic way. (1980: 9)

The claim that moral issues in intercultural encounters remain overlooked is an exaggeration; a lot of research has been done in this area (Asuncion-Lande, 1980; Sitaram & Cogdell, 1976). However, the call for a more systematic study of ethics in intercultural communication is justified. A **metaethic**—a general foundation for successful (ethical) intercultural communication—is needed to transcend all differences.

Today, globalization makes the need for such a metaethic more urgent than ever. **Globalization** refers to the intensified compression of the world and our increasing consciousness of cultural processes that extend beyond the collective identity of any one culture (Robertson, 1992). The process of globalization has a huge potential for development of each and every culture. At the same time, globalization has a dark side in the form of many challenges facing all people. Among the challenges listed in the book entitled *Introducing Global Issues* (Snarr & Snarr, 2002) are weapons proliferation, migration, health, and protection of the atmosphere. These challenges transcend all differences (political, social, economic, etc.) and require an ethical framework that serves the concerns of all people on the planet. And the most fundamental concern is clear—survival, understood as remaining alive or in existence (Morris, 1982: 1296). There can be no doubt that "cultures—like any other organic system—strive to affirm life" (Rodriguez, 2002: 2).To put it bluntly, unless people are alive, they cannot meet the more specific challenges of dealing with weapons proliferation, migration, health, and protection of the atmosphere. Thus, "our newly interdependent global society, with its remarkable possibilities for linking people around the planet, gives us the material basis for a new ethic . . . that will serve the interests of all those who live on this planet" (Singer, 2002: B9; see also Singer, 2001). These ideas are emphasized in UNESCO's Charter: "We are beginning to move towards a new global ethic which transcends all other systems of allegiance and belief, which is rooted in a consciousness of the interrelatedness and sanctity of life" (1997: paragraph 116). This new global ethic, or metaethic, is found in the idea of sustainability.

Sustainability is a dynamic state requiring that decisions be made in such a way that something is kept in existence (maintained). Sustainability by definition involves thinking about forever. Sustainability is a fundamental concern of humankind, and there is a large amount of literature discussing its ideas (Dresner, 2002; Tonn, 1999). Sustainability has a number of dimensions. For example, ecological sustainability concerns conservation of nature, political sustainability concerns preserving democracy, economic sustainability concerns appropriate industrial development, and social sustainability concerns maintaining peace and equity.

In this text we are concerned with intercultural sustainability because "culture . . . has a central place in the complex notion of sustainability" (UNESCO, 1997: paragraphs 111–112). Intercultural sustainability is a dynamic state wherein people must make decisions in such a way that their cultures are continually maintained (kept in existence). Earlier, it was shown that no culture can make such decisions alone; both universalism and relativism are, in fact, forms of ethnocentrism because they present an ethical code from only one point of view—that of Self. Intercultural sustainability requires that each culture pay attention to its environment, which includes all other cultures (the Other). When we pay attention to people from other cultures, we decide how to interact with them. In this connection, "ethics and morality are correlative with the purpose of avoiding damage to the rights and interests of people—preeminently *other* people" (Rescher, 1977: 80). Intercultural sustainability is not just a matter of morality but also of rationality: A decision is considered right if it helps people to sustain their culture. So asking the question "Why be ethical?" is the same as asking the question "Why be rational?" As Lewis puts it, "Cognitive correctness is itself a moral concern, in the broad sense of 'moral'" (1969: 163).

Thus, the global metaethic is found in the idea of intercultural sustainability. Let's see how people must make decisions in order for their cultures to be continually maintained. In other words, let's see what communicative strategies people must use so that their actions are considered ethical (rational).

Strategies of Intercultural Sustainability: Tolerance, Trust, and Resistance

Tolerance. All people living together in perfect harmony is the ideal of intercultural communication. In real life, interactions that are far from harmonious continue to take place between people from different cultures. It is not surprising, then, that "the demand for an understanding of tolerance and intolerance seems to be at an all-time high" (Baldwin, 1998: 24).

Tolerance is defined as "the capacity for or practice of allowing or respecting the nature, beliefs, or behaviors of others" (Morris, 1982: 1351). This capacity makes it possible for people from one culture (Self) to allow people from another culture (the Other) to cross the imaginary boundary line separating them and enter what Self considers its own territory, its own side of the intercultural continuum. As was shown in Chapter 8, if intercultural communication is based on the flexible-sum perception, people from one culture can move into the space occupied by another culture. This move may be viewed as potentially dangerous because new meanings are brought in, meanings that until now have not been part of Self. It is not easy to deal with new behaviors different from your own; you may not be accustomed to eating with chopsticks, as people do in many Asian counties, or standing during a church service, as people do in Russia. But in intercultural interactions we must be capable of handling such challenges; we must tolerate such different behaviors. Tolerance is not the same as acceptance, which implies agreement; people from one culture may or may not agree with the way things are done in other cultures. However, people from different cultures cannot communicate effectively unless they recognize the need to allow these differences to exist. Tolerance is considered a primary virtue (Barnes, 2001) because no culture owns the truth alone. On the contrary, we must tolerate other people's behaviors because everyone knows something of the truth. As was stated earlier, the Truth is the Whole.

Thus, tolerance is the capacity of one culture to deal with the presence of another culture in its territory. Through interaction, every culture establishes a dynamic limit on this capacity: People from every culture decide to what extent they will allow a different system of meanings in their territory. It depends, of course, on how different another culture's meanings are and what the consequences of dealing with such meanings might be. For example, if the Other brings new eating utensils, such as chopsticks, then Self is likely to tolerate this new meaning and maybe even borrow it. However, if the Other brings new eating habits, such as eating dogs or frogs, then Self is less likely to tolerate this new meaning. In each intercultural encounter, a dynamic boundary line is drawn between Self and the Other; if both Self and the Other agree on where this line is, it is possible to speak of tolerance as a communicative strategy leading to intercultural sustainability.

It might seem as if tolerance were a passive process, a form of silent stance. However, tolerance does not mean that people from different cultures must adopt—or are not allowed to challenge—each other's positions. On the contrary, the value of tolerance is to encourage an open exchange of ideas. "Fighting for toleration is not a matter of attempting to align other groups with a preexisting order, but a form of dialogue in the course of which the picture of what toleration is and requires gradually becomes clear" (Walker, 1995: 112). The idea of tolerance is for people from every culture to find out their best position on every issue, including eating preferences and religious rituals; this can be done only through interaction with other cultures. In Chapters 4 and 5, we discussed how cultures come to better understand other worldviews, as well as their own worldview, by engaging in interactions and seeing how they measure up against each other. This task cannot be accomplished without intercultural tolerance, because only by allowing others to share their codes of behavior can people from every culture determine what meanings must make up their collective identity. The word *tolerance* is derived from the Latin *tolerare*—to bear. In a way, people from every culture decide what meanings they can bear, or deal with comfortably.

Thus, intercultural tolerance is impossible without flexibility. People must be open to an exchange of ideas and must be flexible enough to allow new ideas to be part of their own cultural space. It is clear, however, that true intercultural sustainability requires not only tolerance but also trust.

Trust. The word *trust* is derived from the Middle English *truste,* meaning confidence or firmness. **Trust** is firm reliance on someone's integrity; it is confidence that someone will act as expected or as previously agreed upon. As we saw in Chapter 9, without trust it is impossible to solve the prisoner's dilemma and work toward synergy. Trust is crucial for effective intercultural communication because people from one culture can tolerate people from another culture only if they are confident that the people from that culture will not cross the boundary line previously established. For example, suppose people from one culture allow those from another culture to discuss its dog-based cuisine in their territory, but do not allow the selling of products made of dog. If members of the dog-eating culture nonetheless start selling such products, then trust is broken and tolerance is upset. Trust in intercultural communication depends on an unspoken promise to share one's behaviors only to the extent agreed upon by all cultures involved. As long as this promise is kept, intercultural communication can be effective and intercultural sustainability can be maintained. Effective intercultural communication presupposes integrity on the part of all cultures involved in interactions; then it becomes possible for people from different cultures to rely on each other and sustain their collective identities.

Thus, intercultural trust is impossible without firmness. One culture must firmly believe that the other culture will show its integrity and keep its promise not to cross the boundary line previously established. Tolerance and trust form a default mechanism in intercultural communication. This mechanism is in effect as long as one culture establishes a dynamic limit on the other culture's inroads into its territory and trusts that culture not to cross this boundary line. If this line is crossed, as in the example above, the other culture's integrity is questioned and trust is broken. The promise to share one's meanings is now perceived as an intention to impose one's meanings; there is a difference between acting on an invitation and carrying out an invasion. As a result, intercultural sustainability is in danger, and the default mechanism of intercultural communication switches to a different mode—that of resistance.

Resistance. **Resistance** is any force that works against something; in our case, cultural resistance opposes actions from another culture perceived by people as dominant and therefore dangerous to their collective survival. A culture must resist (fight back) if its people can no longer tolerate another culture's behavior in their territory. Obviously, intercultural communication in this case is less effective because it is no longer a cooperative process; now, people from different cultures work not with, but against, each other. At the same time, resistance as a communicative strategy is crucial for intercultural sustainability: Its main goal is to help people from different cultures to resume harmonious interactions and maintain their collective identities. Ultimately, successful resistance is aimed at bringing intercultural communication back to the dynamic state of intercultural sustainability.

So, tolerance, trust, and resistance are all interconnected, as shown in Figure 1.

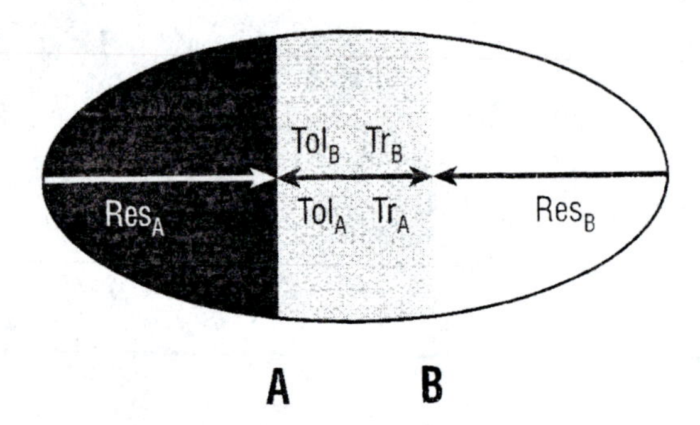

FIGURE 1

The figure also shows that in the process of intercultural interactions a shared zone is created and continuously maintained, based on these strategies of tolerance, trust, and resistance. This zone is bounded on its two sides by lines A and B. Each culture targets—wants to reach—the other culture's boundary. For example, suppose people from the Korean culture (culture A) want to share the practice of eating dogs, part of their cuisine, with people from France (culture B), while people from the French culture want to share the practice of eating frogs with people from Korea. The Korean people are trying to reach line B (part of the French culture), while the French people are trying to reach line A (part of the Korean culture). Let's say that each side decides to present a lecture on the subject for the other side. If each culture allows the other one into its territory and the other culture keeps its promise—that is, simply delivers a lecture—both cultures' targets are reached, thanks to the strategies of tolerance and trust (Tol_A Tr_A and Tol_B Tr_B, respectively). This way, for example, the French can learn that, although such dishes as dog stew and canine cutlets are eaten in Korea because of their alleged health-giving qualities, not all Koreans eat dogs; their diet consists mainly of vegetables, not meat. And the dogs they eat are a special type raised at special farms; such dogs are killed by electrocution (just like the cows and pigs eaten in many Western cultures). Also, the pet industry is rapidly growing in Korea. Similarly, the Koreans can learn about the practice of eating frogs' legs in France.

But suppose each side chooses to add to its lecture a little demonstration, offering the audience a dish made of dog or frog. Or, even worse, what if each side chooses to replace the other's cuisine with its own? In these cases, the culture is seen as moving beyond the boundaries previously set, and the two lines A and B immediately change from target points into points of resistance. Each side, for instance, may react defensively to the other culture's move by requesting that the demonstration be stopped, asking the audience to leave the room, or putting up some other form of resistance. As you can see, the arrows of resistance (Res_A and Res_B) point in the direction opposite that of the arrows of tolerance and trust.

Earlier, it was noted that intercultural tolerance is impossible without flexibility, and intercultural trust is impossible without firmness. The relationship among tolerance, trust, and resistance is now clear: People from culture A can be flexible and display tolerance only if people from culture B are firm in their commitment to act as agreed upon by both cultures. If culture B is perceived as defecting from that agreement—as not firm—then culture A stops being flexible and becomes firm. That is exactly how tolerance turns into resistance; to *resist* means to "remain firm against the action or effect of" (Morris, 1982: 1106). Resistance is a very important communicative strategy (Deyhle, 1995; Duncombe, 2002), and it is crucial that resistance be identified as such. For example, the practice of Islamic veiling is usually discussed in terms of freedom and presented by Westerners (especially feminists) as a case of gender oppression in Islamic cultures. Yet many Islamic women are said to participate in this practice voluntarily and claim it as an important part of their cultural identity and a mark of resistance to the Western morals perceived as wrong (Hirschmann, 1997). Obviously, interacting with Islamic women depends to a significant degree on how one views their practice of veiling—as a form of cultural oppression or resistance.

Notice that we are speaking of resistance as a communicative strategy, as opposed to violent or militant resistance. Peaceful resistance is best exemplified by Mahatma Gandhi and his technique of **satyagraha.** This term "has variously been translated as 'passive resistance,' 'nonviolent direct action,' and even 'militant nonviolence' " (Weber, 2001: 494). In dealing with intercultural tensions, Mahatma Gandhi always focused on issues, not personalities, and saw his opponents as partners, not enemies. He was committed to an open exchange of ideas in search of a fair resolution for all parties involved rather than having his opponents be humbled and destroyed. It is clear that he searched for intercultural sustainability, and if more people in more cultures shared and practiced his technique of satyagraha, the world would be a better place.

The situation in which the strategies of tolerance, trust, and resistance are in perfect balance is an ideal of intercultural communication; this does not mean, however, that we should give up trying to achieve it. On the contrary, if we can envision an ideal, we can present it as an optimal overall strategy. Then people from different cultures will strive for that ideal, continually improving their interactions and sustaining their collective identities.

The global metaethic can therefore be identified with intercultural sustainability. According to this metaethic, if people use the communicative strategies of tolerance, trust, and resistance to maintain their cultures, their actions will be considered ethical (rational). The ideal situation of intercultural communication is a balance, or equilibrium, of the strategies of tolerance, trust, and resistance. This view is expressed especially well by the Systems Theory of intercultural communication. According to this theory, "intercultural communication always takes place in embedded systems" (Ting-Toomey, 1999: 23). All cultures seek to achieve a state of balance or equilibrium—that is, a stable pattern of interactions.

Thus, the situation in which the strategies of tolerance, trust, and resistance are all balanced—that is, are in a state of equilibrium—represents the best case of intercultural sustainability. "There is a way to interpret 'best sustainability ethic' that can provide a general formula for an optimum sustainability strategy" (Durbin, 1997: 50). If we know the formula for the best sustainability ethic, we can calculate the point where intercultural interactions are the most efficient—the

Pareto optimality discussed in the previous chapter. As you may remember, Pareto optimality is an ideal for which people from different cultures must strive in their interactions. So, what is this ideal? What is the best ethic of intercultural sustainability? What is this magic formula?

Formula for Intercultural Sustainability

Earlier, we discussed five golden approaches to ethics—the golden law, the golden purse, the golden consequence, the golden mean, and the golden rule—and their implications for intercultural communication. These approaches can be supplemented with one more golden approach, which takes these ideas further and provides a mathematical formula for intercultural sustainability. This approach is the Golden Ratio approach.

You may have heard of the Golden Ratio as the Golden Number, the Golden Section, or the Divine Proportion. Indeed, the **Golden Ratio,** while it is defined mathematically as a number, in reality describes a proportionate or harmonious relationship between different parts of something. Euclid of Alexandria, who first defined the Golden Ratio around 300 B.C., used the example of a straight line cut into two parts, as shown in Figure 2.

While the whole line AB is longer than the segment AC and the segment AC is longer than the segment CB, the ratio of the length of AB to that of AC is the same as the ratio of the length of AC to that of CB. This ratio is represented by the never-ending and never-repeating number 1.6180339887. . . . This number, which can be rounded down to 1.6, is the value of the Golden Ratio.

You may be wondering what this number has to do with intercultural communication. To begin with, as we have already stated, the Golden Ratio is not so much a number as a relationship: It reflects a proportion between different parts of something. And these parts, no matter how large or small, can remain themselves (i.e., retain their identity) as long as the proportion between them equals approximately 1.6! Moreover, this value continues indefinitely, getting closer and closer to the ideal relationship between these two parts as digits are added. Thus, the Golden Ratio reflects the ideal (the "right") way for different parts to relate—for example, for different cultures to interact.

Let's look at a concrete example of how all this works. Instead of a straight line, we will take a semantic space (a continuum, as discussed in Chapter 6) representing the meaning of "what is right to eat." For the sake of simplicity, let's suppose this semantic space includes only two meanings (two parts): dogs (Korean

FIGURE 2 **Euclid's Golden Ratio**

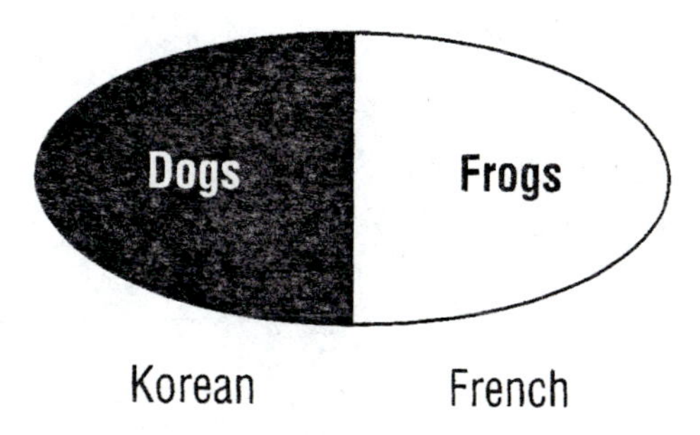

FIGURE 3

culture) and frogs (French culture). We will divide this semantic space equally between these two meanings, as shown in Figure 3.

People from both cultures are curious about each other's eating habits, so they must deal with each other. Let's describe three possible scenarios for their interaction, briefly mentioned earlier in the chapter, and three decisions made in this process.

As the first scenario, suppose the Korean people want to introduce dishes made of dog into your (French) culture as a replacement for frogs' legs; in essence, they want to replace your part of the semantic continuum for "eating" with their own. Then the whole continuum (all 100 percent) would be made up of only one meaning, representing one culture that was not yours. Would you give up half of the overall semantic space (your 50 percent) in an encounter with the Korean culture? Most certainly not! You would resist giving up your part of the continuum because otherwise your own culture would cease to exist, as shown in Figure 4.

As the second scenario, suppose the Koreans offer to arrange a food demonstration for you, preparing dishes made of dog and then distributing samples of them. This is obviously not as radical as completely replacing your cultural cuisine, but it is still quite intrusive. In your eyes, it would equal 25 percent of the overall continuum (see Figure 5). Would you be willing to allow such a demonstration? Very likely not. In other words, you would still resist, finding it risky to give half of your own cultural space to people from another culture whose conduct you find so different from yours.

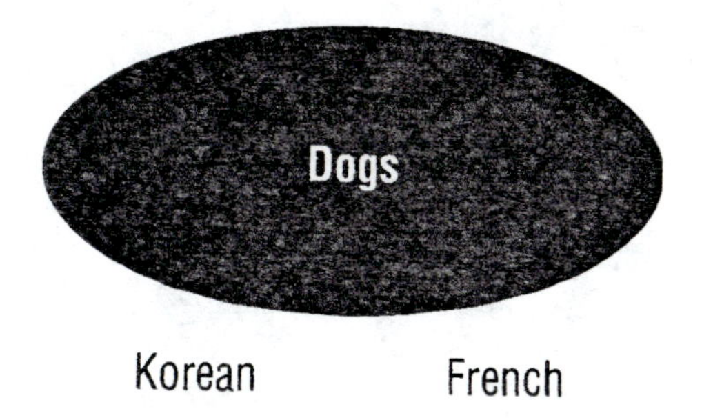

FIGURE 4

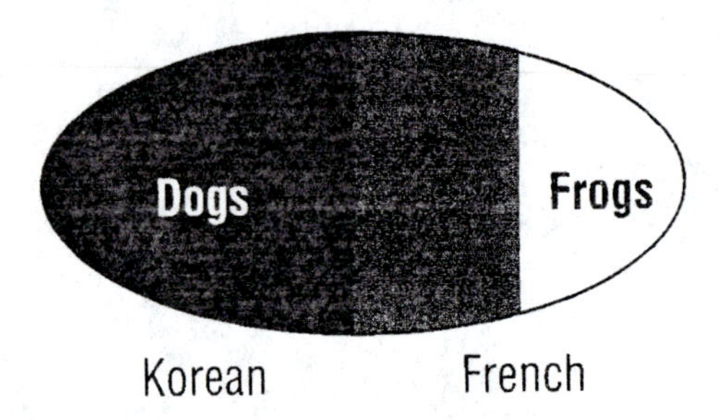

FIGURE 5

What percentage of the overall continuum would you be willing to let another culture use for its own purpose? You refused to sacrifice your total space (50 percent) in the first scenario and then half of that (25 percent) in the second scenario. Would you be willing to let another culture use half of that 25 percent (12.5 percent, rounded down to 12 percent)? Most likely, yes. Suppose the Koreans were to ask you if they could just present a lecture on their cultural cuisine to your people—not a very intrusive action. Would you be against that? Most likely not. You would allow the Koreans to move into your cultural space and present their lecture (see Figure 6).

Now, let's see what we have. First of all, we have the overall intercultural continuum, which equals 100 percent (space AB in Figure 7). Next, we have two different parts of this continuum, each representing one of the cultures: the Korean culture's space AC, which now equals 62 percent (50 percent is its own space, and 12 percent is French cultural space), and the French culture's space CB, which is made up of the remaining 38 percent. Like the line segments in Figure 2, the whole space AB is larger than the space AC and the space AC is larger than the space CB, but the ratio of AB to AC is the same as the ratio of AC to CB! And this ratio is represented by the number 1.6 ($100 : 62 \approx 1.6$ and $62 : 38 \approx 1.6$).

Suppose the Korean culture were to interact with the French culture in the same way—refusing to replace its cuisine with frogs and refusing a food demonstration, but allowing a lecture on French eating behavior. Now the French culture is being allowed to use 12 percent that is Korean semantic space. As a result, now the French culture's space DB equals 62 percent (50 percent is its own space, and

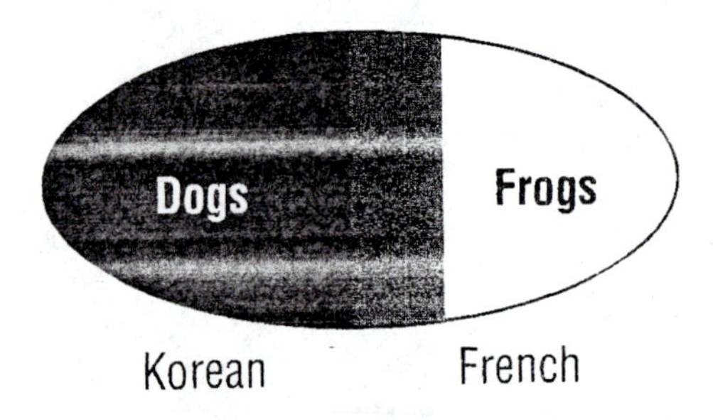

FIGURE 6

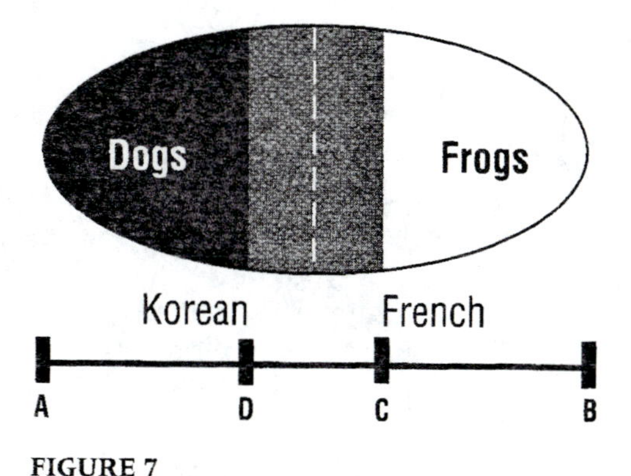

FIGURE 7

12 percent is Korean cultural space) and the Korean culture's space AD is made up of the remaining 38 percent. But, the ratio between the two cultures (DB to AD) is still the same and equals 1.6! (See Figure 7.)

Now, if we go back to Figure 1, we can see that the ideal situation for intercultural interactions, where tolerance, trust, and resistance are in perfect balance, exists when the boundary lines are positioned so that the ratio between the cultures' spaces equals the Golden Ratio (Figure 8).

Generally, people are willing to trust and tolerate a culture that occupies up to 62 percent of the total territory. If that line is crossed without mutual consent, the mechanism of resistance is activated. Naturally, we cannot always calculate our intercultural interactions with mathematical precision. Yet we can usually sense quite well when to tolerate and trust other cultural behaviors and when to draw a line and resist them.

Like the never-ending and never-repeating number 1.6180339887 . . . , intercultural communication never stops; it continues always, trying to reach, but never reaching, that perfect balance. The Golden Ratio defines an ideal dynamic point where each interacting culture is able to preserve its relationship with itself (sustain its collective identity) and consume the least amount of energy (symbolic resources) doing so. As long as oscillations continue to take place between two cultures, the result will be stable and sustainable intercultural communication. Real oscillations fall short of or go beyond the ideal point; such oscillations will be

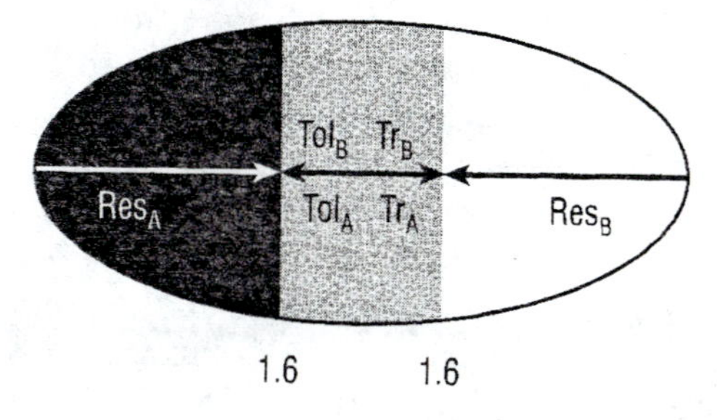

FIGURE 8

tolerated (if mutually agreed upon) or resisted (if not). Intercultural communication is always a process of trial and error, always an exploration.

If people from two cultures make a decision to treat each other based on the Golden Ratio approach, their interactions will be harmonious because neither culture will lose; on the contrary, both cultures will win because they are able to remain whole—that is, sustain their collective identities. The value of the ratio between the space occupied by the overall intercultural continuum and that occupied at least in part by each interacting culture is the same as the value of the ratio between the spaces occupied by the two interacting cultures—1.6—and it represents intercultural sustainability. In terms of the areas in Figure 7, AB : AC = 1.6, AB : DB = 1.6, AC : CB = 1.6, and DB : AD = 1.6. While continually changing, both interacting cultures and the overall cultural continuum remain themselves, intact and whole. Thus, intercultural sustainability presupposes not only that cultures maintain their collective identities, but also that the whole process of intercultural communication be maintained. That is why we do not speak simply of cultural sustainability but of *inter*cultural sustainability.

Intercultural sustainability is a principle that can be used to determine how people from all cultures ought to interact with each other, generating a general rule that helps people decide what behaviors are right and what behaviors are wrong. This principle is a matter not just of morality but also of rationality, as was stated earlier. Similarly, the Golden Ratio is a matter of morality and ratio-nality. If we are not moral and not rational—that is, if we reason badly and treat people from other cultures poorly—we make poor decisions. As a result, we do damage to them as well as to ourselves! Any immoral/irrational behavior is self-destructive, as it undermines intercultural sustainability. Intercultural sustainability tells us that we ought to build our relationships with other people based on the Golden Ratio. The "ought" here is not simply "an *ethical* 'ought,' but one of the cosmic fitness of things. It . . . represents an idealized vision of the optimal arrangement of the world. The world *ought* to be a place where things go properly" (Rescher, 1977: 82).

Thus, when people from different cultures accept intercultural sustainability as a principle underlying their interactions, their actions fit both the universalist and the relativist approaches to ethics. On the one hand, people's actions are culture-bound; each culture has its own ideas about what is right and wrong. As a result, people's actions are judged in terms of that culture's ethical system; for instance, eating frogs is considered the right behavior in the French culture. On the other hand, people's decision to base their actions on the Golden Ratio is applicable to all cultures; it is the correct way for people from all cultures to interact with each other. So, each culture, while maintaining its own codes of conduct, works for the universal good; at the same time, the universal code, represented by the Golden Ratio, makes it possible for each culture to practice its own behaviors. To put it simply, each culture works for Self (relativism) and for all others (universalism). What is good for Self is good for all—or, all for one, and one for all!

"In the professional mathematical literature, the common symbol for the Golden Ratio is the Greek letter tau . . . which means 'the cut' or 'the section' " (Livio, 2002: 5). This meaning of the Golden Ratio relates to the nature of intercultural interactions extremely well: In each encounter, the relationship between two cultures must be "cut" in a certain way. In Chapter 6, we compared cultivating an interaction to cutting around a plant's roots so that it can bear better fruit. The Golden Ratio tells us where this cut must be made in order for intercultural communication to continue and cultural identities to be sustained. This cut corresponds to a line between interacting cultures, and the success of intercultural encounters depends on where this line is drawn.

We began our journey in Chapter 1 by asking the question "What is in a line?" Now we have come back to this issue and discovered the best way to draw a boundary line in intercultural interactions—so as to create a ratio with a value of 1.6. Reaching this point is the overall goal of intercultural communication. But, as was shown many times throughout this text, it can never be reached once and for all. This point is an ideal: It never stops moving and never repeats itself. It is simple yet complex—like life itself. All we can do—all we must do—is go after it, traveling to different places and meeting people from all kinds of different cultures, living this life and keeping it alive.

The Sustainability Principle Defined

Now we can give a more concise formulation of the Sustainability Principle, based on the above discussion of its three parts.

First, the idea of intercultural sustainability represents the global metaethic for today's multicultural world. Intercultural sustainability is seen as a dynamic state wherein people must make decisions in such a way that their collective identities are continually maintained (kept in existence). No culture can make such decisions alone; both universalism and relativism are forms of ethnocentrism because they present an ethical code from only one point of view—that of Self. Intercultural sustainability requires that each culture pay attention to its environment, which includes all other cultures with their codes of behavior. In this sense, intercultural sustainability is a matter not just of morality but also of rationality: A decision is considered right if it helps people to sustain their culture.

Second, according to the global metaethic of intercultural sustainability, people use the communicative strategies of tolerance, trust, and resistance to continually maintain their cultures. Then people's actions are considered ethical (rational). The ideal of intercultural communication is a balance of tolerance, trust, and resistance; this situation represents the best case of intercultural sustainability—the most stable outcome of intercultural interactions.

Third, the best sustainability ethic (the optimal sustainability strategy) is based on the Golden Ratio value, representing the ratio of the space occupied by intercultural communication in general to that occupied at least in part by each culture and the ratio between the spaces occupied by the two interacting cultures. Thus, intercultural sustainability presupposes not only that cultures maintain their collective identities, but also that the whole process of intercultural communication be maintained.

In a nutshell, the Sustainability Principle can be formulated as follows:

Intercultural communication is a process whereby people from different cultures display mutual tolerance, trust, and resistance, sustaining their collective identities and the overall process of their interactions.

This principle shows that no culture owns the truth—that is, knows the only right way of doing things. At the same time, each culture knows something of the truth because it knows its own way of doing things. As long as people from different cultures display mutual tolerance, trust, and resistance, their interactions will be maintained as one whole process of intercultural communication, and each culture will sustain its own relationship with itself, remaining whole. As was said earlier, the Truth is the Whole.

Summary

In this chapter, we set out to show why cooperating and integrating their resources is the right behavior for people from different cultures. Thus, we approached intercultural communication from an ethical point of view. We emphasized that ethics is important in intercultural communication because, in dealing with people from other cultures, we must make decisions about what behaviors are right and what behaviors are wrong.

Next, we discussed two broad approaches to ethics—the universalist and relativist approaches—and their ramifications for intercultural communication. Both universalism and relativism were shown to contain an ethnocentric bias, approaching ethics from the perspective of only one culture. No universal ethical code can be formulated based only on the moral standards of one culture without including views that exist in other cultures; universalism presupposes relativism. By the same token, without some universal ethical foundation, the multicultural world risks plunging into fragmentation and chaos; relativism presupposes universalism. Thus, intercultural communication was presented as oscillating between the poles of universalism and relativism, without settling on either. In other words, we showed how all ethical systems involve a tension between what is universal and what is relative.

We then discussed five specific approaches to intercultural ethics, each of which tries to reveal the nature of this tension: the golden law, the golden purse, the golden consequence, the golden mean, and the golden rule. We showed that the approaches most successful at balancing tensions between universalism and relativism are based on the idea that, in making ethical judgments, we need to focus on the Other's perspective as well as our own. In making decisions, it is crucial that attention be paid both to Self (one's culture's ethical code) and its environment (the Other, or other cultures' ethical codes). Thus, the idea of the relationship between a culture and its environment was emphasized.

Based on these ideas, we introduced the Sustainability Principle underlying intercultural communication. We pointed out that the need for a metaethic is more urgent today than ever because of the many global challenges facing all people. These challenges transcend all differences and require an ethical framework that serves the concerns of all people on the planet. And the most fundamental concern is clear: survival, understood as remaining alive or in existence. We claimed that the idea of sustainability can be viewed as a metaethic—a general foundation for successful (ethical) intercultural communication—for today's multicultural world.

We then analyzed three main strategies of intercultural sustainability—tolerance, trust, and resistance. Tolerance was presented as the capacity of one culture to deal with the presence of another culture in its territory. Through interaction, every culture establishes a dynamic limit on this capacity: People from every culture decide to what extent they will allow a different system of meanings in their territory. Trust was presented as firm reliance on someone's integrity; it is confidence that someone will act as expected or as previously agreed upon. Trust is crucial for effective intercultural communication because people from one culture can tolerate people from another culture only if they are confident that those people will not cross the boundary line previously established. If that line is crossed without mutual agreement, trust is broken, and the default mechanism of tolerance and trust turns into resistance. Resistance was presented as a communicative strategy, opposite to tolerance and trust, whose goal is to bring interactions back to the harmonious state of intercultural sustainability. Thus, tolerance, trust, and resistance were shown to be interconnected, acting as the main communicative strategies of intercultural sustainability.

Finally, we showed that the best sustainability ethic is represented by the Golden Ratio between the space occupied by intercultural communication in general and that occupied at least in part by each culture, as well as between the spaces occupied by the two cultures. This Golden Ratio can be seen as representing the formula for intercultural sustainability. Thus, we showed that intercultural sustainability presupposes not only that cultures maintain their collective identities, but also that the whole process of intercultural communication be maintained.

Based on these ideas, the Sustainability Principle was formulated.

CASE STUDY
AN ETHIC OF CULTURAL EXCHANGE

This case study is based on the article "An Ethics of Cultural Exchange: Diderot's *Supplément au Voyage de Bougainville,*" by Claudia Moscovici (2001). As usual, it is recommended that you read the article in its entirety; below is a summary of the article. Also, you may have to research how the French and Tahitian cultures have changed over the past two centuries.

Be ready to identify and then discuss the following topics:

1. The stages of cultural exchange, as presented in the *Supplément*
2. The communicative strategies that can help the two cultures to sustain their identities
3. How the real exchanges between these cultures over the past two centuries affected intercultural sustainability

Denis Diderot (1713–1784) was a French writer and philosopher known for his novels, plays, satires, letters, and essays. His *Supplément* is a fictitious essay describing a French explorer's visit to Tahiti. The text raises a key ethical question: How can one culture treat people from another culture fairly without giving up its own standards of behavior? The text consists of a series of monologues and dialogues by representatives of the French and Tahitian cultures.

One of the main exchanges described in the *Supplément* is between the explorer Bougainville and the Tahitian chief Orou, presenting two perspectives on cultural behaviors. The Tahitian leader compares his culture before and after its contact with the French culture. He claims that before the French army and their General Bougainville came to Tahiti, the Tahitians had lived a natural and virtuous life. After contact with the French, this idyllic existence was destroyed, the innocence of the Tahitian people corrupted. To the chief, the French culture represents evil itself. He refuses to know more about the Europeans and their behaviors, calling upon his people to "cry misfortune" about the arrival of these mean and ambitious visitors. In Orou's view, the Tahitian culture is clearly superior to the French one.

As an example of ethical behavior, Orou presents the Tahitian practice of exchanging women among men for the purpose of cultural reproduction. He explains that in Tahiti wives and daughters are freely shared among men; this Tahitian cultural practice is presented as natural and innocent, in contrast to unnatural and immoral European monogamy. Unlike the French, the Tahitians make no mistake about gender. In one significant scene in the *Supplément,* Diderot describes how a female European servant, dressed in a man's clothes, was raped by a group of Tahitian men. Corrupted by centuries of artificial morals and no longer able to recognize sexual difference, the European officers had failed to notice the "true" sexual identity of the servant, but the more natural Tahitian men guessed her gender from the first glance. Again, the Tahitian culture is presented as natural and superior to the French culture, with its arbitrary and conventional moral foundations.

The *Supplément* also contains a dialogue between two Frenchmen, called simply A and B, who express a typical Enlightenment view. One of these men has read

(continued)

Bougainville's account of his travels to the exotic Tahiti, and the two characters compare the cruel and primitive cultural practices of people in Tahiti with the civilized life in Western cultures. In their view, the savage life of Tahitians lies far behind the more complex and civilized life in the West; the two characters praise the rationality, civilization, and morality of the Western cultures. The characters feel that the sharing of higher and more valuable knowledge with less advanced cultures justifies Western expansion.

The *Supplément* develops this topic further, presenting a more complex view of different perspectives on cultural behavior in the form of a conversation between the Tahitian chief Orou and the French chaplain. This conversation seems to resemble the exchange between the Tahitian chief and Bougainville, yet it is different. The chaplain is a guest at Orou's home, and the two men discuss the issue of moral sexual behaviors. The chaplain defends the French culture with its sexual prohibitions against, for instance, incest and extramarital sex. He refuses to engage in sexual relations with Orou's wife and nubile daughters, and Orou and his family feel offended. However, the chaplain does eventually give in to Orou's wishes and engage in sexual relations with Orou's youngest daughter.

The chief claims he does not understand any restrictions because, in his culture, sexuality is not suppressed by any morals. In Tahiti, Orou explains, there is no incest taboo, no rule against premarital or extramarital sex, no disapproval of single motherhood. Children are welcome in Tahiti because they are seen as the source of material riches, contributing to the strength of the culture. However, the chaplain points out, Tahitian women and men not at the peak of their fertility (because of age or impotence) cannot engage in sexual acts. Thus, the chief fails to convince us that the Tahitian culture is natural, nonhierarchical, and free. It becomes clear that the Tahitians have their own moral conventions, in an ethic based on fecundity and age. The Tahitians tie "natural" behaviors to reproduction in order to remain ethical.

At the end of the *Supplément*, another conversation takes place between characters A and B, but the two Frenchmen have changed so much that they are almost unrecognizable. They admit that both cultures have certain constraints on behavior (e.g., forbidding certain sexual relations) and that both cultures are trying to develop their own codes of conduct (e.g., sexual mores). The exchange between Orou and the French chaplain is seen as an attempt to have an open-minded and mutually beneficial dialogue about the validity of their codes of conduct. In the conclusion, one of the Frenchmen urges readers to question the ethical norms not only of different cultures but also of their own and to be tolerant toward behaviors different from those of their own culture. Thus, the question of how one culture can treat people from another culture fairly, without giving up its own codes of conduct, is transformed into an open-ended discussion about what constitutes intercultural exchange in general.

DISCUSSION

Now let's see how this case study can be seen as an illustration of the Sustainability Principle of intercultural communication.

1. The stages of cultural exchange, as presented in the *Supplément*. In the *Supplément*, three views of ethics in cultural exchange can be identified, each representing a stage in the development of intercultural sustainability.

(continued)

AN ETHIC OF CULTURAL EXCHANGE CONTINUED

Stage 1: "One's Bias Displayed." This stage is represented in the *Supplément* by two conversations—the one between Bougainville and the Tahitian chief Orou and the first one between characters A and B.

In the conversation with Bougainville, the Tahitian chief claims his people lead a natural and virtuous (ethical) life, while the French culture is unnatural and evil. In Orou's view, the Tahitian culture is clearly superior to the French one. As an example of unnatural (suppressed) behavior, he describes how a female European servant, dressed in a man's clothes, was raped by a group of Tahitian men. He says that the French are no longer able to recognize sexual difference, having been corrupted by centuries of artificial morals, while the natural Tahitian men guessed her gender from the first glance. Clearly, Orou presents the ethical code of the Tahitian people as positive and that of the French people as negative. This view of intercultural ethics can be represented as follows:

CONVERSATION BETWEEN	VIEW OF ETHICS	
Orou and Bougainville	Tahitian +	French –

In the first conversation between the two Frenchmen, A and B express a typical Enlightenment view. Based on Bougainville's account of his travels to exotic Tahiti, the two characters compare the primitive cultural practices of people in Tahiti with the civilized life in Western cultures. In their view, the savage life of the Tahitians is inferior to the complex and civilized life in the West, with its rationality and morality. They claim their system of moral standards (Self) as the only acceptable ethical code, justifying Western expansion. Clearly, they present the ethical code of the French people as positive and that of the Tahitian people as negative. This view of intercultural ethics can be represented as follows:

CONVERSATION BETWEEN	VIEW OF ETHICS	
Characters A and B	French +	Tahitian –

Thus, the view of ethics found at the first stage is extreme and has an ethnocentric bias. Each culture tries to reduce all morals to its own system of ethical standards, claiming its own code of conduct as the only acceptable one.

Stage 2: "One's Blind Spot Revealed." This stage is represented in the *Supplément* by the conversation between the Tahitian chief Orou and the French chaplain. At this stage, a step is made by both cultures toward engaging the other's perspective on moral behavior.

On the one hand, the chaplain defends the French culture with its sexual prohibitions. However, he gives in to Orou's wishes and engages in sexual relations with Orou's youngest daughter. Thus, his ethical stance appears self-contradictory: Forbidding certain sexual relations only enhances desire. This blind spot in the ethical code of the French culture would not have been revealed without interaction between French people and people from another culture, such as that between the chaplain and Orou's youngest daughter. An important piece of ethical knowledge about themselves is revealed to the French, a piece that had been hidden from their view until this point.

On the other hand, the chief defends the Tahitian culture with its absence of sexual restrictions. According to Orou, children are welcome in Tahiti because they are seen as the source of material riches, contributing to the strength of the culture. It appears that sexuality cannot be suppressed by any morals. But it turns out that women and men not at the peak of their fertility (because of age or impotence) cannot engage in sexual acts. Thus, the Tahitian culture, with its ethical norms based on fecundity and age, appears to be just as conventional as the French. This blind spot in the ethical code of the Tahitian culture would not have been revealed without interaction between Tahitian people and people from another culture, such as that between the chaplain and Orou. An important piece of ethical knowledge about themselves is revealed to the Tahitians, a piece that had been hidden from their view until this point.

Naturally, these blind spots are revealed to the two cultures gradually; the dialogue between the chaplain and Orou is only a step in that direction. However, it is very important because at this stage the representatives of the two cultures come to be aware of an inherent vulnerability of their ethical claims. Clearly, neither ethical code can be presented as positive. This view of intercultural ethics can be represented as follows:

CONVERSATION BETWEEN	VIEW OF ETHICS	
Orou and the chaplain	French –	Tahitian –

Stage 3: "Open Exchange." This stage is represented in the *Supplément* by the second conversation between characters A and B. The eyes of the two cultures have been opened up to their blind spots, as it were. It is now clear that no culture owns the truth—that is, no culture can present *the* ethical code of conduct. What seems natural to people from one culture may not seem natural to people from the other. Natural behaviors are always conventional behaviors, and these conventions can be established to each culture's satisfaction only through an open exchange.

The first two stages can be seen as steps toward an open-minded and mutually beneficial dialogue between people from the two cultures about the validity of their codes of conduct. Now that the ethical norms of both cultures have been presented (stage 1) and questioned (stage 2), it is time to move on to an open exchange of ideas about what is moral (stage 3). In the conclusion, one of the Frenchmen urges readers to be tolerant toward behaviors different from those of their own culture. Clearly, the ethical codes of both cultures are being presented as positive and valid. This view of intercultural ethics can be represented as follows:

CONVERSATION BETWEEN	VIEW OF ETHICS	
Characters A and B	French +	Tahitian +

Thus, intercultural ethics are transformed from a biased view (Self only), through a critique of one's blind spot (Self through the Other), into an open-ended discussion about what constitutes intercultural exchange (Self and the Other).

2. The communicative strategies that can help the two cultures to sustain their identities. First and foremost, intercultural sustainability cannot exist without mutual tolerance and trust. Tolerance and trust form the default mechanism

(continued)

AN ETHIC OF CULTURAL EXCHANGE CONTINUED

of intercultural communication; as long as people from different cultures tolerate and trust each other, intercultural communication can be effective.

The initial interactions between the French and Tahitians lack both tolerance and trust. The Tahitians view the French as evil, destroying their natural and virtuous way of life and corrupting their innocence. Orou does not want to know more about the Europeans and their behaviors, calling upon his people to "cry misfortune" about the arrival of these mean and ambitious visitors. On their part, the French view the Tahitians as primitive people whose savage behaviors cannot be tolerated and who cannot be trusted to build a civilized way of life by themselves. However, further interactions between the two cultures begin to display rudimentary tolerance and trust. For example, the French chaplain's visit to the chief's house builds on these communicative strategies. Gradually, these two people open up their minds to each other's ways of behaving. The chaplain, while defending the French culture with its sexual prohibitions, gives in to Orou's wishes and engages in sexual relations with Orou's youngest daughter. And Orou listens to the chaplain's critique of the Tahitian culture, which is presented by the chaplain as just as conventional, with its ethical norms based on fecundity and age.

When different behaviors are imposed, intercultural sustainability is in danger; then the default mechanism of tolerance and trust switches into the mode of resistance. For example, Orou's insistence that the chaplain engage in sexual relations with Orou's wife and daughters could have been perceived by the chaplain as overbearing and dangerous for the collective French identity with its sexual prohibitions. Then the chaplain would have resisted and firmly refused to engage in sexual relations with Orou's wife and daughters. Or the female European servant might have resisted the rape by the group of Tahitian men even though, back then, it would have been almost unthinkable. Of course, the European officers could have come to her rescue, putting up a resistance against the savage Tahitian behavior and defending the European morality. On their part, the Tahitians would certainly have resisted if the French had tried to introduce and enforce a rule against premarital sex on the island. In all these cases, resistance as a communicative strategy would have been crucial because it would have been aimed at bringing intercultural communication back to the dynamic state of intercultural sustainability. Thus, the two cultures cannot sustain their collective identities without using the strategies of tolerance, trust, and resistance.

3. How the real exchanges between these cultures over the past two centuries affected intercultural sustainability. Tahiti is the principal island in the Territory of French Polynesia, which lies in the South Pacific. French explorer Louis-Antonine de Bougainville arrived there in 1768 and claimed the island for France. In 1880, King Pomare was forced to abdicate, and a French colony was proclaimed. In 1957, the territory was officially named the Territory of French Polynesia.

The Western missionaries did everything possible to eliminate Tahitian culture: Temples and carvings associated with native religion were destroyed; traditional dance, music, and tattoos were banned; and so forth. Not surprisingly, the last two centuries saw a number of nationalistic protests as Tahitians searched for independence from France. Today, some people in Tahiti still resist the French influence.

Over the years, culture in Tahiti has undergone many changes due to the French influence, with some old behaviors disappearing and new behaviors taking root. For example, Christianity is now a strong part of life in Tahiti, and Sunday is a day of worship for many people there. Family is modeled after the Western concept, and incest is no longer an accepted behavior. Because of French technological and health innovations, life expectancy is now 75 years, and the population growth rate is 1.8 percent. The French presence is felt even in the local cuisine, which has a French flair. It is possible to trace Tahitian influence on the French culture as well. The laid-back Tahitian lifestyle certainly affected the cold rationality of the Enlightenment and helped people in the West to loosen up. As a result, people became a bit more emotional and less suppressed. Along the same lines, the influence of Tahiti on French arts and literature is strong; the best example is Paul Gauguin, the French painter who chose Tahiti as his home and depicted the beauty of its people and heritage. His art exerted a strong influence on modern painting all over the world. Also, elements of Tahitian dance, dress, and crafts have found their way into French culture. Tattooing, for instance, one of the oldest Tahitian customs, now enjoys popularity in many Western countries. (The words *tattoo* and *taboo,* now part of every European language, are said to be Polynesian words.)

It is clear that the cultural exchange between the French and Tahitian cultures has been quite active over the years. The culture of the island, which still remains highly dependent on France for its survival, has seen a rebirth in recent years. The Tahitian language is now an official language alongside French; it is again taught in schools and used in government meetings. The traditional crafts, music, and dance are widely celebrated. Tourism to the island is growing, and local people actively participate in planning and organizing tourist activities.

SIDE TRIPS

1. Recently, Saudi Arabia's religious police—or, as they are known in the country, the Committee for the Propagation of Virtue and Prevention of Vice—declared Barbie dolls a threat to morality because of their revealing clothes and shameful postures (Barbie dolls a threat, 2003). Barbie dolls, said to have been modeled after a real-life Jewish woman, are considered offensive to Islam. Schoolchildren and their parents are reminded of the doll's negative qualities. Although illegal, Barbies are found on the black market. Do you think Western manufacturers of Barbie dolls ought to give up on the Saudi Arabia market? If not, how can interactions between the West and Saudi Arabia with respect to this toy be made more successful?
2. In an article on business ethics and intercultural communication, Brinkmann (2002) mentions the many political groups that, during the apartheid period in South Africa, claimed that businesses had a moral duty to boycott—not to do business with—the apartheid regime. However, many other groups, especially some "staying" companies, claimed that they ought to use their influence to better the life of the discriminated-against majority. Whose side would you take in this case? Why? You may want to become familiar with a number of other classic cases of intercultural business ethics mentioned in the article.
3. In his book *Who Owns Native Culture?*, Brown (2003) raises the question of whether cultural resources ought to be treated as the private property of particular groups of people. For example, what happens when Native American Lakotas object to the desecration of a sacred site by mountain climbers and New Age religious worshipers, and this sacred site happens to be a monument located in a public park in Wyoming? What communicative strategies would you use to help all involved cultures sustain their collective identities in this case? In general, how would you answer the question posed by Brown: Who owns native culture?

CHECK YOURSELF

Morality
Ethics
Universalist approach
Relativist approach
Golden law
Golden purse
Golden consequence
Golden mean
Golden rule
Metaethic
Globalization
Sustainability
Tolerance
Trust
Resistance
Satyagraha
Golden Ratio

REFERENCES

Asuncion-Lande, N. (Ed.). (1980). *Ethical perspectives and critical issues in intercultural communication.* Falls Church, VA: Speech Communication Association.

Baldwin, J. (1998). Tolerance/intolerance: A multidisciplinary view of prejudice. In Hecht, M. (Ed.), *Communicating prejudice* (pp. 24–56). Thousand Oaks, CA: Sage.

Barbie dolls a threat to morality, Saudis say. (2003). *The Spokesman-Review,* September 11, p. A2.

Barnes, B. (2001). Tolerance as a primary virtue. *Res Publica,* Vol. 7, No. 3, pp. 231–245.

Barnlund, D. (1980). The cross-cultural arena: An ethical void. In Asuncion-Lande, N. (Ed.), *Ethical perspectives and critical issues in intercultural communication.* Falls Church, VA: Speech Communication Association.

Barnsley, J. (1972). *The social reality of ethics.* London: Routledge.

Brinkmann, J. (2002). Business ethics and intercultural communication: Exploring the overlap between two academic fields. *Intercultural Communication,* Issue 5, http://www.immi.se/intercultural/.

Brown, M. (2003). *Who owns native culture?* Cambridge, MA: Harvard University Press.

Deyhle, D. (1995). Navajo youth and Anglo racism: Cultural integrity and resistance. *Harvard Educational Review,* Vol. 65, No. 3, pp. 403–429.

Dresner, S. (2002). *The principles of sustainability.* London: Earthscan.

Duncombe, S. (Ed.). (2002). *Cultural resistance reader.* New York: Verso.

Durbin, P. (1997). Can there be a best ethic of sustainability? *PHIL & TECH,* Vol. 2, No. 2, pp. 49–57.

Fleischacker, S. (1994). *The ethics of culture.* Ithaca: Cornell University Press.

Goodpaster, K. (1992). Business ethics. In Becker, L. C., & C. B. Becker (Eds.), *Encyclopedia of ethics* (pp. 111–115). New York: Garland Publications.

Gudykunst, W., & Kim, Y. (2003). *Communicating with strangers: An approach to intercultural communication.* New York: McGraw-Hill.

Hall, B. (2002). *Among cultures: The challenge of communication.* Belmont, CA: Wadsworth/Thomson Learning.

Hirschmann, N. (1997). Eastern veiling, Western freedom? *The Review of Politics,* Vol. 59, pp. 461–488.

Howell, W. (1982). *The empathic communicator.* Belmont, CA: Wadsworth.

Kale, D. (1994). Peace as an ethic for intercultural communication. In Samovar, L., & R. E. Porter (Eds.), *Intercultural communication: A reader* (pp. 435–441). Belmont, CA: Wadsworth.

Kant, I. (1959). *Foundations of the metaphysics of morals.* New York: Liberal Arts.

Levins, R. (1998). Dialectics and systems theory. *Science and Society,* Vol. 62, No. 3, pp. 375–399.

Lewis, C. I. (1969). *Values and imperatives.* Stanford: Stanford University Press.

Livio, M. (2002). *The golden ratio: The story of phi, the world's most astonishing number.* New York: Broadway.

Martin, J., & Nakayama, T. (2000). *Intercultural communication in contexts.* Mountain View, CA: Mayfield.

Morris, W. (Ed.). (1982). *The American Heritage dictionary of the English language.* Boston: Houghton Mifflin.

Moscovici, C. (2001). An ethics of cultural exchange: Diderot's *Supplément au voyage de Bougainville. CLIO,* Vol. 30, No. 3, pp. 289–307.

Pedersen, P. (1997). Do the right thing: A question of ethics. In Cushner, K., & R. Brislin (Eds.), *Improving intercultural interactions: Modules for cross-cultural training* (Vol. 2). Thousand Oaks, CA: Sage.

Rescher, N. (1977). *Dialectics.* Albany: SUNY Press.

Robertson, R. (1992). *Globalization.* Newbury Park, CA: Sage.

Rodriguez, A. (2002). Culture to culturing: Re-imagining our understanding of intercultural relations. *Intercultural Communication,* Issue 5, http://www.immi.se/intercultural/.

Singer, P. (2001). *One world: The ethics of globalization.* New Haven, CT: Yale University Press.

Singer, P. (2002). Navigating the ethics of globalization. *The Chronicle of Higher Education,* October 11, pp. B7–B10.

Sitaram, K., & Cogdell, R. (1976). *Foundations of intercultural communication.* Columbus, OH: Charles E. Merrill.

Snarr, M., & Snarr, N. (Eds.). (2002). *Introducing global issues.* Boulder, CO: Lynne Reinner Publishers.

Ting-Toomey, S. (1999). *Communicating across cultures.* New York: Guilford.

Tonn, B. (1999). Sustainability and supra-communitarianism. *Foresight,* Vol. 1, No. 4, pp. 343–352.

UNESCO's Charter. (1997). Educating for a sustainable future: A transdisciplinary vision for concerted action.

Walker, B. (1995). John Rawls, Mikhail Bakhtin, and the praxis of toleration. *Political Theory,* Vol. 23, No. 1, pp. 101–127.

Weber, T. (2001). Gandhian philosophy, conflict resolution theory and practical approaches to negotiation. *Journal of Peace Research,* Vol. 38, No. 4, pp. 493–513.

CONCLUSION

And now our journey is coming to an end.

The goal of this text, set in the introduction, was to help you become more competent in intercultural communication—that is, to help you build a system of intercultural communication competence (ICC). Together, we have been building this system over the course of ten chapters. It is my hope that now you know more about intercultural communication (cognitive component), feel more open-minded, curious, and empathic (affective component), and are ready to apply your knowledge and skills in real-life situations (behavioral component).

Your ICC has been built with the help of ten fundamental principles. These principles, based on the study of the most important concepts, propositions, and theories in the field, reveal the general nature of intercultural communication. Each of the ten chapters discusses one such principle; at the end of every chapter, a new problem question is formulated to lead you into the next chapter. Thus, the text appears as a story, or whole narrative. Let's take a quick look back and see how this story unfolded. This way, we will see how all ten principles are interconnected.

Chapter 1. Here, we focused on the process of cultural identification. Our objective was to understand how and why cultural identities are formed. We showed that cultural identities are created by drawing a boundary line between one group and another group (in-group and out-group, Self and the Other). Thus, boundary lines were shown to play a crucial role in the formation of cultures or cultural identification. According to the *Punctuation Principle,* formulated in Chapter 1, intercultural communication is a process of searching for a mutually acceptable boundary fit, which is an agreement of people from interacting cultures on a boundary line between them. "Boundaries" became the key theme for Chapter 1.

But, to establish a boundary fit, we must venture beyond our boundary lines and gain knowledge about how to interact with the Other. How does the nature of knowledge affect intercultural communication? This question led us to the next chapter.

Chapter 2. Here, we focused on the general nature of knowledge and how it affects intercultural interactions. Our objective was to show the inherent uncertainty of intercultural communication. We showed that uncertainty is an unavoidable aspect of intercultural communication; at the same time, uncertainty forms a basis for intercultural communication. According to the *Uncertainty Principle,* formulated in Chapter 2, intercultural communication is a process whereby people from different cultures continually search for knowledge of how to interact with each other against a backdrop of uncertainty. "Uncertainty" became the key theme for Chapter 2.

If uncertainty is an inherent part of intercultural communication, how do we deal with it? How do people get out of the maze of uncertainty? In other words, what is the means to meaning in intercultural communication? This question led us to the next chapter.

Chapter 3. Here, we focused on how people search for meaning and create order when interacting with each other. Our objective was to show how intercultural communication is performed. We showed that intercultural communication is always a joint effort, an activity performed by Self and the Other. As a result of this activity, cultural meanings are enacted. According to the *Performativity Principle,* formulated in Chapter 3, intercultural communication is a reiterative process of enactment of meanings. "Action" became the key theme for Chapter 3.

But if the cultural meanings that are enacted are different, where do these different meanings come from? What happens to cultural meanings as they are performed and enacted? This question led us to the next chapter.

Chapter 4. Here, we focused on the process of constructing a system of meaning; we looked at this process as charting out a cultural map. We showed that cultural maps are dynamic formations and contain such categories as beliefs, attitudes, values, norms, and worldviews. With the help of these categories, cultures establish their specific orientation in the world, or position themselves. According to the *Positionality Principle,* formulated in Chapter 4, intercultural communication is a process whereby people from different cultures engage in interaction and claim authority for their vision of the world. "Specificity" became the key theme for Chapter 4.

But if everything is a matter of a specific position, is it possible for people from different cultures to communicate at all? Is there anything general that people from *all* cultures can relate to—some common ground? This question led us to the next chapter.

Chapter 5. Here, we focused on general standards that make intercultural communication possible. Our objective was to reveal the inherent common nature of people from different cultures—that is, to find out what makes it possible for people to communicate with each other. We identified three forms of meaning that people from all cultures can relate to: image-schemas, concepts, and symbols.

These forms represent meaning at three different levels: corporeal (most concrete), cognitive (intermediate), and semiotic (most abstract). According to the *Commensurability Principle,* formulated in Chapter 5, intercultural communication is a process whereby people from different cultures compare their maps and search for common ground, using the same forms and levels of meaning representation. "Generalness" became the key theme for Chapter 5.

But how can it be that cultural knowledge always comes from a specific point of view and at the same time conforms to some general standards—that is, is the same? This question led us to the next chapter.

Chapter 6. Here, we focused on reconciling the arguments put forward in Chapters 4 and 5—that is, on proving that intercultural communication somehow combines both uniqueness and sameness of meaning. Our objective was to show how people can construct meanings that are different, yet the same. We showed that when people interact with each other, they form a connected and bounded space (a continuum) that continually changes yet remains stable. In this space, meanings exist as *different* positions along the *same* continua. According to the *Continuum Principle,* formulated in Chapter 6, intercultural communication is a process whereby people from different cultures continuously construct a shared space where meanings are discernible by their distance from each other. "Distance" became the key theme for Chapter 6.

But there must be something that makes it possible for a shared space (continuum) to change yet remain stable. What is the driving force of intercultural communication as a continuum? This question led us to the next chapter.

Chapter 7. Here, we focused more closely on the dynamics of intercultural interactions. Our objective was to reveal the contradictory nature of intercultural communication and show why intercultural communication is always in a state of flux. We showed how distances between different cultural meanings create tensions, arising from different needs and motivations. Thus, the contradictory nature of intercultural communication was shown to lie in the ongoing interplay of opposing forces. According to the *Pendulum Principle,* formulated in Chapter 7, intercultural communication is an ongoing and interactive process that simultaneously connects and keeps apart people from different cultures, producing multiple voices. "Tension" became the key theme for Chapter 7.

In the process of interactions, people must continually decide how to make sure the pendulum swings in such a way that their voices are heard and acknowledged by others. How do people resolve their tensions so that the pendulum can swing? This question led us to the next chapter.

Chapter 8. Here, we focused on the process of resolving intercultural tensions. Our objective was to show how tensions can be negotiated. We noted that intercultural communication is more effective when people perceive their transaction as flexible-sum and are willing to integrate their resources. People then can carry out their transactions more effectively, resolving tensions. According to the *Transaction Principle,* formulated in Chapter 8, intercultural communication is a process whereby people from different cultures move within a negotiation zone from positions to interests, in search of an acceptable resolution. "Resolution" became the key theme for Chapter 8.

Everything points to integration as the best approach to intercultural transactions. Why exactly is intercultural integration so important? This question led us to the next chapter.

Chapter 9. Here, we focused more closely on the nature of integration in intercultural interactions. Our objective was to emphasize the importance of intercultural collaboration. We showed that intercultural communication can be viewed as a synergistic process wherein people realize their potential and the outcome of their interaction is a new state. According to the *Synergy Principle,* formulated in Chapter 9, intercultural communication is a process whereby people from different cultures integrate their resources, attaining an optimal result that cannot be achieved by any culture individually. "Cooperation" became the key theme for Chapter 9.

There must be something about intercultural synergy that all people can benefit from. Why, in the final analysis, is synergy the right approach to intercultural interactions? This question led us to the next, and final, chapter.

Chapter 10. Here, we approached intercultural communication from an ethical point of view. Our objective was to show why cooperative behavior is ethical (right) in intercultural communication. We emphasized that ethics is important in intercultural communication because, in dealing with other people, we must always make decisions about what behaviors are right and what behaviors are wrong. We demonstrated how the idea of sustainability can be viewed as a metaethic—a general foundation for successful (ethical) intercultural communication—for today's multicultural world. Intercultural sustainability presupposes that cultures maintain their collective identities and also that the whole process of intercultural communication be maintained. According to the *Sustainability Principle,* formulated in Chapter 10, intercultural communication is a process whereby people from different cultures display mutual tolerance, trust, and resistance, sustaining their collective identities and the overall process of their interactions. "Survival" became the key theme for Chapter 10.

It is possible to view each chapter as a step in our journey and each key theme as a stepping stone. Viewed this way, the gist of our narrative can be presented as follows:

Cultural identification is based on the idea of boundary lines (Punctuation Principle).

↓

Intercultural boundary lines always contain uncertainty (Uncertainty Principle).

↓

To deal with uncertainty, people must perform actions, enacting meanings (Performativity Principle).

↓

As meanings are enacted, different cultural categories are established, or grounded, so everything depends on a certain position (Positionality Principle).

↓

Although cultures take specific positions, universal forms and levels of meaning exist that make intercultural communication possible (Commensurability Principle).

↓

People find a way out of this seeming contradiction by constructing a shared space (continuum) where meanings exist as different positions along the same continua, so it all comes down to a distance between meanings (Continuum Principle).

↓

Distances between different cultural meanings create tensions, arising from different needs and motivations and producing multiple voices (Pendulum Principle).

To resolve intercultural tensions, people must create a negotiation zone in which to carry out their transactions (Transaction Principle).

The best way to resolve intercultural tensions is through cooperation, thereby finding a resolution that cannot be achieved by any culture individually (Synergy Principle).

The decision by people from different cultures to cooperate is the right decision because it leads to the survival of their collective identities and maintains the process of intercultural communication (Sustainability Principle).

We had to break our narrative into chapters because the only way to study anything is step by step. But in real life, intercultural communication is a holistic process, where all these steps are taken at the same time. In other words, intercultural communication is all about boundaries *and* uncertainty *and* action *and* positionality *and* compatibility *and* distance *and* tension *and* resolution *and* cooperation *and* survival! All ten principles, therefore, are interconnected and are best viewed as a circle. You can view this circle as a compass, with each principle as one of its directions. With this compass in your hand, you should never be lost, and your intercultural journeys will be more exciting, rewarding, and successful.

GLOSSARY

acceptance reception and approval of the Other

acculturation secondary socialization process of people in another culture

actions level level of performativity in which performance is directed toward a certain goal

activity level level of performativity in which performance is driven by a certain motive

adjustment stage stage of culture shock in which one learns to live with new cultural practices

analogic communication type of communication in which meaning is represented by a likeness to something else

anxiety affective equivalent of uncertainty

arbitration approach to conflict in which a third party is authorized to make a decision for the parties in conflict but not to control the process of their interaction

arm's-length prejudice engaging in positive behaviors toward people from other cultures only in certain settings

artifact any object created and used by people for a specific purpose (e.g., clothing and vehicles)

assimilation disregarding one's own cultural tradition in favor of the tradition of another culture

attitude predisposition to respond positively, negatively, or neutrally to certain objects and practices

authority ability to lay claims that are accepted

avoidance staying away from the Other; approach to conflict that may be adopted when neither side is really concerned about the outcome

BATNA best alternative to negotiated agreement

belief attribution of some characteristic to an object

binary thinking thinking that divides everything into two separate entities

boundary fit agreement among people from interacting cultures on the function of a boundary line between them

chronemics use of time in communication

closure process whereby an incomplete stimulus is perceived to be complete

cognitive look approach to meaning focusing on the mental process, or faculty, by which meaning is acquired

collectivism high degree of integration of people into groups

colonialism policy by which one culture maintains or extends its control over other cultures that depend on it

communication practice of creating and exchanging meanings as symbolic resources

compromise approach to conflict in which resources are split 50/50, with each side showing moderate concern for both Self and the Other

concept basic notion resulting from our mental segmentation of the world

conceptualization process of generalizing or typifying

conflict perceived disagreement over resource allocations

continuum continuous succession, no part of which can be distinguished from neighboring parts except by arbitrary division

contradiction interplay between opposing tendencies

convergence act of approaching the same point from different directions

corporeal look approach to meaning grounded in sensory experiences of the body

crisis stage stage of culture shock in which one feels confused and rejected

cultural appropriation the taking away of symbolic resources

cultural gaze a culture's way of looking outward into the world

cultural loci positions from which a culture views the world and its own place in it

culture system of symbolic resources shared by a group of people

culture shock reaction people have when they attempt to adjust to new situations

determinism view that people behave in patterned, predictable ways, often seen in terms of cause and effect

dialectics art of discussion or debate, through which truth is sought

digital communication type of communication in which meaning is represented by distinct and separate symbols

dis-closure process of simultaneously sharing and filling in information

disclosure process of regulation of information flow between the self and the outer world

discrimination biased action whereby people from another culture are treated disadvantageously

disparagement derogating or discrediting the Other

divergence act of moving in different directions from a common point

dual concern model model for analyzing conflict in terms of concern for one's own culture's outcomes and concern for the other culture's outcomes

empathy understanding so intimate that feelings, thoughts, and motives of the Other are readily comprehended

enculturation primary socialization process of people in their own culture

engagement process whereby people from different cultures present claims that their narratives represent the true vision of the world

environment natural elements, such as physical landscape and temperature, affecting the way people communicate

epistemology branch of philosophy that studies knowledge, or how people know what they claim to know

ethics study of the general nature of modes of behavior and moral choices made by people in relationships with others

ethnic identity group membership based on a common symbolic heritage

ethnic tourism special practice whereby people are invited to experience other cultures

ethnocentric affirmation process whereby people from interacting cultures exercise equal authority

ethnocentric negation process whereby one culture simply disregards another culture as not Self

ethnocentric reduction process whereby people from one culture force people from another culture to start doing things according to the first culture's frame of reference

ethnocentrism central point of reference from which a culture understands the world and itself

ethnography method of interpreting actions in a manner that generates understanding in the terms of those performing the actions

ethnolinguistic vitality extent to which a culture can function as a collective entity because of the range and importance of its language usage

evaluation process of appraising or judging

experiment examining the validity of a hypothesis

explanatory uncertainty inability to explain why people behave as they do

face the cultural identity one presents to others

facework process whereby people present their identities to each other

femininity emphasis on such values as modesty, nurturing, caring, and the like

fixed-sum perception perception that the value arising from an interaction is fixed and must be divided

flexible-sum perception perception that the value arising from an interaction is flexible and subject to change

flow states peak experiences when people realize their potential and find optimal solutions

folkways everyday cultural practices that are widely accepted

frame definition or interpretation of what a certain situation means

fundamental attribution error tendency to overestimate the negative influence of dispositional factors and the positive influence of situational factors in explaining others' behavior

generalization putting experiences in general categories, or types

globalization intensified compression of the world and people's increasing consciousness of cultural processes that extend beyond the collective identity of any one culture

golden consequence ethical stance according to which ethical decisions are based on what will bring the most good for the most people

golden law ethical stance according to which all actions are said to be inherently ethical or unethical, regardless of who performs them

golden mean ethical stance according to which ethical choice is a happy medium between two extremes

golden purse ethical stance according to which the one with more power rules

Golden Ratio proportionate (harmonious) relationship between different parts of something

golden rule ethical stance according to which we should act toward people from other cultures as we would have them act toward us

grand narrative recounting of a sequence of events claiming universal truth

grounding process of establishing a cultural system of meanings

haptics use of touch in communication

hard boundaries lines that are deeply engraved within a culture and difficult to change in the process of intercultural interaction

hermeneutic circle circular process of understanding meaning in which distance-experiences and near-experiences are in constant rotation

high-context communication type of communication in which most of the information is either in the physical context or internalized

"honeymoon" stage stage of culture shock in which one is excited about the new things one encounters

horizon of knowledge degree of reach of knowledge

identity membership in a group in which all people share the same symbolic meanings

identity confirmation process through which individuals are recognized, acknowledged, and endorsed

identity disconfirmation process through which individuals do not recognize others, do not respond sensitively to others, and do not accept others' experiences as valid

image-schema mental representation that grows out of primary bodily experiences

in-group group whose members identify and associate with one another

individualism low degree of integration of people into groups

integration approach to conflict in which each side shows high concern for both Self and the Other

intercultural communication process of interaction between groups of people with different systems of symbolic resources

intercultural communication competence system of knowledge and skills enabling us to communicate successfully with people from other cultures

interests underlying needs and desires that motivate people to take a certain position

interview asking questions

introspection using one's own frame of reference in dealing with others

Johari Window model model describing four areas of awareness (Open, Closed, Blind, Unknown) in the context of interaction between Self and the Other

kinesics use of body movements, such as gestures and facial expressions, as a means of communication

lacuna empty space or missing part (usually in a language system)

language a means of communication consisting of combinations of symbolic elements used to accomplish various tasks

language games dynamic structures created by people for accomplishing various tasks

laws cultural practices that are codified and usually written down

linguistic imperialism term for the global spread of a language, used by those who perceive it to be a negative development

linguistic landscape language of public signs and symbols, billboards, street names, and so on

linguistic relativity view that the way people in a culture think and act depends on their language

looking-glass self our view of ourselves based on the view of us held by people from other cultures

low-context communication type of communication in which most of the information is vested in the explicit code

Manifested category all that has been accessible to senses and represented by culture; meanings that are established

Manifesting category all that is in the process of becoming representation; meanings that appear in the form of new experiences

masculinity emphasis on such values as assertiveness, ambition, performance, and the like

mediation approach to conflict in which a third party is authorized to control the process of interaction of the parties in conflict but not to impose a decision upon them

metaethic general foundation for successful (ethical) communication, transcending all differences

monochronic time orientation orientation that emphasizes compartmentalization and segmentation of measurable units of time

morality customs and traditions of a given culture regulating relationships and prescribing modes of behavior

mores cultural practices that carry moral connotations and impose stricter constraints on people's behavior than do norms

narrative recounting of a sequence of events that is told from a particular point of view

national identity group membership based on a historico-political formation with a specific space and an administrative apparatus

needs inner strivings underlying cultural behaviors

negotiation zone the spread between two resistance points

nemawashi cutting around the roots of a tree before transplanting it, enabling the tree to bear better fruit

nonnormative stereotype self-projective overgeneralization through which people project a concept from their own culture onto people of another culture

nonsummativity idea that separate entities working together and integrating their resources can achieve results that none could achieve individually; the whole is greater than the sum of its parts

norm shared standard for accepted and expected behaviors

normative stereotype overgeneralization based on limited information

objective approach view that knowledge is an objective reality external to people

objective ethnolinguistic vitality culture's linguistic position as defined by available hard data such as demographics

observation paying attention or noting a phenomenon

observer's paradox fact that scientific findings are always influenced by the observer's subjective viewpoint in spite of the fact that the observer tries to be neutral and objective

operations level level of performativity in which activity is performed through operations, or automatic skills, that depend on conditions

out-group people who are kept at a physical and emotional distance by the in-group members

paralanguage meaningful sound characteristics, such as rate, volume, and pitch, that are not phonemes

Pareto optimality solution that cannot be improved on without putting one of the interacting sides in a worse position

perception process by which people select, organize, and interpret sensory stimulation

performance manifestation of performativity

performativity reiterative process of enacting meaning

phoneme distinctive sound that is a basic element of spoken language

polarization approach to conflict in which each side is highly concerned about Self and has little or no concern for the Other

polychronic time orientation orientation emphasizing involvement of people and the completion of tasks

polyphony human capacity for engaging one's own voice with other voices

position stance one takes on a certain issue

power distance degree to which people accept and expect that power is distributed unequally

pragmatic dimension dimension of language covering the relations between its elements and the people who use them

praxis concrete practices by which people choose how to resolve the tensions of the moment

predictive uncertainty inability to predict what someone will say or do

prejudice premature judgment based on little interaction with people from another culture

preliminary stage stage of culture shock in which one forms expectations about people from another culture and how to deal with them

principle essential quality or basic source of an object

prisoner's dilemma the game in which the outcome of one party's decision depends on the other party's decision

proposition statement put forth about how two or more things are related

proxemics use of space in communication

punctuation process of perception through which people organize their ongoing interactions into recognizable openings, closings, causes, and effects

racial identity group membership based on alleged biological and physical characteristics

relativist approach ethical view that people's actions are culture-bound, that is, each culture has its own ideas about what is right and wrong

resistance any force that works against something—for example, actions opposing another culture perceived by people as dominant and therefore dangerous to their collective survival

resistance point stopping point beyond which each side will not go, preferring to break off interaction

ritual structured sequence of actions, the correct performance of which pays homage to a sacred object

satyagraha Gandhi's technique of peaceful resistance or nonviolent direct action

self-shock people's reaction to changes in their own cultural identity while trying to adjust to new situations

semantic dimension dimension of language covering the relations between its elements and what they designate in the world

semiotics discipline that studies signs—that is, anything that can be used to represent something else

sensitivity being susceptible to the circumstances of the Other

separation favoring one's own cultural tradition and disregarding the tradition of a new culture

soft boundaries lines that are not deeply engraved within a culture and relatively easy to change in the process of intercultural interaction

stereotype overgeneralization or fixed perception of something

strong version of linguistic relativity view that linguistic structure determines the way people think and act

subjective approach view that knowledge is constructed by people in various situations of interaction—that is, cultural meanings are internal to people

subjective ethnolinguistic vitality culture's linguistic position as perceived by its members

sustainability dynamic state requiring that decisions be made in such a way that something is kept in existence

symbol anything that can stand for something else and has meaning

synergy process whereby people work together, integrating their forces, to achieve an effect that they could not achieve individually

syntactic dimension dimension of language covering the relations between its elements

target point goal that each side wants to achieve in a transaction

theory system of interrelated concepts and propositions that explains the nature of a certain object

tokenism engaging in relatively effortless behaviors toward members of another culture (e.g., donating a small amount of money) in order not to appear prejudiced against them

tolerance capacity for or practice of allowing or respecting the behaviors of others

topology study of the properties of geometric configurations invariant under transformation by continuous mapping

transaction interaction that affects both sides and results in some kind of resolution

trust firm reliance on someone's integrity; confidence that someone will act as expected or as previously agreed upon

uncertainty our cognitive inability to predict or to explain our own or others' feelings and behaviors in interactions

uncertainty avoidance degree to which people feel uncomfortable in ambiguous, unstructured situations

universalist approach ethical view that there is one correct way for people from all cultures to do something

value shared idea within a culture about what is important or desirable

voice position from which one expresses oneself

voluntarism view that people do not behave on impulse but rather make decisions through free will

weak version of linguistic relativity view that linguistic structure influences the way people think and act

worldview overall way people from a certain culture see reality

zero-sum perception perception that interaction has no value

INDEX

Aaker, J., 83
Abdel-Nour, F., 90, 98
Abraham, 95
Acceptance, 148
Acculturation, 58
Actions level, of performativity, 68, 69, 71, 273
Active strategy, of uncertainty, 40
Activity level, of performativity, 68, 69, 71
Activity Theory, 67
Adjustment stage, of culture shock, 65
Advanced Micro Devices, 234–236
Affective component, of intercultural communication competence, 5
African, worldview of, 85
African-American culture, 54, 81, 86, 190
Afro-Brazilians, 81, 94
Agar, M., 116
Ainu people, 23, 24, 25, 86
Albers-Miller, N., 140
Al-halqa, 73–75
Alora, A., 168
American culture, 13, 15, 55, 82, 132, 220–221, 234–236. *See also* African-American culture; White-American culture
American Indians. *See* Native Americans
Amine, K., 72
Amish culture, 20, 55, 211
Amurians, 24, 25
Analogic communication, 148–152, 153
Analyzing Cultures (Danesi and Perron), 35–36
Anderson, J. L., 104
Anderson, R., 16, 58, 149
Anglo-American culture. *See* White-American culture
Anglo-Saxon culture, 20, 55, 190, 241
Annan, K., 188
Anschutz Exploration Co., 81, 82
Anxiety, 36
Apache tribe, 49, 69, 162–163, 240, 241
Apartheid, 266
Arab-Americans, 189
Arab culture, 20, 91. *See also* Palestinian culture; Saudi Arabian culture
Arapaho tribe, 82
Arbitration, 197
Argumentative ground, 101, 103
Aristotle, 245
Arm's length prejudice, 147
Artifact, as nonverbal language, 54, 55
Asad, T., 125
Ascuncion-Lande, N., 246
Asian culture, 8–9, 10, 37. *See also specific countries*
Asian Vikings, 23, 24
Asimov, N., 167
Assimilation, 66
Atman, 85
Attitude, 5, 104
  cultural, 94, 270
  definition of, 82, 83
  toward the Other, 148, 149
Australian Aboriginal culture, 168
Australian culture, 94, 180–182
Authority, positionality and, 95–96, 97, 98
Avenhaus, R., 224, 225
Avoidance, 147, 228, 230, 231
  in conflict, 193, 196, 197, 206
Azande people, 81
Aztec language, 110

Bakhtin, M., 169
Bald Man Fallacy, 144
Baldwin, J., 31, 32, 247
Bardot, B., 84, 88
Barker, C., 13, 17, 95
Barker, V., 165, 166
Barnes, B., 248
Barnlund, D., 246
Barnsley, J., 242
Basso, K., 69
Bateson, G., 16
Bateson, M., 43
BATNA (Best Alternative to Negotiated Agreement), 202
Baxter, L., 174
Bedouin, 95
Behavior, influence of cultural beliefs on, 81–82
Behavioral component, of intercultural communication competence, 5
Beliefs, 81–82, 270
Bell, V., 67

Bennet, M., 13, 149
Berelson, B., 80
Berger, C., 40
Bergin, T. G., 118
Berlin Wall, 18, 21
Bernstein, D., 40
Beyond the Cheers: Race as Spectacle in College Sports (Springwood and King), 223
Big Five dimensions, 137
Bilingual education, 166–167, 170–173, 175
Bilingual Education Measure, 167, 172, 173
Binary thinking, 142–146, 152, 153
Black History Month, 190
Blair, J., 87, 89, 98
Blind Window, 37, 38, 40
Blommaert, J., 9
Bochner, S., 64
Bohr, M., 32
Bond, M., 138, 139, 150
Bougainville, L.-A., 264
Boundary, 15
  hard, 21
  soft, 21
Boundary fit, 20, 21, 25, 30, 269
Boundary line, 12, 13, 229, 247, 255, 269, 272, 273
  as conceptualization, 16, 17, 24–25
  constructive versus destructive, 17–19, 21
  as mark of cultural identity, 25
  punctuation principle and, 21–22
Boundary Lines (Stapp), 17
Boyer, P., 115, 116
Boylan, P., 52
Bradac, J., 42
Brahman, 85
Brazilian culture, 94, 220–221
Breadth, of self-disclosure, 39
Bredella, L., 119
Brett, J., 197
Brewer, M., 13
Brinkmann, J., 266
Brislin, R., 88, 147, 221
British culture, 83, 97
Broome, B., 4
Brown, M., 266
Brown, R., 61
Brunner, B., 157
Buddhism, 96
Bullfighting, 216–218, 223, 226
Burrel, G., 32
Bush, G. W., 104
Butler, J., 60

Calori, R., 138
Canada, 183
Cantor, N., 80–81, 86
Case study, 3
  on Coca-Cola scare in Europe, 154–156
  on conflict between Japanese and Western cultures, 208–210
  on ethic of cultural exchange, 260–265
  on history of Russo-Japanese frontier, 23–25
  on interacting with Kobon, 180–182
  on Israeli-Palestinian encounters, 101–103
  on performing al-halqa in Morocco, 72–75
  on problem of *chou*, 128–131
  on shock of the Other, 46–48
  on unleashing intercultural potential at AMD, 234–236
Categorical imperative, 244
Categorization, 80, 226
Catholic identity, 190
Chang, H.-C., 49
Change, cultural, 176–177
Chavez, L., 82
Chen, G. M., 4, 36, 89
Chinese culture, 138, 176
Chinese language, 49, 53, 128–131
Chou, 128–131
Christianity, 54, 96, 188
Chronemics, 55
Citizenship, 12
Clark, D., 215
Clifford, J., 95
Closed Window, 37, 38, 39
Closure, 40, 41, 47
Coca-Cola, 154
Cochiti culture, 183
Cogdell, R., 246
Cognitive component, of intercultural communication competence, 5
Cognitive level, of commensurability, 120, 121, 126, 127
Cognitive look at meaning, 115–117, 271
Cohen, R., 37
Collective identity, 255, 256, 272, 273
Collectivism, 138, 141, 143, 144–146, 150, 153, 170
Collier, M., 12
Colonialism, 168–169, 180–182
  cultural, 235
Columbus, C., 46, 47
Comanche tribes, 82
Coming-of-age ceremony, 84
Commensurability
  forms and levels of, 120–123
  implications of, 123–126
  nature of, 119–120
Commensurability Principle, 119–126, 271, 273
  case study of, 128–131
  defined, 126
Committee for the Propagation of Virtue and Prevention of Vice, 266
Common ground, 100
Communication. *See also* Intercultural communication
  analogic, 148–152, 153
  definition of, 9–10
  digital, 147–148, 152
  as drama, 60–61
  high context versus low context, 140, 141, 153
  influence of language on, 113
  language as means of, 52–60
  time in, 55
  touch in, 55
Compromise, 194–195, 196, 197, 200, 206, 228, 229, 230, 231
Concept, 1, 115, 116, 120, 121, 126, 127, 270

Conceptualization, 214, 215–220, 232
Conflict
avoidance in, 193, 196, 197, 206
compromise in, 194–195, 196, 197, 200, 206
constructive versus destructive, 191, 206
definition of, 188–190
dialectic nature of, 190–192
dual concern model of, 192
identifying roots of, 188–192
integration in, 195–196, 197, 200, 206
polarization in, 194, 196, 197, 199, 206
positions and interests in, 204–205
resolution of, 201, 204–205
transactions in, 196–198
Conflict of interest, 188
Conflict of opinion, 188
Confucius, 245
Conquergood, D., 62
Constitutive view of language, 59
Context, 140
Contextual rule, 58
Continuum, 143, 144–146, 164, 172, 228, 252–255, 271, 273
Continuum Principle, 271, 273
analogic communication and, 148–152, 153
case study of, 154–156
defined, 152–153
digital communication and, 147–148, 152
overcoming binary thinking in, 142–146, 152, 153
Contradiction, 170–174, 177, 181, 271, 273
Convergence, 171
Conviction, 222, 226
Cooperation, 225, 272, 273
Coptic culture, 54
Corporeal level, of commensurability, 120, 121, 126, 127, 271
Corporeal look at meaning, 117–118, 126
Council on American-Islamic Relations, 84
Cows
Hindus and, 88
Masai and, 81, 82, 240, 241
Craig, R., 59
Crisis stage, of culture shock, 65
Cronen, V., 59
Crow tribe, 82
Csikszentmihalyi, M., 227, 235
Cultural appropriation, 20
Cultural attitudes, 94, 270
Cultural colonialism, 235
Cultural diversity, 188
Cultural exchange, 260–265
Cultural gaze, 86–92, 93, 99, 100, 215, 219
ethnocentrism and, 88–92, 99
Cultural identity, 8, 11–15, 22, 269, 272
boundary lines as marks of, 25
conflict in, 189–190, 191
performance in, 61
as reflective self-image, 13–15
Cultural interests, 204–205
Cultural knowledge, 53, 98
Cultural loci, 92
Cultural map, 80, 82, 83, 86, 87, 99, 270
Cultural needs, 162–165
Cultural positions, 96–97, 204–205
Cultural self-image, 15, 26
Cultural spiral, 122, 126
Cultural symbiosis, 235
Culture. *See also* Global cultural dimensions
change in, 176–177
definition of, 8–9, 189
prejudice in, 220–224
stereotypes of, 215–220
Culture shock, 33, 64–65
al-halqa and, 74
Cupach, W., 61
Cushner, K., 221
Cyprus, 4–5

Danesi, M., 35, 42, 115, 118
Darwin, C., 47
Davidson, A., 147
Davis, P., 115
Defection, mutual, 225
DeFleur, M., 15
Degabriele, M., 138
Demographic imperative, 4
Dennis, L., 168
Depth, of self-disclosure, 39
Descartes, R., 117, 118, 142
Determinism, 31, 34
De Vries, R. E., 163
Deyhle, D., 251
Dialectical Theory, 170
Dialectics, 170, 171, 173
change in, 176–177
conflict in, 190–192
Dialogue, 169, 226. 232
engaged, 101, 103
Diderot, D., 260
Digital communication, 147–148, 152
Dinar, S., 189
Disclosure, 39, 43
Dis-closure, 41, 44
Discrimination, 90, 147, 223
Disparagement, 147
Disposition, 221
Distance, 271, 273
in communication, 54–55
on continuum, 149–150, 151
Divergence, 171
Divine Proportion. *See* Golden Ratio
Dog, in cultural cuisine, 84–85, 88, 242, 248, 249, 250, 252–255
Draft, D., 154
Drama, communication as, 60–61
Dresner, S., 246
Drinking, cultural views on, 176
Dual concern model of conflict, 192
Duncombe, S., 251
Durbin, P., 251

East Asia, 174, 192, 193
East German culture, 234–236
East Timor, 91, 95
Eating habits, cultural differences in, 84–85, 88, 242, 249, 250, 252–255
Eccles, J., 14
Economic imperative, 4
Ecuadorean culture, 211
Edward, A., 13
Efficient frontier, 231, 232

Ego-defensive function, of prejudice, 221
Egypt, 54, 189
Eisenberg, E., 43
Eisenstadt, S., 13, 15
El País, 132
Ellis, D. G., 101
Embodiment perspective, 117
Empathy, 148
Empowerment, 139
Enculturation, 58
Enemies, 199
Enfield, N., 94
Engaged dialogue, 101, 103
Engagement, 96–98
English language, 183
  global spread of, 166, 240–241
English-only movement, 166, 167
Environment, as nonverbal language, 53–55
Epistemology, 30–36, 44
Ethical imperative, 4
Ethics, 240–242, 272
  in cultural exchange, 260–265
  relativist approach to, 242–244, 245, 247
  universalist approach to, 242–244, 245, 247
Ethnic cleansing, 90
Ethnic cultures, 163
Ethnic identity, 13, 20, 22, 25
Ethnic tourism, 86–87
Ethnocentric affirmation, 91–92
Ethnocentric bias, 243
Ethnocentric negation, 90–91, 99, 170, 243
Ethnocentric reduction, 89–90, 99, 170, 243
Ethnocentrism, 87, 88–92, 99, 243, 257
  Positionality Principle and, 99
Ethnography, 62–64
Ethnolinguistic vitality, 165–168, 178
Euclid of Alexandria, 252
European culture, 91, 176
Evaluation, 214, 232
Experiment, 63
Explanatory uncertainty, 36
Ezo, 23, 24, 25

Face, 61
Facework, 61
Facial expressions, 54
Family, intercultural, 229–230
Faure, G., 189
Female circumcision, 82, 84
Femininity, 139, 141, 153
Fennimore, B., 237
FIFA, 220
Figure/ground effects, 93, 125
Fijians, 163, 164
Fisch, M., 118
Fisher, R., 204
Fisher, W., 96
Fixed-sum perception, 199, 201
Fleischacker, S., 38, 95, 96, 242
Flexible-sum perception, 200–201, 206, 247, 271
Flow states, 227, 232, 233
Folkways, 83
Followable rule, 58
Fong, M., 11, 12
Foreign language, learning, 53, 98, 115
Frame, 61, 69, 76
Free will, 34, 35
Freedom of expression, 189, 190
French culture, 250, 252–255, 256
  versus Tahitian, 260–265
Freud, S., 47
Friesen, R., 203
Fromkin, V., 52, 53
Full Circles, Overlapping Lies: Culture and Generation in Transition (Bateson), 43
Fumhan, A., 64
Fundamental attribution error, 221, 222

Gaijin, 132
Gale, Xin Liu, 128, 129
Game theory, 224
Games, language, 58–59, 61
Gandhi, M., 251
Gannon, M., 138, 140
Gauguin, P., 265
Geertz, C., 66, 90
Gelb, B., 140
Gender oppression, 251
Gender roles, 139
Generalization, 226
  versus stereotyping, 215–220
Geography, as function of culture, 87
German culture, 234–236
Gestures, 52, 53, 54, 56
Giles, H., 165
Gillo, M., 234, 235
Global cultural dimensions, 136–142, 155
  High-Context/Low-Context Communication as, 139–140, 141, 153
  Individualism/Collectivism as, 138, 141, 153
  language and, 157
  Masculinity/Femininity as, 139, 141, 153
  Power Distance as, 138–139, 141
  Uncertainty Avoidance as, 139, 141, 153
Globalization, 246
Global metaethic, 251, 257
Goffman, E., 61
Golden consequence, 245, 258
Golden law, 244, 245, 258
Golden mean, 245, 258
Golden Number. *See* Golden Ratio
Golden purse, 244, 245, 258
Golden Ratio, 252–257, 258
Golden rule, 245, 258
Golden Section. *See* Golden Ratio
Gollobin, I., 177
Goode, B., 49
Goodpaster, K., 241
Görlich, J., 180
Graham, M., 85, 86
Grammar, 110
Grand narrative, 95, 97
Great Tartary, 23, 25
Ground, argumentative, 101, 103
Grounding, 94, 98, 101, 102–103, 125, 273
Group inclusion function, 11
Gudykunst, W., 1, 11, 30, 34, 35, 36, 39, 61, 83, 88, 215, 242

Hall, B., 54, 95, 97, 208, 241, 243, 244, 245
Hall, E. T., 54, 55, 138, 140
Hall, J., 54
Hampden-Turner, C., 137, 174, 227, 234
Haptics, 55
Hard boundary, 21
Hatfield, D., 237
Hattori, Y., 197–198
Hegel, G. W. F., 244
Heggy, T., 230
Heider, F., 221
Heisenberg, W., 35, 36, 42
Heraclitus, 162, 174
Hermeneutic circle, 65–67, 71
Hersh, R., 115
Herthans, H., 142
Hesselgrave, D., 85, 86
Hierarchy of needs, 164
High-Context Communication, 139–140, 141, 153
Hinduism, 55, 85, 88, 204, 211
Hirschmann, N., 251
Hispanics, 17, 166, 167, 183
Hiwasaki, L., 86
Ho, D., 201
Hoffmeyer, J., 42
Hofstede, G., 136, 138, 139, 150, 155
Holquist, M., 169
Hon, L. C., 157
"Honeymoon stage" of culture shock, 65, 74
Hopi language, 110
Hoppo, 24, 25
Horizon of knowledge, 39
Howell, W., 243
Humanistic approach to knowledge, 32
Human rights, 103
Hussein, King of Jordan, 189

ICC, 4–5
Identity, 11–13, 14. *See also* Cultural identity
  Catholic, 190
  ethnic, 13, 22, 25
  Jewish, 190
  national, 12, 22, 25
  racial, 12, 22
Identity confirmation, 17
Identity disconfirmation, 17
Identity Management Theory, 61
Identity Negotiation Theory, 1
Ideographic writing, 53
Image-schema, 118, 120, 121, 122, 123, 126, 127, 129, 270
Images of the U.S. Around the World (Kamalipour and Tehranian), 26
Imahori, T., 61
Imperatives, 4
Imperialism
  linguistic, 166, 240
  stereotypes and prejudices as, 223–224
Incas, 81
Indeterminacy, 49
Indeterminacy principle, 35
India, 55, 85, 88, 116, 204, 211
Indian Voices, 168
Individualism, 138, 141, 143, 144–146, 150, 153, 170
Indo-Fijians, 163, 164
Indonesia, 86, 91
In-group, 11, 12, 15, 22, 269
Integration, 228, 230, 231, 272
  intercultural, 224–226
  in resolving conflict, 195–196, 197, 200, 206
Interactive strategy, of uncertainty, 40
Intercultural communication
  approach to, 1–3
  boundary fit as goal of, 20–21
  change and, 176–177
  contradictory nature of, 170–174
  as culture shock, 64–65
  definition of, 10, 15
  disclosure and closure in, 40, 41
  epistemology and, 30–36
  ethics and, 240–245
  as ethnographic encounter, 62–64
  ethnolinguistic vitality and, 165–168
  as hermeneutic circle, 65–67
  imperatives in, 4
  Johari Window Model and, 37–38, 39, 40, 44
  necessity of, 124
  as negotiation zone, 202–204
  perception and, 80–86
  as performance, 59–60
  possibility of, 123–124
  as praxis, 174–176, 177
  as shared space, 155
  tensions in, 162–165
  as topological space, 143, 144
  voice in, 168–169
Intercultural communication competence (ICC), 4–5
Intercultural conflict, 188–190. *See also* Conflict
Intercultural integration, 224–226
Intercultural synergy
  flow dynamics and, 227–228
  nonsummativity and, 229–230
Interests, 204, 206, 209, 272
Interpretive approach to knowledge, 32
Interview, 64, 140
Intimate spatial zone, 54
Introducing Global Issues (Snarr and Snarr), 246
Introspection, 63
Inuit language, 111–112
Irwin, H., 169
Islamic culture, 73, 176, 251, 266
Israeli culture, 20, 95, 101–103, 188, 189
Ivester, M. D., 154

Jackson, D., 16
Jain, N., 85
Jandt, F., 9, 54, 55, 88, 116
Japan, 23–25, 76, 86, 116, 132, 175, 191, 208–210
Japanese language, 53
Jermanok, S., 19
Jewish culture, 20, 95, 96, 174, 176
Jewish identity, 190
Ji, L.-J., 176
Johanson, A., 145, 150, 151
Johari Window Model, 37–38, 39, 40, 44

Johnson, B., 165
Johnson, M., 117, 118
Johnson-Laird, P., 113
Jordan, L., 55

Kale, D., 242
Kamalipour, Y., 26
Kant, I., 244
Kapchan, D. A., 60, 72
Karma, 85
Kashima, E. S., 136, 157
Kashima, Y., 136, 157
Katriel, T., 20, 95
Keating, M. A., 137, 138
Kempen, H., 142
Kennedy, H., 104
Kenya, 81
Keres language, 183
Kim, A., 103
Kim, J.-B., 157
Kim, Y., 9, 11, 30, 31, 35, 36, 39, 61, 83, 88, 215, 242
Kinesics, 54, 55
King, C., 223, 224
Kirn, W., 82
Klopf, D., 80, 88
Knapp, M., 54
Knowledge, 270
  cultural, 98
  horizon of, 39
  nature of, 30–31
  objective approach to, 31–32, 34–36, 44
  subjective approach to, 32–36, 44
Kobon culture, 180–182
Koch, P., 93
Koehler, W., 93
Koester, J., 4, 15, 39
Korean culture, 88, 242, 250, 252–255
Krauss, C., 183
Kurds, 13
Kussman, D., 85

Lacan, J., 14
Lacey, M., 82
Lacuna, 112, 126, 130
Laing, D., 17
Lakoff, G., 117, 118
Lakotas, 266
Language, 35, 121
  Aztec, 110
  as boundary line, 18
  constitutive view of, 59
  culture and, 157
  definition of, 52–53
  dimensions of, 56–57
  English, 166, 167, 183, 240, 241
  ethnolinguistic vitality and, 165–168
  Hopi, 110
  influence on communication of, 113
  Inuit, 111–112
  Japanese, 53
  Keres, 183
  learning, 53, 98, 115
  linguistic relativity and, 110–115, 124, 129
  Maa, 82
  native, 98
  nonverbal, 52, 53–55, 71, 87
  Quechua, 81
  as resource, 189
  rules of, 57–60
  shared, 13
  spoken, 53, 55
  Standard Average European (SAE), 110, 111
  translation of, 128–131
  Uto-Aztecan, 132
  verbal, 52, 53, 55, 71, 87
  worldview and, 113, 114
  written, 53, 55
  Yaqui, 132
Language games, 58–59, 61
Laos, 94
Larson, G., 39
Larson, R., 175
Latvia, 165, 166
Laws, 84–85
Lax, D., 230
Learning to Hate Americans (DeFleur and DeFleur), 15
Lee, C., 36
Lee, M., 91
LeGrand, J., 168
Leont, A. N., 67
Levins, R., 244
Levi-Strauss, C., 119
Lewicki, R., 199, 202
Lewis, C. I., 247
Linguistic determinism, 112
Linguistic imperialism, 166, 240
Linguistic landscape, 166
Linguistic relativity, 110, 124
  strong version of, 110–113, 129
  weak version of, 113–115
Linguistic space, 49
Littlejohn, S., 9, 10, 30, 31, 35
Livio, M., 256
Looking-glass self, 14
Low-Context Communication, 139–140, 141, 153
Lubatkin, M., 175
Luft, J., 37
Lumitao, J., 168
Lustig, M., 15, 39
Lying, 245

Maa language, 82
Makela, L., 176
Manifested category, 125
Manifesting category, 125
Maoz, I., 101
Marchese, M., 139
Marris, P., 35
Marsella, A., 137
Martin, J., 4, 12, 15, 30, 31, 32, 35, 36, 97, 170, 241
Masai culture, 81, 82, 84, 240, 241
Mascho-Piro tribe, 46, 47, 48
Masculinity, 139, 141, 153
Maslow, A., 164
Mattson, M., 162
Maya, Hindu concept of, 85
Maya language, 110
Mayan identity, 17
Maybury-Lewis, D., 46, 47, 48
McGregor, A., 86, 87
McKie, D., 96
McLaughlin, M., 58
Mead, G. H., 14
Meaning, 9, 108–118, 273
  cognitive look at, 115–117
  cultural, 270
  grounding of, 94
  group membership and, 12
  language and, 59
  manifestation of, 125–126
  semiotic look at, 109–115
Mediation, 197
Mediterranean culture, 55
Merriam, S., 97
Mestizo, 17
Metaethic, 246, 247, 251, 257, 258

Michael, M., 54
Miller, N., 13
Mitchell, M., 81, 94
Mohawk culture, 203
Monochronic time orientation, 55, 113–114, 123
Montgomery, B., 176
Morality, 241–242. *See also* Ethics
Morani, 84
Mores, 84, 104
Morgan, G., 32
Morocco, 72–75
Morris, E., 2, 8, 9, 12, 16, 111, 118, 143, 148
Morris, W., 56, 246, 247, 251
Morris-Suzuki, T., 23
Moscovici, C., 243, 244, 260
Motivation, 164, 271, 273
Munshi, D., 96
Muslim culture, 12, 54, 84–85, 91, 188, 215
Muttawa, 63

Nakayama, T., 4, 12, 15, 30, 31, 32, 35, 36, 170, 241
Narrative, 95, 97, 100
  grand, 96, 97
  moralistic historical, 69
  oral, 168
National identity, 12, 22, 25
Native Americans, 81, 82, 83, 90, 162, 168, 237, 240, 266. *See also individual tribes*
  stereotyping of, 223, 224
Natural resources, 189
Navajo people, 81
Navarro, M., 17
Needs, 271, 273
  cultural, 162–165
  hierarchy of, 164
Negotiations, 176, 197, 271
Negotiation zone, 202–204, 205, 206, 228, 230, 231, 272, 273
Nemawashi, 191
Neuliep, J., 36, 55, 59, 80, 114, 147
Nietzsche, F. W., 47, 60
Nirvana, 85
Nivkh people, 23, 25
Noguchi, M., 208
Nonnormative stereotype, 215
Nonsummativity, 229–230, 232, 233
Nonverbal language, 52, 53–55, 71
  artifact as, 54, 55
  chronemics in, 55
  cultural map as, 87
  environment as, 53–55
  haptics as, 55
  kinesics as, 54, 55
  paralanguage as, 54, 55
  proxemics as, 54–55
Normative stereotype, 215
Norms, 83–85, 94, 103, 270
Northwest Airlines, 84
Nöth, W., 14, 56

Oberg, K., 33, 64
Objective approach to knowledge, 31–32, 34–36, 44
Objective ethnolinguistic vitality, 165, 178
Observation, 63
Observer's paradox, 32
Occidental Petroleum, 189, 197
Oil resources, 189
Okhotsk people, 23, 24
Ollman, B., 173
Olson, M., 205
Oonk, G., 169
Open Window, 37, 38
Operations level, of performativity, 68, 69, 71
Oral narratives, 168
Organic view, of time, 114, 149
Orthodox Jews, 176
Other, 14, 15, 22, 30, 40, 43, 62, 64, 66, 71, 73, 75, 147, 148, 149, 151, 177, 224, 228, 243, 245, 247, 248, 258, 269
Out-group, 11, 12, 22, 269
Overconvergence, 173
Overdivergence, 173

Pachamama, 81
Palestinian culture, 101–103, 188
Palmer, G., 132
Panta rhei, 162, 174, 177
Papua New Guinea, 180–182
Paralanguage, 54, 55
Pareto frontier, 231
Pareto optimality, 230–231, 232, 233, 252
Parom, 180, 182
Passive strategy, of uncertainty, 40
Peace imperative, 4
Pearce, W., 58, 59
Pedersen, P., 243
Pendulum Principle, 169–177, 271, 273
  case study of, 180–182
  contradiction and, 170–174, 177
  defined, 177–178
  intercultural communication as praxis in, 174–176, 177
Perception, 205, 214–224
  fixed-sum, 199, 201
  flexible-sum, 200–201, 206, 247
  fundamental attribution error in, 221, 222
  intercultural communication and, 80–86
  prejudice in, 220–224
  stereotypes in, 215–220, 232
  zero-sum, 198, 201
Performance
  face and, 61
  flow of, 70
  frames and, 61
  intercultural communication as, 59–60
Performativity, 60
  dramaturgy as, 60–62, 71
  as reiterative process, 62–67
  structure of, 67–70, 71
Performativity Principle, 60–71, 270, 273
  case study of, 72–75
  defined, 70–71
Perron, D., 42
Perron, P., 35, 118
Personal spatial zone, 54
Petronio, S., 20
Philipsen, G., 175
Phillipson, R., 166
Phoneme, 53
Phonetic writing, 53
Pinxten, R., 108
Pitts, Leonard, Jr., 8
Plato, 170

Polarization, 228, 230, 231
  in conflict, 194, 196, 197, 199, 206
Polychronic time orientation, 55, 114, 123
Polyphony, 169, 178
Pomare, King of Tahiti, 264
Popper, K., 14, 218
Porter, R., 85
Position, 164, 204, 205, 209, 272, 273
Positionality, 99
  authority and, 95–96
  as grounding, 92–95, 99
  as process of engagement, 96–98
Positionality Principle, 2, 92–98, 163, 270, 273
  case study of, 101–103
  defined, 98–99
Power, 95, 98, 99, 100, 244
Power Distance, 138–139, 141, 155
Power relations, 101, 103
Pragmatic dimension of language, 56, 57
Praxis, 174–176, 177, 192
Predictive uncertainty, 36
Prejudice, 220–224, 236
  arm's length, 147
  versus conviction, 221–222
  origins of, 220–221
  stereotyping and, 222–224
Preliminary stage, of culture shock, 64
Prescriptive rule, 58
Principle, 2
Prisoner's dilemma, 224–225, 227, 228, 232
Proposition, 1
Proposition 227, 167, 170–173
Proxemics, 54–55
Pruit, D. G., 192
Public spatial zone, 54
Puddifoot, E., 26
Pueblo tribe, 183
Punctuation, 16
Punctuation Principle, 269, 272
  boundary fit in, 20–21
  boundary lines in, 16–19
  case study of, 23–25
  defined, 21–22
Putnam, L., 168

Quebec, 183
Quechua language, 81

Race, as boundary line, 17
Racial identity, 12, 22, 76
Racial profiling, 26
Ramey, B., 144
Rasmussen, S., 49
Reality
  as outcome of transactions, 201–202
  stereotype and prejudice and, 224
Reflective self-image, 14–15, 30, 44
Relativism, 256, 257, 258
Relativist approach to ethics, 242–244, 245, 247
Religion, as source of conflict, 190. *See also individual religions*
Religious police, 63, 64, 266
Rescher, N., 247, 256
Resistance, 97, 249–252, 255, 257, 258, 264, 272
Resistance point, 202, 203
Resolution, 204–205, 210, 230–231, 272
Resources, 271
  intangible, 189, 190
  language as, 189
  natural, 189
  shared, 241
  as source of conflict, 189, 199, 200, 203, 204–205
  symbolic, 8–9, 10, 189
  tangible, 190
Rhee, D., 157
Riahi-Belkaoui, A., 140
Ring gesture, 54
Ritual, 175–176, 180, 182, 248
Ritual performances, 87
Rivera, R., 183
Robertson, R., 246
Rodman, R., 52, 53
Rodriguez, A., 246
Rogers, E., 9
Roles, in communication, 61–62
Room, R., 176
Rorty, R., 98
Rosegrant, S., 231
Ross, V., 16, 58, 149
Roth, W.-M., 94
Rothman, J., 205

Rubin, J., 189, 192
Rudmin, F., 215
Rules
  conflict over, 190
  contextual, 58
  followable, 58
  of language, 57–60
  prescriptive, 58
Russian culture, 23–25, 53, 97, 166
Russian Orthodox church, 58
Russo-Japanese frontier, case history of, 23–25
Ryan, D., 36

Sack, K., 183
Sadat, A., 189
SAE, 110, 111, 124
Sakoku, 132
Samovar, L., 85
Samuels, D., 49
San Carlos Apaches, 49
Sapir, E., 110, 111, 115, 124
Satyagraha, 251
Saudi Arabian culture, 59, 62, 63, 64, 65, 266
Schatz, R., 166
Schechner, R., 60
Schwartz, A., 12
Schwartz, S., 136
Sebenius, J., 230, 231
Sebeok, T., 115
Seeds of Peace project, 103
Segall, M. H., 88
Self, 14, 15, 22, 40, 43, 62, 64, 66, 71, 73, 75, 177, 222, 224, 230, 243, 245, 248, 256, 258, 269
  looking-glass, 14
Self-awareness imperative, 4
Self-disclosure. *See* Disclosure
Self-image, 13–15, 26, 44
Self-labeling, 97
Self-shock, 33
Semantic dimension of language, 56, 57
Semantic space, 252
Semiotic level, of commensurability, 120, 121, 122, 123, 126, 127
Semiotics, 109–115, 271
Senses, 80, 117
Sensitivity, 148

Separation, 66
Sexual harassment, 55
Sexual mores, 261
Shakespeare, W., 66
Shared space, 155, 172, 202, 228, 271, 273. *See also* Continuum
Shibui, 116, 117
Shimanoff, S., 58
Shirato, T., 10
Siberia, 23
Sikhs, 204
Simmel, G., 9
Singer, P., 246
Sitaram, K., 246
Situation, 221
Snarr, M., 246
Snarr, N., 246
Soccer, 220–222, 223
Social spatial zone, 54
Socrates, 170
Soft boundary, 21
South Africa, 266
South Korea. *See* Korean culture
Soviet Union. *See* Russian culture
Spaniards, stereotypes of, 214, 216–218, 223, 226
Spatial zones, 54
Spoken language, 53, 55
Springwood, C., 223, 224
Standard Average European (SAE) language, 110, 111, 124
Stapp, P., 17
Starosta, W. J., 4, 36, 89
Stauffer, D., 230
Stein, J., 220
Steiner, G., 80
Steinfatt, T. M., 112, 113
Stereotype, 215–220, 226, 232, 236, 237
  versus generalization, 215–220
  nonnormative, 215
  normative, 215
  prejudice and, 222–224
Stewart, E., 13
St. Martin, 19
Strong version of linguistic relativity, 112, 129
Subjective approach to knowledge, 32–36, 44
Subjective ethnolinguistic vitality, 165, 178
Sullivan, N., 166
Sumner, G. G., 83, 88
Survival, 246, 258, 272, 273
Sustainability, 246–247, 272
  Golden Ratio and, 252–257, 258
  strategies of, 247–252
Sustainability Principle, 245–257, 272, 273
  case study of, 260–265
  defined, 257–258
Symbolic resources, 8–9, 10, 12, 189, 241, 255
Symbols, 8, 109, 113, 120, 121, 123, 126, 127, 129, 130, 270
  artifacts as, 54
  conflict and, 209
  Indian images as, 237
Synergy, 227
Synergy Principle, 226–232, 272, 273
  case study of, 234–236
  defined, 232
  flow dynamics in, 227–229
  nonsummativity in, 229–230
  Pareto optimality in, 230–231
Syntactic dimension of language, 56, 57
Systematic experimentation method, 235
Systems Theory, 251

Tagae culture, 211
Tahitian culture, 260–265
Tajfel, H., 11
Tana Torajia culture, 86, 87
Tanno, D., 9
Target, of self-disclosure, 39
Target point, 202, 203
Tattooing, 265
Taylor, C., 17
Taylor, M., 154
Technological imperative, 4
Tehranian, M., 26
Tejano, 17
Teleological view, of time, 114, 149
Ten Commandments, 242
Tension, 230, 271, 273. *See also* Conflict
  created by language, 165–168
  cultural needs as, 162–165
  dialectic of, 171, 177
  zero, 165
Text, 140
Thailand, 13, 162
Theory, 1
Theory of the Dialogical Self, 169
Thomas, J., 59
Thomas, M., 12
Thompson, E., 147
Thompson, L., 188, 189, 198
Time
  in communication, 55
  monochronic orientation toward, 55, 114, 123
  polychronic orientation toward, 55, 114, 123
Ting-Toomey, S., 1, 11, 14, 15, 17, 39, 40, 67, 88, 189, 251
Tokenism, 147, 157
Tolerance, 247–248, 250–252, 255, 257, 258, 264, 272
Tonn, B., 246
Topology, 143, 144
Touch, in communication, 55
Tourism, ethnic, 86–87
Transaction, 196–198, 273
Transaction Principle, 198–205, 272, 273
  case study of, 208–210
  defined, 205–206
  negotiation zones and, 202–204
  perception and reality in, 198–202
  positions and interests in, 204–205, 206
Trans-Amurians, 24, 25
Travelers, 31, 86–87
Treaty of Nerchinsk, 23
Triandis, H., 138
Trompenaars, F., 137, 174, 227, 234
Trust, 241, 249, 250–252, 255, 257, 258, 264, 272
Turkey, 4–5

Uncertainty, 270, 273
  closure and, 40, 41
  defined, 36
  disclosure and, 39–42, 43
  explanatory, 36

Uncertainty (*cont.*)
  intercultural contact and, 47, 48
  order out of, 42–43
  predictive, 36
  strategies for dealing with, 40
Uncertainty Avoidance, 139, 141, 153, 155
Uncertainty Management Theory, 36–37
Uncertainty Principle, 36–44, 270, 273
  case study of, 46–48
  defined, 43–44
  horizon of knowledge in, 36–39
Underdal, A., 228
UNESCO, 246, 247
United Nations, 91, 188
United States. *See* American culture
Universal, 108, 115
Universalism, 256, 257, 258
Universalist approach to ethics, 242–244, 245, 247
Unknown Window, 37, 38, 40
U.N. World Conference on Women, 104
U.S. Soccer Federation, 220
Usunier, J.-C., 13
Uto-Aztecan language, 132
U'wa Indians, 9, 189, 197

Valence, of self-disclosure, 39
Valley of the Chiefs, 81
Value-expressive function, of prejudice, 221
Values, 82–83, 94, 103, 104, 270
van Dijk, T., 221
Vatikiotis, M., 12
Veiling, 251
Verbal language, 52, 53, 71, 87, 109
Verdu, V., 132
Verhovek, S. H., 18
Vietnam, 13, 98
Violence, in cultural conflict, 180, 182, 190, 191
Vitality Theory, 165
Voice, 168–169, 177, 273
Voluntarism, 32
Voting, 175–176
Vygotsky, L., 14

Walker, B., 248
Wall of Death, 208–210
Wang, A., 55
Warren, J., 12, 60, 67, 76
Wars, 90
Wason, P., 113
Watkins, M., 231
Watzlawick, P., 16, 147
Weak version of linguistic relativity, 113–115
Weber, T., 251
Wertsch, J., 67
Western Apache culture, 69
Western culture, 37, 81, 208–210
Western languages, 129
West German culture, 234–236
White, R., 224
White-American culture, 54, 97, 138, 237
White Mountain Apache tribe, 162–163, 240
Who Owns Native Culture? (Brown), 266
Whorf, B., 110, 111, 115, 124, 125
Winkelman, M., 64
Wiredu, K., 115
Wiseman, R., 4
Wittgenstein, L., 58
Wong, I., 138
Wood, C., 81, 94
Wood, J., 59, 62
Word, 109. *See also* Language
World Rainforest Movement, 211
Worldview, 85–86, 124, 270
  language and, 113, 114
  tolerance and, 248
Written language, 53, 55

Xavante tribe, 46, 47, 48

Yaqui language, 132
Year of Dialogue among Civilizations, 188
Yell, S., 10
Yeltsin-Hashimoto Plan of 1997, 24
Yoga, 85
Young, R., 97
Yugoslavia, 20

Zaharna, R., 33
Zero-sum perception, 198, 201
Zero tension, 165
Zhifang, Z., 124, 130
Zulu, 13